MEMOIRS OF A
LONGSHOT

Other books by W. Cothran Campbell

Lightning in a Jar
Rascals and Racehorses

MEMOIRS OF A
LONGSHOT

...A Riproarious Life

W. COTHRAN "COT" CAMPBELL

To order additional copies of this book, contact:
Xlibris Corporation
1-888-795-4274
www.Xlibris.com
38100

CONTENTS

DEDICATION

For Anne

The reader of this book will understand why

PROLOGUE

At the height of my drinking career in 1954, I left New Orleans and went to New York City to make my fortune in the advertising business. The plan was to stay in the dormitory at the YMCA Sloane House to save money, while I sought a position with one of the leading agencies. Instead I checked into the Algonquin Hotel, holed up in my room ordering Gin and Tonics sent up from the bar, and later bounced a $10 check. When I returned to the room one evening and found the door bolted from the outside, I sought other accommodations. After several days in a flophouse, I borrowed enough money to catch a Greyhound Bus back to my hometown, Rome, Georgia. An ignominious retreat.

In 2001, I came back to New York with my wife, family and friends, staying at The Pierre. We were there to attend a spiffy cocktail party hosted by "21" Club. Four of America's leading Thoroughbred racing stables were having their racing colors enshrined into the picturesque entrance gallery of "21" jockeys. This ceremony was a highly cherished, world famous salute to the elite of the sporting world. And the green and gold colors of my Dogwood Stable were among those honored at this glamorous affair. I had returned to New York many times under happy circumstances since that dark time a half-century earlier. But this occasion had a stunning significance for me—a significance none of the other honorees and guests could have possibly fathomed.

W. Cothran Campbell
Aiken, South Carolina
September, 2006

CHAPTER 1

THE ELEMENTS:
WHISKEY, AIR, COTTON, BLACK GOLD

No one has ever had a more fascinating existence on this planet than me. I am not too far from eight decades of life, and during my days I have done nothing that will make me immortal in the big scheme of things. I am certainly not a famous man. No monumental contributions, no legendary deeds.

But how delicious it is to me that the early part of my life—so tumultuous, so often exciting, and so frequently miserable by my own doing—really made possible the absolutely, indescribably wonderful latter part of it. I love the idea that this is so.

I have lived as a rich person, and I have known complete destitution. I have been a drunkard that people would want to cross the street to avoid; and I have become one of the most highly respected members of my industry, my community, and my state.

I have tasted every pleasure and even invented a few. And I have demonstrated discipline that you would not believe.

I have been in jail in sixteen different cities, from Shanghai, China, to Tampa, Florida. And I have been honored by industry and civic organizations. My reputation, impeccable now, has been the very epitome of degradation. I have been described on numerous occasions as the prototype of a "Southern Gentleman." And I know well that the term "bum" is one that was synonymous with "Cot Campbell" during a significant portion of my life.

There is no gamble, no chance, no challenge that I have not swarmed all over. I have leapt at opportunities that were reckless and harebrained and, through sheer enthusiasm, made some of them successful.

I have seen much of the world, and I have made my living in the wildest conceivable manner of ways. I have worked in jobs that were the very meanest. And I have started and made flourish two highly respected, greatly emulated businesses. I had an insignificant amount of education and benefited not at all from what there was of it. Yet I have written two highly-lauded books.

My life has been tragic, funny, inspirational, rewarding, admirable, shameful, exhilarating, colorful, important, frustrating, happy, and entertaining. And I would not change one iota of it.

I think it is worthy of a book, and I have written this one. I have "seen the elephant" as it was said of battle-hardened Confederate soldiers. My life has inevitably thrown me into the paths of some memorable, colorful, and wonderful characters that were also looking for and viewing that beast.

So this *Memoirs of a Longshot* is going to relate one splendid journey.

But I will struggle to avoid what is a pet peeve of mine: voluminous details of dreary family trees. There is nothing more tedious than struggling with minutiae concerning great great grandfather Olaf's journey from Oslo to Staten Island!

The erratic, illogical nature of my life was crafted, quite naturally, by me from seventeen years of age onward. However, the frequent changes of environment, geography, and circumstances during my childhood and adolescent period were solidly in the hands of one who could be described as restless, brilliant, mercurial, lovable, complicated, difficult, nerve-racking, and completely unforgettable. This would be my father, William Theodore Campbell.

*   *   *

We would not want to go further in this story at this time without a description and establishment of the personalities and backgrounds of my parents. They were both vivid, interesting characters. They bred in me the character traits and frailties that have caused me to inflict anguish on myself, and they also gave me the tools to extricate myself from seeking and traveling calamitous paths.

My father came from a financially comfortable, conservative, and well-respected family from the North Georgia town of Rome. He fit in there "like a bastard at a family reunion."

As an attractive-looking youngster, with a marvelous personality and an irrepressible, infectious charm about him, he was enormously popular. When his mother died when he was twelve, his father sent him to military school, simply because he did not know what else to do with him. Excessively high spirits caused him to go to several, and the handwriting was on the wall—early on and clearly recorded—that here was a young man who was going to be a bit of a handful.

He attended the University of Georgia in Athens, where he was a cheerleader, sang in the Glee Club (writing and performing a song called "Prohibition Blues," which portrayed a frame of mind that would have been right down his alley), and in general was a joyful and enthusiastic participant in the more frivolous side of campus life. He was known as "Whiskey Bill." He was easy to like, unless you were an academician.

Surprisingly, in 1917 he graduated. That event coincided with the outbreak of World War I, and, typically, he was among the first to join the Army. He applied for a brand new branch of the service, the Air Corps. Bill Campbell went to flight school in Dayton, Ohio, soloing late on the first afternoon of his training! He was born to be an aviator and looked and acted the part. He was commissioned a Second Lieutenant, and was soon after assigned to Love Field in Dallas, Texas, for more training.

So great was the frenzy to turn out aviators at this crucial stage of the Great War, that it was not hard to become a veteran (if you survived learning to fly in those old crates!). In several months he was made "Officer in Charge of Flying" at Love Field. He made First Lieutenant and soon after was promoted to Captain.

His primary mode of conveyance in the Army Air Corps was the legendary old bi-plane, the Curtiss Jenny. In that plane (which was so lacking in air-worthiness that on a very hot day it could not achieve enough lift to get off the ground and into the air), he broke several world records.

He was the first to fly upside down. And on Armistice Day in 1918 he celebrated in spectacular fashion by doing 151 consecutive loops in that Jenny, a record-breaking feat never equaled.

He established quite a reputation as an aviator, even though he did not go overseas. Lord knows he tried because combat in the air would have been right down his alley. He had "ace" written all over him!

After the war, he formed a barnstorming attraction known as "Wild Bill Campbell's Aerial Circus," which toured throughout Texas and Oklahoma. My father did the flying, and the icing on the cake was supplied by his parachutist Chauffeur Botrelle, and his "wing walker" "Daredevil Slim" Spain. They performed wherever they could find a field decent enough for the Jenny to land and take off. The plane had been purchased thriftily from the government, which certainly had an over-supply.

My father quickly gained considerable familiarity with the territory, and it did not take a genius to deduce that there was feverish activity in the oil fields of Oklahoma and Texas. He knew nothing about the subject, but the idea of wildcatting for oil tended to have an ambiance about it that got his attention. His personality fit the job description of a "wildcatter."

So when the saturation point came with the "Aerial Circus," when every small town had been thrilled, every Indian reservation milked, and every rube in the Southwest who was itching to ride in an airplane had been flown once around the field for a dollar, he decided to sell the Jenny. He took the proceeds of the sale, along with those gate receipts still remaining, said farewell to Chauffeur and Slim, and went seeking "black gold."

His modus operandi was to buy up ground leases from the Indians and sink some drilling wells, promoting and funding the production costs of the venture through the sale of shares in the wells (always named for the Indian, or whoever, who owned the land). Thus, an investor might own one tenth of "Silas Littledog Number Three" or a twentieth of "Lizzie Blacktree Number One." Bill would clear a share or two for himself and provide for some personal expense money.

He knew nothing about geology, but he hired some veteran roughnecks and roustabouts that knew about oil and how to drill for it, and he freelanced the services of oil geologists to give the venture some guidance and, you may be sure, to provide a feeling of substance to the operation, very important to the attraction of investors. Then, too, it never took my father long to be able to talk the talk and walk the walk. He was a great salesman. And he was selling a great opportunity at a great time in a great place.

He was up one day and down the next. He might be broke today but he knew he'd be wearing diamonds tomorrow. And he was often right. He wasn't afraid of anything, he was lucky at first, and he was riding high. There were enough gushers to make up for the inevitable dry holes.

Some of his investors were from New Orleans, and through visiting those connections he renewed his acquaintance with a highly-respected family that he would have easily known back in Rome, Georgia. This was the family of Harold Dickson Cothran, a gentleman who was to become my grandfather.

Dick Cothran was a cotton speculator who had started in Rome, when cotton was king of the Agricultural South, but then found it expeditious to move to New Orleans. Here was the site of the New Orleans Cotton Exchange—the place to be if you were serious about trading in the commodity of cotton.

Dick Cothran was a distinguished-looking man, a charming gentleman, and he had flourished in every way in New Orleans. He served as president of the Cotton Exchange and traditionally made the initial trade to start each day's proceedings. He was known in that environment as a "lightning calculator," which translated to mean he was a fearless gambler and was damned quick about the mathematics that governed decisions on trading of cotton. It was not a game where one spent hours pondering the efficacy of a move. Seconds perhaps.

Mr. Cothran was a civic leader, well connected socially through memberships in the prestigious Pickwick and Boston Clubs. He loved the opera and took delight in entertaining for dinner at his home each year the world-celebrated diva, Madame Schuman-Heinke. He also adored betting on the horses and was a founding member of the New Orleans Jockey Club.

The Cothrans had a lovely home on Prytania Street in the Garden District of New Orleans. They had two daughters, Adelaide and Lila. My father had known both these girls slightly back in Rome, but they had been too young for him during his adolescent years in that town.

In 1924 in New Orleans my father re-discovered the younger daughter, Lila. She was truly a smashing young lady, and Bill Campbell had little difficulty convincing himself that she was no longer too young.

She was quite beautiful, very petite, full of fun, and a legitimate belle of New Orleans. She had been presented at court in England, and had just reigned as Queen of Osiris (tantamount in those days to being Queen of Mardi Gras). By day she played mahjong and bridge and tended to her rather undemanding civic responsibilities of Junior League membership; by night there was absolutely no shortage of merriment, and she would have been more than a welcome participant in any phase of it.

While the young boulevardiers of New Orleans were glittering and gay, there were no Bill Campbells in the bunch. This dashing ex-aviator, visiting from the oil fields of Oklahoma, just naughty and wild enough to be exceedingly glamorous, but with the proper background of a gentleman from good old Rome, Georgia, quickly became heavy on Lila's mind. They got to know each other quite well before he had to head on back to the Oklahoma barrens of Okmulgee, Burkburnett, and Whiz Bang, and the quest for oil.

New Orleans investors in the Campbell Drilling Company soon noticed a sharp increase in the amount of personal reportage from the principal of the company. He was often in "The City That Care Forgot." He became good friends with Dick Cothran, who even invested some money in a few oil wells and returned the favor by introducing my father to horseracing which he, predictably, found very intriguing.

During these visits Bill and Lila fell very much in love.

My grandfather might have been slightly more comfortable with a well-established, sound and safe New Orleans "boy." But perhaps not. The old boy was a bon vivant of the first order himself, and he identified rather warmly with Bill Campbell.

My grandmother, on the other hand, definitely had a strong inclination toward the local talent. However, other than drifting about being elegant, she would not have had any really significant contribution to the proceedings. Addie was more decorative than anything else. She was not a mover and a shaker and could always be "handled." My father recognized the necessity of handling her, but the two of them predictably had little rapport.

After about a year of these visits, to the surprise of practically no one, Bill Campbell called on Dick Cothran and asked his permission to marry Lila. It was given, ninety-five percent wholeheartedly.

In the spring of 1925 they were married in a quiet "in-home" ceremony. My father had been married before for a few months while he was at Love Field in Dallas. This previous union with "Agnes Cherry-Campbell" was never a matter of much significance to anyone, but technically its existence was enough in those prim and proper days to dictate a discreet and understated nuptial ceremony.

One of the attendants was a lifelong friend and beau of my mother. This was Dick Barlow, who rather dramatically sent her a telegram when the wedding plans were announced. It read, "Lila, darling. Be sure it's the right thing for you . . . then go ahead."

This decidedly qualified sentiment probably expressed accurately the outlook of practically all those who knew both the bride and groom.

After the wedding luncheon Lila and Bill caught the afternoon train for Tulsa, Oklahoma. It was wisely decided not to subject so delicate a flower as my mother to Indian culture and the rigors of oil field life right off the bat. Tulsa, a relatively civilized city but nevertheless still a far cry from New Orleans, was selected.

My father had hit a few good wells about that time, and he was flush. So the newlyweds were able to buy a very attractive house in Tulsa, and they settled in happily, accompanied only by Bruno, a spectacularly wonderful-looking Chesapeake Bay Retriever about the size of a Hereford calf. He was accustomed to being with my father in the oil fields, but his job now was to stay with my mother when his master had to spend the night at the drilling rigs, located some distance from Tulsa.

Those were happy days, made even happier when it was discovered that my mother was "with child." I was the child, and I was to arrive in the fall of 1927. But my mother returned to New Orleans for the blessed event.

Contrary to the expectations of the disappointed suitor, Dick Barlow, the marriage *was* "the right thing." It was never to be the *easy* thing. But for Lila Cothran Campbell it was the *only* thing. Lila was sure of it then; and really she was sure of it for the rest of her life.

She was wildly in love with my father and would always be. As time went by, he could and did often drive her to distress. He was worrisome and could be enormously difficult, but he was fascinating, unpredictable, colorful, usually considerate, protective—and he loved her mightily. He was her best friend. Neither could have done without the other, through good times and bad.

The post-nuptial good times did indeed take a rather sharp nosedive several months before I was born. The first of many Campbell family economic slumps was very much in evidence.

That year my father had drilled one dry hole after another one. And now he had gambled everything he had in sinking six wells on a piece of ground he had leased from an Indian woman named Ruth Brinton.

The drilling bits were down plenty deep, and all the wells were yielding was salt water. He had borrowed from the banks to keep drilling, and he was about out of that money. It did not seem wise to continue—geologically and financially.

Bill Campbell was broke, didn't know how he would pay back what he had borrowed, had a wife about to produce their first child, and the six oil wells looked to be dusters. He was plenty discouraged and had a right to be.

He shut down five of the six wells and decided to concentrate just one more night on the most promising one. When he left the rig at "Ruth Brinton Number Three" in early evening, he told the night crew boys to "take her on down another twenty feet, and then in the morning, we'll see what we've got."

That night he uncharacteristically admitted the worst to Lila, "Honey, I'm afraid it looks bad. Looks like we've got another dry hole. I'm going out in the morning and shut the last well down, salvage what money I can through selling the equipment, and then . . . God knows what we'll do."

It was rare for him to disclose a bleak outlook and admit that he didn't have a promising "Plan B" in the works. This time he was whipped.

After a sleepless, worrisome night, he got out of bed around five a.m., took Bruno with him for much-needed company, and started driving east toward the drilling site some forty-five miles away. His head was spinning with details that were going to have to be handled. Bill Campbell had never been lower.

The sun was coming up now, and when he drove up the last hill before arriving at the location of the well, as he topped that rise he could not believe the sight that he beheld. The sun, rising out of the horizon in the East, was practically obliterated by this gigantic plume of black. Black Gold, it was.

The Ruth Brinton had hit. That rich, illusive seam of oil he had been probing for had been penetrated in that last twenty feet of drilling. The result was a gusher of major proportions.

The oil was pouring onto the highway. Police cars had arrived and were holding up traffic for about a quarter of a mile. What a mess! What a glorious, miraculous, stupendously wonderful mess it was!

Bill made his way to the well and helped the crew cap the mighty gusher. Later in the day when it was brought under control, he sent down to a little roadhouse, bought a couple of quarts of whisky, and he and the crew celebrated. The police, disgruntled at first by the complications caused by the gusher (though they understood the nature of such problems in that part of Oklahoma), even stayed and joined enthusiastically in the festivities.

He called my mother and told her the fantastic news and said he would be home when he could. That night when he and Bruno stumbled in, black and greasy and exhausted, he engulfed her, much to her complete approval, and shouted, "By God we're going to New York, and I'm going to buy you the most expensive mink coat in the whole damned town." They did, and he did.

"Ruth Brinton" was a personage I felt on intimate and grateful terms with all my life. Her name was spoken often. Her largesse did not last but it was wonderful for my parents at the time.

In later years, I named a racehorse for the old girl.

CHAPTER 2

THE DEPRESSION AND SOLUTIONS

Cash flow from "The Ruth Brinton," bountiful though it was, was tested to the fullest extent by the Campbells, and finally dissipated. There was no help, unfortunately, from the drilling of subsequent oil wells, and there was inevitably one dry hole too many. That, coupled with the Depression, dried up investor interest in The Campbell Drilling Company.

My father was broke, and so was most everyone else, including my grandfather, Dick Cothran. He had been wiped out in the nosedive taken by the cotton market in 1932.

Papa, as I knew my grandfather, partially solved his dilemma by—of all things—buying a book on how to play poker. Though he had never played poker, he read and completely absorbed this book, memorized the percentages and, in no time could tell you the exact mathematical likelihood of drawing to an inside straight or turning two pair into a full house.

He was essentially a gambler anyway. For years when he was rolling high in the cotton market, he maintained in his suite of offices a special room in which he had ensconced a professional horseracing handicapper with telegraph and telephone hook-ups to every major racetrack in North America. And he bet the horses, through bookmakers, every day of his business life. I remember so well as a child, when I visited his offices, listening with delight to a race call of, say, the fourth at Belmont Park, or the eighth at Churchill Downs.

On top of that he was, after all, a "lightning calculator." If he knew the rules, why wouldn't he be a superb poker player? Thanks to the book, he did. And he was.

For the first half of the decade of the Thirties, he supported his wife (his other daughter, Adelaide, had married a well-to-do West Virginia man) and himself by playing poker three times a week at the better social clubs of New Orleans.

When cotton made a comeback, he resumed trading, but thank God for poker in the meantime!

Bill Campbell did not embrace this particular resource to solve his fiscal woes. But he did have an idea. It centered around Atlanta, Georgia; and to have access to that town, he, Lila, and five-year-old Wade Cothran Campbell moved back to nearby Rome. There, life was simpler, kinder, cheaper; and, with numerous family connections, the odd opportunity to make a little money existed.

It was absolutely imperative that he keep up appearances, look like a winner in a land of losers. He had concocted a splendid idea, but to sell it, he needed to reek of success, Depression or no Depression. He had a wonderfully creative scheme involving a return to the field of aviation, and the burgeoning Coca-Cola Company in Atlanta was a tailor-made partner.

My father had been intrigued with an exciting and revolutionary new aircraft being built by the Pitcairn Aircraft Company in Philadelphia. This was the Autogyro, an open-cockpit, single-wing airplane with a gigantic rotor blade on top. This strange-looking craft, the forerunner of the helicopter, could fly around 120 miles per hour but had the advantage of being able to land and take off in very short spaces. It couldn't hover like a helicopter, but it could sure set down or take off on anybody's football field. My father would ultimately land one on top of the post office in Philadelphia!

Bill wanted to sell the Coca-Cola Company on the idea of buying the first of these planes. It would be painted in the red and white Coke colors with the logo emblazoned on the fuselage. Of course it would be flown by none other than William T. Campbell, the very same Captain "Wild Bill" Campbell of Curtiss Jenny, 151-loop, World War I fame.

Here was the pitch: This Coca-Cola Autogyro would be flown around the United States. With doors opened by Coke bottlers in practically every worthwhile burg in America, permission would be gained to land on the athletic field at Harvard or Clemson or Ohio State or Stanford or whatever!

What a sensation this would be. The students, never having seen such a thing, would never forget it. Once on the ground, Captain Campbell would then repair to the assembly hall, where he would make a speech on the future of aviation, having logically been introduced by—and made possible by—the local Coca-Cola bottler. From there it would be a simple matter to motor downtown to address the local Rotary Club, catch the Kiwanians the next day . . . the possibilities were limitless. There would be opportunities with youth groups, charity organizations, every sort of civic and social organization.

Since times were hard, there were not that many exciting attractions floating around, especially for free. America was looking for cheap entertainment and diversion.

This tour would simply be a most significant, highly creative public relations project for the Coca-Cola product, and would endear the parent organization to every franchisee in the land.

It was truly a natural-born, superb idea, and the Coca-Cola Company (headed at the time by the legendary Robert W. Woodruff) would have to recognize it as such. Still, that great organization didn't get where it was, and is, by eagerly jumping on every sharp-sounding scheme that came along. To sell the idea there would be plenty of appointments to be arranged, many meetings at many levels, *pro formas* to be developed, and much due diligence to be performed. And my father was starting at ground zero. He didn't know them. They didn't know him.

During this difficult and tedious time, while Lila, Bill, and their child were trying to exist and at the same time seem to be affluent, they had secured lodging in Mrs. Frith's Boarding House on Second Avenue in Rome. This was a rather up-scale establishment catering to other well-connected—but temporarily down-at-the-heels—tenants. It certainly wasn't the big time, but neither was it a soup kitchen.

It was at this time that young Cothran took action on a matter that contributed significantly to livening up the doldrums of the Depression.

Mrs. Frith had a dining room where lodgers took their meals, if they were at all economy-minded. The dining room seated around thirty guests, and the serving was done by two black staffers, Will and Fannie Mae. Will was a general handy man around the Frith domicile, and Fannie Mae was primarily a maid. Both doubled as dining room wait staff.

Naturally, Will and Fannie Mae were thrown together frequently in their daily routines. Will was a middle-aged, rather frail, slightly effeminate (but amply warm-blooded) man with a very pleasant personality. Fannie Mae was a zaftig and handsome young woman.

Will was a bachelor. Fannie Mae was married to a fellow known as "Big Sam," who worked in the nearby lumberyard. I adored all of them. I would see Big Sam almost every evening when he would come to wait on Fannie Mae while she cleared the supper dishes.

Will had developed for Fannie Mae a fondness that far exceeded that normally associated with one co-worker for another. He had a major crush on Big Sam's wife. And one day, when thrown together in close quarters in the Frith pantry, Will vigorously pursued his ardor by seeking to kiss Fannie Mae. Little of any significance was accomplished, but I was entering the kitchen at the time and did witness Will's clumsy gropings. While I had not yet been indoctrinated on the activities of the "birds and bees," I grasped enough of what was taking place for it to make an indelible impression on me.

That evening in our small apartment I related this highlight of my afternoon's activities to my mother and father, and I was pleased that it was a news item that seemed quite noteworthy to them. We talked about it, and I remember them saying that all the guests knew that Will was "kind of sweet on Fannie Mae." Thus, I had received confirmation that what I had seen had, indeed, been a pretty significant happening.

———

At supper the next night in the communal dining room, after polishing off our salmon croquettes and cabbage and waiting on the arrival of our banana cream pie, I looked out the window toward Second Avenue, and there sauntering down the street came Big Sam, arriving to fetch his wife.

I quickly excused myself and darted out into the yard to fraternize with my friend, Big Sam.

Shortly afterwards my father glanced out the window. His heart immediately sank. He beheld this small figure, in earnest and animated conversation, gesticulating furiously. Bending over him intently, listening with surprising absorption, hungrily devouring every morsel, was the giant black man. My father understood in a flash what was transpiring. His child had decided that he had unearthed the ideal news item to share with Big Sam, and was relating, with some embellishments probably, that romantic episode in the pantry between Will and Fannie Mae.

He jumped up quickly, found Will in the kitchen, and told him to get the hell out of there. Another look toward the front yard confirmed his worst fears. Big Sam had broken off the discussion, needing no further details to formulate his next course of action. He was advancing resolutely toward the house, with mayhem on his mind.

My father intercepted Big Sam about ten feet from the front door and, seemingly casual, asked, "What in the world have you and that little boy of mine been talking about, Sam?"

"Been telling me about that goddamned Will fooling around with my wife! That's what!"

"Aw, Sam, I can't believe you'd pay any attention to a crazy story like that from a little child!" He had Sam slowed down, but the day wasn't saved yet by a long shot.

I quickly squeezed by the two men on the porch and scooted into the house, sensing that somehow the item of gossip I had selected for my chat with Big Sam might have been ill-chosen.

By this time Will had departed with no concern over the completion of his daily chores, and my mother had wisely decided to alert Fannie Mae to what she felt sure had been the conversational topic covered by Big Sam and me in the front yard.

My father, meanwhile, was making headway with the irate husband and, by this time, had convinced him of the extraordinary imagination possessed by this strange little child. Indeed, by then, Sam had been convinced of the fact that I was practically mentally unbalanced.

The incident cooled the ardor of Will. And, it served as a slight retardant toward my camaraderie with Will, Fannie Mae and, of course, Big Sam. But this was a small price to pay for avoidance of what would have been a major disturbance.

Another factor that somewhat livened up Depression Days in Rome was the frequent presence of my Uncle Al. Al was actually a resident of Atlanta, where he lived with his wife, my father's sister, known as "Baby," or to me as "Aunt Baby."

Albert Dabney Irving was a native of Charlottesville, Virginia. He had a rather distinguished family background there. And he was a professional Virginia gentleman. Compared to Al, you'd have thought that Robert E. Lee was a foul-mouthed, degenerate carpetbagger. Al had gone to "The University" (of Virginia, of course). He had served his country in France in World War I and, before and after in civilian life, he had spent much of his time riding to the hounds, fornicating (voraciously, but with relative style and discretion), drinking, and avoiding any form of work.

Al was a handsome fellow with the head of Rudolph Valentino, but with the kind, crinkly eyes of Edmund Gwenn (Santa Claus in *Miracle on 34th Street*). He had "rich boy hair." He parted it about an inch off center, and it was then swept back on either side, having been so arranged by use of a wide-tooth comb. Liberal usage of Kreml Hair Tonic then gave it a sort of permanent, shiny, and etched-in-stone look.

Al was kind. He truly liked everyone and wanted the entire world—and certainly himself—to be happy. He could in a genuine manner charm the birds right out of the trees.

Inexplicably, he married neither a beautiful nor a wealthy woman. He probably could have. And should have.

As a testimony to his conviviality and joie de vivre, he once made himself legendarily synonymous with those characteristics while within the confines of the staid old Piedmont Driving Club in Atlanta.

His brother-in-law, George Campbell, was a member, and on a warm, spring evening shortly after the end of the War, Al and "Baby" were socializing with a sizeable coterie of friends—some of Atlanta's "beautiful people." There was considerable merriment and frolic at this al fresco affair on the lawn at the Club, and Al, as usual, had imbibed quite heavily and was feeling no pain. During a bit of a lull in the revelry at his table, Al decided that it behooved him to liven up the proceedings.

Quietly slipping into the nearby men's locker room, he went to George's locker, borrowed his bathing suit, disrobed, and excitedly slipped it on. Then, gleefully he flung the door open, hurtled out onto the lawn, and sprinted madly for the nearby pool, shrieking, "The last one in is a rotten egg!"

With all the spirit of an Australian lifeguard entering the surf, he dove enthusiastically into the pool.

There was no water in the pool.

That broke up the party. And it sure as hell broke up Al. He spent the night in a nearby hospital suffering from a fractured collarbone, with a severe hangover in the making!

In the post-war years, Al's business career had not been promising. He had launched several short-lived entrepreneurial ventures. Al could find employment, thanks to his attractive nature. But due to his character frailties, in a job market greatly favoring the employer, he did not last long at any of them.

The Great Depression had the nation in its grips; and to give credit where it was due, Al was pursuing much more vigorously than was his usual wont promising money-making opportunities, especially ones he deemed "suitable." It is here that we encounter the venture that introduced me to the job market, and Uncle Al was the architect of it.

It was 1933. And at the age of six, I was engaged as a "Sales Representative for the Sav-A-Rip Company" in the Rome, Georgia, territory. The Sales Supervisor, and the franchisee, was, of course, Uncle Al, who operated solely on commission in this door-to-door enterprise.

Sav-A-Rip was a rather gluey substance that was spawned by the Depression, and was marketed as a preservative product that would prevent "runs" in women's stockings.

Al hit upon an idea of considerable ingenuity. He employed the services of me and my cousin Dabney Irving (his son), age eight (transported in from the Atlanta market, where he had had some brief indoctrination in the Sav-A-Rip "approach," and thus was senior to me in every way). The marketing theory—conceived by Al, not Sav-A-Rip—was that Dabney and I were to canvas the neighborhoods, ringing doorbells, and counting on our cuteness to "open the door." At that point we would notify Uncle Al by surreptitious signal, so that he could come smilingly in to close, first dismissing us so that we wouldn't "bother this lovely lady." We would then move on down the line, while he "canned the fruit."

If the prospective Sav-A-Rip-ee was comely, Uncle Al might easily have been inclined to do more than help her prevent runs in her stockings. Indeed, he might have caused a few.

Times were tough, God knows. And neither the cuteness of Dabney and Cothran, the attributes of the product, nor the suavity of Uncle Al could make this a viable undertaking, and after several weeks of toiling in the hot Georgia summer, the Rome territory was surrendered back to Sav-A-Rip headquarters. The project was abandoned. The sales force was dismissed, and Uncle Al moved on to greener pastures—charmingly full of optimism and high spirits.

Meanwhile, the Coca-Cola Autogyro project was consummated, much to the supreme joy of the Campbell family. It was a marvelous coup in the economic climate that existed in this country. It was seemingly a great idea, and my father deserved great credit for conceiving it and for selling a gigantic company on the idea. And Coca-Cola deserved plaudits for gambling on such an undertaking in a most unpropitious promotional climate.

My dad went immediately to the Pitcairn headquarters in Pennsylvania to get checked out on the Autogyro. He had not flown since the days of the Aerial Circus, and this aircraft was a trifle on the tricky side. But he was a top pilot and mastered the technique quickly.

The gyro was purchased and painted to Coca-Cola specifications, and Bill flew it back to Atlanta so that all the company headquarters people could get properly enthused about the upcoming tour. Logically, the nationwide tour was to start in the Southeast.

My father hired a mechanic named Henry Whitebirch, and the two of them would travel together from that time on. Both men were outfitted in attractive, white aviator jump-suits.

To test the impact of this promotion/attraction, it was publicized in Atlanta that the Autogyro, Coke's revolutionary new flying machine, would circle twice and then land on the athletic field in the city's centrally-located Piedmont Park, on an upcoming Saturday morning at eleven o'clock.

About thirty thousand people came to see that.

With scores of police on hand to maintain a clearance for the gyro to set down, Captain Campbell, his long, white scarf streaming dramatically behind the cockpit, whipped the ship down over the silver maples surrounding the field and floated that baby onto the ground.

He taxied up to a roped-off ceremonial area. The Mayor of Atlanta welcomed him and the Coca-Cola plane, company officials and my father were then introduced, and they discoursed on being in the vanguard of aviation history. There was much clapping and picture-taking. The newsreel cameras cranked away.

To thunderous applause, Captain Campbell and the trusty Henry then climbed up on the wing and scrambled into their tandem cockpits. He fired her up, taxied down to the end of the field, turned into the wind, gunned it, and lifted into the air in about eighty yards.

Admittedly this was Coke's hometown. But if the reception was any indication, the Coca-Cola Autogyro Tour was going to be dynamite.

And it was.

My father spent the fall and winter of 1933 working Florida and the rest of the Southeast. My mother and I continued to live in Rome, but with my father's new position we had vacated Mrs. Frith's and moved into a nice apartment. Depending on his itinerary, we sometimes traveled along behind by train in order to meet up with him.

Sometimes on a short hop from Atlanta to Chattanooga, say, I was permitted to fly with them. I sat in the front cockpit with good old Henry. If the flight got bumpy—and it often did—I would automatically throw up on Henry. I remember well the terror in the poor man's eyes, intensifying as he observed my worsening color and expression, knowing what was coming (I never learned the knack of leaning my head out of the side of the cockpit!) Henry was a good sport about it. After all, things were tough all over.

What an indescribable thrill it was to stand near the runway of an airport (there were not many rules about that in those days) and watch my father bring the gyro in, no more than fifty feet away.

First a tiny speck would appear in the sky (and in those days there weren't too many other specks up there. It *had* to be him). As it got closer, the murmur of the crowd would increase in volume. Then the gyro would approach the runway. Sometimes my old man—especially if he knew Mom and I were there—would "hot dog" it up a bit, just touching the ground and spinning the wheels before climbing again and coming around for his landing. This was accompanied by a dramatic wave, of course. Man, was I proud! And when he would get out and eventually come over to us, I would hug him for five minutes (making sure the crowd understood the connection).

And so it went. After my father finished in the Southeast that winter, my mother and I moved up to Huntington, West Virginia, and lived with my Aunt Adelaide for about six weeks, while my father covered the Eastern Seaboard.

In June, we moved up to Boston and rented an apartment, as the Autogyro was covering New England. By then the word had spread. Powered by the Coke public relations machine, the considerable publicity generated in southern climes was having its effect all over, and the Coca-Cola Autogyro was eagerly awaited and well-heralded wherever it went.

My father (and my mother, when she was available) was exceedingly popular on the cocktail circuit. And Bill Campbell was just the man for the job. He was about thirty-eight years old, attractive looking (sort of a Spencer Tracy type, I always thought), lots of fun, and rapidly becoming a bona fide celebrity during a time when the populace was hungering for celebrity and diversion. There was plenty of fun to be had after the airplane got on the ground, and the Captain meant to have his share of it. He was drinking plenty during the times it was deemed appropriate to do it, and he was handling it pretty well. Then.

The tour moved westward, and my mother and I moved back to Rome so I could go to school. He would fly in from time to time . . . from Dayton, or Milwaukee, or St. Louis. Otherwise there would be long periods when my parents wouldn't see each other. It was tough on them both. My father was busy and accessing numerous opportunities to have a good time, but he was crazy about my mother, and he did miss her terribly.

When spring came in 1934, we picked up and caught a train to Salt Lake City, where we took an apartment.

After several months there, we followed him by train on to Cheyenne, Portland, and Seattle, staying in hotels. And then we moved on down to San Francisco.

My schooling was erratic, to put it mildly. Some places I enrolled in school for awhile, in others I was privately tutored, and during other times we just didn't worry about it.

My mother and I inevitably became especially close. We really only had each other during this hectic, nomadic existence. It was terribly difficult for her, caring for a small boy while living in trains and hotels and moving constantly. I was like most small boys—not easy. Yet I remember periods when it was particularly tough on her, and I must have curbed the obstreperous part of my nature. It was tough, but she was only thirty-one years old, with a distinct taste for adventure. She handled it better than most.

Whoever is reading this, I wish you could have known my mother. She was splendid. My mother was quite small, very pretty, with lovely, expressive, light brown eyes. She smiled easily and radiantly. She was exceedingly witty, a wonderful storyteller and mimic. Talk about lighting up a room!

Lila Campbell was always "up" and anxious to make things easy for the rest of the world; and she smoothed out the many bumps in her particular road of life through her irresistible charm. After several hours on a train, the porter, conductor, and dining car waiters were all eating out of her hand. She was one of the most likeable, charismatic, and popular human beings I ever encountered.

She adored me, and I adored her. Though I did not bring her much happiness during my early adult years, I tried hard to make up for it in our later years together. I think about her often now, and find myself wondering where she is, what she could be doing. Weird, I know.

We had several interesting brushes with celebrities during our travels. In fact, one unforgettable incident was far more than a brush. Mom and I got on the train in Portland, Oregon, one night, and we were headed south to California. The porter saw to it that we were ensconced in the seat that was part of our lower berth unit. Departure time came and went, and the porter—usually well informed about scheduling departures—could only surmise that they were holding the train for some reason. My mother decided that we should take this opportunity to walk back to the Club Car and look around, and then see what time the diner would be serving.

As we moved into the vestibule between cars, there was a loud, clanking noise accompanied by much shouting from the station platform, and a very tall man bounded up the steps while looking back and waving. This big oaf slammed into my mother and me and knocked us flat.

It was Gary Cooper. Even I recognized him, and my mother certainly did! In his typically bumbling, stammering way, he swept off his fedora, clutching clumsily at both of us as we struggled up from the iron-grated vestibule flooring, and murmuring apologies all the time. Simultaneously he was vaguely trying to acknowledge the shouts from some well-oiled, highly vociferous companions who were seeing him off. One I can hear plainly now: "Kill a goddamned moose for me, Gary!"

Cooper was on his way to Idaho for moose hunting (with Ernest Hemingway, perhaps?), and they had, indeed, held the train for him, ample testimony to his incredible popularity at that time.

He continued to pursue us, brushing us off, patting us and, in general, trying to make up for what was not the heroic role in which he usually found himself.

We saw him later when he came into the diner. He gave us that funny little simper of a smile of his, with the apologetic, raised eyebrows. Certainly no harm was done, and the incident provided my mother and me with a topic of enormous conversational value.

California was to be the last region of the Coca-Cola Autogyro Tour, and it was reckoned to be a very productive one.

My folks and I moved into a furnished apartment on Nob Hill in San Francisco. (At this point my father was benefiting from considerable relaxation of the expense account purse strings by the Coke finance department.) It was October of 1934, and we were to stay in the Golden State until the public relations "gold" was deemed to be depleted.

It might take awhile, because situated in California and ready to do battle for the cause was one who was to be Coca-Cola's door-opener extraordinaire. This was a gentleman who was one of Coke's biggest stockholders, one of the world's most vivid and recognizable characters, and perhaps the supreme baseball player of all time: Ty Cobb, "The Georgia Peach."

Cobb had retired from baseball several years earlier and was simply clipping the numerous coupons he had caused to come his way. He was a very astute investor. As he had made money through his career, he had socked it away, steadily and significantly, in Coca-Cola stock; he was a very wealthy and somewhat grateful man.

Coke had assiduously steered clear of publicity associating the Cobb name with their pristine product. While he was enormously admired as a ballplayer, he would not exactly have been a strong candidate to win the "Albert Schweitzer Humanitarian Award." During his playing days he had the disposition of a piranha and the aggressiveness of a pit bulldog. He adored a fight.

But now Coke had perceived the ideal role for Ty. And they sought his cooperation. And he pledged it. He was to be the California host for Captain Bill Campbell. Who could be more ideal to get him in the right places (and perhaps some of the wrong ones)? If Cobb picked up the phone, or knocked on any door, he could make things happen.

The great hitter had little to occupy himself with at the time. He whiled away the days hunting, drinking, and looking for someone to pick a fight with. He was intrigued with aviation, he loved Georgia, his home state . . . and here came a lively young fellow from Rome, Georgia, who could fly the hell out of this funny-looking flying machine. It was a splendid match.

They had a lot in common. They quickly became great drinking companions. My father loved to hunt, and that helped. Further, Bill Campbell, like the rest of America, hero-worshipped the ferocious old Detroit Tiger. Cobb's reputation for pugnacity did not make him easy, but it did make him fascinating (as one might admire the qualities of a gamecock or a pit bulldog) to most other men.

All in all, the two new friends cut a wide swath through California, and the Coca-Cola public relations aspirations in that important state were more than realized. My mother and I were certainly not much involved in the activities of Cobb and my Dad. She was happy not to be, and there was certainly no reason for the pilot's little son to be in the equation.

Until, that is, there came a time that November when Ty Cobb invited my father and family to attend the East-West Football Classic at Kezar Stadium in San Francisco.

We were to come to lunch at the Cobb home and then drive to the game with the Cobbs. Mr. and Mrs. Cobb and their son Jimmy, age thirteen, were to represent that family, while my Dad and I would be the only Campbells. My mother was not a Cobb enthusiast, and decided to take a pass on the occasion.

I was keen to see the game, but at my young age hanging out with Ty Cobb, the celebrity, would not have rung my chimes. And there was a decided darkness about him and his name that even I sensed. I had certainly picked up on some of the conversational nuances about him. But still my wariness was unusual—and maybe I'm imagining it now, after increased awareness of the legend of the man has had its impact. He was really not a fearsome man physically. His countenance could have belonged to a druggist, or a judge, or a doctor. But even I grasped the fact that where there was all that smoke, there must be some fire. Most of the entire world knew: he was some kind of mean son of a bitch!

Dad and I showed up at their rather impressive estate in the suburbs of San Francisco. After the adults had a drink or two, we were served lunch, and then it was off to the game on a rather dreary, gray day.

We had wonderful seats right on the "50," of course. All was going nicely, and it was a great occasion. Cobb was quite jolly and had been a perfect host. Then in the second quarter it started to rain lightly. Most of the fans had brought umbrellas, and they opened them up and kept them open during a shower of maybe five minutes. Then it stopped raining, and the umbrellas throughout the stadium were closed. All but those belonging to two men in our section. They had been imbibing heavily, and they were seated two rows directly in front of us. These guys had been pretty annoying right along, but now the umbrellas were particularly effective in making them quite obnoxious.

Their neighbors suffered in silence for awhile. Then Cobb leaned over the row just in front of him and—in a pretty civil manner, really—tapped one of the men on the shoulder and said (and I can hear it now!), "Say, fellas, how 'bout putting your umbrellas down so a paying customer can see the game?"

That started it.

The two drunks had struck pay dirt. Now they had one clearly defined, responsive target. They immediately turned and gave Cobb the finger, accompanied by considerable hostile repartee. This kept on, with Cobb, his face as red as a beet, not saying a word.

But on and on it went. Everyone within twenty feet of us was tuned in to an unpleasant situation.

Finally, after the two revelers unleashed a particularly offensive tirade at Cobb, a fan in front of them, fed up himself, turned and said, "Boys, you ought to know . . . that guy you're getting so tough with back there is Ty Cobb."

WHAP! Those umbrellas came down like a shot.

The umbrella owners then gave a pitiful, little obsequious wave back at Cobb as if to say, "I hope this is satisfactory now, sir!" Then they hunched their shoulders to make themselves as inconspicuous and inoffensive as possible. Indeed, they would have liked very much at that point to disappear from the face of the earth.

They remained that way, silent and still as church mice, until the half. Then they jumped up and bounded up the steps and through the exit.

They had no more than cleared the area, when Cobb nonchalantly stood up, stretched a little, and said, "Jimmy, how about going down and getting us some Coca-Colas?" Jimmy left on his assignment.

No more than sixty seconds later—with a quick glance at Mrs. Cobb (who knew what was coming!)—he said, "I wonder what's keeping Jimmy? I'd better go down and see where that boy is." With that, he rushed out of there.

Mrs. Cobb immediately looked over at my father and said, "Oh Bill, I wish you'd follow Ty! I just know he's going to do something to those two men." That was not the most surprising news my father had ever received. He told me to sit tight and then he was gone, leaving Mrs. Cobb, nervously twisting her hankie, and me.

My father descended into the lower regions of the stadium to the men's room. When he approached it he saw Cobb hiding behind a gigantic, square concrete pillar, peeking out toward the exit door. About that time, the two men, considerably more sober than they had been, stepped out.

Ty pounced. He throttled one in each hand, and was in the process of selecting the one he was going to annihilate first, when my father rushed up. After quite a bit of cajoling, amidst a steady stream of apologies, their release was secured.

Even though there was no more rain during the second half, there were two empty seats near us.

CHAPTER 3

HORSES, EGGS, AND STORMY TIMES

Soon all the Rotarians, Kiwanians, Boy Scouts, and other West Coast targets were covered, and the Coca-Cola Autogyro Tour of America had run its course. And a very successful one it was, but that was the end of it.

So my father flew the gyro back to Atlanta. My mother and I—inveterate train travelers by now—booked passage on the Southern Pacific.

My father had done well by Coca-Cola, and they wanted to keep him around. They created a position for him: "Director of Research and New Outlets." No sooner had he launched his career in this rather nebulous slot in corporate life than he got wind of the fact that a bottling franchise in Des Moines, Iowa, was buyable. Sounded right down his alley, but he didn't have any money.

During his tour Bill Campbell had met—and hit it off with—a wealthy family in Birmingham, Alabama, which controlled a number of Coca-Cola bottling plants around the country. He went to see Crawford Johnson Sr., patriarch of this soft drink clan. He quickly sold him on putting up the money to acquire this franchise (my father clearing a minority, but still significant, interest for himself). It was a good property even though it was in a state that not many Southerners had much interest in or knowledge about. "Where in the hell is I-O-WAY?" people wanted to know.

We moved to Des Moines in the spring (thank God it was not winter) of 1935.

My folks, with their Southern accents, charming ways, and quasi-glamorous backgrounds, knocked that smallish city for a loop. Soon Bill and Lila belonged to the best country club and were welcomed into the top social strata. Bill was regularly playing squash and frolicking afterwards in a generally harmless manner with the younger "business leadership" of Des Moines.

Demonstrating his customary drive and zip, my father soon had this portion of the Corn Belt drinking more Coca-Cola than had been its custom. He understood selling the "sizzle." And he had fire in his belly. In a short time, so did the collective employees of the plant.

My father, when he began to enjoy some success in the soft drink field, decided that he must own some three- and five-gaited saddle horses. Typical of him, he flung himself and his family into this hobby with great fervor, and soon Shoestring Stable ("started on a shoestring") was a significant stable. I began to ride the horses and, in time, to help train them, and I was assigned several to groom.

I was a rather rotund little fellow at the time, and had enormous trouble getting on top of the horse. Once I did get astride, with the help of two huffing and puffing grown men, I could ride one pretty well, ultimately becoming Champion Amateur Rider of Iowa, Nebraska, and Missouri.

For actual show ring competition, I was outfitted exceedingly well, with some expensive butternut brown and dove gray riding outfits. These ensembles were traditionally very tight and form-fitting, and with my form, they caused me to look like a very plump link sausage.

It was absolutely essential that show horse riders wear this type of restrictive garb, both then and now. No way around it. To wear anything else (a nice Hawaiian shirt or a loose-flowing muumuu, for instance) would certainly have been more forgiving esthetically, but in the show horse world it would have been considered unthinkably bush.

Any self-consciousness in connection with my obesity—and there was considerable—was put to the test one night in Lincoln, Nebraska.

I was showing a horse at the Nebraska State Fair. I was outfitted in my brown garb, complete—of course—with a derby hat of the same color. I had perhaps added five or six pounds to my already hard-to-define frame since being fitted for this suit, and every nook and cranny was easily discernible through the tautly stretched fabric.

This was a night event and the arena was packed. Included in the crowd were about seventy-five boys from the famous Father Flanagan's Boys' Town, an orphanage for wayward and homeless boys.

This group was positioned in a bloc, in the cheap seats at the end of the ring, and they were a lively, excited bunch, entirely ready to be entertained by practically anything. It would not take much to set them alight.

When young Campbell and his fancy three-gaited horse popped into the ring, and I went energetically posting past this group, it got their attention. The idea of seeing this fat child, clad in such raiment and vastly overweight (and flaunting it), was more than their decorum could stand.

Such catcalls, whooping, whistling, and gesticulating you cannot imagine. The fact that I was riding and showing the horse quite well was completely beside the point. I was simply a very tubby kid, all duded up in such a manner as to accentuate my fatness (and richness), and fair game.

Unfortunately their manner of recognition for my efforts was contagious, and soon the entire assemblage in the Lincoln Show Arena was in complete harmony with the lads from Boys' Town. It made for a miserable thirty minutes. I think the judge "tied" me second or third. Technically I may have deserved to win, but no judge would have been brave enough to have given me the blue ribbon. Not with that crowd on that night. We were all probably better off with those results.

This memorable event can probably be thanked for my present-day obsession with weight control. The early involvement with show horses was my introduction to a lifelong love affair with the horse.

Simultaneously, though, I had an intense love affair with the chicken. Why, I really do not know. I was suddenly beset with an insatiable appetite for any and all matters having to do with poultry. Perhaps during a motor trip with my parents through the agriculturally-oriented Iowa countryside, my attention fell on an attractive grouping of White Leghorns in some neat, picturesque farmyard. And I was simply, inexplicably smitten.

I subscribed to the two leading publications in the world of chickens, *The Poultry Tribune* and *The Poultry Journal.* I knew every major poultry producer in America through the advertisements. My favorite was the clearly established Queen of the Poultry World, Gusta B. Atz, of Moline, Illinois.

I was soon able to identify any breed of chicken (and a smattering of ducks and geese) known to the world of poultry.

At the time—1937—"taking a ride" was a favorite family pastime, either to escape the heat of summer or general boredom anytime, and I drove my parents crazy during these "relaxing" outings as I would scream out periodically, "Look, there's a Buff Cochin!" or "Have you ever *seen* so many Rhode Island Reds?"

Since I essentially liked the bird—the chicken per se—as an individual, the egg-producing side of the game certainly appealed to me more than that of producing chickens *to be eaten!*

My enthusiasm for chickens continued to grow, and I inevitably yearned to be "hands-on," to get down in the poultry trenches. I wanted to *own* chickens. Since we lived in a rather nice, typical, upper-income, residential section of Des Moines, having a chicken operation of any size was not entirely feasible. Still I yearned to be a "Poulterer."

The haunted, wistful look in my eye, after consuming the most current issue of *The Poultry Tribune,* must have melted the resistance of my parents, who were inclined to be indulgent anyway.

As the Christmas season approached in frigid Des Moines, my father conceived the gift of all gifts for his son—the surprise to end all surprises. He would establish for me a chicken operation in our very own backyard.

First he commissioned the maintenance workers at the bottling plant to construct—off site—a rather sizeable chicken house to fit within a surrounding wire-mesh, recreational pen, for future positioning in our backyard.

At the same time he put in an urgent call to Gusta B. Atz, with whom—through constant hearsay—he was quite familiar. After considerable consultation with Mrs. Atz, he secretly arranged for the delivery of six White Rock hens and one White Rock rooster, this breed having been recommended as the most practical from the standpoint of hardiness, adaptability, and "production capability." The hens were purchased to lay eggs, while the job of the rooster was to be cosmetic and, of course, convivial so as to provide stimulation of hen house morale.

None of this I knew, of course.

Christmas Eve came, and when I had finally gone to sleep, a phone call to the plant summoned the poor fellows standing by to come out to our house with the henhouse and material for the surrounding pen. They would bring with them the seven chickens which had been domiciled for several days in the temporary shipping crate in the Coca Cola plant garage.

They were aided in this late-night construction endeavor by Alec, our "houseboy." Alec was a young black man from Georgia who had been brought up to Iowa by my father. Alec was a man of many duties. He went about all of them in a somewhat tentative manner and was possessed of a very lugubrious outlook on life. He served as chauffeur, butler, gardener, sparring partner to the young boxing enthusiast in the house, was called upon to be the appreciative audience for my father's jocularities . . . and had many another role in our family life.

On Christmas morning I awoke with my usual zeal for the job at hand, but little did I dream what was in store for me. After my folks had had a chance to get somewhat organized for the day, they mysteriously announced that the three of us—attended by Alec, of courseshould go outside. The thermometer read eight degrees, but it was really a decent enough day for Des Moines in December. We put on considerable outerwear, I was then blindfolded, and we made our way into the backyard.

Our foursome shuffled through the gate of the pen, the door to the henhouse was flung open, and the blindfold was removed.

What a sight! What ecstasy! Never had I known such joy. *Chickens*!

I looked upon my chickens with unbridled adoration. The chickens, huddled miserably in the corner of the excruciatingly cold henhouse, glared back at me, clearly yearning to be back in Moline in the heated facilities of the Gusta B. Atz chicken complex.

There then began a long period of admiration and speculation concerning the unlimited future possibilities of the chicken operation. Alec was called upon frequently to contribute to the general enthusiasm, and he performed gamely. However, Alec wisely deduced that after a flurry of feverish concern for the chickens, the heavy duty of poultry maintenance would fall right into his domain.

Mrs. Atz had sent along various feeds, tonics, and medicines for predictable poultry maladies. Assisted by Alec (with whom I was flaunting my expertise), we fed and watered the new feathered residents, then decided that we should leave them alone so that they might begin to feel at home and commence laying eggs.

Back in the house I opened the rest of my presents, somewhat anti-climactically, and then rushed to the phone to begin soliciting egg orders from neighbors and close friends of the family. Though this exercise was worrisome to my mother, I was permitted to push on, and the requests for orders went swimmingly. Like Girl Scout Cookies, there were few turndowns.

The production requirements, therefore, would need to be quite strong, with little margin for slow days or frigid Iowa weather not conducive to laying eggs. But I had complete confidence in my White Rocks. Alec looked pained when I told him how well the reception to the new egg business was going.

I made numerous trips to the henhouse that day—some of them surreptitiously so as to not interfere with the acclimation process. There was nothing startling to observe. The hens and the rooster still seemed to favor the leeward corner of the henhouse. None of the hens had yet gone to nesting. Plenty of time for that though, I reasoned. How long could it take to lay an egg?

Christmas night I occupied myself with other gifts, but my mind was on the chickens and I yearned for the next morning when I could start collecting the eggs from a band of well-adjusted chickens, fully acclimated and happy to be in residence at 33 Foster Drive.

I overslept the next morning, and when I raced through the kitchen on my way to the henhouse, with my basket at the ready, I sang out to Alec who was busily preparing to serve breakfast, "I'm going to gather the eggs." Alec simply looked disgusted.

I rushed into the henhouse. None of the hens were in, or near, their nests. But optimistically I began probing in the deeply bedded nests for the first of the eggs. Number One was empty. On to Number Two. Empty. So were Three, Four . . . all of them! Not one egg after having a full day to acclimate. I was flabbergasted. What *was* the problem?

Alec then entered the henhouse, having been firmly instructed to help me get started. I whined to him, "These chickens haven't done one single thing!"

With a resigned look at me, he said, "Them old chickens ain't gonna lay no eggs, cold as it is."

I was close to tears when I got back in the house. I told my mother about the disappointing lack of developments. She counseled me to be patient, that after all it had been just one day. We called my father. He weathered the news admirably, but said if something didn't happen by the third day, by God, he would give Mrs. Atz a ring.

My mother suggested that I notify a few of the egg customers who would be expecting deliveries at any moment that things were running a little behind schedule.

On the next morning, my suspense did not have to endure long. As I went through the kitchen, Alec, seated at the kitchen table reading a comic book, looked up and gloomily announced, "Ain't no eggs out there." Alec was not exactly the sparkplug of my team. But, alas, he was right. Nor did any eggs appear at any time during that dark, windy, mid-winter day.

That evening my father, always one to insist that things work as they were *supposed* to work, put in a call to Gusta B. Atz herself. Mrs. Atz listened sympathetically and even suggested that perhaps we would like to send the chickens back. This was the bluff of a seasoned campaigner. Mrs. Atz knew that the logistics of our crating and shipping seven White Rock chickens back to Moline, Illinois, was not an option we would likely undertake. No, no, my father assured her, we *wanted* the damned chickens! Of course! But did she have any suggestions? After several questions about their consumption of feed and water, she suggested patience.

I had gone into a stunned period of resignation, so when the fourth day in the egg business went completely eggless, it didn't take any more of the wind out of my sails.

That night at dinner, it was clear that the joy of the Christmas Chicken Presentation had diminished to a clear, deficit position. My parents—with some half-hearted assistance from Alec—sought to jolly me up.

When I retired that night my parents faced the facts: Thus far, the chickens had supplied about twenty-four hours of pleasure and a great deal more of despair and disappointment.

They made a wise decision. They hatched a plan that would give me another fabulous twenty-four hours and then—unless the miracle of miracles occurred—we would all have to bite the bullet and call it a day, poultry-wise.

The next morning, one of the last I had free before school was to take up again, I got up and headed for the kitchen for some breakfast, where I encountered Alec, who was showing considerably more animation than usual. He asked me if I was going out to the henhouse. When I told him I was going to have my breakfast first, he asked me to go out there to see if there were any eggs, since the refrigerator was short on that commodity.

I looked at him as if he were demented to even make such a suggestion. But there was a significant aura of optimism about his demeanor and, believe me, this stuck out on Alec like a sore thumb.

Putting on my heavy weather gear, I trudged through the snow to the henhouse and made my way into the gloomy interior. As always, the rooster and his six girls were huddled dispiritedly in the corner. But I began checking the nests.

Would you believe that my eye and hand collided simultaneously with a rather chilly, white, spheroidal object. IT WAS AN EGG! I was staggered with the import of this totally unexpected development. I went to the next nest and discovered another one. Just going through the motions, I was sure, I nevertheless moved on down that line. I hit pay dirt again at Number Three. Number Four yielded an egg, as did Five . . . as did Six!

Man, my White Rocks were in the groove, finally. I knew they could do it! The period of homesickness and strangeness was over. We were now one big happy family.

Being careful not to drop any of the precious eggs, I crept along the snowy path back to the kitchen door, flung it open, and screamed loudly, "You'll never guess what I have GOT in this basket!" Alec looked as if he might have at least a fighting chance to determine the contents.

But my parents were now seated at the breakfast room table, and they, at least, seemed very, very curious. Exuding excitement, they got up and came over to peer in my basket. They did a fine job of sharing my excitement and optimism about the future, but when I rushed to the phone to inform my egg customers that the problems of production were behind us, my mother frantically and firmly interceded. She counseled me to cool it.

Several times during that happy day I returned to the henhouse, not only on routine maintenance chores but also to observe and evaluate the conduct of the chickens. I definitely perceived a change for the better in their general attitude. I was certain there was more of a "Can Do" approach to life. While I did not have a right to expect it, I did check the nests several more times, thinking that they might wish to make up for lost time. There was no further production; but, hey, that was perfectly all right! One egg per day per chicken would be quite satisfactory.

All in all it was a glorious day for a Poultry Man. Alas, it would turn out to be the last glorious day.

When I breathlessly checked the nests the next morning, much to my horror there were zero eggs. Naturally I was crestfallen. I puzzled over this erratic production pattern during the post-Christmas period. Neither my mother nor Alec was able to shed much light on this mystery, but both suggested that my father might have some theories when he came home from the plant.

He did. It was bullet-biting time. He sat me down and told me that after the three adult principals had mulled over the problem of the chickens' poor performance, it was decided that there existed a troublesome combination of inadequate urban facilities, unfriendly climate, and—despite my general expertise—perhaps a slight deficiency in experience. These factors made continuation in the chicken enterprise quite impractical, it was felt. He confessed that he had instructed Alec to place the eggs in the nests so as to avoid another day of heartbreak for me.

At this point my enthusiasm for a career in poultry produce had waned considerably. So I did not protest the consensus of the rest of the team. I felt that the chicken game was one of ups and downs. After seven days as a Poulterer, I had experienced two wonderful ups but had been thoroughly devastated by five distinct downs. It was not going my way.

The chickens were donated to a better-equipped agrarian operation outside of town; the backyard accouterments were removed; Alec breathed a sigh of relief . . . and I was out of the chicken business.

Unbounded enthusiasm was typical of my father when a project seized his attention. His sponsorship of my chicken venture was a good example.

Now his adventurous spirit introduced us all to an awesomely monumental undertaking, and we quickly forgot about chickens and refocused on another breed of horse.

Logic had nothing whatsoever to do with his announcement of a surprising, precipitous change from a secure, conventional life in Des Moines, Iowa, to a harebrained endeavor near the small country town of Franklin, Tennessee. But logic and my father were not running mates. And a secret idea that had been germinating suddenly had to be born.

My father abruptly sold his interest in the Coca-Cola bottling plant in Des Moines, vacated the presidency thereof, bought a farm in middle Tennessee, and decided—by God—to go into the racehorse business.

The truth is that five years of the soft drink bottling business was a little on the tame side for Bill Campbell. Then too, he did not suffer supervision smoothly. The Johnson family—majority owners of the Des Moines business—recognized that while he had done a superb job of increasing sales, it was clear that he was living pretty high on the hog and had a tendency to brush off any suggestions that they might make—not an endearing quality for a minority stockholder. This clearly rankled the Johnsons, and they let it be known.

But think about it. Here was a man who had been a record-breaking World War I aviator, had later barnstormed with his "aerial circus," had gone from that into wildcatting for oil, and then went on to touring the nation in the Coca-Cola Autogyro. Was managing a bottling plant in a provincial Midwestern town likely to keep him stimulated for very long?

My father was a romantic; he had supreme, often unfounded confidence; he didn't sweat the small stuff; he didn't want to be confused with the facts when his mind was made up . . . and he was drinking hard at the time—not a good combination for sound business decisions.

During his entire life, my father had either been up or down. He was now about to embrace what would become a "down" from which he would never recover economically. But the establishment of Shoestring Farm was a project loaded with panache, if nothing else. Whiskey had played an important role in his resignation from the ever-so-bountiful Coke franchise and certainly in his subsequent purchase, for $18,500 (pretty big money in 1940), of a lovely, if run-down, farm with a spectacular antebellum home as the keystone of the operation. It was an absolutely nonsensical thing to do. My father never gave a thought to the security of his family. As far as he was concerned, he was simply going to support them in the business of Thoroughbred racehorses . . . somehow. I don't know if he intended to do this through betting on them, breeding them, winning purses with them, or a combination of all three. Nor did he know. He would figure it out as he went along—the way he had done a lot of things, some of them very successfully.

Much to the delight of the sleepy little community of two thousand traditionally horse-oriented souls that was Franklin, the 112 acres of Shoestring Farm were soon literally churning with construction activity. A huge barn was being built, a half-mile race track was under construction, fences were going up, and "The Big House" was undergoing refurbishing and was being decorated to the desires of my mother, although she was understandably leery of the entire venture. But she had been there before; she was risk-averse.

At age twelve, with some of my aforementioned chubbiness on the wane but still not conquered, it was felt that manual labor in the hot Tennessee sunshine would not be a bad idea, so I was put to work on the farm crew. The rest of the farm crew consisted of an adult black man and two black teenagers hovering on the brink of puberty, as I was.

Much of the summer was spent eradicating weeds with a sling blade, but often I was moved over to the barn to help with the horses, which I adored. I constantly looked for reasons why my time might be better spent at the barn, and actually I was more productive there than flailing away with the sling blade.

The Shoestring endeavor definitely did not have the sweet smell of success about it. At my age I did not fret much about the fiscal soundness of the Campbell family, but even I sensed that pushing ahead full blast in the racehorse business was not the thing to do.

The preposterous nature of my father's latest venture began to demonstrate itself, and his drinking began to accelerate.

Bill Campbell really knew nothing about racehorses, relatively speaking, and every fast operator in the game was seeking to unload bad horses on him. The fact that in America war clouds were definitely hovering made the outlook for the Shoestring operation even more ominous.

My father harbored some forlorn hope that his ex-partners in the Coca-Cola plant in Iowa were considering a further cash settlement as part of his severance. There was much illogical talk of this severance. My mother, I am sure, knew that the chances of this were slim to none. But she also knew that her husband was not one to be counted out.

To add to the difficult times, some very inconveniently shocking news surfaced at this juncture. My mother was pregnant with my sister.

The collective mood of the Campbells was grim indeed, with excellent justification for it.

I decided at this time that it would be a good idea for me to start drinking.

CHAPTER 4

EDUCATION IN DRINKING

In case you deduce that the launch of my full-fledged drinking career was precipitated by concern over unsettled conditions within the Campbell household, this was not really correct.

Like many teenagers before and since, the young lads around Franklin found drinking and getting drunk the thing to do. It was what the hotshots did, and it was a sign of maturity, or at least that maturity was within hailing distance. In my case it provided my persona with a rather zesty ingredient, and the persona of this particular chubby thirteen-year-old was probably in bad need of something to "get it up on its feet."

I was enrolled in a new school—Battle Ground Academy (BGA)—which is always a stressful time. While I generated some interest because of my Shoestring Stable connection, this was not enough to make me cool with my peers. The fact that I was eager (at a pretty early age) to hit the roadhouses and get polluted with all the older "in crowd" did give me a modicum of panache, and I badly wanted that. I became sort of a mascot.

Franklin had more than its share of roadhouses, and they were rough and ready establishments, situated out on the highways (not in the town where the citizenry could clock the comings and goings of patrons). The proprietors of roadhouses asked no questions, did not concern themselves with the morals of the youth of the community, and exhibited an every-man-for-himself outlook on entertainment, conduct, and life itself. They did not know the meaning of the word "minor."

The roadhouses bore such plebian names as Taylor's, Harry's, White Way Inn ("bloody way out"), and The Globe.

The architectural configuration was invariably quite simple. In the front room there was usually a bar with stools, where one could imbibe, or dine, if desperately hungry. A spacious open doorway led one into another much larger room where there were booths or tables around the circumference of an unusually ample dance floor. Occasionally on Saturday nights there might be a three-piece band, but for the most part a juke box sufficed for dance music. And the music was strictly "hillbilly," as it was known in that era and locale in the heart of Grand Ole Opry country.

Little thought had gone into restrooms. Usually there was only one, for whichever gender got in there first. A door simply opened from the dance floor abruptly to reveal the business part of the bathroom, with no thought of an ante-chamber, and rarely did one encounter a stall or even "modesty panels" surrounding the toilet. The only other equipment in the small room might possibly be a wash basin.

One of the indelible memories of my life came from a hilarious scene during a festive evening at Taylor's roadhouse. A very drunk man had answered a call of nature. After staggering into the small bathroom, the requirements of his relief necessitated that he seat himself on the commode. Unfortunately for his dignity, while the couples on the dance floor glided by to the strains of "You Are My Sunshine", someone—perhaps a mischievous dancer—flung open the door.

During the rest of the number, this disgruntled occupant of the restroom, caught in the very midst of that which had brought him there, and stymied as to how to bring "closure" to the operation, remained seated on the commode, his britches down around his ankles, his forearms resting on his knees, muttering threats and gesticulating vaguely and angrily toward the dancers cavorting past.

Some kind soul finally shut the door.

The first time I felt the effects of alcohol came when three of us split a pitcher of Gerst Beer at The Globe. It was quite a large pitcher and it cost a quarter. I liked the daring nature of what we were doing, the way the beer made me feel, and the taste of it. Altogether, it was a very satisfactory exercise.

Where had this been all my life? I certainly intended for it to be there for the *rest* of my life. From that time forward, alcohol, in some form—beer, wine, liquor, whatever was affordable—would play a major role in my existence. Life without drinking was simply not an option.

At this time I was an eighth grader at BGA. This was what I would describe as a country prep school—and the finest institute of learning I ever knew. There were only 120 students, and perhaps half were dormitory students. There were rich boys, along with some local boys whose parents struggled with even the modest tuition of $85 per year. There were incorrigibles in need of strict disciplinary measures. And there were afflicted boys—mentally and physically—who would be schooled in specialized institutions today. BGA, struggling through the shank of the Depression, was up for any challenge.

Regarded today as one of the more fashionable prep schools in the South, Battle Ground in 1940 was ranked below such Tennessee institutions as McCallie, Baylor, Montgomery Bell, or Castle Heights Military Academy.

I adored it and was happy to immerse myself in its world, although certainly as a "day student" I continued to live on our farm, no more than two miles away from the shabbily attractive little campus.

The Headmaster of BGA was a legendary disciplinarian who had cut his teeth at the hard-case Webb School in Bell Buckle, Tennessee, which offered its young men amenities comparable to Alcatraz. His name was George I. Briggs.

There were but six other men on the BGA faculty, and there was much doubling in brass. From this group of seven came the coaches of football, baseball, and basketball. Mr. Briggs was the cheerleader for all athletic events—literally. Always clad in a three-piece suit, he often led the entire student body in vigorous cheering practice at our daily assemblies. For days before the start of football in the fall, motorists driving by our hallowed halls could be startled by the cacophonous roar of "BGA, rah! rah! Who rah? Who rah? Battle Ground rah! rah!" And woe to the student who not did show a frenzied enthusiasm for this drill. The BGA Wildcats might not win the game but there would be a hell of a lot of noise in support of their efforts, led by "'Fessor" Briggs, red in the face, striding up and down the sidelines and pumping his arms furiously.

Every young man in the school became either a "Plato" or a "Greer." There was no real reason for these organizations other than to determine the rosters for the annual—and highly celebrated—BGA Tug of War. At the start of the school year, committees of senior Platos and Greers would, at a gathering of the entire student body, choose from the new students.

Accompanied by much loud, vocal comment from existing members concerning the wisdom of certain selections of new Platos and Greers, this embarrassing undertaking would, of course, result in the better specimens being selected early on while the geeks, nerds, crippled boys, and wheelchair types stared at the floor and went last.

The Tug of War took place each spring. With the citizenry of Franklin assembled along the route, the entire BGA student body—120 strong, along with seven faculty members and "Uncle Henry," our janitor—would march importantly down the long hill into the small town. With the rope stretched out on our shoulders and with ear-splitting shrieks of "Plato" and "Greer," we paraded through the tiny business section and onward to the Harpeth River, where the idea would be for one side to pull the other through the cold waters of the Harpeth. The townsfolk and scores of dogs, seriously stimulated by this dramatic magnification in the tempo of city life, would follow along behind us and excitedly assemble themselves on the concrete bridge overlooking the site of battle.

When all combatants were ready, proper instructions having been given, 'Fessor Briggs would ring a cowbell and the struggle would ensue. After considerable straining and grunting, one side would begin to lose ground, and soon their front boys on the rope would be dangling over the Harpeth, an indication that the end was near. Bodies would drop into the river and the coup d'etat would see the rest of the losers being pulled through the river, with the boys on the tail end of the rope jumping in just for the sheer hell of it. The winners did not jump in, of course, because dry clothes were an indication of a winning effort.

I was a Plato. The Plato coach was a young teacher named Turney Ford. He was also the football coach, having been a pretty good halfback at Vanderbilt. He taught some uncomplicated subjects (civics?). One year he devised a plan for us that would assure victory. However, it was one whose successful implementation would depend on absolute secrecy, somewhat difficult to achieve with sixty boys in possession of the details of the scheme.

One of our number—presumably not an able-bodied Plato with pulling power—was to sneak off in the woods nearby; when the serious pulling began, he would fire a shotgun, with which he was to be provided for the occasion. At the sound of this unmistakable signal, all Platos would drop the rope. The straining Greers, already back on their heels from pulling, would end up flat on their backs. We Platos would then seize the rope and simply pull the disorganized Greers through the Harpeth.

The vital job of firing the shotgun was assigned to a very frail young man, with a bad leg from an attack of polio. His name was Billy Perrin, but for some inexplicable reason he was known as "Rhumba Pete." The gun was owned by Mr. Ford.

Rhumba Pete had been schooled very thoroughly in the execution of his task, and the necessity of maintaining firearms safety measures had been strongly stressed. He was to go off a "safe distance" into the woods, count to fifteen after hearing the cowbell signal, and then fire the gun—into the air to be sure.

The day arrived. As we all trekked down to the river, Rhumba Pete marched to the side, waving gaily to the crowd and brandishing a strange, long object, thickly wrapped with burlap. Pete's demeanor did definitely bespeak the fact that he would somehow play an important role in the upcoming event.

The opposing sides got to the river and moved into readiness for the start. With our Plato teeth gritted and our knuckles white on the rope, we awaited the cowbell. Rhumba Pete had earlier slouched off into the woods. Unfortunately—safety having been imbedded heavily in his mind—to play it cautiously he had decided to go a good quarter-mile upstream!

The starting bell sounded, and the straining see-sawing began. The townspeople cheered lustily and loudly from the bridge. Fifteen seconds into the struggle a faint "pop" was heard in the distance. Heard by *half* of us, that is. Thirty Platos dropped the rope. Thirty did not. Of course, the original plan depended on absolute unanimity for its success. At that point, it was a simple matter for the Greers to whisk us half-staffed Platos through the river quickly and easily.

Never in the history of Battle Ground had there been such an ignominious, swift, and overwhelming defeat in the Tug of War.

Rhumba Pete was lustily berated for "going to the next county to shoot the goddamned gun!" Turney Ford, seeking a dramatic breakthrough in his first year at BGA, had fashioned a plan instead that resulted in making asses of us all, and he was furious.

The tug of war was but one of many reasons for me to love Franklin, and I remember it sixty years later as a jewel of a truly bygone era. But bygone it is. Today its charm is besmirched by a dreadful procession of Burger Kings, Popeye's, Captain D's, Taco Bell, Po Folks, McDonald's, Wendy's . . . you name the franchise, it's there in all its ghastly glory!

Two thousand mostly easy-going souls lived there in 1940. It was a charming little town, eighteen miles south of Nashville, and it reeked of history and glorious tradition. During the Civil War, the gory Battle of Franklin squandered the lives of nine thousand men from both sides, and during that engagement four Confederate generals were slain on the front porch of a fine old home.

Franklin's economy then was entirely dependent on agriculture—livestock, various food crops and tobacco. So the town was quiet through the week but teeming with activity on Saturdays, when farmers came to town with their families to trade, shop, listen to the leather-lunged street preachers around the square, shoot pool, and/or get drunk.

In those days one often saw a team of workhorses trotting down Main Street with the farmer/daddy at the reins and his family spilling over the sides of the wagon. They would do their shopping and gossiping at the dry goods, feed, hardware, or grocery stores. Then the children might be deposited at the picture show, and the wife would find a little visiting to do. The head of the house and maybe the oldest boy would settle in at Ham's Pool Room, strategically situated between West Point Grill and Baker Lane's Barber Shop, clearly an environment of conviviality in Williamson County.

In those simpler days before Nintendo, television, the internet—ad infinitum—the citizens of a town like Franklin pretty much had to confine their leisure time activities to talking, making music (or listening to others make it), watching the high school sports team, participating in church activities, shooting pool, and/or drinking. There was plenty of all of those things.

Ham's Pool Room was an establishment of simple proportions but enormous intrigue and drama. It was a building perhaps twenty feet on the street by sixty feet in depth, with a small counter and uncomplicated cash register up front, and four exquisitely balanced, impeccably clean pool tables in a row. The back door was of keen interest to the prep school students, as Ham's was off limits. Many a pool game was aborted when one of us saw a faculty member peering in the window. Battle Ground administrators (especially Mr. Briggs) sought to have Ham bar us from admittance, but Ham was decidedly anti-establishment. He was on our side; besides, he wanted the nickels for Nine Ball and the dimes for Rotation!

It was an unwritten law that the caliber of players competed on tables in descending order. The hotshots played on Number One. If we happened, during a slow period, to be playing up front, as soon as good players came in we would quickly finish our game and move aft.

For some reason, Middle Tennessee was a mecca for great pool players, and there was much gambling on Straight Rotation, Nine Ball, Eight Ball, Bank, Kelly, and a smattering of Billiards. Franklin had its share of pool sharks, and the good ones moved easily from Ham's establishment up the pike to Nashville, to the vaunted basement parlor of the Maxwell House Hotel, where the action was ferocious.

The great pool players of Franklin definitely enjoyed some celebrity, and much of the town speculated on who could beat whom at what particular game. And, believe me, no game or sport could offer up more drama, theater, intrigue, and excitement. Why? The men who played it. They were colorful characters, tinged with at least a smidgen of larceny in their souls, essentially gamblers, with gamblers' guts and nerves of steel. Another reason for its intrigue was the personality of the pool halls where it was played. They were deliciously dark and forbidding places, suggestive of sinister doings.

Our stars were James Lilly, Bob Polk, Leroy (Bertha) Hardison, Featherlip Trabue, Ham Scranton (proprietor), Grady Ray, Shotgun Gentry, Leonard Lankford (Lank), and one who enjoyed *regional* prominence and distinction. He is enshrined as one of my all-time favorite sports heroes.

His name was Andrew Morrell. And he was known as "Mister Andrew" or, more accurately, Mist' Andra. Never was he referred to as "Andrew," "Andy," "Morrell" or anything else.

I had occasion to know him because my good school friend, Andy, was his son. The Morrells lived on a small recreational farm, in a beautiful house halfway between Nashville and Franklin. While Mist' Andra was by no means to the manor born, he had married into a very wealthy, socially prominent family in Nashville. He co-existed peacefully, if not warmly, with this distinguished clan. They asked and expected little of him, and that suited Andrew Morrell perfectly. Often he would be absent for rather long periods of time, but then he seemed to flow easily back into the household, with no questions asked and no explanations given.

"Mystique" could have been his middle name. He was about forty-five, handsome in a pock-marked, dissipated way. He was medium-sized, trim, neat, with very small, delicate hands. Mist' Andra was a salesman for a wholesale grocery company—not typical employment for a man with his connections.

He drove a black '38 Plymouth Coupe. He was always dressed in blue serge pants and a white shirt with a bow tie, and he wore a popular belt of the time, leather with a flat, silver buckle plate that had his "A. M." monogram embossed on it. From April to October he wore a jaunty sailor straw hat cocked down over one eye. This was replaced with a brown fedora for the colder months. He was a handsome figure, and one that would capture your interest immediately—one reason being that he clearly didn't give a damn if he did or not.

He was quick to flash a quiet, shy, brief smile, but he said very little; when he did make an utterance it was in a soft, genteel Southern drawl. I remember once when I had spent the night with Andy, his father drove us to school the next morning. We rode along in silence with the radio playing typical big band music. Suddenly, the Tommy Dorsey Band cut loose with their rendition of "The Jersey Bounce," an emphatically up-tempo arrangement of a very lively swing tune of the time. The entire brass section was hard at it, with the trumpet man showing the way, demonstrating trill after trill, "triple-tonguing," hitting every high note with enormous gusto. They were slamming this number home, selling it!

The three of us rode along in stunned admiration. At the end of the number, Mist' Andra looked over at me, grinned shyly, and drawled, "That man was gettin' a right smart music outta that horn."

He was an alcoholic. And he would go on week-long binges every couple of months, which certainly helped explain his prolonged absences from home. When he drank he did not shoot pool. When sober, he did. And his reputation among the billiard parlors of Tennessee was comparable to that of Doc Holliday around the saloons of Tombstone.

He had an instinctive, unpremeditated flair for avoiding overexposure. He did not appear often in Ham's Pool Room in Franklin. Sometimes when he did come in, he would watch for awhile, smoke a few cigarettes, shake off an invitation to play, and move on. Every penny-ante player in the territory was gunning for him, hoping to make his reputation. But Mist' Andra, with a gut feeling for the dramatic, would know when to lay it on the line.

Had there been a "Commissioner of Pool," he would have decreed that there take place a championship match between Andrew Morrell and Grady Ray. Grady was the best in Franklin, and he had been shooting his mouth off about his desire to "relieve Morrell of some of his bankroll in a little Nine Ball competition." The public had been clamoring for it. It was simply an event whose time had come!

Saturday afternoon at about three o'clock was perhaps the optimum time of the week for Franklin pool room activity. One September day at such an hour, this fourteen-year-old was in Ham's. I had audaciously copped one of the tall, wire stools with wooden arms, and was reared back watching a game of Bank Pool. Hardison and Lankford were playing a couple of guys from Murfreesboro.

Grady Ray was sipping on a beer and watching the same game.

I heard someone say, "Lord, God, look-a here!" Sauntering across the square came Mr. Andrew Morrell.

He opened the screen door, came in, and stood with his hands in his pockets, surveying the crowd with a vague, pleasant little smile on his face. There was a murmuring of greetings, and the writer enthusiastically tossed off a "Hey, Mist' Andra," which he returned with a wink.

As if it had been prearranged, he looked over at Grady, nodded, and then simply raised his eyebrows quizzically. Grady said, "Let's do it."

It was as if a siren had sounded through the streets of Franklin. Within minutes, there could not have been a human being in that Tennessee community who did not know—by telepathy?—that the long-awaited pool game of the century between Grady Ray and Andrew Morrell was about to happen. Stores emptied, and every person that could get inside Ham's did. Norman Rockwell would have loved it, surely focusing on Baker Lane, our one-armed barber (he cut with his right, with a strong rubber band holding the comb on his left nub) and his portly patron, still adorned with the barber's sheet. They had come from next door with no hesitation, having easily agreed to a hiatus in the tonsorial treatment. Both were jammed behind the cash register. It was truly like the "Gunfight at the OK Corral."

Very thoughtfully, Mist' Andra came over to me and handed me a package he had brought in with him. "Hang on to this for me, Cot." He figured if he assigned me such an important task, I would be permitted by Ham to keep my seat and not be bumped to accommodate a more prestigious patron. Lord, I appreciated that. I had never seen this man shoot pool, and like a fellow who was about to see Babe Ruth hit, I did not want to be robbed of the opportunity.

Both parties milled about while the occupants on the first table hurriedly finished up. All other tables ceased play. The combatants first painstakingly washed their hands, applied talcum powder, and began the process of selecting their cue sticks, an important undertaking.

When Table Number One became open, Ham very importantly announced that Ray and Morrell would play Nine Ball. The object of Nine Ball was to run all the balls in rotation so as to get to the Nine Ball. He who sank that ball, having called the proper pocket so as to eliminate blind luck, won the game and got to break in the next game.

"For how much, fellows?" Ordinarily this question would have been verboten, but surely it was unthinkable that the scope of THIS game would not have entitled the community to be privy to the information.

"How about five, Grady?" Mist' Andra asked. Grady blinked quickly a couple of times, his Adam's apple did a strange little number, and then he nodded, "Sure."

This was big money. The average stakes for a pool game in Ham's was maybe two bits. Heavy hitters played for a dollar perhaps. This was 1940, and gambling five dollars a game for Nine Ball in Franklin, Tennessee, was plenty strong. But, under the circumstances, it needed to be strong. Each man took out a five-dollar bill and stuck it in a corner pocket, as was the custom (you don't play pool on credit).

You could have heard a pin drop when Ham flipped the coin. Grady called heads, and it was heads. He would break. A significant development, because in Nine Ball a strong break would see two or three balls sunk, and the rest of them spread out pretty well on the table. A good player could often go ahead and run the table.

Grady broke. It sounded like an explosion. Two went in. Other than heavy breathing and the buzz of a few flies, there was no sound. One heard only the click of the balls and the squeak of the chalk on the cue sticks, done painstakingly by the players to be sure that the all-important "English" they put on the cue ball would take it to the right position after the shot.

Grady ran the rest of the balls, and loudly and dramatically slammed the butt end of his cue stick on the wooden floor, the universal pool room signal that the game is over and the balls need to be racked. He reached in the table pocket and gently extricated the two fives.

Mist' Andra simply leaned lazily up against the wall, with his eyes squinting through the smoke from the Chesterfield in his mouth.

They anteed up again, and Grady broke, sinking the Five Ball. He cut the One into the corner, left himself an easy straight-in on the Two, made it, but then found that he had his first problem. The cue ball was frozen on one rail and the Three Ball was frozen across from it on the other side rail. He had to bank it in the corner. Tough shot.

He missed.

Mist' Andra's eyes looked like those of an alligator half submerged in the water and pretending to be a log, while a plump doe moved gingerly near him to get a drink.

He adjusted his straw boater, threw the cigarette down, shot his cuffs, chalked his cue, and went to work. Did he go to work! It was 3:35 when his turn came.

At 4:20, Grady threw his stick on the table and said, "Aw shit!" Morrell had run eight straight racks of Nine Ball. He never missed. Moving steadily and smoothly around the table, his eyes narrowed, and never glancing at anything other than the table, he had done what he had come to do. He *was* like a predator. It was a hell of a thing to see. No bowl game, no World Series, no heavyweight championship ever offered a greater build-up, more tension and excitement, and a more satisfactory conclusion (for me) than that pool game in the little Tennessee town.

Mist' Andra nodded at Grady, hung up his pool cue, gave Ham a little tip, and moved toward the door. He came by me, and I handed him his package. I had an enormous smile on my face. He winked at me and then reached up and pulled my baseball cap down over my eyes. My proudest moment ever, perhaps. Then he walked out of the pool room. We had whipped 'em!

Meanwhile, back at Shoestring Farm, our thoroughbred racing venture—struggling with a decidedly disastrous marketing plan—was having another nail driven into its coffin by the outbreak of World War II.

Not much good was happening in 1941 and 1942. My mother had delivered my sister Sally in August of '40, and her existence was a happy enough ingredient in our lives. But complicating life considerably was the fact that my grandfather, Dick Cothran, had had a stroke, and he and my grandmother had been forced to come live with us at the farm. Ghastly timing.

The hopes of the oft-dreamed-about "financial settlement" that my father felt was due him as severance from the Des Moines Coca Cola bottling plant were pretty well abandoned. He was drinking hard; the racehorses were hardly running, nor, God knows, were they winning anything.

When the United States entered the war, many racetracks were closed as "non-essential wartime activities." Gasoline was rationed and getting exceedingly hard to come by, and it was almost impossible to transport horses. In fact, by the time 1942 was half over, you literally could not *give* a horse away, much less sell one. Bill Campbell was not exactly in a growth-oriented business.

The Shoestring operation was now known to be financially very shaky. The contractor who had built the splendid barn, constructed the racetrack, and put up all the white board fences had not been fully paid. Things were understandably getting nasty, and lawyers were becoming involved. Things were flat going to hell.

It really was a terribly depressing time. I made it worse.

My folks had a period of conviviality and "relaxation" before dinner each night. My mother's custom—all her life—was to have one highball before dinner, one glass of beer with one cube of ice at 10:00 p.m., and a cup of black coffee and a shot of bourbon at 11:30 p.m. That was it—never more, but always that. Odd.

My father had no such structured pre—or post-prandial pattern for libations. Either he was drinking nothing, or he was drinking everything! The latter program prevailed during these troubled times.

My curfew at this early fourteen-year-old stage was ten p.m. This was precisely when my mother was having her beer, and when my father would be joining her with any number of alcoholic possibilities. It was our custom that I would come in and join them for a few minutes before going to bed. They wanted to know, naturally, something about the nature of my evening's entertainment.

One evening after several of us had tackled a generous amount of our beloved Gerst Beer, with maybe a little muscatel wine thrown in, I reluctantly joined my mom and dad, and they quickly observed that I conversed as if I had a mouthful of marbles. I was obviously tight.

"What's the matter with you? Have you been DRINKING?" they asked incredulously. They stared hard at me. They hadn't counted on this particular unhappy development.

I took a fling at being innocent. Wide-eyed and wounded, I answered, "Drinking? What do you mean? Of course not!" But my thick tongue gave me away, and I surrendered pretty quickly, admitting that I had tried "a little beer."

A short, but to-the-point, talk ensued. A few questions were asked, but I was dismissed pretty soon so I could go to bed and participate in another conversation on the morrow, when my head would be clearer.

That conversation did take place the next morning—Thanksgiving Day, it was. I listened, agreed with all their points, made all the right sounds, and promised faithfully to be satisfied with a token drink, only at home under their supervision. This would have meant a third of a glass of beer, or a Toddy with a couple of teaspoons of bourbon on festive occasions—all very nice, but it would not have accomplished the bonhomie of an evening at The Globe.

The conversation was concluded with good feelings by the three of us. And I did regret bringing further unhappiness into an already understandably dismal family atmosphere.

But two nights later I did the same thing. Throughout the rest of the fall and the following spring the influence of strong drink in my demeanor was detected on several occasions. They got so they pretended not to observe it. But they did.

Was I not supervised? Well, by today's rather ridiculous standards, I was practically under house arrest. But I was not on a tight rein. My parents were middling-conscientious parents, but their sophistication leaned them toward unstructured child rearing. Their subconscious attitude was that the sooner I became a peer and could be treated as an adult, the better. There were not a lot of intimate, instructive chats, and there was zero coverage of the birds and bees. Even if they had been inclined in that direction, the desperate, disconcerting nature of this period in their lives would have nudged child rearing to the back burner.

As far as church was concerned, my folks had a warm, pleasant feeling toward the Presbyterian Church but never attended it. The only guidance I got from church came from weekly attendance at the Franklin Church of Christ—instigated by me. The Church of Christ, or Campbellite Church in Middle Tennessee, was a big deal. I went there for social reasons, strange as that may seem. It was fun to go there and sing with friends.

There were no musical instruments allowed in that church. I once asked one of my friends—a sanctified, anointed, baptized member in good standing—why that was so. He explained, "Because Jesus didn't play a musical instrument." I don't to this day know the real reason, but I don't think my pal had it right. His answer to me simply conjured up visions of Jesus attempting the saxophone or the slide trombone. Still, the Church of Christ congregations were noted for their sharp harmony. Singing was a big pastime in that small town in that era, and it was terrific to cut loose on Sunday mornings with "Love Lifted Me" or "Beulah Land."

Despite my church activity, my parents decided that life in Franklin and at Battle Ground was a little swifter than was in my best interest. In the fall, my high school sophomore year, I would become a dormitory student at Darlington School for Boys in Rome, Georgia. This was our ancestral hometown, and a distant cousin was headmaster of that rather rigid institution.

This was a grievous development for an adolescent, enthusiastic indeed about tasting the seamier and exciting side of life. I was convinced that Franklin would offer more of it than would Rome, Georgia. So were my parents.

At age fourteen, I had become a rather accomplished drinker, having graduated to whisky on occasion. While at this point I was certainly not a full-fledged, clearly-defined alcoholic, I might easily have been voted "Most Likely to Succeed."

Girls were now beginning to interest me, although my achievements in the distaff department lagged alarmingly behind the partying. My appearance was still too chubby to give me the swashbuckling Errol Flynn image that I sometimes imagined I could bring off.

Nor did I possess a gift of gab that some of my peers and older companions seemed to possess. I had been counseled by some of the local Lotharios that I needed "a line." I was not precocious, and I really couldn't quite grasp what "having a line" or being "slick" or "smooth" entailed. Whatever it was, I had not yet located the key.

When the evening's activities were to feature drinking, I was always a welcome addition to the group. When romance was the mission, it was made clear by my buddies that my presence was a distinct liability.

In addition to my general backwardness as a budding ladies man, the fact that I had not yet learned to dance was a further retardant to my progress with the thirteen—and fourteen-year-old girls of Franklin.

I remember well an incident that was symbolic of my image of suavity, or complete lack of it. On Saturday and Sunday afternoons, five or six girls and twice as many boys would often meet at one of the girls' homes. Records would be played, there would be dancing, the bottle would perhaps be spun, and there would be much conviviality, flirting, and a little minor league petting perhaps.

My friend William Brittain—whose social dexterity was in the same league as mine at the time—and I heard one Sunday that "everyone" was going to Rebecca Chandler's house. We decided to go. Invitations were certainly not ever extended; it was just a matter of instinctively knowing who belonged. And who did not.

William and I, decked out in ensembles that we were sure bespoke nonchalant sharpness, strode up to the Chandler front porch and optimistically twisted the doorbell handle. Nothing happened. We did it again. Still nothing.

Peering through the glass, we thought we could see shadowy figures, and we heard much subdued giggling and the vocal strains of Helen O'Connell rendering "Green Eyes." Did we detect the sound of footsteps seeking a hiding place? Someone was home. We beat on the door glass, but a response never came.

William and I departed, neither of us choosing to acknowledge the fact that we were clearly not wanted.

"Wonder where they are?" William asked.

"Maybe they've gone swimming out to Willow Plunge."

"Yeah."

Neither of us could fail to observe the seven or eight bicycles strewn around the yard. Gentlemen callers.

Perhaps this slight was a subliminal stimulus for me to achieve the status that would come with visiting a whorehouse, since I was clearly not welcome in the Chandlers' parlor, though I hasten to point out that the rewards of those two environments were certain to be decidedly dissimilar.

Some of the older "boulevardiers" of Franklin decided that I—perhaps with another friend who was equally inexperienced—should be introduced to the joys that were to be found in Nashville's Red Light District, "down behind the Capitol." The idea was scary but in no way unappealing.

Three older guys (age seventeen) made up the orientation committee. After several long, enthusiastic, and most exhaustive sessions of indoctrination, it was decided that Tuesday afternoon would be a good time for our de-virgination (Saturdays were busy days and no time for the introduction of amateurs). My friend Billy Clemens and I were to catch the Interurban from Franklin to Nashville, then transfer to a city bus, get off on Capitol Avenue, walk one block west, and look for the three-story brick building with the Southern Bell Public Telephone sign out front, a dead giveaway that something unusual would be going on inside.

We had been counseled and counseled some more about the technique that would maximize the enrichment of a whorehouse experience. I was led to believe if I implemented all of this properly, the lady would perhaps insist on giving me back my two dollars! I might even *make* money from the pleasure I would provide!

The day came. Both Billy and I went to the Interurban station just off the square in Franklin and skulked about surreptitiously for fear that some meddlesome adult would interrogate us on the nature of our journey.

We were nervous as hell. And both of us, I am sure, would have loved to have aborted the project—which would have been absolutely unthinkable!

The trip to Nashville took forever, although we were in no hurry whatsoever. Once in the city we caught our bus, got off at our stop, and strolled nonchalantly toward the brick building, easily identified from numerous descriptions.

Billy and I had fantasized that we would be ushered into a parlor where there would be numerous beautiful girls, all excited over our arrival. We would each pick out our partner, much to the disappointment of the rejects, and then go upstairs and put into practice that which we had been taught.

We rang the bell. No one came. We rang it again. Nothing. Oh Lord, not another experience like the one at the Chandlers'. We rang it again and simultaneously rapped on the glass.

Inside we heard a weary, "Yeah, yeah—hold your horses!"

The door was opened by an older woman who certainly could have been our grandmother. She had been pretty, but not lately. Clearly she must be the madam!

We had been told to say, "I would like a date." I did say it.

"Me too," said Billy.

She looked us up and down, smiled coyly, and said, "Well, there's just me. My name is Peg, and I'll do you right! Who's going to go first?"

Billy took the words out of my mouth, "You go ahead. I'll wait."

"Come on then," Peg said, and we traipsed upstairs. I surrendered my two dollars. Preparations were made, and the big moment had arrived. After a few half-hearted attempts to put into play some of the tactics in which I had been schooled, Peg showed me how it was going to be . . . and about thirty seconds later, it *had been*! Thank God.

When I slunk downstairs, I gave Billy a knowing wink, indicating that I had accomplished everything I set out to do, though he certainly grasped the fact that it had been a mighty short visit.

Peg, having completed some abbreviated ablutions, called down to "send the other kid up."

Billy didn't stay up there very long either.

We said farewell to Peg, who had never turned two tricks any more efficiently—from a time standpoint, that is.

Off we hurried to catch our bus and then the Interurban back to Franklin. After all, we had much to discuss and many details to provide during what was left of the summer.

In the fall I would leave Franklin. And I would leave it much wiser in the ways of the world than when I came to it.

CHAPTER 5

"GODDAMNED SHIT SCHOOL"

It was 1942, World War II was spilling out all over the planet in frightening fury, and the outlook was dicey indeed for the Allies. God knows, our guys in Italy, North Africa, and throughout the South Pacific were taking the worst of it. At home, there were some Americans who were making a killing from profiteering, and there were those who were taking it on the chin economically.

The Campbells fell into the upper echelons of that latter category. Bill Campbell was struggling just to find homes for "those damned racehorses" and at least eliminate the expense of caring for them. He had no hope of selling them. And he and my mother were using all their imagination, charm, and what was left of their resources to avoid bankruptcy. I can't imagine how they paid for me to enroll in Darlington School for Boys. But enrolled I was.

So that fall I got on a Greyhound bus in Nashville and headed two hundred miles southward to Rome, Georgia, and my sophomore year in a new school. My folks would have certainly taken me, but between gas rationing and having their hands full at the beleaguered farm, they had no choice but to send me on the bus.

Being a new kid on the first day in a new school is not easy at any time, and I had played that role often (in grammar school it was my custom to establish my presence on opening day by throwing up on the desk!). Adding to my difficulties on the first day in a new school was the fact that as a young boy—regrettably—I was called "Cothran." Invariably this would cause confusion. You could stake your life on the fact that someone from the principal's office would breeze into the room the first morning of school and ask, "Is there a little girl in here named CATHERINE Campbell?" When I was forced to raise my hand, this, of course, would launch my school year in spectacular fashion, creating an indelible impact with my fellow students.

But this particular situation was especially difficult. In the first place, I do not recall many bus trips in my lifetime that had about them an aroma of triumph. This lonesome journey was no exception. I seemed to be the only adolescent civilian among what seemed like at least a division of soldiers and sailors, with a generous sprinkling of nursing mothers, and a couple of whores in transit.

I stood up all the way to Chattanooga, disembarked, waited a couple of hours, and then transferred to an Atlanta-bound bus that went through Rome.

There was not much relief upon my arrival in that town. While it was the hometown of my parents, it was essentially an unfamiliar place to me, and I was plenty homesick before I reached its environs. I now had to report, unsupported, to a new school where I knew no one. I took no solace in being a distant cousin of the headmaster—not something I could glamorize with my future fellow students. Indeed, it figured to be more of a liability than anything else.

I got my trunk and a large suitcase off the Greyhound and caught a taxi out to the campus. Darlington was far prettier and more upscale than good old BGA. The elegant red brick buildings nestled attractively around a rather large lake, with swans and other decorative waterfowl swimming languidly about. It was a knockout, the kind of place the parents adore. But Darlington was formidable, and it scared the living hell out of me. Everywhere, except with me, there was fellowship. Affluent-looking, athletic, All-American-type young boys were greeting one another, laughing uproariously at obscure and very inside situations, and definitely paying no attention to me. Nor could I blame them. I understood it, but how I yearned for Rhumba Pete, and the lame and the halt of the Battle Ground student body.

I was "processed" and then shown to my room by a hearty but slightly harassed and preoccupied proctor. There I encountered my roommate and his parents, all enthusiastically engaged in the process of getting settled. My "roomy" was a perky little guy, who had started as a freshman the previous year and had been the representative of that class on the Honor Council. The Proctor introduced him as Sonny (wouldn't you know it!) Schuyler, and pointed out that he was an "old boy." Believe me, he was "Darlington" to the core. This was unappealing to me at the time, as I would have been more comfortable with another green, confused, and miserable neophyte as a roommate. Somehow I got the impression that Sonny was not going to have showing me the ropes as number one on his list of things to do.

The enthusiastic, crew-cutted Sonny had brought an inexhaustible supply of University of Georgia accouterments, which were being positioned on "our" walls. Sonny immediately began interrogating me on my opinion of Frankie Sinkwich, Charley Trippi, George Poschner, and other Georgia Bulldog football luminaries. When I contributed little that was illuminating, he asked me which college team I supported. I rather lamely came up with the Vanderbilt Commodores, and he quickly lost what little interest there had been.

The three Schuylers greeted my arrival with politeness, some decently well-concealed disappointment, but definitely not what you could call keen enthusiasm. Since poise was not exactly my middle name, I couldn't do much to make this new relationship catch fire.

While we were all unpacking, Sonny and the parents seemed very curious about the absence of my family. I did have the good sense to toss in my kinship with Ernest Wright, the beloved headmaster. This struck a blow, but by no means carried the day.

As the afternoon wore on, there was a steady stream of exuberant visitors who popped in our room to greet this popular little fireball from Summerville, Georgia. He was clearly, because of his size, cuteness, and peppy ways, a crowd-pleaser; faculty and boys alike seemed to be overjoyed that he had returned for another year at good old Darlington.

They would check me out surreptitiously during their benign scuffling and horseplay and then glance back at him sympathetically as if to say, "Not what you were hoping for, is it old boy!"

The school year commenced. The roommate situation unfolded about as I figured. Sonny and I got along adequately, but there was no warmth between us. I was quite insecure to begin with, and Sonny was not going to be the man to solve that problem and make me feel "a part of the Darlington family."

When I had arrived on the campus, I was under the clear impression that I knew no one at the school. But I was mistaken. The first evening when the students of 1942-43 went to supper, I encountered my dear old first cousin, Dabney Irving, he of Sav-A-Rip door-to-door fame and the son of Uncle Al. In Des Moines, Uncle Al had worked for my father at the Coca Cola bottling plant. He fired him when he learned that Al interpreted his job description as Sales Manager to include going horseback riding with one of his lady friends almost every afternoon.

This unhappy event resulted in the relocation of the Irving family from Iowa back to the friendly environs of Atlanta, Georgia. The relationship between the Campbells and the Irvings was distinctly chilly, and Dabney's attitude toward me reflected this. Thus, prior to my arrival I did not know of Dabney's selection of Darlington as a place to finish out his high school career.

When we encountered each other, we went through the motions but hardly more than that.

Interestingly, while I had a roommate that was not ideal for me, Dabney had drawn the lemon of all lemons. Since leaving Des Moines, Dabney had matured rapidly and had blossomed into a rather accomplished social animal. He had learned to dress well and had inherited some of Uncle Al's oily charm with the opposite sex. He was part of a coterie of Atlanta boys attending Darlington. They were categorized in the jargon of that city as "jellies." They were pretty slick articles, far more precocious and knowledgeable in the ways of the world than their sixteen years entitled them to be. They would quickly become the "In Crowd."

For this reason, it would have been a matter of supreme importance to Dabney that he be assigned a roommate of similar inclinations and suavity.

Instead he had been domiciled with the dreaded Richard Bush-Burke, also an "old boy." This young man was the son of a famed physician in Atlanta. While he was not afflicted or handicapped, he was sickly, frail, most unattractive, and exceedingly strange. He was alarmingly thin and had the complexion of cookie dough, a shock of very unruly red hair, bright red liver-like lips, and a huge nose that constantly housed unspeakable contents. Personal hygiene was not high on Bush-Burke's priority list.

Further, he had no personality, zero sense of humor, and his very existence was singularly abrasive. He was undoubtedly brilliant, but not the roommate that old Dab would have selected to further embellish his own image as one of the "beautiful people" of Darlington. Bush-Burke was a serious liability in the plans of Dabney Irving to conquer the student body.

Richard Bush-Burke had been sent the previous year to Darlington with hopes it would "bring him out." But not much progress was ever to be made in this endeavor. He was the immediate target for bullying and serious harassment. Children and adolescents are mean as hell for the most part, and Darlingtonians—despite accent on the Honor Council and Young Men's Christian Association, etc., etc.—were not deficient in this capacity. When it came to making the life of Bush-Burke miserable, Dabney led the onslaught. He was constantly infuriated about having to live with this nerd of all nerds, and he took out his frustration directly on the nerd.

Occasionally neighbors on our floor would hear a blood-curdling scream of rage from the Irving/Bush-Burke room, and one would know that Dabney had pushed "Bushy" to a complete frenzy. At that point the victim had an oath that seemed to sum up his rage and indignation. He would shriek, "Goddamned SHIT School!!!"

We loved it when this colorful epithet would be evoked. And indeed "Goddamned Shit School" became sort of a sub rosa school battle cry.

And I had reason to appreciate it to the fullest extent.

To help defray my tuition I had been able to get a job as a waiter in the school dining room. Being on the "shift" meant that you set up the tables, served the food, and cleared the dishes at either lunch or the evening meal. You were given financial credit for each meal you worked. I opted for the supper shift.

I had been assigned two tables of twelve. One of the tables included a young faculty member (Mr. Maddux), his very pretty wife, and ten boys. Alas, included in this number were Dabney and young Master Bush-Burke.

The latter student was not one you would seek out as a dining companion, because of his aforementioned untidy hygienic patterns. These characteristics, demonstrated at mealtime, repulsed and angered his unfortunate tablemates. And consequently this could bring on an intense wave of mealtime teasing and harassment, despite the supposed vigilance of the faculty member (who was probably also disgusted by the young man, if the truth were known).

As the server, I remember all too well one evening when several young men—led by Dabney, of course—had concentrated their abuse on Bush-Burke, while Mr. and Mrs. Maddux had seen fit to look the other way.

Shortly after the Jello salad had been consumed, and the heart of the meal—beef hash, mashed potatoes, and creamed spinach—had been placed by me in front of the students, Bushy reached the saturation point. He had had enough!

He took his plate in both hands and, with a maniacal look in his eyes, hurled it straight above him against the ceiling (no mean feat!) and screamed in a frightful voice that could have been heard in downtown Rome: "GODDAMNED SHIT SCHOOL!"

You could have heard a pin drop. Boys and teachers alike stared in stunned silence at this spectacular display of protest.

The ceiling was covered with spinach, potatoes, and hash, as were numerous diners within range of the explosion. Suddenly, Bush-Burke's tablemates became quite busy with the innocent consumption of their own evening meals, as high-ranking faculty types rushed to our table to deal with this obvious crisis.

This outbreak did not solve Bushy's problems of harassment, but it did make for smooth sailing for the rest of the evening.

At this point, I was not hearing much from my folks back in Franklin, and no news was bad news. They had reached the point in the winter of 1943 of being absolutely hemmed-in financially; they could not move. The only way out was to auction off Shoestring Farm, the property and all of our belongings. They were preparing for this unhappy event, and it took place in the spring. Our periodic exchange of letters (phone calls were too expensive) never prepared me for these dark developments. The first I knew of the auction was when several of my Franklin friends wrote me that they had gone together and bought my shotgun at the sale and were holding it for me. This thoughtful gesture (from teenagers no less) is perhaps as nice a compliment as I have ever gotten.

While my family was arranging its ignominious departure from Franklin, with plans for a desperation retreat to their old hometown of Rome, Georgia, I was yearning to swap places with them. I wanted to get back to Franklin and good old BGA. Darlington was just not my place. It was a little too buttoned-up for me. The students were somehow stereotyped into a rather slick blandness. I guess if I hadn't adored Battle Ground, I might have liked it fine. But I missed the old combination Battle Ground offered up: cripples, misfits, a zesty touch of mild mental derangement, good old country boys, and a batch of well-heeled, small-town Southern boys.

I had an average sort of year at Darlington. I went out for football (Junior Varsity second string), my grades were fair, and I somehow got inveigled into being on the counsel of the Young Men's Christian Association, which meant I was orchestrating the chapel presentations, mandatory for all students.

Being a dormitory student at Darlington was not conducive to developing my drinking career, which had certainly begun to blossom when I was in Tennessee. However, this involved only a temporary hiatus; when conditions permitted, it would be resumed with gusto.

I had many great-aunts and uncles, cousins, etc., in Rome, but none of them represented an exciting way to enrich my social calendar. During my year there, I did force myself to have what was known as a "parlor date" (in the young lady's parlor). I had only one, and I could have done without that one. The procedure for a parlor date was first to work it out with the girl. Then one made check-out arrangements with the school, with the clear understanding that the student (caller) must quit the parlor so as to arrive back at base by ten p.m.

In my case, I caught a bus into town, transferred to the West Rome bus, and arrived—with rather sweaty palms—at the home of Helen Murray, sometimes known as "Whale Tail."

Helen was a lively young woman, quite comely of countenance, but considerably "high in flesh." As one might guess from her rather unflattering nickname, much of her avoirdupois was housed in her behind. Her niceness, chipper manner, and cute face tended to make up for her less-than-ideal form.

My arrival for our date came as the Murray family finished their dinner hour. This necessitated several minutes of convivial exchange with the father and mother. After this sparkling repartee, Helen and I repaired to the sun porch to "consummate"—to use the term very loosely—our date.

This lasted until about 9:15, with a mid-date break for some lemonade, at which time Helen badly needed to reload her conversational arsenal. During the two hours we were together, I perhaps contributed three badly strained minutes of dialog. When the date was mercifully terminated that evening, I am sure even the gregarious Helen returned to her boudoir longing for solitude and silence. She had carried a heavy load and had done it with grit and gameness. I, on the other hand, wondered how in the first place I could have possibly subjected myself to such a daunting test of my social graces. At one point during our date, Helen good-naturedly exclaimed, "I don't know what I have to do to bring you out!"

I knew that I had failed miserably. Two other things I knew when I left that poor girl's house. One, a pitcher of Gerst beer, instead of that lemonade, would have moved me up immeasurably. Two, the burden of the young lady in social intercourse is often even more crucial and exacting than in the other kind.

Another social engagement that was unforgettable also occurred when I was at Darlington, and it created a lifelong devotion to a very unlikely beneficiary.

There was a day student at Darlington whose name was Ed Hine. Ed was something of a misfit. He had a rather raucous personality that contributed to incompatibility in most cases. He was a big fellow, fattish in a strong sort of a way. His hairline appeared about two inches above his eyebrows, and his tonsorial treatment seemed to have been created with an eggbeater. Ed was loud, loutish, and sputtered and sprayed the air as he tried unsuccessfully to be funny much of the time. In general, he wanted to fit in but was not ever going to be one of the "beautiful people."

But you could not have a better, more loyal friend. And he was one of the few truly fine, kind people I have ever known.

My first real encounter with Ed came when Darlington announced that an upcoming Sunday was going to be "Visitation Day." This meant that any day student could invite a dormitory student to his home for Sunday dinner, if both parties were so inclined (and few on either side were).

Ed, in his earnest, square, and clumsy way, was enthusiastic about the concept, and surprisingly he invited me. Before I had a chance to prepare a feasible regret, I had accepted.

Ed's father ran a laundry in town, and his mother was dead. Ed helped out at the laundry from time to time, and he and his old man had an amicable relationship, but I don't think either one wanted a steady diet of the other one. Ed Hine lived with his maternal grandmother and her daughter, who was retarded significantly with Down Syndrome.

Their home was a little, one-story, white house with a wraparound porch, modest but situated in a high-class section of Rome. The house had an impecunious and distinct grandmotherly look about it.

I arrived at 12:30 to begin my Visitation Day. Ed met me at the door, oozing hearty good cheer, and ushered me into the parlor. The inside of the house had an atmosphere that I have always equated with down-at-the-heels Southern aristocracy. It was dark, musty, with the faint odor of lilacs, cat litter, old folks, and a trace of onion. A few pictures of Robert E. Lee and Nathan Bedford Forrest looked down on heavy, overstuffed velveteen furniture, and the entire house was teeming with bric-a-brac.

The grandmother (Mrs. Randolph) and her retarded daughter, Sarah, came bustling in from the kitchen, and Ed did the introductions, pointing out that I was the great nephew of Isabel Gammon, the Rome *News Tribune* Society Editor.

Mrs. Randolph could have been the perfect understudy for Josephine Hull, the sweet, vague, very dotty aunt in *Arsenic and Old Lace*.

Sarah was a tiny woman of about forty with typical Down features and the innocent, enthusiastic personality that invariably goes with that affliction. Her wispy black hair was cut in sort of a "Dutch boy" style. She was bubbling with excitement over this pathetic "special occasion." Sarah had been schooled on

61

shaking hands, and she shook mine several times after we seated ourselves for the obligatory pre-Sunday dinner social spell. After discussing my progress at Darlington, a little war news, and Aunt Isabel, we all went into the dining room and had our Sunday dinner.

There was nothing remarkable about any of this event, really. But more than sixty years after that dismal Sunday dinner I am still blown away as I remember the pure goodness, the absolutely wonderful, dogged, un-self-conscious spirit of Ed Hine. Was I blown away on that day? Of course not. I thought, "What the hell kind of nut is this guy, inviting me out here to have a meal with this goofy old lady and her moron daughter?"

I would have suffered the tortures of the damned rather than be observed by my peers while in the company of my mother or father, and they were attractive people. This unjustified attitude would have been true of most boys or girls fourteen or fifteen years old.

Not Ed. This lady and her daughter were who they were. They were his people, his family. I was a guest. So let's all have a nice time. Nothing complicated about it.

During this period, lasting several hours, Ed served energetically as moderator, busy complimenting his grandmother on the quality of the meal, encouraging me in any conversational sallies I might find fruitful and, for my comfort, deflecting in his kind way the off-the-wall offerings from the mentally deficient Sarah.

While I did not appreciate at the time that I was seeing a wonderful example of unadulterated goodness, I am happy to say the light came on in my brain shortly after leaving that strange little threesome. And I thought a lot about it. Ed Hine became my good friend. Later he got me a job on a surveying crew, and I needed that job. Still later, in college, he once scraped together $40 to loan me, and that $40 would be like $400,000 today. No exaggeration.

Ed stayed in Rome, Georgia, went into the cotton brokerage business, made a lot of money, married a fine girl, and produced some very high-class descendants. Then he died, earlier than he should have.

Late in the spring of 1943 my family moved to Rome, acknowledging an agonizing, humiliating defeat. While I was finishing out my year as a Darlington boarding student, they arrived in town and rented a respectable but cheap house for themselves, my sister Sally, and their two dachshunds.

My mother got a job as a salesperson at Wyatt's Book Store; my father took a job as a clerk in an insurance agency. They probably would not have landed those jobs—so ignominious to them—had it not been wartime with a severe shortage of manpower. What a shocking comedown!

I have often thought of this. Usually if a family (or a person) has risen to a certain level of standing in society or in the community, and then had their fortunes plummet, losing everything, there is a sort of communal safety net, made up of connections, that stops a complete fall. The "system" will simply not let them sink too low. There is an unidentifiable, unrecognized infrastructure hazily in place, and it clicks into motion and prevents that entity from economic self-destruction. This is especially true if there are strong family connections in the community.

My mother had never worked a day in her sheltered life, and had been a prominent member of the loftiest social structure wherever she had been. Junior League, presented at Court, queen of an ultra prestigious Mardi Gras Ball—suddenly this woman is now going to wait on the public in a bookstore?

My father was a noted aviator, a public speaker of great accomplishment, a pal of the great Ty Cobb, president of a Coca-Cola Bottling Company—really a celebrity. A big shot! Now he could do no better than a menial job in a small business that sold homeowner's insurance. Just doesn't happen that way. This was a descent that had surely spiraled completely out of control. There was no safety net here.

When June came and the school term ended, I was able to get a job as a delivery boy and general handyman, joining my mother on the staff of Wyatt's Book Store.

The summer was not bad for me. For my parents it was rough. Predictably, my father lasted about sixty days at the insurance agency before a disagreement caused him to tell someone in authority to go to hell.

On the other hand, my mother was a natural-born salesperson and quickly became a terrific asset at Wyatt's. She had good connections in Rome and became highly sought after by Roman matrons in search of furniture, books, or gifts. It wasn't very long before she and Mr. Wyatt were discussing the viability of starting an antiques department.

My father had an inspiration. It seemed an impractical scheme, but one that would restore the aura of prestige that he not only craved but could not live without. He would write a book. Based on his immediate past history, he would write a novel based on the development of the Coca-Cola Company. Could he write? Who knew? Again, he would figure that out. How difficult could it be?

In perhaps his masterpiece of salesmanship, he had the unmitigated gall to approach a casual friend of the family with the preposterous idea that this Rome lady of some means would invest in this venture!

She did.

She advanced him five thousand dollars (during World War II!) for twenty-five percent of the net profits of the book. Now he would require the appropriate setting to stimulate his creative juices. He bought a typewriter and the required office paraphernalia and rented a small office above a downtown retail establishment. He got set to write a book he would ultimately title *Big Beverage*.

So things were looking up financially. I chose mid-summer as a time to launch my campaign to get back to Franklin for the fall semester. Rather cleverly, I first implored Lila and Bill for permission to join the Merchant Marine when I became sixteen that September. You could actually do that, if you had written permission from your parents. Naturally they did not buy that idea, but as a consolation prize, they agreed that I could return as a boarding student to Battle Ground.

In September, I caught "Big Blue"—for me, bus travel was the realistic (practically the only) form of transportation during the war years—to Nashville, rode the Interurban down to beloved Franklin, and trudged up the hill to BGA. There was much yelling, shoving, and punching one another in the belly, as old boys reunited and registered for the 1943-1944 school year. I was back where I belonged.

I was assigned, along with fifteen other mostly juniors and seniors, to Barton Hall, which was about as much a "hall" as would be a phone booth. Barton Hall was a funny-looking stucco house, with a lot of front porch. It was somehow reminiscent of a mushroom house. There were six dormitory rooms, with two or three boys occupying each. I drew Cecil Oliver, a wealthy boy from a cotton plantation in Arkansas. I knew him well and liked him. We had a third roomy. His name was Arthur Smith, he was from Mobile, and he came to be known as "Same Shirt." Personal hygiene was not Arthur's strongest point.

Barton Hall offered no living room, nor any kitchen. There was one bathroom. One. It was constantly in use. It was in the back corner of the house. Next to the bathroom was the smoker, a room perhaps twelve by twelve feet. In it were a few cane bottom chairs and, in the middle of the room, a kettle of sand. The room was designed exclusively for our smoking pleasure, and in those days we all smoked—but supposedly only in the smoker, and with written permission from your parents.

The room next to the smoker and on the other back corner of the house was the dwelling of Mr. Eldon Lambeth, our faculty supervisor. "Professor" Lambeth was typical of what the lower-end prep schools could recruit during World War II. He was probably twenty-six years of age, a graduate of an obscure college, and had been wounded in the back while on duty in 1942 with the U.S. Coast Guard. Lambeth was decidedly junior on the small BGA faculty.

The noteworthy thing about this man was that he had a wife of perhaps twenty-one years of age, and she was some kind of a stone-cold killer in looks. Her name turned out to be Tanya, but she was, of course, addressed as "Mrs. Lambeth." She was the outstanding occupant of Barton Hall.

Outrageously, this poor couple inhabited a meager little room and had to share the bath with only sixteen others! When this young woman, who worked as a stenographer in Franklin, wished to take her daily bath, she had to pass through the smoker. Once her schedule for daily ablutions was established as a pretty certain late afternoon occurrence, the smoker would be jammed to capacity.

With a pretty little smile on her face and her nylon bathrobe tightened to indicate clearly every heavenly nook and cranny, she would wend her way through the smoker amidst sudden silence, intense stares, and a great deal of heavy breathing. We would all then imagine what that lovely creature was doing in that grimy little bathroom.

But we really didn't have to imagine too long. One of our Barton Hall stalwarts, "Greasy" Grantham, had a room adjacent to the Lambeths'. And soon Greasy was enjoying unforeseen popularity, for he had drilled a small hole in the common Grantham-Lambeth wall, and thus gained visual access to the most intimate activities of the young couple. He permitted those of us in his favor to come in during the prime times and be enormously grateful voyeurs.

Often in late afternoon, when Tanya disrobed for her bath, the fires of passion were ignited in Professor Lambeth, and he would indicate unmistakably his desire to make love. This usually suited Tanya. The procedure never lasted long, it seems now. But when it was about to be consummated, knowledge of it spread as if by some sort of mental telepathy, and Greasy practically had to barricade his door. Greasy was certainly cognizant of the fact that discovery by the authorities of the splendid hole in the wall would have dire consequences for him. Therefore, his rules of the game were stringent. He exacted a heavy price (cigarettes, extra desserts, help with homework) from participants.

For quite some time, all other activities at Battle Ground were pretty well subordinated to interest in our unlikely "housemother."

A postscript of the Tanya Lambeth saga: The following year, after I had left to join the Navy, she and the star halfback were discovered by our legendary headmaster, Professor Briggs, engaged in "petting" one evening in the darkened gymnasium. There could not have been a greater indiscretion. The Lambeths left the campus shortly afterwards, and later, I'm told, that marital union was severed.

BGA was quite strict, and we were super-cautious about skirting the rules. The penalty for drinking was immediate expulsion, so my high school years at both Darlington and BGA were not productive for advancing my drinking career. However, I would soon catch up and make up for lost time.

The war was beginning to go better for the Allies, and all of us were interested, though never desperately concerned even in darkest times (that being the nature of mid-teenagers). From time to time, servicemen, who had been seniors during my freshman year at the school, came back for visits and were swarmed over for war stories. Some had seen some action; some were on the verge of going overseas. From time to time word would come back to the school about casualties of BGA servicemen that we had known. There would be plenty more to come.

I was an average student, and not terribly active in what meager student body politics and extra-curricular activities existed for the more ambitious boys. I was fairly popular. In class superlatives, I was voted "cutest" (aided somewhat by the fact that I was still a bit chubby), and also "wittiest." I sort of liked the latter. I managed to stay out of trouble and slog my way through the year.

In June I went back to Rome for the summer. My little sister was three and was generally in the daily care of a colored nurse, as my mother was becoming more of a vital fixture at Wyatt's. The antiques department was being formed, and Lila had made several buying trips to Tennessee, Kentucky, and Ohio.

My father was writing his book but having difficulty finding the most productive, inspirational atmosphere in which to exploit his creative talents. He was not one to make do at the kitchen table, nor was his small, downtown office proving stimulating. There was talk of his finding a creative refuge in the Georgia mountains or perhaps at the shore near Darien, Georgia—a location that had paid big dividends for Tennessee Williams. My father had taken a bit of a hiatus from *Big Beverage*, and he had been working on a couple of short stories. One of these was excellent. "A Snowball in Hell" was bought and published by *Esquire*. It was a story about a small black child in a hostile white world, and was chosen in a highly respected anthology as one of the best short stories of 1944. The old boy could deliver the goods.

I renewed my job at Wyatt's and was permitted to wait on customers. The ladies' section at Wyatt's was staffed with stylish young matrons who were working while hubbies were in the service. The exception was my mother.

I would have my seventeenth birthday on September 27, 1944, and the Navy would take me if I had the permission of a parent. The war was going our way in the late summer of that year, and I struck hard for permission to join up. The climate was right, and my parents agreed.

When we visited the recruiting office, I learned that since my birthday was on a Saturday, I could not join until Monday, the 29th. I would catch the bus to Macon during the weekend and be sworn in with other young patriots from Georgia on Monday.

In early September some of the more social types at Wyatt's gave me a going away party, and there was much talk and frivolity about my upcoming career as a seaman.

I was absolutely thrilled to be joining the Navy. Unnecessary though it might have been, there was still a hellacious war going on, and I was mighty anxious to "do my bit." As it turned out I came back in one piece. No one fired a shot at me in anger or any other way, and it was one of the great experiences of my life. Not a great accomplishment perhaps, but joining the U.S. Navy at age seventeen was something of which I have always been exceedingly proud.

I worked at Wyatt's on that last Saturday. And near the end of the workday, my mother and I walked together out the back door of that establishment and strolled down the alley to the street where we said goodbye. Typical of her—and most any mother—she was devastated by the idea of her son being involved in the war, but she was plucky about keeping the farewells as upbeat as possible. We hugged, she cried (of course), and I walked on home to get my bag and catch the evening bus to Macon.

My father was not there, because the Air Force had pressed him into temporary, part-time service as a civilian basic flight instructor at a nearby, small military installation. This interrupted his writing career but did bring in ready money. He wasn't there to see me off because he couldn't be there. But he was heavily invested emotionally in the project. For the next two years I would get a letter from my father practically every day, and he wrote regularly to many others in the service.

On Monday afternoon—September 29, 1944—a small draft of Georgians was jammed onto the northbound train, on our way to Great Lakes Naval Training Station, about thirty miles north of Chicago.

CHAPTER 6

THE MAKING OF A SIGNALMAN THIRD CLASS

Great Lakes Naval Training Center in the fall of '44 was gigantic—probably about the size of Toledo. Boot camp was to last three uninterrupted months, and the program was somewhat foreboding. When we arrived there, our little band of Georgians, bonded by both apprehension and geographic union, had become a pretty close-knit group. We were a bit overwhelmed when our bus from the train station made its way onto the massive base. But at age seventeen, being overwhelmed is quickly dissipated.

We were issued uniforms, equipment, and haircuts, done shockingly fast and without regard to styling that would accentuate our better features. Physicals were next, and then we were taken to our barracks, where 125 extraordinarily diverse young men were to exist—as Company 2067.

Simply by happenstance we were made up of a large draft from the mountains of Virginia and some Chicagoans, and from Youngstown and Steubenville, Ohio, came an ornery aggregation of pretty tough customers (mostly Italian). There were some other states and regions with very minor representation, including us Georgians.

A rough sort of camaraderie existed. There was always much jawing back and forth about the invariably unattractive characteristics of certain geographic origins. The Virginians inevitably invited the designation of "hillbillies" (and they were). But, considering the close quarters and the constant fatigue, our lives were pretty harmonious.

One of the indelible memories of my life came from boot camp and those barracks. I was on top in a double-decker bunk. Beneath "Campbell"—alphabetically decided—was (John) "Burke," a quiet, little fellow from Wheaton, Illinois. Burke was really an unremarkable youth, rather uninteresting, but touchingly earnest.

He was a very devout Catholic. And each night just before taps, he would kneel by his bunk, with his clasped hands under his chin, and say his prayers. There might be a noisy crap game or some other melee going on ten feet away, but Burke was going to say his prayers. It took some guts. He was not seeking attention, but neither was he going to abandon a nightly procedure that was a vital part of his life.

There were raucous, rough, and ready guys (sometimes me) in those crap games. Burke's prayer ritual certainly did not slow down the action, but from time to time you would see a gambler cut his eyes over—curiously and respectfully—at the kneeling John Burke.

I loved the Military, the Navy. I have always tended to be a "lead, follow, or get out of the way" type of guy. In this case it was strictly "follow," of course, but I was happy to do that. I liked the structure of the service, in that you did what you were told by a superior, and that superior was doing the bidding of another superior, and he got his direction from another superior, and on and on. No questions asked. You simply did it. Ridiculously, some tried to fight it. I liked drilling and military protocol, and I had a flair for doing it with panache. When the brass came to inspect our company barracks, I was automatically chosen as the guard on the door, the one who popped to attention, saluted snappily and sang out, "Attention! Company 2067 dormitory guard reporting, sir!"

Of great appeal to me were the authentic and archaic forms of communication. We were woken up by the P.A. system blaring out, "Now hear this! Heave out and lash up" (get up). Or, "Now hear this! Campbell, Signalman Third Class, lay up to the bridge, on the double" (report to the place where the officer of the day was located—quickly). I quickly put into use the salty, Navy names for things: "Hubba Hubba," "the head," "skivvies," "scuttlebutt," "chow," "ditty bag," and expressions like "I steamed outta there with both boilers lit off and no smoke showing" (left in a hurry).

I made one very close friend in boot camp. This was Charlie Evans, who had been one year to college when he joined the Navy to avoid being drafted and ending up in the infantry. Charlie had played backup to the great L.S.U. football halfback, Steve Van Buren. We were separated after boot camp but were reunited a half century later, after he retired as one of Georgia's leading real estate moguls.

Charlie Evans was in love with a lovely Georgia girl when he went into the Navy. They corresponded daily and I got a vicarious kick out of their love affair. I was delighted to learn later that he had married Mary Lib.

After boot camp, we all got a five-day leave before we were assigned to either sea duty or secondary training. I was slated for the latter, tests having indicated that I was well suited to being a Signalman. (I could spell.)

After meeting my mother and father in Cincinnati and having a wonderful time with them, I caught the train back to Great Lakes and reported for Signalman School, which was to take another three months. I would learn how to send and receive semaphore and blinking light (Morse code), and the practice of communicating with signal flags.

We had wonderful instructors, salty older Chief Petty Officers and Signalmen First Class petty officers—guys who had served with the fleet, had seen plenty of action, and had been brought back to Great Lakes for some easy duty.

Now that we were in Signalman School we were given liberty almost every weekend, and it was on these junkets to Milwaukee or Chicago that I was able to regain my touch for some bona fide drinking, encouraged by the fact that it was part of being a sailor.

Great Lakes ran trains to and from both cities with great frequency, and when you got to either destination you literally could not spend a dime. A sailor checked in at the USO, and on a blackboard was a list of places, parties, and events you could attend gratis. The Daughters of Hadassah, The Hibernians, Sons of Italy, The Kozciusko Society—they were all offering hayrides, dances, drinking bouts of some sort. If you did not improvise some place to sleep, there was always the YMCA or church recreation halls, where there were seas of cots for those in need.

All wars are horrible, of course; but from the standpoint of patriotism, national unity, morale, general good nature, and forced homefront joie de vivre, there never was one like World War II. And nowhere were those virtues practiced with more fervor than in those two great Midwestern cities. You could walk into a bar—any bar—sober as a judge, and leave knee-walking drunk without having spent a cent. Transportation, food and drink, lodging, and sweethearts were yours for the asking if you were a sailor in Milwaukee or Chicago. It was a great thing to observe, and startling now to think back on those years. And this boy did enjoy them.

I graduated from Signalman School, and most of us were assigned to the Pacific Fleet. The night before we were to embark for the coast on a troop train, four of us went into Chicago on liberty. One of our group was Art Versen, the son of a rather well-to-do Chicago couple, and an outstanding fellow. Art was one of our platoon leaders, having had some military training at Culver Military Academy.

We went to Calumet City, a rather rough area on the South Side, and had a great deal to drink. When time came for us to return to our base, we caught a train and, for some reason none of us ever remembered, we got off at the fashionable North Shore suburb of Lake Forest. All of us were quite drunk, and we lolled obnoxiously about the station waiting for the next train to take us to Great Lakes, some thirty miles north.

While there, Art (the drunkest of all) wandered away. Pieced together later was the fact that he staggered forty or fifty yards up the tracks and was leaning over a railing perhaps three or four feet away from the track, throwing up, when the streamliner express known as the "Illinois Central 400" (Chicago to Minneapolis in 400 minutes) came through at full blast. It was not a local.

We never saw Art again.

The train did not know it, we did not know it, but the Station Master did. He called the police, and we ended up back at Great Lakes several hours later being interrogated by the Shore Patrol.

The facts surrounding the tragedy were pretty well established. No one thought our remaining threesome was guilty of anything other than being completely inebriated. Still it was necessary for the Navy to conduct a formal inquiry into the affair.

We were detained indefinitely from departure for California until the matter had been completely resolved, and it was, of course, deemed appropriate that we attend Art's funeral two days later in Chicago.

Nothing was ever more difficult than visiting the Versen home and attending the funeral, accompanied by several officers from the base and the other two miscreants. We were ashamed at our role in the tragedy. Theoretically we could have been more watchful about Art, but the truth is that it could have been any of us. The Versens could not have been kinder, going to great lengths to absolve us of any blame.

The Navy Board of Inquiry did not make the same effort. But after two weeks of several brief and perfunctory questioning sessions and endless waiting, we were given orders to proceed to Treasure Island Naval Base in San Francisco via troop train.

It was now July, and the journey from Chicago to the West Coast took four horrendous days, including a one-day hiatus in the dreadful Mojave Desert when the train broke down. During this period we were taken off to do calisthenics in the hot sand and indescribable heat. Other than this, the only noteworthy happening in this stifling trip occurred in Hutchinson, Kansas, while we were confined to our cars during a stop for the train to take on water and do some other maintenance. Whatever whiskey had been smuggled aboard—and a good bit had—was long since consumed, and we were bored, uncomfortable, and irritable, to put it mildly.

Suddenly, out of a bar just across the main drag from the railroad station, a woman (fairly decent looking and in a state of high good humor) darted out and rushed over to our cars. She announced that she was going "to kiss every damned gob on this train." While the occupants of the bar came out to watch and cheer her on, she proceeded to stand on her tiptoes, work her way down the line, and take a good run at it. And despite the rather unwholesome nature of the job, she had plenty of takers, and did provide us with a break from the stultifying tedium of the trip.

We finally got to Treasure Island, our orders were processed, and we commenced to wait, and wait, and wait. Several weeks went by.

The USO—God bless them!—was very active on the base and tried mightily to relieve the tedium. One exciting project of theirs was the selection of "Miss Treasure Island." It was announced by the base newspaper and the ubiquitous public-address system that this honoree would be selected by vote from a slate of four luscious candidates.

"You sailors will choose the lucky lady from four of the world's most beautiful women. They are Hedy Lamarr, Lana Turner, Betty Grable . . . *and* Dale Evans," we were proudly told. Well, if you are familiar with that era you know that three of these gals *did* fit that description. Dale Evans, whose main claim to fame was that she was Roy Rogers' wife, was attractive but did not exactly break the mold when it came to beauty. We all voted strong for Hedy or Lana or Betty, but when the votes were "tabulated," guess who was the winner. Old Dale, of course. She would have been the only one at the time available to perform even the meager duties expected of "Miss Treasure Island." She came to the base, entertained us, and was well received despite our skepticism of the balloting.

Finally, we were told that on August 22 we would ship out on a troop transport to the Pacific (nothing more specific) where we would get our fleet assignments.

On August 15 the Japanese surrendered. This sparked in San Francisco one of the most uproarious celebrations in history, and I participated as hard as I could.

A week later we did board the USS Feland, a troop transport bound for the Philippine Islands. It was the wartime practice for troop departures to be sent off by a military band, banging out stirring martial airs while the boys strode up the gangway. Even though the hostilities were over, the custom continued, and we rushed aboard with blood in our eyes, anxious to attack someone, some place!

At sunset, the Feland got underway, steaming toward the Golden Gate Bridge, with the strains of "Anchors Aweigh" fading in the distance. When we sailed under the fabled bridge, we were "pumped," to put it mildly.

That night around midnight, it was clear that the engines had stopped. Soon, we learned that one of the propellers had burned out a bearing. We must return to the port for repairs. What a downer!

When the sun came up the next morning, we were slowly chugging our way back to San Francisco, the decks awash with disconsolate sailors, our patriotic fervor completely deflated.

But as we neared the Golden Gate Bridge, we saw a curious and completely unexpected sight. On that great span there must have been twenty-five thousand human beings shouting and screaming. A band was playing "When Johnny Comes Marching Home," flowers were cascading down on us, and a tremendous banner hung from the bridge emblazoned with "Welcome Home, Boys." A loudspeaker was booming out "God bless our fighting men. Well done, boys, and welcome home!"

I remember thinking, "Gee, what a nice gesture. These people sure do like us. We've only been gone for fifteen hours."

It seems that morning the renowned naval port was expecting the arrival of the first troop transport from the South Pacific, returning the brave veterans of Guadalcanal, Iwo Jima, Saipan and other bloody battles. They assumed we were it.

Well, we played it to the hilt. Posturing as we thought heroes might and dramatically throwing salutes aloft, we sailed under the Golden Gate to one of the most tumultuous welcomes imaginable. That we were completely undeserving was beside the point. We seized the moment.

I just hope the throng on the bridge hung around for a while, and that the real heroes didn't miss out on the welcome they had coming.

We sure enjoyed ours.

Two weeks later we arrived in the Philippine Islands. We got our various assignments while briefly at a base known as Tacloban. I was assigned temporarily to PT Boat Base 17, on the island of Samar, in the Leyte Gulf, where some of the fiercest naval battles of the war had occurred. I was thrilled and immediately envisioned myself on the bow of a speeding PT Boat, leaning against the wind as we shot through treacherous waters (the war was over, I repeat), ready to send my signals!

PT Boat Base 17 was rather primitive, one could say. There were probably two hundred men on the base. It had been cut out of the jungle, with a great deal of jungle remaining. I was assigned to a tent with three other guys, and an impressive crop of rats domiciled with us. The head (bathroom) was a quarter mile away and offered only cold water.

There was little action involving the six or seven tired, old PT Boats docked there.

I was immediately assigned to "base maintenance" and was put to work on a crew repairing the roofs on the few wooden buildings and Quonset huts that existed there. The regimen tended toward loosey-goosey. We worked all day, and at 17:30 we lined up at the mess tent and were each issued three cans of Iron City beer. No refrigeration, of course, and it had been sitting under tarps beneath the hot Philippine sun. Still, all things are relative, and we enjoyed that "cocktail hour."

However I made an adjustment in my drinking pattern. I had a buddy who worked at the tiny ice-making facility, most of its output being enjoyed by the fifteen officers on the base. I would trade him one of my daily rations of three beers, and he would supply me—on the q.t.—once a week with a fair amount of ice. I was entitled to twenty-one beers a week, I had to give the iceman three, so I decided to go on the wagon during the week, horde most of my remaining allotment of beer until Saturday night, ice it down, and try to drink all on that occasion. This philosophy was based on the old Chinese proverb, "One cup of wine is better spilled."

On the base a movie theater had been fashioned. This consisted of a cleared space of about forty feet square, with rows of logs for seating, a very antiquated movie projector, and an erratic supply of very old films, which were traded haphazardly with Navy ships and bases in that area.

Two things you could count on nightly at the "Roxy," as it was called: (1) The film would break, and the projectionist would suffer the worst sort of verbal abuse while he struggled to mend it, and (2) there would be a torrential downpour lasting about fifteen minutes, and it would cause no interruption whatsoever. We would simply sit in the rain and watch the film.

My modus operandi was to take my bucket of ice cold beer to the movies every Saturday night and have a rip-roaring good time. Any attending officers invariably escorted the two USO women that were assigned to the base, and they customarily sat together on the reserved front row of the Roxy.

Sometimes if we got too rowdy, the officers sought to restore decorum to the situation, but their threshold of pain was sufficiently high so we were permitted to have pretty jolly evenings.

A highlight of life overseas was "mail call"—an exercise in which there was much subliminal drama. A sailor stood on the table during noon chow and screamed out "mail call"; there was a stampede to surround him, and you hoped that your name was called. Some guys got multiple letters with consistency, and others rarely got one, causing great speculation among other bystanders. When a perfumed letter arrived for some fortunate recipient, there was a chorus of catcalls, much jostling, and some highly suggestive commentary. On the other hand, when a sailor who was known to have a steady girlfriend back home did not get the usual familiar envelope there was always a lot of lewd explanatory commentary. No letter from one's steady girl was most embarrassing.

I had no sweetheart correspondence, but I got letters at every mail call. My father wrote me almost every day—two pages single-spaced on the typewriter. I was kept closely posted on the progress of his writing. The reports were consistently optimistic but sometimes forced, you could tell. He had placed a few more short stories in minor publications, and he was struggling with his novel. His letters were most entertaining. He thought about me constantly. I'll never forget that.

Christmas came in the jungle, and it provided a really hilarious example of the fact that all things in life are relative. We were told that there would be no traveling USO Troupe to entertain us, "But every man on the base will receive Christmas presents!"

The USO girls told us to line up on Christmas morning at the Roxy beginning at 08:00, at which time Santa would have delivered the goods.

Well, by 07:30 every man on the base was in the line that stretched well back into the jungle. In very oppressive heat, the two hundred sailors (clad in our usual cut-off dungaree shorts, no shirt, and an assortment of white sailor caps or the khaki, short-billed caps usually identified with the Marine Corps) made a few half-hearted passes at "Jingle Bells" and "Silent Night." Around 08:30 the girls arrived, and the line began to inch forward with keen anticipation.

Soon, those in the front of the line had received their gifts and were filtering back through the jungle past those of us not yet rewarded.

"What are we getting?" we yelled out.

The gifts were held aloft as the sailors shuffled past us. For Christmas we would each receive a short, black pocket comb, *and* a paper cup of warm grapefruit juice.

But, what the hell, they didn't have to give us anything, and we got a kick out of going through the Yuletide motions.

P.T. Boat Base 17 really wasn't too bad. I was playing second base on the baseball team, I had lots of good pals, and my tent mates were okay guys. I was cruising along enjoying life on Samar—glorying in the fact that I was indeed serving in the Navy on the other side of the world . . . when after four months, I received orders that I was being sent to the Naval Base at Subic Bay near Manila and would be assigned to sea duty.

Several of us were transported by ship the one hundred miles up to Subic. We got off the small transport and were lined up on the dock. My name was called, and then I was walked about a half mile, passing one ship after another and staggering under the weight of my sea bag, to the gangplank of the USS Bull, a sleek destroyer escort. The Bull was an old veteran that had seen considerable action in the North Atlantic and throughout the Pacific. And now she was short one signalman, and a pretty green and rusty one was what she was getting.

I went aboard, remembering to salute the flag and the Officer of the Deck. I was taken in hand, unenthusiastically, by the Chief Boatswain's Mate and shown to my bunk. He then yelled out to a sailor shaving in the nearby head, "Hey, Irvin, here's your new skivvy waver!" Irvin was a Second Class Signalman and head of the four-man Signal department. He wandered over, shook hands, asked me where I had been and what I had been doing, and then asked where I was from, noticing a Southern accent. I told him "Rome, Georgia." His face lit up and he bellowed, "Well, goddamn, I'm from Elberton (Georgia)!" This was a good development. I had a friend.

The Bull carried a complement of 120 men and was being used at that point to ferry Marines who had been in heavy combat up to Shanghai, China, for some rest and relaxation. With no immediate orders, the ship was doing some repair work while waiting for the next assignment (more Marines to Shanghai, it was assumed).

"H. C." (Irvin) took me under his wing and brushed me up on my blinking light, semaphore, and some actual sea-duty procedures, differing in some cases from what we had been taught back at Great Lakes.

The first night on the Bull I experienced a neat thing. One of our signal lights had a high-powered, twenty-four-inch-diameter lamp. Manila was sixty miles away from where we were tied up in Subic Bay, with a mountain range in between. When the night was clear we could actually bank our light off the big, fluffy cumulus clouds and contact a Signalman in Manila. At night, in this manner, private messages could be sent from Bull sailors to ex-shipmates on ships or with shore facilities in Manila.

Two days later, the Bull received orders. So did every other Naval vessel in that part of the Pacific Ocean. A fierce typhoon was raging toward the Philippines and all ships were to get underway immediately for the open sea. The docks were to be cleared. There were no specific instructions, except to steam at will and go where the typhoon would not be. We would be kept advised by the fleet command with weather bulletins.

It would be one of the worst typhoons ever recorded in the Pacific Ocean.

CHAPTER 7

THE GREATEST DRINK EVER DRUNK

Within four hours of receiving our orders the Bull was steaming hard away from the storm with our sister ship, USS Farley, about one thousand yards behind us. Every Navy ship sought company under those conditions.

Over the next three days, we avoided the eye of the typhoon, but we sure as hell caught the outskirts of it, and it was a bitch. The swells were monstrous, with unbelievably deep troughs, often causing us to lose sight of the Farley, so the idea of communicating by blinking light was out of the question. We were both on our own anyway, outrunning the typhoon. The idea generally was to try to go with, or into, the seas but not quarter them or run parallel to them. A pitch—as horrible as it was—was preferred to a roll.

The bow of the Bull would rise toward the sky and then hurtle down into the trough and the next oncoming wave. The destroyer, not the ideal vessel for heavy weather, trembled ominously.

I am sure at no time were we in peril, but I did not know this. The officers and seasoned deck hands did not seem frightened, but the storm definitely had their attention. No one ventured on deck unless it was absolutely imperative. We were all sick as dogs but were encouraged to get to the head and not heave over the side.

Our ship carried four Quartermasters, and their primary job was to be on the helm, especially in critical times, each man standing a four-hour watch. Because of the severity of the storm, the watches were split into two-hour segments. The secondary job of Signalmen was to serve as back-up helmsmen. We were certainly needed due to seasickness and fatigue. What an experience. A full right rudder was necessary when the force of the gigantic running seas pushed the ship's forward progress to port, or left. As soon as it began to respond and come right you had to give it full *left* rudder and so forth. In this manner we were able to keep the Bull roughly on course. But it was nerve-wracking work. I was introduced to sea duty in an unforgettable way. But through the years, since that great typhoon of '46 during which several Navy ships were lost, the conversational opportunities it afforded me have made that ordeal well worth it.

After several more days of random steaming, the weather improved and we made our way back to Subic Bay. That facility was plenty roughed up but operating.

After about a week, here came the Marines! And we were off to Shanghai, China. There were about eighty of them. They seemed somber and, I suppose, war-weary, though we really saw little of them. The wintry weather was bitter, and they stayed below in the quarters that had been fashioned for them during the two-day journey to Shanghai.

Oh, Lord, arriving there was a thrill! We steamed up the Yangtze River and into the Huang Pu River, passing great naval vessels of many countries. The entire Bull crew was turned out in dress blues for what was a very ceremonial exercise, and I adored the pageantry of it all. If a ship outranked us (based on her captain's flag), we would face her, snapping to attention as we sailed past and saluting at the bugle's command. That ship would then return the salute. There were French, English, Chinese, and American battleships, cruisers, destroyers, and smaller ships. The river part of the journey took several hours, and we would repeat the same procedure as we steamed southward several days later. This was a perfect example of why I loved the Navy.

The definition of the word "mystique" was "Shanghai." Just saying the name was exciting. The weather was gray; the city was gray and simmering with intrigue and wayward behavior. I was freshly turned eighteen, and I ate it up.

The marines were cut loose for some serious debauchery before we would return them to Subic Bay. Each of the Bull sailors got liberty two out of three nights, and we "debauched" right along with the best of them. I tasted just about everything Shanghai had to offer. Among the less productive ventures involved four of us visiting a Shanghai nightclub and paying a handsome stipend for Chinese ladies to dance, sit with us, and drink very expensive ice tea that was supposed to be whiskey. Very stupidly we harbored hopes that a more intimate relationship would blossom from this arrangement. It did not, of course, but we paid a dear price to learn this. We did have the nightclub photographer make what turned out to be a very colorful picture of our little octet. Sadly, I lost the picture in a fire later on. Oddly I remember my "girl's" name was Wong Wong Li.

I did leave Shanghai with something more tangible. If you were in the Navy and had done duty in Shanghai it was considered imperative—if not in compliance with Navy regs—to have the inside of your jumper cuffs and collar sewn with silken material depicting very garish and unmistakably Oriental dragons. There were a number of tiny tailor shops that specialized in this "art." This would definitely contribute to my saltiness when I got back to the States.

Shanghai is a voguish travel destination today, offering all sorts of glamorous state-of-the-art facilities and sensational advances in industrial technology. But it would not be for me; I would not want to go there. Like a lot of places in my past, I prefer to remember it as it was when it took my breath away sixty years ago with its delicious wickedness.

We spent the spring of 1946 operating out of Subic Bay either in training operations or on the Shanghai run with more Marines needing R and R as they awaited their rotation to go back to the States.

In mid-May during a routine afternoon, while underway in the China Sea returning from China, the Captain came on the P.A. and surprisingly announced, "We have just received orders to proceed to Long Beach, California, where this ship will be decommissioned, and some of our personnel are to be mustered out of the service." There was a mighty roar, and then the wheelhouse got the Captain's order to "come left to 110 degrees, maintain that course, and steam with all engines at flank speed."

When we dropped the anchor at Long Beach, a few miles from Los Angeles, there were new orders awaiting me. I was to report to a nearby dry dock where I would find LSM 630, my new ship. An LSM is a very large landing craft, the "M" standing for "mechanized." It certainly did not have the panache of the destroyer escort. Still I had heard rumors that this ship was going eastward through the Panama Canal and on to New Orleans where it would be decommissioned and the personnel discharged. And at this stage—July 1946—there was something to be said for this. I was coming up on two years of Navy service, and it had been a wonderful and very eventful two years with absolutely no harm having been done to me. I was still eighteen years old, the age of most college entrants.

I went aboard the LSM as the one obligatory Signalman among a crew of only twenty sailors. The Captain, an Ensign, was the lone officer, and he looked to be about my age. He was a very immature, singularly silly fellow, with no vestige of spit and polish about him. He had served briefly on one other ship and really had no interest in the Navy. It is shocking now to realize that our lives depended on this fellow's judgment.

We got our sailing orders and we were indeed headed through the Canal with Mobile, Alabama, via New Orleans, as our official destination.

As we chugged out of Long Beach Harbor we went closely past the Bull, and I signaled a goodbye message. They answered very enthusiastically, my pal H. C. Irvin semaphoring that he would see me back in Georgia. He did, once.

Years later in Atlanta I would also renew a nodding acquaintance with the Bull's Executive Officer, a "Mister Karp." Also, long after the war one afternoon on a New York commuter train to Connecticut, after a very long, liquid lunch,

I spied a man on my car who looked like my Captain Chambers of the Bull. I rushed over and fell upon him with great exuberance. Indeed, he was Captain Chambers, and pleasant enough, but he quickly determined that this was a conversation that should not be prolonged. I do not blame him.

With my new vessel, the trip though the Canal took a while, and it was not an exciting journey. We had a hand-cranked Victrola on the LSM but only two playable 78 rpm records. One was Pearl Bailey singing "Tired" and the other a forgettable number called "Cement Mixer." Our Captain liked to sit up in the conning tower of the little ship, with his feet on the railing, and chime in loudly on that chorus: "Cement Mixer! Putty Putty!"

When we reached the Canal there was heavy traffic, with many warships from the Pacific Theater heading for decommissioning on the East Coast. We were under the complete control of pilots and the remarkably skilled Panamanian line handlers, and a fascinating experience it was.

We then set our course for the port of New Orleans. But when we got there it did not fulfill its promise as "The City That Care Forgot"—thanks to my own misdeeds.

We tied up at the Poydras Street docks around two p.m. to refuel. We were to spend the night and then to shove off for Mobile at eight a.m. The captain granted liberty for most of us, drawing straws to see who would not go ashore. I got lucky and was given a pass, which stated that liberty ended at one a.m.

The fact that I was not exactly inspired by my ship and most of my shipmates, coupled with the fact that I had not had a drink since I left Shanghai, had definitely put me in the mood to tie one on. I was in the right town to do it but had an inadequate amount of time to get it done.

In my sparkling clean Navy dress whites, unworn for many months, I headed for Bourbon Street. It was not to be an auspicious re-acquaintance with the city of my birth. First I called my folks in Rome telling them that I was in the States and soon to be discharged and headed for home, and that more details would follow.

Then I got down to business. Actually, from a legal drinking standpoint I was a minor, but the bars in New Orleans were never inclined to sweat the small stuff, such as closing time, election days, underage drinking, etc. And I visited most of the ones on Bourbon Street.

Around ten o'clock I was getting up a pretty good head of steam, and I wandered into the rather high-toned Hotel Monteleone, went into the lounge there, and seated myself at the round bar. Across from me were another sailor and a pretty good-looking girl. I got the impression from her rather loaded glances at me that she was not enchanted with her companion. Our eye contact became more significant—discerned, to be sure, by her escort.

Then, I got the signal from her that she was about ready to "jump ship." She excused herself and headed for the powder room, on the other side of the lobby. After about thirty seconds, I left the bar and headed in the direction she had taken. While I was waiting for her to emerge, her date sauntered up. We had words. The young lady then came out, and the action heated up.

With the lady trying to maintain a somewhat neutral position, there was some pulling and tugging, and then the sailors started fighting. We were going at it with great gusto, spilling out into the center of the lobby. There was then a lovely water fountain in the Monteleone lobby, and this young man and I were in and out of this fixture, adding immeasurably to the conspicuous nature of the altercation. Hotel staffers rushed out onto Royal Street to summon the Shore Patrol, always in plentiful supply in the contentious French Quarter. They broke up the fight quickly, but in the process one of the Shore Patrolmen's elbows struck and broke my nose. I began to bleed like a stuck pig.

The Shore Patrol would routinely break up a number of fights that night, without making a big deal out it. However, inasmuch as I was injured rather gorily, it was decided to transport me to the Marine Hospital Brig in Algiers, Louisiana, across the river from New Orleans. This would necessitate my being charged with disorderly conduct.

Arriving there, my nose was popped back into place, I was tidied up a bit, my blood-stained whites were removed, and I was given some pajamas with "P" (for "prisoner") prominently displayed on them. I was placed in a cell. At this point I had sobered up considerably, and I realized that I was in trouble—in jeopardy of my ship sailing without me, a very serious no-no. I decided I should summon a staff member and seek to avert this ominous eventuality.

When a Marine sergeant strolled up, he asked sweetly, "What do you want, you son of a bitch?" I told him my predicament. He glared at me, sneered, and left.

The next day came and went without much improvement in hospitality. I was keenly aware that my ship was by now tied up at the docks in Mobile, sans one Signalman. My nose was sore but operative, and I was most anxious to bring closure (as we say today) to this unhappy situation.

Finally I was hauled out of my cell and taken to the Officer on Duty. This Marine Lieutenant interrogated me about my unruly conduct and permitted me to tell him about my problem with my ship. He left the room for about ten minutes, and when he returned he said, "The toughest discipline for a dumb bastard like you is to send you back to your Captain and let him sock it to you. We'll put you on the 10:30 train to Mobile tomorrow morning. When you get to your ship at the Mobile Dry Docks, your Captain will confirm to us that you are back aboard. Out!"

This was pretty good news. Knowing the flakey nature of the young Ensign who was commanding on the LSM, I had reason to think the punishment would be lenient, if at all. My spirits were on the incline.

But the journey from the brig to the New Orleans Train Station was a nightmare. Two Marines with sidearms came into my cell and handed me my dirty, wrinkled, bloody white uniform and a government voucher for a train ticket to Mobile.

"Get dressed, sailor boy," they instructed.

"What will I wear?"

"Same thing you came in with."

The two Shore Patrolmen, with guns and a big "SP" on their sleeves, put me in a paddy wagon, and we three were dropped off on Canal Street around six blocks from the train station.

We got out and began a humiliating trek to the station. Bear in mind Canal Street is the main thoroughfare in downtown New Orleans, and this was an hour at which many shoppers would be stirring about. I thought of the times I had gone downtown with my grandmother and trod this same route.

Our little formation consisted of me in front, the blood on my white uniform discernable three blocks away, followed two paces behind by the burly, stern, seriously-armed Shore Patrolmen. If Ringling Brothers Circus had paraded down Canal Street, it would not have generated more attention. That march was excruciating. At the station, the guards waited until the train pulled out for Mobile.

About an hour out of New Orleans, in stifling hot weather, with cinders blowing in the open window and children and adults walking past to ogle me, I was slumped down in my seat, wondering (stupidly) if the Navy had seen fit to tell my folks about my bad behavior. It was then that things began looking up.

A tall sailor walked up and kneeled down by my seat. He asked, "Is your name Campbell?" I nervously admitted that it was, and he then asked, "Are you from Rome, Georgia?" I perked up and said "Yes."

"I'm Jack Dockery. From Rome? I used to see you around the Corner Drug Store. Man, you look bad. What the hell happened to you?" Jack inquired.

I told him, and he sympathized with me.

He thought for a moment, and then he asked, "You see that water cooler down at the end of this car? It's full of crushed ice. And when I got on in New Orleans, I put a quart of Four Roses bourbon in that cooler. It ought to be ice cold. You reckon you could use a big drink about now?"

I looked incredulously at Jack Dockery. I said, "Jack, you are my man! I need about four fingers in a washtub."

Old Jack fished his bourbon out of the cooler, and we went to work on it. By the time we were rolling through Pascagoula, Mississippi, my outlook on life brightened considerably, and my lifelong affection for Jack Dockery was well established.

When we got to Mobile, I said goodbye to my new friend who was traveling through to Atlanta. I walked to the dock where the LSM was tied up, and reported to my captain. He was taking a nap. He looked up groggily, heard my story, shook his head, and said, "Behave yourself!"

After another week in Mobile, I was told to report to the Navy Recruiting Office, where I was given my Honorable Discharge from the U.S. Navy. Shortly thereafter I caught a bus to Rome, Georgia.

CHAPTER 8

THIRSTING FOR KNOWLEDGE

When—thankfully—I got off the bus in Rome, having stood up halfway from Mobile, I was greeted by my mother, father, and sister. It was a happy occasion, although clearly my baby sister was somewhat dubious about my homecoming. My sister Sally—one of my favorite human beings—is thirteen years younger than me. At this point, she had not seen me in the two years since she was three years old.

My folks had her turned out in sort of navy jumper, in my honor, and when I stepped off the bus, they gave her an encouraging little nudge. The idea was for her to rush forward and fling herself into the arms of her brother "back from the wars." However, her memory of me was not so vivid that she was dead certain who in the hell I was. She approached the welcoming project in a very wary manner. But she warmed up quickly.

I was mighty glad to be home. It was a good time for all of us, and my foolish concern that the Navy would see fit to report my unseemly behavior to my parents had not materialized.

My father's drinking pattern at this stage was that he would stay on the wagon for as long as several years and then go on a binge for a month or two. He would get dried out and then turn over a new leaf. His rather fragile morale was high when I got home. He had just sold a short story to a literary magazine in Texas and was going great guns on his novel *Big Beverage*. A publisher was making encouraging sounds. Developments of this sort affected the mood of the entire household.

For me—and later for my sister—Bill Campbell had always been something of a cheerleader. He was always in my corner. If I made some minor accomplishment it became an incredible achievement. And if I had erred, he turned that "sow's ear into a silk purse." While he had lots of suggestions—ideas about what to wear or drive, insurance matters, how to deal with bankers—they were always very tactfully suggested and usually beneficial.

His drinking, moodiness, and impulsive behavior made for a parent who was not easy, but he was never dictatorial. On his day, he was enormous fun. You could not have a better friend, and my father never talked down to me from the time I was a little boy.

When he surmised that my Navy days would be drawing to a close, he suggested to me that since the Veterans Administration had decreed that servicemen would get high school credits for service time, perhaps he could put the wheels in motion to get me into college (which, of course, the VA would also underwrite).

College admission was no piece of cake. There were millions of servicemen seeking college educations. We (he) tried the University of Georgia, Georgia Tech, and Emory University . . . but no dice. Because he had sold his short story to *Southwest Review*, the literary magazine published by Southern Methodist University in Dallas, he had an in with that college, and they took me. I was to leave in early September.

After a brief sojourn in Rome, the day came. My dad drove me to the Atlanta Airport, a facility in 1946 that could be housed inside a present-day Boeing 747. I got on a Delta DC-3 and many hours later landed at Love Field in Dallas.

When my taxi arrived at SMU, I was astonished to see the teeming masses of knowledge seekers. A year before, the student body of Southern Methodist had been 1,900. On this day there were 6,000 in the process of matriculating. The campus had some lovely buildings, but they were subordinated by the prefabricated trailer-like classrooms and offices scattered about.

I was assigned to a dorm. I dragged my gear up to the second floor to my room, and there I encountered my roommate—Sidney Campbell.

Sidney was lounging on his bed, reading a "girlie" magazine. Sidney leapt to his feet and greeted me with a startling fervor that was certainly more than was called for.

My new roomy looked to be about twenty-eight or thirty. He was short, swarthy, and muscular. Sidney sported a spectacular hair treatment, in length, density, and styling. It swept back from his forehead in wave after wave of cascading blackness, kept intact by a generous application of "Lucky Tiger" hair oil. His pillow attested to this.

Sidney enthusiastically welcomed me to Dallas and SMU and guaranteed me that I would love it (he had arrived just the previous evening!). He explained that he was from Michigan and had served in the Army, mostly in the Aleutian Islands. He had seen eighteen months of duty there and had been wounded—twice, in the head. He had been given a medical discharge several months earlier. Sidney had never been to college.

This old boy had a slightly maniacal demeanor about him, but still, I thought he seemed rather surefooted.

While I unpacked, Sidney explained quite a few things about college life to me. It was then about dark, and he suggested that we catch the bus downtown and have supper, and then he wanted to introduce me to some friends that he thought could be helpful. Didn't this guy say earlier that he was from Michigan, and that he had just arrived in Dallas?

I explained to my new roommate that while my name was Wade Cothran Campbell, I was called Cot.

Sidney protested, "Oh no! To me, you're going to be Wade." This did not go down well, but I thought we'd get it worked out later.

We caught the bus downtown, and when we arrived in front of the famous old Adolphus Hotel, Sidney announced that this was our first stop.

We walked up to entrance to the Adolphus and encountered the doorman. Sidney grabbed the doorman's hand, shook it vigorously, and said, "I want you to meet my roommate. This is Wade Campbell."

The doorman went along with it, and shook my hand suspiciously. Then Sidney said goodbye, and we walked on down the street.

Soon, we encountered a policeman. "Hi there!" old Sidney sang out. "Have you met my roommate from Georgia? This is Wade Campbell."

On it went for awhile. I became acquainted with a few more doormen, a druggist, and one or two passersby, before I said, "Sidney, I'm getting a little tired. I think I'll head back to the dorm." I thought to myself, "Oh my God! What have I got here!"

Long story short: Sidney was nutty as a fruitcake. Tragic that service to his country had caused it, but nutty is nutty, and he was not going to be the ideal roommate.

Beside the rigors of life with Sidney Campbell, the rest of SMU did not blow me away. I had pledged a fraternity in which the pledge class numbered a whopping 125 (120 from Texas, I bet). It was about as fraternal as belonging to the public library. The college had too many people. One of them left after nine weeks and headed back to Georgia.

In Rome I got a job on a Georgia Power line-surveying crew, and in the evenings raised a little hell around town with some other returning veterans (keeping an eye out for my hero, Jack Dockery, he of the much-enjoyed quart of Four Roses bourbon). At the same time, I unenthusiastically plotted my future and the education it would require. Some Rome connections suggested the University of the South (Sewanee). My father spearheaded the drive to gain admittance for me, and the job got done. I was to report in February 1947. I did not appreciate at that time how lucky I was to get in this really wonderful college in the Tennessee mountains, with only 525 students (all-male).

I think during this brief sojourn in Rome my folks were concerned about the amount of drinking I was doing but chalked it up to well-deserved high jinks of returning servicemen, and there was some validity to that. But I was setting a blistering pace, and could not imagine a night without some serious drinking. I think I recognized that a troubling dependency on alcohol was developing, but I thought, "Aw hell, I'm going to give it a good run!"

My old friend Ed Hine had also enrolled at Sewanee, so when the time came, my father drove the two of us to Tennessee to enroll in the winter semester.

Ed and I were housed in the same pre-fabricated dormitory—shades of SMU, but the Sewanee student body increase was relatively only a drop in the bucket compared to that school's.

Sewanee was fabulous. The campus was dripping with tradition and class—architecture of ancient-looking stone, lovely trees, upper classmen clad in gowns, and all students wearing coats and ties. The place had been there a long time and looked it.

This was an unusual time to be in college. The student body was a combination of young men who had missed the service and much older, weathered, and wiser types (many of whom had seen some horrendous wartime action). The attitude of this contingent was that "I've been doing some hard traveling, and I've got an education coming, but, along with it, I'm due a hell of a good time."

A lot of them—myself included—had been buying a war bond during each month of service time. When cashed, they yielded a good stash.

An amusing indicator of how college life was changing had to do with the wearing of beanies, or rat caps, traditional head garb to intimidate lowly freshmen. One day a nineteen-year-old sophomore started raising hell with one of the new arrivals because he was not wearing his rat cap. The object of the sophomore's indignation was a fellow named Guy Carr. Guy was twenty-seven years old and had been an infantry Captain, decorated for bravery a week after the Normandy Invasion. Guy went to his room, got his rat cap, handed it to the sophomore, and explained in very vivid terms what he could do with it. Shortly thereafter the practice of wearing rat caps at the University of the South was discontinued.

I struggled with my grades and did just enough to get by. I re-pledged the SAE fraternity, soon knew just about everyone on campus, loved the place, and had the time of my life being there. There were no girls but they did come in often for very elegant dances we had frequently, and we spent weekends in Nashville and Chattanooga from time to time.

Every college has its legendary drinking establishment with quaint customs and traditions about which alumni wax nostalgic into their dotage. But Sewanee truly had one of the all-time greats: "Clara's." It had sort of a 1928, corny, Appalachian rustic motif. It was vintage roadhouse atmosphere, smelling of cigarette smoke, onions, and beer. The front room offered a bar, with booths lining two of the walls. Then a large opening led you into the back room where most of the collegiate conviviality (with a great deal of singing, of course) took place.

Next door to Clara's was a nondescript dwelling. This was a rather low-key bootlegging establishment run by "Tubby" and "Mrs. Tubby." The latter would sell you a pint of bourbon for five dollars (a nice markup, then) while the proprietor lounged, half drunk in his bed, listening to the radio. If you did not have ready cash and wished to hock your watch, this could usually be done but did necessitate waking Tubby for his approval.

Mrs. Tubby was not bad looking, although a little shopworn. Imagine a 1933 photograph of a fairly handsome Oklahoma woman who had weathered the worst of the dust bowl. Occasionally a young customer, emboldened by John Barleycorn, would seek a romantic assignation with her, when it was clear that Tubby was "in the arms of Morpheus." Undoubtedly, she would have been willing, but her standard answer was always, "He'd kill you and me both!" That usually ended the quest.

Clara's was also referred to as "The Eagle," as in "Let's go to the Eagle," the establishment being located in the quietly stylish summer resort town of Monteagle, about four miles from the college campus.

Clara (Shoemate) was a tiny woman, resembling the actress, Claire Trevor. She was quiet, unflappable, and always wore a faint smile, even when in the act of restoring proper order in her establishment. Her husband, Tom, was a big, burly fellow with a fearsome countenance. But his ire, when aroused by customer misconduct, was effective only for a few minutes, whereas "Miz Clara's" soft rebuke would "settle your hash" for the evening.

She was one of the truly fine human beings. Students, faculty, mountain folk, and ritzy summer residents held her in high regard. Oddly, she was quite fond of me. She permitted me to run a tab with her—more later on that subject when I deal with my fiscal program at its lowest ebb.

At the end of the first college semester, there occurred the usual musical chairs with roommates. Ed Hine had been rooming with Walter Bryant, tailback on the football team, a great guy and one who would one day become the beloved Athletic Director of the University. They got along fine, but Ed was intense and could grate on one after so long. My own roommate was all right but nothing to write home about, and I was receptive to a change. Walter and I had become great friends—and remain so to this day. He and I decided to room together. Ed, being thick-skinned Ed, understood it all.

The first semester I struggled by academically. The second semester my heart was at Clara's, and I flunked almost everything. The Chancellor of the school, Dr. Alexander Guerry, and I had some mutual Rome alumni connections; he had taken note of me, and he certainly knew Walter well from football. One day he encountered Walter and reportedly said, "I want you to do two things for me. Get Reed Bell (former Sewanee star fullback, who had moved to Florida State University) to come back to Sewanee next fall. And get Cot Campbell to quit drinking."

Walter accomplished the first. I did not quit drinking, but I slowed it down significantly and hit the books pretty hard. Consequently, I made the Dean's List that semester, and chalked up my one pitiful collegiate accomplishment.

But the next semester it was back to just getting by, and the next one—spring of '48—I emphatically flunked out of the University of the South.

Most young men in college have hair-raising stories about wild and wooly behavior and how "it's a wonder I survived!" My crowd at Sewanee truly set a standard of outlandish, outrageous behavior that will rarely be threatened. As most of us were veterans, we felt an entitlement to raise pluperfect hell. We did so, on and off the mountain.

One unfortunate venture of the off-the-mountain variety came when a young lady in Rome, a student at the very straight-laced Shorter College, invited me to come back for the annual Shorter Halloween Dance at that Baptist institution. Because I thought it would be nice to see my folks in Rome, I decided to go. I knew the dance would be dry and thus heavy going, to put it mildly. Therefore, I got pretty well fortified beforehand. And I armed myself with a new pint of whiskey to take along with me, housed in the inside pocket of my suit coat.

The dance got underway, I was repairing to the gent's room frequently to take a good swig of the bourbon, and I was having a very enjoyable time, although being cautioned worriedly by my date about my rather conspicuous exuberance. Little did she know what was to come. Around ten o'clock—considered the prime of the evening by the Shorter merrymakers—the authorities released a rather discouraged-looking cluster of balloons tethered near the dance floor. We male dancers began to leap excitedly into the air so as to capture a balloon and present it to one's young lady. With such force did I leap that my pint bottle of bourbon came cascading out of my pocket and crashed noisily in the middle of the dance floor, scattering chinks of glass all about and creating quite a large pool of bourbon.

The gaiety ceased. You could have heard a pin drop. And all eyes were on me, most of them glaring disapprovingly. My date began to weep dramatically, and the Dean of Students advanced toward me with blood in her eye. In no uncertain terms, she told me to leave the Shorter campus immediately.

I did leave, and I was never invited again to a social event at that college.

Soon thereafter, and back at Sewanee, I received my non-passing grades in four of the five courses I was taking. Erasing any doubt I might have had about my status was an easily understood, official letter from the University of the South saying that I was no longer a student there. I called my mother and father, who were not flabbergasted by any means. I told them I thought it was time to begin my "business career." They agreed. I headed for Rome to plan my next conquest.

—

CHAPTER 9

SETTING FLORIDA ON FIRE

Construction!

There's where my future lay. The war was over; America had to have new roads, homes, office buildings . . . you name it. My road to success was clearly in construction. It was here that I would make my mark. What training prepared me for this new undertaking? Well, none actually. But I would work my way up from the very bottom, hopefully not taking too long about it.

One of Georgia's biggest highway construction firms was Ledbetter Construction Company, headquartered in Rome. Al Ledbetter, the head man, was a distant cousin, so he had to see me when I called. The meeting did not take long. I told him I felt that I was cut out for a career in construction and was willing to take a lowly job with Ledbetter. He looked rather pained, and picked up the phone and muttered, "Tell Bohannon up on the LaFayette job that Cot Campbell will be up there in a day or two, and to put him to work on the road gang." Done.

The next day I caught the bus to LaFayette, where a highway was being constructed from there to Chattanooga. I found a boarding house (this was to be the beginning of an eventful boarding house era for me) and that night I called Mr. Bohannon at his "tourist court." He told me to be at the town square at 6:30 the next morning. The shuttle would pick me up and take me to the construction site.

The shuttle (a dump truck) did pick up and then deposit me and other assorted construction types at a barren, hot, rock-strewn stretch of ground that would someday be a highway. There I met Mr. Bohannon, a red-faced, sour little man. During my acquaintanceship with him he constantly smelled of bourbon, but his outlook on life never seemed to brighten. He looked me up and down with some ill-concealed skepticism. Mr. Bohannon, or "Bossman" as he was known, got me together with a sledgehammer and told me to start making little rocks out of big rocks. During the day Bossman cruised up and down the line in his pickup so as to keep us inspired.

I had worked up a pretty good sweat by noon that first day, at which time I discovered that I should have brought something to eat. I did not bring it, and I did not eat.

We knocked off at six, the shuttle dropped most of us back at the town square, and I staggered off to my boarding house, where they served supper, fried Spam being a popular entrée. There were very few nocturnal attractions in LaFayette, and after swinging that big hammer in the hot Georgia sun for about ten hours, I would have had little heart for night life anyway.

Through June and July my life followed this grim routine. We did cease work at noon on Saturdays, so I could hitchhike to Rome and paint the town red that night. Thank God for those respites, but I did have to be back in LaFayette Sunday night so I could answer the bell Monday morning.

I was certainly involved in the world of construction, but, thus far, I felt that I was not being sufficiently exposed to the rudiments. Or, maybe I was!

After two months, I was eight pounds lighter, brown as an ancient walnut, pretty fit, slightly flush with unspent money, and bored out of my mind.

One Tuesday morning I heaved out at six a.m., glanced out of my window at the dreaded shuttle pick-up spot on the square, and the thought struck me: perhaps construction is not exactly what I seek. I tossed my work clothes in the closet, put on some decent garb, threw some meager toilet articles in a shoe box, told some of my co-workers on the square to pass the word that I would not be on the sledgehammer that day, and proceeded to the tiny bus station, where I bought a ticket to Monteagle, Tennessee.

I set sail for Sewanee. When the bus got to Chattanooga, during the rest stop I disembarked, ran across the street, and purchased a quart of fine bourbon, concealing it in my shoe box.

Late that afternoon I strolled into the Student Union at the University of the South, where I found many of the old pals on the mountain for summer school. We went to good old Dopey McNeill's room, where several of us finished off what I had left of the quart, and then we headed for Clara's. For several days I made up for lost time, feeling that I had it coming. I then found a ride to Atlanta with a student, but dropped off in LaFayette to spend one more night in my charming quarters and settle up with my landlady. I called Bohannon and told him I had another opportunity. He grumbled that he had been on the verge of offering me the job as timekeeper (a step up from breaking rocks with a sledgehammer). I expressed my appreciation for his confidence, but said, "So long, Bossman!"

Back in Rome there was another family confab about where and how I might seek my fortune, with my father—as usual—being the most productive with ideas. This time he was pushing Florida, which was flourishing post-war, offering a myriad of opportunities for a bright young man. My dad had an old friend residing in Winter Haven, Florida. This was George Chambliss with whom he had flown during World War I. He had done well as a citrus grower and lived right in the smack dab middle of that rich Florida citrus belt. Dad would call George, if I agreed, and see what the lay of the land was. He did, and George said, "Send Cot on down. We'll figure something out."

The next day I was hitchhiking my way to central Florida, and I got all the way to Tallahassee the first night. In those days—with both gas and trust plentiful—you could travel fast on your thumb. Interestingly, the first leg of the journey dropped me off in LaGrange, Georgia, on the corner of the First Baptist Church, near the Courthouse Square. Little did I dream that eleven years later I would marry Anne Dodd there.

The next evening I arrived in Winter Haven, a passenger in a citrus truck. I called Mr. Chambliss, who sent his daughter in to pick me up. I had dinner with the Chambliss family and spent the night in their lovely home. Winter Haven was truly the heart of the citrus belt, but it was also the location of one of America's leading tourist attractions: Cypress Gardens—a breathtakingly beautiful horticultural attraction, and the birthplace of the sport of water skiing. It billed itself as the "Home of the Cypress Gardens Aquamaids and Water Ski Champions." Many local youngsters worked there during the prime season, and George Chambliss thought this was an ideal place for me to seek employment and gain a foothold in the Sunshine State. He had already made inquiries on my behalf to E. Malcolm Pope, who owned the electric boat concession at the Gardens. Ten or twelve of these boats operated during the peak season, each of them transporting tourists through the winding waterways of the gardens, with a young man driving and explaining the flora and fauna and answering questions.

The next morning, Lucy Chambliss, an attractive young lady about my age, drove me around Winter Haven, then took me out to Cypress Gardens where I was to meet Mr. Pope.

Malcolm Pope was the freest of free spirits. He was a man of about forty-five years and a former world champion motorboat racer known as the "Lookin'-back Kid," a moniker earned from a logical mannerism when he was on the lead in a race. Malcolm was keenly interested in having fun, and he had a bit of a "roving eye." With Cypress Gardens teeming with beautiful models and scantily clad female water skiers, he was in the right place to indulge the latter interest.

The Gardens had been established by Malcolm's older brother, Dick Pope, and he had built it through his genius in the art of creating publicity. Enormous crowds poured into Cypress Gardens all winter (and a fair number came in the summer months). They were lured by their familiarity with the inviting bathing beauty photos shot at the Gardens (and distributed relentlessly to every metropolitan daily in America, where they were frequently used as filler to make up a newspaper page). All day, every day, at the Gardens, alluring pictures were being shot on the artificial photo beach and during the water-ski shows.

Dick Pope was a charmer but not quite the fun-loving type as his younger brother. Indeed, Malcolm was something of an albatross to the head of the gardens. I think his ownership of the electric boat "fleet" had been arranged as a trouble-free and safe business haven for the maverick brother.

The interview went well. Malcolm absentmindedly asked me a few questions and then said, "Well, the season's not here yet, but I'll find something for you to do."

I found lodging at a pleasant boarding house in town, and hiked over to Malcolm's house the next morning, as I had been told to do. That day was spent riding around in his car, then washing his car, but mostly listening to Malcolm's stories. He told me to report to the boat dock at the Gardens the next day, and he would have Chuck, a sort of electric boat harbormaster or foreman, check me out on my future duties as a boat driver and guide (the latter term being used very loosely for some time to come.).

When I reported I was issued a little red and blue, horizontally striped tee shirt, vaguely reminiscent of a British seaman. Then Chuck, clad likewise, put me in a boat with a few tourists and we weaved creepingly through the Gardens in a twenty-five-minute trip, with Chuck smacking his gum and explaining in a very singsong manner some of the wonders we encountered. I got the impression that Chuck—even though the head man at the boat dock—was not essentially a botanist. I spent the rest of the morning taking trips with several of the other boys.

One technique that did impress me came at the termination of the journey. As the boat glided back to the dock, all but the legally blind could not help but note that there was a sign posted conspicuously on a tree that read "TIPS ARE PERMITTED." As the sign loomed up, the driver of the boat obsequiously intoned, "I hope my explanations have made the trip more enjoyable for you!" Then he directed that passengers disembark from front to back, one seat at a time. When the front passengers climbed onto the dock, the driver would loudly exclaim, "Oh, thank you very much." at the same time making sure those in the other seats got a gander at the dollar bill extending quite visibly between his fingers (his own legal tender if the front seat were tightwads).

To give validity to the work of the guides, we were given an introductory trip with Mrs. Werthmeir, the bona fide Gardens botanist and the sister of the Pope boys. She also took test trips from time to time to make sure we were doing a decent job. It was now decided that I should take my Werthmeir indoctrination trip and then perhaps solo.

93

I did start being my own captain, and one thing I had learned from earlier passenger trips was that it did not make much difference what you said during your spiel. Hardly anyone knew the difference. Most of them were too busy anyway looking at the pretty young girls bedecked in antebellum hoop skirts, smiling coquettishly and waving from strategic points along the way.

When I got into the swing of things and got a little confidence, part of my delivery included this gem: "Ladies and gentlemen, note the shaggy-barked tree up ahead on the right. This is the *Cajeput Melecalucalucadendron*—better known as the 'punk tree.' Now the leaves of this tree are used in the process of making nose drops, while the bark we utilize in the preparation of 'punk sticks' with which we light our fireworks on the Fourth of July!" To this day, I have never heard of a punk stick. But all the people would point to the tree and nod their heads knowingly. When I was asked a question about a certain plant or flower, and I did not know the answer, I would always sing out—with never any trace of hesitation—"Oh, that's the Bell Flower" (Tree, Plant, etc.). The safety valve, if questioned, was to imply politely, "You might think it's something else, but that's how it's known *around here!*"

Talk about a fun place to work: Cypress Gardens was heaven. I got to know all the boys and girls working there, and we had frequent parties in town at night. The world's greatest skiers were there, and so were the prettiest of pretty girls; the place was constantly swarming with magazine photographers, newsreel cameramen and celebrities. You would have paid to work there.

There were four water-ski shows a day. During most of the year, the announcer for these was Chuck, the leader of us jolly boatmen. In the prime part of the season (January, February, and March) a man named Bill Carter, announcer on the Miss America Pageant, was brought in to work the shows.

Chuck, a somewhat battered and fragile veteran of the War, did a decent job with the show, but in the same singsong manner in which he did the electric boat tour spiel. Also, Chuck liked to drink a little, and about twice a year he went on a toot that might last a week, disappearing from the scene.

In October after I went to work in August, Chuck did go on one of his benders, and one morning when it came time for the first show there was no announcer. Word went out frantically for a volunteer. God knows why, but I volunteered.

I did that show and loved doing it, gaining confidence as I went on. They asked me to do the other three shows that day. Chuck didn't come in the next day, so I filled in again, and also the next day. When Chuck finally surfaced, red-eyed and contrite, he had lost that part of his job. And I had a new one, and that experience was to play a major role during the rest of my life.

This new job gave me a lot more exposure and wallop at the Gardens and undoubtedly enhanced the glamour of my image with the young ladies there. If I enjoyed life at Cypress Gardens before, I reveled in it now.

The evenings were always festive in Winter Haven. While I lived at a nice "Christian" boarding house in town, I took no meals there, nor did I partake of the regular sessions of bonding and fellowship in the parlor. However, I did get the full attention of the proprietors a few weeks after I moved in.

One evening after having a great deal to drink, I stumbled home pretty much the worse for wear. I retired but thought I would have one last cigarette while reflecting on the highlights of the day. Alas, the sandman visited prematurely, and the lighted cigarette fell upon the bed clothes. After about an hour, I became rather hot. I awakened and could not help but notice that the bed was on fire.

In my room was a small Coca-Cola fountain glass (you will recall the type). The common, second-floor bathroom (and nearest source of water) was down at the end of the hall. My only course of action, therefore, was to sprint to the bathroom, fill up my tiny glass, rush back, and hurl its contents on the bed. This I did about fifteen times (quietly, I am convinced), and this brought the conflagration under control. The presence of smoke on the second floor was rather apparent to me, but the nocturnal peace of the house did not seem to be disturbed, and I appeared to have gotten by with what is a decided boarding house rule violation. I went back to sleep, and my open windows helped to minimize the smell. But what to do with the bed? The sheets where quite charred, and there was a fairly significant hole in the mattress.

I decided that I would smuggle the sheets out of the house, thinking that I would purchase new ones in the very near future. As for the mattress, I took the out of sight, out of mind approach. I turned it over. Since my landlady did not service the rooms on a daily basis, I thought this plan of action might carry the day. When I left the house that morning, nothing seemed amiss with the authorities or with my housemates.

That evening I noticed that the mattress had been turned back over, exposing the burned hole. Therefore, I was not completely surprised on the following morning when the landlady did announce to me that a beloved former boarder ("practically a member of the family") was returning to Winter Haven. She was sure that I would understand that she felt obligated to give him his old room back. Perhaps I could make other arrangements as quickly as possible.

I was able to arrange accommodations in a small house with two of the skiers from the Gardens and a third man, a Winter Haven policeman named Poncho. They offered me a bed for five dollars per week. However, these arrangements quickly became tenuous, also through another incident provoked by excessive use of alcohol.

About a week after I moved in, I returned to my quarters late one evening after I had spent a great deal of time and energy at an affable neighborhood bar known as The Hob Nob. Perhaps I was in a confused state of mind when I climbed into bed. At any rate, I woke up several hours later, sensing that something was amiss.

Suddenly I discovered that a large animal had gotten in and was roaming about the house! I could make out dimly its furtive form moving through the darkness of the living room. So I moved into action. First I unlocked and propped open the front screen door, then found a broom and began to herd this animal out of the house. Finally after several abortive efforts I shooed him out in the yard. I breathed a sigh of relief and went back to bed.

The next morning I was awakened by a loud conversation taking place in the kitchen. I wandered in and found Poncho and Jumper Boyle, the Gardens' number one skier and the leaseholder on our humble dwelling. Boyle looked up at me and asked, "Do you know anything about Poncho's dog?"

"No, I don't know anything about any dog. But I do know some kind of big animal got in here last night. I found him about two o'clock and had a hell of a time getting him out of here. But I did," I added proudly.

The two of them looked at me incredulously. Poncho screamed out, "Goddamn, man! That was my purebred Collie that I bought in Lakeland yesterday. That dog cost me eighty dollars. You stupid . . ."

It seemed wise at that point for me to volunteer for the neighborhood search that was to begin immediately. That morning it proved fruitless. However, in the afternoon Poncho did locate the Collie and returned him to our abode. Profuse apologies kept me from being evicted from my quarters again, but it was a close call.

I was creating some problems for myself with my drinking, but life was fun, and my body at age twenty-one was resilient enough to take the beating I was handing it.

I was, of course, Master of Ceremonies of the water-ski shows and still driving the boat (which I had risen above at this point, but that big sign at the end of the dock was helping to generate some significant "walking around money"). Mr. Dick Pope had me doing a little modeling at the Gardens, and he tossed some other odd assignments my way.

One day he gave me the cushy task of being the escort of the Tangerine Queen in the Thanksgiving Day Parade in Orlando, where she was to be the feature of the Cypress Gardens float. The Tangerine Queen was a girl named Neva Jane Langley, who was to go on and become Miss America. She and I and some others from the Gardens did go to Orlando, but I did not do much escorting, spending most of my time in the bar at the Angebilt Hotel.

Years later I met Neva Jane again when I was speaking at a convention in Palm Beach. She was married to a wealthy gentleman from Georgia. She was gracious enough to act as if she remembered me, but did not recall the Thanksgiving Day Parade in Orlando in 1948. As a matter of fact, I didn't remember it much either.

I had two great friends in Winter Haven. They were Clyde May and Columbus (Lumby) Smith, both native "Havenites." We did a lot together, and the three of us enjoyed hunting and fishing. With one hundred lakes within a fifty-mile radius of Winter Haven, the bass fishing and the duck hunting were first rate.

Right after Christmas the three of us and another older fellow decided that we would spend a couple of days duck hunting at Kissimmee Lake. We would go on Thursday evening and come back Saturday afternoon, in time for New Year's Eve when we all had important social obligations. I was into heavy dating with a Gardens skier and model named Jane Strickland who, incidentally, would some years later marry my friend Clyde May.

Off we went in Clyde's car, towing his inboard motor boat. We spent the night in a motel, drank a lot of Scotch, and got up early to launch the boat and head for Bird Island, where incoming ducks could be expected. After fair morning sport, we lolled around on the island and took naps after eating our packed lunches. We were waiting for sundown and another flurry of incoming migrating ducks.

Not a one appeared, so at sundown we decided to head out for the mainland. We got in the boat, and Clyde cranked it up. There was a terrible grinding noise, and then a smoky discharge from the engine. Oh Lord! We discovered that the boat had swung around with its twin propellers right in the middle of a fish trap made of chicken wire. When we'd started the engine, a hell of lot of chicken wire had wrapped itself around the propeller. A very gruesome predicament! Now it was practically dark, the temperature was dropping alarmingly, and there was little choice but to sleep on the island and tackle the boat problem the next morning in daylight.

We had six ducks and a little Scotch. We lit a fire and consumed that, seeing no need to ration. We then retired and were freezing our tails off when New Year's Eve dawned. (We later learned that the temperature hit 28 degrees that day, setting a new record in Florida.)

We developed a plan of action: one of us must strip and dive under the boat and try to unwrap the chicken wire. We drew straws to see who would get this enviable task.

Me. I got it! It was unspeakably horrible. I dove and dove and grappled with the wire, and I got nowhere. Finally that approach was abandoned, and there was none other except to sit by the fire we had started and wait for help. We knew that when we did not return to Winter Haven that night, all of our connections would begin to worry and take action. Several of them knew where we had planned to hunt.

Another night on Bird Island, no food or drink, and the weather seriously cold. Sunday morning—New Year's Day—around eleven o'clock, we spied a Piper Cub circling overhead, and we began to take heart. He obviously saw us and wiggled his wings to let us know it. By then we had not eaten in almost two days, and we were exceedingly tired of one another.

What a beautiful sight it was two hours later when we saw the Game Warden's boat headed toward us. He beached his boat, waved casually, and then cutely asked us if we were ready to head back. We piled in after tying a towline to Clyde's boat, and we headed home, our faces blackened by the smoke of the campfire.

Lumby Smith, seated next to the boat driver, discovered, in the well of the dashboard, two Peter Paul Mounds candy bars. You will recall that that product offered two morsels in each package. Without any permission or conversation, Lumby simply reached in and got them, and we devoured them.

When we returned to Winter Haven Sunday night, we were quite the celebrities. The local papers, the Associated Press, and various radio stations had been alerted about our disappearance on Saturday night, and they had all been carrying the news.

We were photographed on Monday, in a reenactment mode, nonchalantly leaning against the boat. My forced "heroics" of diving under the boat in the cold waters was recounted, adding much spice to the story.

It was a sorry experience, but we sure got a lot of mileage out of it when we got back.

CHAPTER 10

HANGING WITH JACK DEMPSEY

Summer came, and tourist activity had tailed off. I was ensconced in still another boarding house. I had been rooming with Bill Carter, the prime-time announcer at the Gardens (gone now to Atlantic City for Miss America Pageant duties, leaving his brother Ed, the number one model at Cypress Gardens, to share my quarters). My tenure with Boyle, Poncho, and the Collie dog had been lacking in harmony ever since I had "fouled the nest," albeit in a well-meaning, but admittedly confused, manner.

It would have been fun to stay at the Gardens into my twilight years, but I began to have twinges of chagrin that I was not embarked on a more ambitious course. Plus, there was the fact that June, July, and August would be a slow time at the Gardens.

It was at this point that I decided I should be a newspaper reporter. Was I prepared for such a career? I think not. Nevertheless, I was convinced that it was an idea whose time had come.

I explained my plan to the Popes, of whom I had grown quite fond, and vice versa I do believe. They bore up under this news. And I left the Gardens' employ.

One of the skiers was going home to Michigan, a summer haven for the sport, so I hooked a ride as far as Atlanta and then caught the beloved Greyhound to Rome, for a nice visit before launching my new career.

I loved this visit. My parents were simply wonderful companions, regardless of kinship, and I was so glad to see them. I told them of my plans, and they—as usual—saw the logic of my being a writer (they had been terribly impressed with my Master of Ceremonies duties in Florida, one of my few accomplishments to date). My father did point out one stumbling block in the way of my new newspaper career. I did not know how to type.

I addressed this problem by going down to a local pawnshop and purchasing a five-dollar typewriter, including a dog-eared chart on learning the touch system. For the next week I sweated over the touch system, practicing with recreated stories of great horse races, most involving Eddie Arcaro, the premier jockey of his day.

During this stay, I became quite close with my little sister, now seven years old. The two of us did a lot, including the rather interesting experience of attending several picture shows together. Sally tended to be quite intense about the movies.

In those days people arrived at the theater whenever it was convenient for them. You stayed until "This is where we came in," an often-heard expression of the time. It was a system that worked fine then but would be unthinkable today.

The trouble with movie-going with Sally was that there never was a point at which she was willing to leave. Invariably a disagreeable row, disruptive to anyone within earshot, came with the suggestion, "Sally, this is where . . . ."

Sally was known to me then, and is today, as "Baby Sister." The primary reason for this appellation is that it tended to annoy her, mildly I think. It was fun to tease her. She was feisty, as we say in the South, and she would always fire back at me with, "I am *not* your 'Baby Sister.' I am your *kid* Sister." This variation seemed to make a great deal of difference.

Her feisty nature was lessened permanently one day by my father. Sally was prone to have tantrums when she was little, and she was reared at a time when tantrums met with stiff opposition from parents. One day things did not go her way, and she responded by screaming like a banshee, throwing things, and pretty much getting out of control. There was a large pitcher of ice water in the dining room. In exasperation, my father seized it and emptied the entire contents in the face of Baby Sister. She stopped in mid-scream, stared at him wide-eyed, and did not make another sound. End of tantrum. This sounds rather extreme of my father, who earlier was described as consistently supportive. But he was also innovative. He did everyone an immense favor by permanently curing the tantrums. Including Sally.

A particular movie episode occurred during that trip, and its details are etched in stone in my memory. I had given Sally a coonskin cap the previous Christmas, and she adored it. The fact that it was suggestive of cold weather made no difference to Sally. She insisted on wearing it all summer long.

On a Saturday afternoon, she and I went to the DeSoto Theater to "enjoy" a film, starring her favorite cowboy, Lash LaRue. The Desoto had two side aisles, and thus, the middle rows were exceptionally long. The theater was packed this day.

We were forced to find two seats in the very middle of one of the long rows. She was, of course, wearing the coonskin cap. When settled in our seats, I insisted that she remove the cap.

After we had seen the film, the cartoon, the newsreel, and a Pete Smith short subject, we had covered it all—once. I firmly announced that it was time to leave. There was some spirited griping, but we did leave the theater and began walking home. When we got almost there, Sally shrieked, "Where's my cap?"

I knew immediately where it was—under a seat in the middle of one of those long rows (only God knew which one). Back we went, Sally distraught over the possible loss of the cap; and I, infuriated that God had visited this ghastly ordeal on me.

With the aid of an usher with a flashlight, after several torturous trips up three or four rows and managing to wipe out about ten minutes of plot continuity for fifty or sixty people, we hit the right spot and found the wretched cap. Home we went again, holding hands, the coonskin cap perched on Sally's head, discussing the heroic accomplishments of Lash LaRue.

The Rome respite was closing, and it was time to get started on my newspaper career, so I hitchhiked back to Winter Haven, armed with my battered pawnshop typewriter. I knew I could get paid for doing the ski shows on Sundays and holidays, and the rest of my plan was to work on odd jobs, giving me the flexibility to venture forth to different cities and call on their newspapers.

I had secured several letters of reference which I thought would aid me in my quest. My mother had somehow become a friend of one of the South's greatest newspapermen. This was the distinguished editor of the *Atlanta Journal and Constitution*, Ralph McGill. He wrote a letter, though he could say little other than that I was a young man from a good family and was seeking a job on a newspaper.

For most of the summer of 1949 I pruned citrus trees, painted houses, and announced the well-attended weekend shows at the Gardens.

I made periodic Greyhound Bus trips to Tarpon Springs, Lakeland, Clearwater, Daytona, Orlando, and Tampa. There were no such things as appointments; you just had to hope that the editor, or someone of authority, would be there. Sometimes they were not, and it was back on the bus to Winter Haven until another trip could be financed.

One evening I fielded a call from Ed Ray, managing editor of the Tampa *Times*. He asked if I could come back to the office; there was an opening. I did, and he hired me. Truthfully, there was only one reason. I'm sure it was the letter from Ralph McGill, his great hero.

I reported the following Monday, being driven to Tampa on Sunday by my good friend Lumby Smith, accompanied by my girlfriend, Jane Strickland. Another boarding house was found. I signed in, Lumby and Jane said goodbye, and I awaited my first day at the *Times*.

I showed up at the city room at 7:30 a.m. I have never encountered a more terrifying place. Every one of about twenty typewriters was clattering, smoke practically pouring from them, and behind each one was a very capable, professional-looking man or woman. I thought, "Oh, my God. Touch system, don't fail me now!"

I walked timidly up to the desk of Hampton Dunn, the City Editor, who was doing about three different things at the same time. He glared at me as I told him Mr. Ray had said to report in to him. He wearily got to his feet, walked me down the awesome aisle between the desks, and stopped at the last desk. "You'll be here, as soon as Leo clears out. He's going to the AP in Daytona. When you get settled in, I'll give you your assignments. This is your first newspaper job, isn't it?" I felt like I had a sign on my head confirming this fact.

Settling in did not take long. I went back to "Hamp's" desk, and he said, "You'll be covering civic clubs, ship sailings, and obituaries. Here, give me a quick rewrite on this news release on the Jaycee's Fun Fair, and then I want you to cover the Rotary Club today at Columbia Restaurant in Ybor City."

I nodded like I thought that would be a piece of cake, went back to my desk, and tackled the rewrite, having no earthly idea what was wrong with the original news release.

Leo had not yet cleared out, and I noticed he was sort of clocking me, with a slight air of empathy. He could not help but notice that I had not yet completely mastered the touch system and seemed to be in heavy weather generally.

He looked down at me and said, "You doing OK?" knowing what the answer was. "Let's see what you've got." He looked at my lead on the rewrite, which started out, "A good time was had by all this Sunday at the Jaycee's Annual Fun Fare . . . ."

"You're writing a goddamn editorial, not a *news* story. Just give 'em the facts, not your opinion. Here, let me show you." He looked at the news release for about fifteen seconds, sat down at the typewriter, and brrrrrrrrrrrrt! I believe smoke did come out of this machine. In a minute or two he tore off a sheet with three short paragraphs and handed it to me. He then gave me a capsuled journalism lesson on "Who, What, Why, When, and Where," said "Good luck, partner," and left for Daytona.

I handed "our" story on the Jaycees to Hamp; he glanced at it and grumbled, "OK." Thanks entirely to Leo, I was off to a satisfactory start. But would there be a Leo in the future when I needed him?

No. And if ever a human being was entirely unqualified for the job he was asked to do—even the meanest of assignments—it was me. I struggled on. The response to eighty percent of my output was "try again." What made it worse was that on the same day that I started, the *Times* added another reporter, an honors graduate from the famed Missouri School of Journalism. He slid easily into coverage of City Hall, as I floundered while covering an insignificant speech at the Civitan Club.

I got better, of course, but I didn't get the impression old Hamp was excited about his new staffer. My only real contribution came with our coverage of a very celebrated murder case.

A Tampa preacher (I forget the denomination) had married a thirteen-year-old member of his congregation earlier, and then quickly moved to another town with his new bride. This had gone down badly with the girl's father.

After some months, the couple came back to Tampa, to test the waters, I suppose. And it had been rumored that the young bride was not wildly happy with her mate, who might have rather forcefully sold her a bill of goods. They were staying at the Tampa Terrace Hotel, rather fashionable digs. When the girl's father got wind of this, he visited the hotel, found his son-in-law in the lobby, and shot him dead. This happened around nine a.m., and we were sitting pretty to nail the story in the afternoon street edition and scoop the vaunted Tampa *Tribune*, our overwhelming competition.

Our ace, Marge Daugherty, was assigned to go to the hotel and interview the young widow, who was under heavy protection by family and police. Getting Marge in to talk to her was going to be a severe problem.

As I was working morosely on my stash of other routine obituaries, Hamp yelled down the newsroom at me, "Campbell, you go with Marge to the hotel and see if she needs your help in some way." Exciting assignment, if rather vague.

The hotel was about three blocks away. As Marge and I hurried there, we discussed strategy. Simply requesting an audience with the girl was hopeless, so we agreed to try to bluff our (Marge's) way in. Marge was a bespectacled, matronly, sweet-faced woman, and I appeared fairly clean-cut, neat, and respectable. We would present ourselves, in a vague but unequivocal manner, as sort of grief counseling specialists from the funeral home and/or the church.

Marge knew which floor we wanted but not the room number. When the elevator took us to seven, it was clear from the activity where the room was. We breezed by a policeman. Marge knew him, and he looked the other way. When we got to the room several people were at the door, and I said authoritatively, "I'm sorry we're late. We got here as soon as we could. I'm sure Viola (the girl) would like to see Mrs. Daugherty now." They nodded respectfully, and ushered Marge into the room, while I waited in the hall (but at a safe distance away so as to avoid any unwanted interrogation). Marge got her story, and it was pretty juicy. It was clear Viola's primary anguish lay with her father's incarceration. Our story was in the early edition, which hit the street at 1:30. Marge got the byline, of course, but my role gained me some points back at the city room.

It was not admirable for us to gain admittance to the bereaved girl's quarters under false pretenses, and today I am not at all proud of my role in it. Regrettably perhaps, it was then—and is even more so now—standard newspaper procedure used to get the story and the inside angle. And, furthermore, at age twenty-one, frantically trying to hold onto a job I shouldn't be in, was I going to tell Marge Daugherty or Hampton Dunn that I did not approve of such tactics?

———

Even my contribution to this good story did not save the day for me. After several months, Ed Ray and Hamp called me into Ed's office one morning, and said they thought I was trying hard and that I had made some headway, but my inexperience, combined with a lack of education, was a stumbling block. "We like you and we want you to stay with us, but we want you to go to night school and get some more education. Think it over, but it's the best thing for you in the long run."

I understood their point, but I loathed the idea of night school. For a few days I agonized over what to do, and then serendipitously I got a call from a friend in Winter Haven with a report that the Winter Haven *Daily News Chief* had an opening for a proofreader, which would lead in two months to a job as a reporter. Man, that sounded good. My stint at the *Times* had been tedious, and life in Tampa had been pretty lonesome. I called the Winter Haven publisher, Bill Rynerson, with whom some groundwork had been laid, and he hired me on the phone for the princely sum of $29 per week. The Veterans Administration would supplement my salary up to $40 per week through the GI Bill.

I was so happy to go back to Winter Haven where I had many friends, a girlfriend, and the Gardens announcing connection, and where I could still continue in newspaper work. The truth is that I was under-qualified for even the *News Chief* job, but the fact that they had hired me from the *Times* gave me some cachet. They did not need to know anything about the night school suggestion.

The *News Chief* was a cozy little daily paper, with a staff of about thirty, five of whom made up the editorial side. The publisher wrote innocuous editorials, and there were managing, sports, city, and society editors. I was the proofreader, being groomed to be sports editor, when the soon-to-depart Managing Editor created a slot down the line. One thing about the Winter Haven *News Chief*, there was no shortages of titles.

The festive but exhausting life continued apace in Winter Haven. I lived there for another year and a half, residing in several boarding houses and an apartment or two, and purchased a 1938 Ford, my first-ever automobile.

I did become Sports Editor, meaning that I covered local sports and anything else that needed covering. I wrote a daily column under the dreadful title "The Hot Box." The publisher was constantly in a snit because I had a strong tendency to give my views about the Kentucky Derby, the Olympics, the Rose Bowl, and the World Series. However, I was slow to address the progress of the Winter Haven High School girls' swimming team, the Blue Devil Hoopsters, or the YMCA's new inter-league softball tournament. Mr. Rynerson felt that I was overly ambitious in selecting my targets.

There were some interesting assignments that logically came my way. I covered the Detroit Tigers when in winter quarters in nearby Lakeland; and one day when the Yankees were playing them, I saw Whitey Ford pitch his first big league exhibition game, and watched the immortal Joe DiMaggio compete in his last one. I saw the greatest prizefighter who ever lived: Sugar Ray Robinson. I covered a fight of his in Orlando. And I even had dinner with the mighty Jack Dempsey, one of my great heroes. This was thanks to a wrestling match.

Wrestling was a big deal in nearby Lakeland, and it was felt that I should cover it because the wrestling promoter, Cowboy Luttrell, advertised in the paper. There was an upcoming match pitting "The Swedish Angel" against "Haystacks" Calhoun, a natural draw. But to add some zest to the proceedings, Jack Dempsey had been engaged to referee the match. Jack was touring the country on a refereeing binge. The unfailing scenario was that the combatants would persist in breaking the "rules" of wrestling. Dempsey would patiently intercede, upholding the standards of good sportsmanship. Finally one wrestler, supposedly enraged with Jack for trying to retard his evil tactics, would rear back and take a poke at the old "Manassa Mauler." The very vocal crowd would shriek in outrageous disbelief. This night "Haystacks" was the bad guy. Dempsey first cautioned the wrestler and then waved them together to continue the match. At this point, Haystacks advanced on Jack, shaking his fist, and swung at him. Now the pièce de résistance: Jack blocked the blow but came back with one of his legendary right-handed haymakers, and the evil wrestler was out of the ring. All of this was cleverly orchestrated. The crowd went berserk. The bad guy had gotten what was coming to him, and he got it from the most popular heavyweight champion of our time. Good theater.

After the matches, Cowboy Luttrell had invited me and another writer from the Lakeland paper to have dinner with him and Dempsey. How could we refuse?

We went to a roadhouse near Lakeland where we had a private room. Jack showed up and had a good-looking dame with him, a corn-fed redhead with a little age on her, but not bad at all.

The evening was good, really thrilling for me. Jack told us about his great fight with Luis Firpo, and the famous "long count" fight with Gene Tunney in which Dempsey cold cocked Gene but then would not go to a neutral corner, and thus delayed the start of the count. Tunney, you will remember, was permitted about fourteen seconds on the canvas instead of ten. He got up in time, backpedaled until he cleared the cobwebs, and went on to outbox and outpoint Jack, thus keeping the championship. It was fascinating to hear the details of this from the man himself.

The evening was great fodder for a column, an opportunity the Sports Editor of the Winter Haven *Daily News Chief* would not normally be privy to. I'm sure I was pretty full of myself at that stage, and I'm afraid I demonstrated it. Despite my hero worship for the great old fighter, I wrote a nasty, sarcastic column about the farcical performance in the wrestling arena, the staginess of it, and how it was really a pretty inferior theatrical production. I discussed Dempsey's girlfriend and her lack of contribution to the repartee at the roadhouse dinner.

All in all, it was a sorry thing for me to do. The column wasn't well done, and it exposed me as an amateurish, immature kid, playing the role of hard-bitten, cynical newspaper man and missing the mark pretty badly. I realized my mistake when I saw it in print the next day and was embarrassed. At least you had to give me that.

At this time, I was making $240 per month as Sports Editor, and I picked up a little extra announcing the Cypress Gardens water-ski shows. I was also the public address announcer at the Winter Haven Blue Devils football games, for which I got a pittance. Funding my night life kept me from being flush, but I was getting by. Lord knows I was having a good time.

But there must have been a seed of ambition incubating within me because I began to think about a new "career path." Of course, I was not one to immerse myself too long in any one line of work, and I had heard of an interesting job from my friend, Clyde May. He had taken a position some months earlier with the Florida Citrus Commission. He was one of twelve merchandising representatives situated around the country. Clyde was in New York, and his purpose was to coordinate—with the big grocery chains—the advertising and merchandising of Florida citrus. The name of the game was to see to it that oranges and grapefruit from Florida got promoted instead of California fruit.

The salary was $400 per month, and get this: you got eight cents a mile for your auto travel and a per diem of $10 on which to eat three meals when on the road. You got to keep what was left over! There was an opening in Chicago, which included the territory of Wisconsin and Minnesota. It all sounded very glamorous, and Clyde thought if he put in a word for me, I could get the job.

I did interview at Commission headquarters in Lakeland and got the job. It turned out to be the dreariest line of work imaginable.

I was told to be sure I owned a felt hat and several "nice, dark suits," to then secure lodging in Chicago, and to report to work by December 1 (a lovely time of year to begin traveling through Wisconsin and Minnesota). Upon my arrival, I would be indoctrinated by the other veteran Chicago rep, whose territory was southward.

It happened that my "sweetheart," Jane Strickland, had started that fall as a freshman at Florida State University and had pledged Kappa Delta Sorority. They were having a big Thanksgiving Dance, and she wanted me to come up to Tallahassee for it. It had also been hinted that it would be nice if we got "pinned" on that occasion—and I looked favorably on the idea of giving her my Sigma Alpha Epsilon fraternity pin.

I gave the newspaper two weeks notice, got my simple affairs in order, said goodbye in a few spots, and drove up to Tallahassee for the double-whammy weekend.

When I arrived, I did give her the pin. She had told everyone who belonged to KD that it was a fait accompli, of course. The dance was the next night, and this night there was to be some sort of function at the sorority house. So, when all hands assembled in the living room—to my utter embarrassment—Jane and I were serenaded, for what seemed like two hours.

Perhaps that caused me to lose my equilibrium. After I had said goodnight, the serenade still fresh in my ears, I left for my borrowed bed at the SAE House. There I encountered some of my newfound brothers drinking beer—a superb idea, I thought. Soon we decided to go back out into the night. Time slipped by, and the next thing I knew I was in a police car with several others, headed "downtown," having been arrested for creating a disturbance (our own version of the earlier serenade) on the front lawn of the Kappa Delta House.

It was equally as bad as the unhappy spectacle, already chronicled, at Rome's Shorter College, and my incarceration did put a serious damper on the conviviality of the next evening. The young lady kept the fraternity pin, but the weekend had not gone too well. I was quite relieved when it was time for me to motor to Chicago.

CHAPTER 11

CONQUERING NORTHERN CLIMES

I got a sensational place to live in Chicago when I arrived there in the winter of 1950. Through my mother's connection with a young matron in Rome, I was able to rent for very little money her parents' garage apartment. Their home was in Kenilworth, a super-fashionable North Shore suburb.

Chicago's other Florida Citrus Commission merchandising rep met with me and explained the details of the job from the viewpoint of a man "in the field." One would call on the regional headquarters of a big grocery chain, say A&P. We would detail to their merchandising people the upcoming impact of our Florida citrus advertising schedule (full page, color ads in *Ladies Home Journal, McCall's*, etc.). Then we would make sure their stores would be in a position to benefit from the stampede caused by this campaign. The rep would go around to the stores and make sure our point-of-sale material was being utilized in the citrus department, offering to build displays if necessary. In my case, I was to do this in part of Chicago and all major markets in the states of Wisconsin and Minnesota.

Since my drive to Chicago, I had had concerns over the unexciting nature of the job, and these were heightened now that I was fully indoctrinated. It was a dull job, and I had restlessly made a dumb mistake.

When I was a young man I certainly did not intend to short change the recreational phase of my life. But I also worked hard at every job I had and gave good value to employers. With the Florida Citrus Commission, I did not. I hated the job because you were not selling anything that anyone ever really wanted to buy. I never encountered anyone who did not wish I was elsewhere. It would have made selling life insurance a piece of cake.

I herewith apologize to the Commission. I was a sorry employee, and I'm glad I did not take their money for very long.

I did love the city of Chicago though, and was charmed by the glamour of the big hotels in the Loop. My favorite activity during one period was to go into the heart of the city to a gymnasium where Sugar Ray Robinson was training for his upcoming championship fight with Jake LaMotta. I would watch the great fighter go through his paces, and then ease over to the Ambassador East Hotel to the storied Pump Room and have a martini, the olives having been stuffed with the hearts of artichokes.

After three or four months of this—with a Christmas break in Rome—I was invited to be in my cousin Adelaide's very chic wedding in Huntington, West Virginia. I made arrangements to go; my mother and sister also were making the trip up from Rome. My father was never very thick with my mother's sister and, therefore, he took a pass. Besides, he was finishing his novel in Boca Raton, Florida, having found first Rome, then the Georgia mountain resort of Cloudland, and then Darien, Georgia, all disharmonious to the creative output.

The wedding was outstanding! What a surprisingly sporty little town was Huntington, filled with a delightful blend of people, and lots of beautiful girls. I had the time of my life and overstayed my visit.

While there, someone told me that I should go to Peru (or was it Chile?), where there were great opportunities in the lumber business, especially for someone who understood public relations. Had I not worked on newspapers? They said I would first have to learn to speak Spanish (or was it Portuguese?). This innocuous conversation would prove to be significant—and troublesome—in fashioning the path of my future career.

When finally I was settled back in Chicago, I was motoring down Sheridan Road one stormy, snowy night when the motorist in front of me stopped too abruptly (I felt), and I slid into his vehicle. It was nothing more than a mild fender bender.

The police came to investigate at the behest of the aggrieved gentleman. Prompted vigorously by the "injured party," the officers did not disagree that the smell of alcohol was in the air, and it seemed to be emanating from me. But there were no charges.

After some time, reports were written and insurance connections were exchanged. Then the police dismissed us. Nevertheless, I had the distinct impression that the other motorist possessed a litigious nature. This fact kept resurfacing over the next few days as I mulled over future lifestyle options. It seemed a good time for me to end my association with the Florida Citrus Commission and absent myself from Chicago.

I resigned and once again returned to Rome, Georgia, to strategize and plan my next move. That move would usher in a period of intensifying absurdity. But now that these outrageous times are behind me, I must admit I wouldn't have done without them, and they may have—in their zaniness—laid constructive groundwork for my future stability. At this stage, the outlook for stability was bleak, indeed. There was no light at the end of that tunnel.

I decided to go to Miami, enroll in the Berlitz School of Languages, become fluent in Spanish, and head for Peru—the land of opportunity for PR specialists in the timber business, according to my cocktail party acquaintance from Huntington (whose name I cannot recall today).

In order to fund my new program until the GI Bill approved my next educational phase, I sold my car (slightly gashed in the front fender). I could get by without a car in Miami, and I certainly could not take one with me to Peru.

I hitchhiked to Miami, spending a couple of nights with friends in Winter Haven on the way. When I arrived in Miami, like a homing pigeon I first located a boarding house. Then, through the want ads, I found employment as a car parker at the Copa City nightclub, one of the grandest anywhere. Since this was nighttime work, it would afford me time to pursue my Berlitz studies during daylight hours. In no time, I would be on my way to Peru, chattering away in fluent Spanish.

Copa City was a fun place to work. It was truly one of America's glamour nightclubs, along with such as El Morocco, The Stork Club, The Brown Derby, Ciro's, and Copacabana, all of which have long since vanished from the entertainment scene. Copa City was the crown jewel of Miami Beach, and its entertainment included such headliners as Jimmy Durante, Sophie Tucker, Martin and Lewis, Joe E. Lewis, and Jackie Gleason. In support, there were gorgeous chorus girls in lavish productions presented twice each night.

Its clientele included heavy hitters in the worlds of sports, crime, politics, entertainment, characters who were simply famous for being famous, and hustlers of every variety (including, naturally, some top-of-the-line "ladies of the evening"). Oh, it was lively!

Along with seven other guys, I reported to the doorman at six p.m. every evening. There was always a little cocktail hour business, but the heavy action started around eight p.m., and lasted until two a.m. No one—but no one—who ever came there considered parking his own car. Making an entrance was part of the deal.

If the customer tipped both you and the doorman, you took it, and then turned it over to the doorman. So lucrative was "the door" that the doorman paid to work there. If you were really hustling during the rush, the doorman might "duke," or tip, you. That, plus the $10 per night, was your pay, but most of the boys had other hustles, including thievery in the case of several. Belongings left in the car—binoculars, sun glasses, golf shoes—might be gone when the client bothered to look the next day.

Every night, Walter Winchell, the famous gossip columnist, clad in conservative business suit and gray fedora, would show up for about an hour.

There was certainly plenty of gossip ammunition inside. Sugar Ray Robinson, wintering in the warm climes between fights, would come wheeling up to the door in his famous fuchsia Cadillac. What a splendid, friendly, charismatic fellow he was. Pristine in his dress and grooming, he loved white ties on white shirts, with a dark blue suit.

Ray usually came to Copa City alone and often would stop and talk with us for a few minutes out front. When asked about his pugilistic success, invariably he would go into a fighter's stance, flash that million-dollar grin, and say, "Just keep your hands up, and your ass off the ground!" The line was not that sensational, but it brought gales of laughter. Ray was a generous tipper. He was a sweet human being, but a lethal windmill of unbridled fury in the boxing ring.

Almost nightly we were privileged by a visit from "Snow White." Reportedly Snow White was a $1,000-per-night call girl, and in 1950 that tab and her looks certainly gave her super-celebrity status. She drove herself to the club in a white Mercedes convertible, top down. She was always dressed in white, with platinum white hair. And her face and figure "would make a boy knock his daddy down!" Old Snow White would park in the middle of Dade Boulevard, wait for one of us to open her door and, if the weather was at all cool, she'd fling a white fox fur around her neck and sashay into Copa City. If Joe E. Lewis was performing there, invariably she would emerge with him much later in the evening. Ah, Snow White. She did have style.

There were some glitches in the processing and approval of my enrollment at the Berlitz School, but I must admit I was not undone about the delay. I was making pretty good money at the club, and when I awakened at noon each day, I caught the bus out to Gulfstream Park and bet on the horses, coming to the club straight from there.

But spring came and the season slowed, and I had to think about another means of making a living. Opportunity then presented itself. Incongruously enough, the club's next door neighbor was a thriving funeral home known as Walsh and Wood. During slack times at the club (and, presumably, at the mortuary), Mr. Wood would stroll over and chat with some of us. He often interrogated me on my plans, sensing that I might be cut out for loftier things than parking cars in a nightclub. He offered me a job.

"Why don't you consider being an apprentice mortician?" he asked. "There's a good future in it down here. Your job would be to help us out with funerals and some other things. Also, we rotate with two other funeral homes in taking Miami Beach emergency police calls at night. You'd be on duty with one of our morticians and would drive the ambulance. You'd have quarters with us in the funeral home."

The latter point was spooky but economical. His proposition had appeal. I envisioned roaring up and down Miami Beach in the big shiny ambulance with the siren screaming, rushing to the aid of wounded citizens. I liked the idea. The Peru project was clearly now on the back burner, the hours of this job would give me plenty of time at the track, and it was a question of "any port in a storm." So I accepted.

First, though, I needed a little vacation back home in Rome.

Auto dealerships at that time were looking for drivers seeking free transportation to Northern destinations. To reduce slack-season inventory, they needed cars ferried to Northern cities, and Atlanta was one. So I hopped in a bright red Ford convertible, put the top down, took off my shirt, and headed for Atlanta. I dropped my auto off in Atlanta at the dealership, where my father was waiting to transport me to Rome.

Bill Campbell had finally finished his novel, *Big Beverage*, a truly provocative history of the Coca-Cola Company, complete with some thinly-disguised Coke luminaries. He was about to send the finished manuscript to an Atlanta publisher with whom he had been negotiating. My mother had opened her own antique shop, and it was going well. So, much of our visit was spent discussing *Big Beverage*, "Lila C. Campbell, Antiques," and my upcoming life as a mortician.

They were remarkable people, my folks. How could they suffer in absolute silence while their only son blundered from one ridiculous line of work to another, with never an upward step? Could they have had confidence that I would someday get myself straightened out? If so, it would be tested strenuously before it was rewarded.

My father, "in need of a break," decided he would drive me back down to Florida and that we would spend a few days at the racetrack before I had to report for duty at Walsh and Wood.

When that time came, we drove into the parking basement of the funeral home. And there we encountered a decidedly menacing and hostile atmosphere. Inside the parking garage, there were maybe twenty hard-looking gents in dark suits. When I piled out with my luggage, you could cut the tension with a knife. Every eye was on us. Then I noticed an open casket, in which reposed a very dead man, evilly handsome, well turned-out, and creatively coiffed. I recognized that man because I had read about his murder in the previous day's paper.

This was Charlie Fischetti, the Chicago gang lord and successor to the Mafia empire of Al Capone. He had been shot down and killed in a Miami coffee shop. The supporting cast hovering about my new place of employment were Charlie's boys, and they were inclined to be in a very contentious mood because "The Man" had been whacked. They were on the alert and were somewhat curious about the nature of our mission, innocuous though it seemed.

Fortunately, the head of the funeral home showed up and identified us tactfully to Charlie's men, then murmured to us, "The departed is being taken back to Chicago on an evening flight."

My introduction to the mortuary was unsettling, to say the least. It was exceedingly disturbing to my father, who was quite reluctant to say goodbye. But Fischetti and his boys were on the verge of clearing out, so once I was settled in, my Dad reluctantly struck out for Rome.

The summer was a slow time on the Beach, and therefore business at Walsh and Wood was relatively draggy. Many nights my sleep was uninterrupted, but there were enough police calls to make life interesting. Most of these were heart attacks, drunks falling in the canals, drunks needing help being taken to hospitals, and occasionally a bloody fight or murder. Activity of the latter sort was more pronounced than in other locales, to be sure. Miami Beach was never noted for its wholesome nature.

Since I was on duty every night, I had the afternoons off. I did various things around the mortuary in the morning—washing the hearse, moving caskets around in the display room, or helping with the heavy lifting at embalming time (not my favorite phase of mortuary life). I can see my employer now, toiling in a casual mode, nonchalantly pumping embalming fluid into a cadaver while munching on a ham sandwich.

On visitation or funeral days, I put on my blue suit, drove one of the procession cars, and helped usher people about, while looking properly doleful. I was learning the ropes.

This routine did not permit me much time for evening carousal. However, I did work out an arrangement with Mr. Wood that during the early evening I could walk over to "Mother Kelly's," a famous Miami Beach watering hole where the legendary singer Billie Holiday held forth nightly. The understanding was that if I was needed (and I was not at the funeral home) I would be at "Mother Kelly's." It was within two hundred yards of the funeral home, so someone could easily reach me if the ambulance needed to go out.

The afternoons were mine. Some were spent on the beach, but most at the racetrack, depending on my finances. One attractive feature of this job was that the driver of the ambulance sometimes got hefty tips (for driving sick or handicapped people to the train station or airport for return to their summer homes). Most of this went through the windows at the racetrack.

The funeral home professionals kept trying to instill in me an enthusiastic, "fire in my belly" attitude toward being an apprentice mortician, but the truth is that I was just looking for a place to light and, despite my lessened enthusiasm for Peru, I justified killing time at the funeral home by paying mental lip service to myself that I was waiting to attend the Berlitz School but was stymied by the foot-dragging and red tape at the Veterans Administration.

Walsh and Wood got their money's worth from me, but now they sought to accelerate my training and move me into burial preparation. This was a natural progression, and I knew it was coming, but I had little stomach for what we might very appropriately call "the nitty gritty."

One day in the embalming room, I was milling about uncomfortably while a very wasted ninety-five-year-old lady was having the finishing cosmetic touches applied by the head man and his wife.

Mr. Wood looked over at me and said, "Cot, why don't you go ahead and 'dress her mouth'—just remove her dentures, then take those rolls of cotton, open her mouth, and put them outside her gums all the way around. Makes her face fuller, you know what I mean?"

I knew, but I couldn't tackle that. The moment of truth in the career of an apprentice mortician had inevitably arrived. And I was found wanting!

"Aw, gee, Mr. Wood, I just can't do that," I replied.

"Well, you'll certainly have to, if you're going to perform this job!"

"I know. But I won't be able to perform the job. I'm sorry."

I left.

Clearly I had just about done South Florida, and some other locale was calling. I decided that Huntington, West Virginia, was the place for me. I had enjoyed myself to the utmost in that town, had connections there (an aunt and uncle), and sensed that my talents would somehow be just the thing for Huntington. I got my mother to pave the way through a conversation with her sister (probably something along the lines that I had not yet "found myself," and perhaps Huntington would be the answer). My Aunt Adelaide was my mother's older sister, and had some of her great attributes—notably charm, intelligence, and a superb sense of humor. But she was slightly stuffy, mostly because she had married the original "straight arrow." This would have been Uncle Luther, known in Huntington as "the Major."

Luther Griffith had served as an artillery officer during World War I and had never forgotten it. He went into the lumber business in West Virginia, worked like a dog, made a lot of money, somehow got himself to New Orleans, and met and married Adelaide. They had two highly successful children. The Major's hobbies were his garden, the American Legion, and the super-conservative wing of Republican politics in his town and state. He was the "Rock of Gibraltar," a fine man, but not a lot of laughs.

Adelaide looked on my settling in Huntington as an unexpected and perhaps lively diversion in her colorless life with the Major. Luther, vaguely familiar with my nomadic wanderings and remembering my festive nature during my visit in connection with his daughter's wedding, was not wildly enthusiastic about taking me on. But he would agree ultimately to anything Adelaide desired.

It was decided I should come to Huntington, stay with my aunt and uncle until I could "get on my feet," and they would put out feelers to find me employment that was suitable—and, based on my résumé to date, God knows what "suitable" would be.

Despite the town's lively nature (discovered on my earlier visit), Huntington was not so overrun with talent in its young social set that it could not use another fresh, attractive bachelor. Given my connections and some titillating rumors about my past activities, my arrival on the scene did generate some mild excitement.

I interviewed at the newspaper, several life insurance companies, and nearby Ashland Oil, and I then was hired as Credit and Operating Manager of Stettler Tire Company.

I had been referred to Mr. Stettler by Billy Campbell, no kin but a young turk who took an interest in me. He was one of America's most celebrated amateur golfers, the darling of West Virginia, a legislator, and a friend of my relatives. Billy, my uncle Luther, and Mr. Stettler were all strong players in the local Republican organization.

Mr. Stettler bought me a car to use, and in his enthusiasm he hinted that perhaps I could be groomed to one day take over this B. F. Goodrich dealership. I think this possibility did not escape the notice of some of the other employees, and they were not keenly supportive in seeing me get off to a good start.

My uncle successfully masked any disappointment he may have felt when I moved out of his house and into an apartment with a new friend who was a local stockbroker. I think Adelaide missed my company.

I worked for a nice man in a harmless sort of a job. I have never been particularly well-suited for undertakings that fell under the mechanical umbrella, so an affinity for the subject of tires was by no means inspired.

Ah, but the social life was magnificent, delicious! I was in demand as a groomsman for a number of festive weddings and was always going to a tea dance, ball, cocktail party, or some impromptu bash. I was twenty-five years old and in my prime physically, so I could drink the moon out of the sky, get four or five hours of sleep, and answer the bell the next morning. During the next few years, this indefatigability would wane. But it had not yet. I think I knew that I was a full-fledged alcoholic, and that some day I would pay the piper. But for the time being, let the good times roll. And, for me, there was never a better place for them to roll than Huntington, West Virginia.

Luther sought to slow my journey to destruction by giving me for my birthday a membership in the Young Men's Christian Association. I was truly touched by this gift and felt badly that while I took an occasional steam bath at those facilities; I surely did not embrace their program for a healthy mind and body.

During my stay in Huntington I knew many young ladies, but for most of my tenure there I went out with a girl named Jane Ellen Queen. She had been Miss West Virginia in the Miss America Pageant, came from a modest background, taught elementary school, and was a very fine human being.

However, we enjoyed a most singular social relationship. While she was unmistakably very fond of me, she was engaged to a man in medical school at the University of Pennsylvania. It was etched in stone that she would marry him (and did, I am told), but she never visited him, nor did he ever come home to see her. Other than to explain to me what her ultimate arrangement would be, she never talked about him. I saw her four or five nights a week. Oddly, when I picked her up at night, she had me wait in the car in front of her house, and never once asked me to come inside to meet the parents.

I was in Huntington for about a year. I gave up my apartment when my roommate was transferred. Seamlessly, I moved into a boarding house where a number of the city's young bachelors were staying. It was a large, three-storied Victorian house, and I was assigned an attractive attic apartment suitable for a single occupant.

Fate—or John Barleycorn—would end my time at that boarding house too soon; so, indeed, would my sojourn in Huntington end.

One summer evening I lingered a long, long time at Martin's Grill, a popular neighborhood bar. I took Miss Queen home and went to my relatively new quarters.

As was my custom, I had a last cigarette before falling "into the arms of Morpheus." I fear Morpheus was ahead of schedule. Around dawn, I began choking. The room was full of smoke, and there were flames everywhere, including on me!

I screamed "Fire!" about ten times. Several boarders came running up the steps, but saw that there was nothing to be done and fled. I threw on a handy pair of pants, having torn away my pajamas, and ran down the stairs and out onto the front lawn, where everyone had gone. The fire department arrived and soon put out the blaze, but the entire attic was destroyed, and some of the house was damaged from water. The boarders were properly glaring at me; the proprietor was most agitated; and the big question was "What the hell caused it?" I mumbled something to the effect that "it must have been faulty wiring." No one was buying.

I lost virtually everything—all my clothes save the pants I put on. Burned up was what little cash I had, a baseball signed by Babe Ruth and Lou Gehrig, all but two antique beer mugs my mother had given me, and some framed pictures of Kentucky Derby winners.

Barefooted and shirtless, much of my hair burned off or at least singed, I got in my car and drove to Stettler Tire Company, which had just opened for the day. Mr. Stettler was shocked when he saw me, then properly sympathetic, when I told him of the circumstances. I borrowed twenty dollars and told him I would return when I had gotten organized.

I then decided that the only thing to do was to go swimming!

I called Jane Queen at her school, told her of the fire, and said I would appreciate it greatly if she would get a substitute teacher and spend the day swimming with me. God bless her, she agreed immediately. I met her at the home of some wealthy friends, Jimmy and Joan Edwards, parents of two of my contemporaries. Their spacious pool was practically a community facility.

The Edwards could not have been sweeter, and it was there that I borrowed clothes belonging to their son. Jane and I then spent the day swimming and drinking some of their beer. As word spread, we were joined by others in my crowd later in the day.

I called my folks and told them what had happened and that I would be coming home. The Griffiths were on a cruise, or I would have gone there for help. And then I called Mr. Stettler and told him I thought it was indicated that I should leave Huntington, and that I would bring in his car the next morning. I think at that point the handwriting was on the wall for him: I was not going to be the next president of Stettler Tire Company, and he did not protest the wisdom of my going back to Georgia.

The news of the holocaust was all over town by now, and that night a large group appeared for a farewell party at Martin's Grill, where I had no trouble borrowing enough money for a bus ticket home.

The next morning I headed for the bus station, traveling mighty light.

In my youth I rode extensively on Greyhound buses, and—as indicated earlier—hardly ever did I associate that mode of travel with a sense of gaiety, anticipation, or adventure. Trips on "Big Blue" were usually pretty depressing. But the ensuing journey to Rome was the worst yet—ghastly! Never had I known such an ignominious departure or such a bleak outlook. It was all my own doing, of course, but bleak right on.

CHAPTER 12

THE SIEGE OF ATLANTA

It was back to the drawing board, big-time. After the bus trip to Rome, the first stop was National City Bank where I borrowed four hundred dollars, necessarily backed by a substantial co-signer. Refurbishing my wardrobe—but not very ambitiously—was certainly a requisite, and following that, employment of some sort.

I decided Atlanta might offer more opportunities for a young man with my talents. Since my aunt on my mother's side had been my sponsor in West Virginia, it was decided that it was only fair that I throw a bone to my father's sister in Atlanta, and perhaps I could rent a room in her modest home. I could, and I did. "Aunt Baby," as Elizabeth was known, was the impecunious widow of the notorious Al Irving, whose escapades were chronicled earlier, and whose liver faltered early, to no one's surprise.

Thankfully, I was able to get an immediate job as an assembly line worker at the Chevrolet plant in Hapeville, an Atlanta suburb. My qualifications for such work were skimpy indeed, but I took a good run at it. I was positioned on the assembly line where the bumper was installed on the vehicle, and it was nerve-wracking at first, because there was absolutely no room for error.

The plant was reachable by bus if one transferred twice. My shift started at 7:30 a.m., so I had to leave Elizabeth's house by 6:15 to make it. The shift ended at three p.m., and I got home about six o'clock.

While toiling at the Chevy plant, I launched a campaign to get a job with an advertising agency, having some valid background for such a quest. I called various agencies seeking four p.m. appointments, the only time slot I could make. When I scored one, on those days I would take my new dark suit, shirt, tie, and shoes to work, change hurriedly when my shift ended—a procedure considered most curious by my co-workers—and hurry downtown, seeking a more "suitable" form of employment.

In those days, advertising was America's voguish, white-collar line of endeavor. The world of advertising was the quintessence of glamour. The agencies had great, mellifluous names, fun to say as they rolled off the tongue: Ruthrauff & Ryan; Batten, Barton, Durstine & Osborn; Foote, Cone, and Belding; and Kenyon & Eckhardt. There were scads of movies and books about the ad game, and magazines and newspapers featured stories of dramatic breakthroughs in the world of commerce, made possible by the cleverness of the gray flannel suits and hatched during three-martini lunches.

I had gotten a taste of big-agency atmosphere when I traveled to New York during my time with the Florida Citrus Commission and spent several days being indoctrinated on our ad campaign by the biggest agency in the world, J. Walter Thompson.

The problem was that competition for advertising jobs was so stiff that you practically had to pay the agency to let you break in with them.

After one got on the payroll, to be successful in the agency business one needed essentially to be a salesman, a tad whimsical, creative, interested in everything, a quick study, and mentally glib.

While fumbling with the bumpers at the Chevy plant, I dreamed of a job with an advertising agency. I was about to get one, and I would spend a substantial portion of my life plying that trade.

I had an appointment with Burke Dowling Adams—another mellifluous name but, in this case, not the names of three men, but the full name of the founder, familiarly known as "Bob Adams." I told him about my newspaper work, the Florida Citrus Commission and, more importantly I think, I told him that I had just come in on the bus from my job on the assembly line at the Chevrolet plant. He loved it. Thought I had moxie. He hired me for $225 per month.

He had the significant Delta Air Lines account and also the biggest banking chain in Atlanta, the Citizens and Southern Bank. Adams had just moved his agency from New Jersey because of Delta's Atlanta headquarters, had only nine employees (I was number 10), and was struggling to staff up. This was the only sensible career move I had made since I went to work for the Tampa *Times*.

I knew quite well how to have fun during the nighttime hours. Now I learned about fun while I was working. The people at BDA were sharp, interesting, witty people who worked hard but laughed a lot while doing it.

Working there as a copywriter was a polio victim (paralyzed from the waist down) named Chuck Shields, who was to become one of my staunch friends. Chuck was an orphan who had been brought up and educated at Boys' Town in Nebraska. He had been a radio announcer in the Midwest and blossomed into one of the finest broadcast copywriters around. Certainly there were none in the

South that could touch him. I was put under Chuck's wing to learn to write radio commercials (there was not much television in 1951).

Soon I was writing all the radio commercials for the bank account and, with Shields supervising, I was writing and producing a weekly, half-hour radio show that was heard all over Georgia. This was "Cavalcade of Song" (" . . . a cavalcade of music and memories, brought to you by . . . etc.").

Shields, seriously handicapped and married with an adopted child, was naturally obsessed with job security but yearned secretly for the life of a boulevardier, and he lived vicariously through my nights on the town.

I got a raise or two, expanded my wardrobe, and bought a car. Quite naturally though, I was having a hard time funding my very active social life. I decided that the only thing to do was to "consolidate my debts" (a phrase I had used in my radio work for the bank). I knew I must secure a loan from my neighborhood Citizens and Southern branch bank.

I went by the 10th Street branch where I had an account, sought out Mr. Johnson, the young manager, and told him I was a virtual employee of C & S, in that I spent my days writing radio commercials on why people should bank there. And that I needed a four hundred dollar loan to "consolidate my debts"—smooth verbiage, I thought. (You have noted by now that four hundred dollars was the magic number in my bank dealings. I was quite conscious of not being too ambitious.)

"What would be your collateral, Mr. Campbell?" he asked.

I explained again about being a virtual employee and that surely that eliminated the normal need for collateral.

He rather pointedly said, "Well, Mr. Campbell, we are familiar with your account history. Without any collateral or a very strong guarantor, I'm afraid we can't help you."

I was flabbergasted, dismayed by this totally unexpected response. Where was I to turn?

Suddenly, I had a stroke of genius. The president of the Citizens & Southern Bank in those days was one of the truly legendary, innovative characters in the history of American commerce. His name was Mills B. Lane, the loosey-goosiest, free-wheelingest maverick in the banking business. I did not know Mr. Lane but I had been told that he had an open door policy. If you wanted to see him, just come on downtown. Here was my answer. Mills B. Lane would set things right.

Off to his office I went. I asked his secretary if I could see Mr. Lane. She looked up and cocked her thumb toward his inner office. I introduced myself to the man, went through the spiel about virtually working for the C & S because I spent my time writing about why people should bank with Citizens and Southern, and then really warmed to my task.

"Mr. Lane, I have been to your 10ᵗʰ Street branch and talked to Mr. Johnson about a four hundred dollar loan for the purpose of consolidating my debts. He turned me down because I didn't have any collateral.

"Now, Mr. Lane, as you know, our advertising theme is 'personalized banking'—the fact that if you bank with C & S you are an individual, not a set of numbers. Our bank looks behind the scenes, to the individual, to the specific situation. We provide PERSONALIZED BANKING!

"There is no way in the world I would jeopardize my job by not paying back a four hundred dollar loan. So I submit to you that if ever there was a person who needed—and deserved—personalized banking, it is me. And I have come downtown to get you to provide some!"

He looked at me as if I were insane. Then his eyes crinkled up and he started to grin. He slapped the desk and started to laugh. His face turned red and tears rolled down his cheeks.

I didn't know what to think, but things seemed to be going my way. He pulled himself together, looked at me, shook his head, wiped his eyes, picked up the phone, and dialed a number.

"Johnson, I've got a fellow named Campbell down here. You turned him down for a loan, and I'm sure you should have. But let's go ahead with it. He'll be back out there to see you. Thanks."

"Mr. Lane," I exclaimed, "you are my man!"

He stared at me a moment, smiled a little, and said, "Get the hell outta here!"

Within an hour I was properly funded to continue my social life.

A prominent fixture in that life was a cabaret/bar called Wit's End. It was run by a very attractive couple, Phil and Nancy Erickson. Phil had been half of a popular night club act known as "The Merry Mutes." The other half was Dick Van Dyke, on his way then to becoming an internationally known film and TV star. The Merry Mutes were, as the name suggests, lip sync artists. That means they performed to recorded novelty numbers, costumed creatively and depending heavily on pratfalls, facial contortions—anything to sell the number.

Wit's End had two nightly shows, and some of the regulars at the bar were coerced into performing. I participated fairly regularly in a number called "Cigareets, Whiskey, and Wild, Wild Women."

One evening, after a good bit to drink, another bon vivant and I decided that we should go to the nearby Biltmore Hotel, where the Shriners were having a convention, and procure a Shriner's fez, the strange looking headgear they wore. We thought it would be very cute to "acquire" (steal) one or two, and return to Wit's End, triumphant in our derring do.

Insanely, we entered the Biltmore, which was swarming with Shriners, and caught the elevator randomly to the fourth floor. We wandered up and down the halls, seeking an opportunity to seize a fez. The door to one room was open and we brazenly went in, hoping to find a fez laying around. Suddenly, in the doorway appeared five or six pretty sizeable Shriners. One of them yelled out what turned out to be a secret cry of alarm: I believe it was "Nobles!" It worked. Soon there were ten surrounding us. Someone called the police. Because of the convention, Atlanta police were patrolling in and around the hotel, and within a few minutes two of Atlanta's finest had apprehended us. Shortly, several plain-clothes detectives joined the group.

We were hustled down to the street and told to lean, spread-eagled, against a police car. We were then handcuffed and searched while we giggled, and about a hundred people watched.

Tommy (I won't use his name in case he's still alive) and I were transported downtown to the Atlanta Jail, where we were fingerprinted, photographed, relieved of our belongings, and then put in separate cells (each with a cellmate, of course). We were booked on "Suspicion of Grand Larceny"—a little more serious than being slapped in the "drunk tank." This charge was quite logical because there had been some thievery going on at the Biltmore during the convention, and we were sure prime prospects. Admittedly, we had gone to the Biltmore with thievery on our minds—"cute" thievery though it may have been.

When we were put in our cells we were full of bravado, of course, yelling and smarting off. However, after spending a night without more alcohol to sustain our joie de vivre, our outlook on Saturday morning was becoming grave. As new loudmouthed inebriates were shown to their facilities near us, we did not find their exuberant behavior very appealing. Our own demeanor went from blustering to obsequious.

We were served hominy grits, baloney, and bread for breakfast, and the cuisine did not become any more desirable as the weekend unfolded.

Furnishings in jail cells tend toward sparsity. There were two very narrow bunks in the eight-by-ten cell, bare mattresses, and a toilet without a seat—standard equipment in penal institutions, I have found.

There is something about a seatless toilet that certifies the dark mood of being in jail. It says you are a jailbird and, understandably, not even worthy of having a seat on your toilet. You don't deserve even this pitiful amenity. While I cannot think as one in charge of a penal colony might, I do believe the absence of a seat also speaks to the fact that you, the inmate, are capable of doing a drastic, self-destructive act or, at the very least, that you are poised on the bubble of extreme violence and quite capable of ripping off a toilet seat and bludgeoning your cellmate with it. Perhaps, even worse, you might be so demented as to destroy city, state, or federal property. Life without a toilet seat is simply depressing as hell.

Then too, one's cellmate is invariably a lugubrious sort, and is not likely to brighten the outlook of jailhouse days.

When you are put in jail simply for being drunk, at least you know that there is a pattern for release: the authorities are anxious for you to sober up and make your phone call for bail, so they can collect their fine and get you out of their hair. Grand larceny is another matter. We were permitted no phone calls, we had no reason to think that anyone at Wit's End or anywhere else knew where we were, and one begins to despair that the entire world is against him, if it has even thrown a thought his way.

This somber outlook continued and intensified for us through Saturday night of what was Labor Day weekend. On Sunday Tommy's black cellmate was released, but not before Tommy gave him the telephone number of a friend of ours and asked him to communicate our need for help. One would not have enormous confidence in the conscientious nature of a cellmate in delivering such a message. But in jail there is sort of an unwritten code that once on the outside you would be honor bound to pass on a message on behalf of an inmate, and certainly a cellmate. No matter how heinous your nature, you would play by this rule.

Sunday was pretty horrible. All day long my family was heavy on my mind, particularly my mother. Whenever I suffered remorse—inevitably induced by drinking—it tended to focus on my mother and how she deserved a positive contribution from me and not the anguish that my sorry behavior caused. Oddly enough, her small size became particularly poignant to me; illogically in my thoughts her "littleness" made her seem more vulnerable.

The innocence and purity of my little sister, and the fact that her brother was in the Atlanta jail, part of the dregs of humanity and thought to be involved in grand larceny, gnawed at me on that dreadful, interminable weekend. Perhaps my father's many indiscretions in his life lessened my pangs of conscience concerning him. In any case, none of the three of them ever knew anything about my predicament.

On Labor Day afternoon, the jailer came and got Tommy and me. We were taken to an interrogation room where the same detectives who arrested us appeared and questioned us briefly. I think they had decided to buy our story of sophomoric high jinks at the Shriners' convention. After several minutes, the door opened and in walked our friend—who *had* been reached by Tommy's cellmate. Thank God he was not away on a holiday weekend because the cellmate might not have persevered.

Our bail was paid by that friend, an older, steady type, and we were released, our high spirits curbed but not eliminated.

At this juncture in the life of the Campbell family, and on a temporarily brighter note, my father's book came out. *Big Beverage* was published by an Atlanta firm, Tupper & Love.

Since it was a satire on the history of the Coca-Cola Company, that organization had never shown much enthusiasm for the project from the time they had first gotten wind of it. In fact, at several points along the way, my father reported, Coke attorneys had offered him a healthy stipend if he would just forget the whole thing. Having poured a significant portion of his life into it, thinking it was pretty good, and dreaming of movie rights and many other happy consequences, he turned these offers down.

Because they could not buy him off and rid themselves of this impending nuisance, Coca-Cola decided to try to suppress the distribution and sale of the book. Before it was known that they would and could do this, there was supreme happiness in the Campbell household that the publication day of *Big Beverage* had finally come. Soon it would be in every bookstore in America.

My father was very proud. So were we all. The book was dedicated to my mother, as well it should have been. I was given a special, leather-bound printer's copy, in which there was this inscription:

"To my good son, my good friend—

"Wade Cothran ('Cot') Campbell

"With humble gratitude for those many virtues which you have always possessed, and which have always made me so very proud to say—'This is my son!'"

The publisher laid on a big luncheon in Rome, and it was a very buoyant time. The reviews trickled in, and some were mediocre but most were very complimentary. But there were expected reviews that were conspicuous by their absence. Then too, there were stores—in Atlanta especially—where the book was unthinkably not available. A call from the publisher confirmed my father's worst fears. Coca-Cola, he was told, was calling in its chits, and many retail establishments—Rich's in Atlanta, I understood, was a prime example—were not going to stock it. There was, of course, never any proof of this, but it was quite clear that the book was not being offered at some locations where it would have sold like hot cakes.

Financially to Bill Campbell, the publication of the book yielded nothing more than the meager advance he had long since received and spent. Feeling that his efforts deserved success or at least a chance to *have* success, the frustration to him, and to a lesser degree his family, was significant. It drastically reduced what wind was left in his sails. He made numerous false starts with other books and short stories, but nothing was ever published after this.

He did stay sober during the ordeal of *Big Beverage.*

CHAPTER 13

"WILEY C. CRANSTON" IN THE BIG EASY

By the time 1954 rolled around, I had learned a good bit about the world of radio and a little bit about television (no one knew much then). My work at BDA took me to various radio and TV stations in Atlanta, and when at WAGA-TV, I got to know the film editor pretty well.

Her name was Lorraine Morgan, and she was not too long out of Stephens College. She was attractive (looked like an exuberant Claudette Colbert, the most recent look-alike I can come up with), had an infectious personality, and soon after her arrival was a vital cog in the smart nightlife world of Atlanta. In the era when moral codes were germane, she had a high one, while at the same time being in the top echelon of party girls in that city. The one outstanding characteristic we both shared in spades was that we loved to drink and have fun.

After some months of seeing each other and visiting her folks in Alabama and mine in Rome, we decided the thing to do was to get married. It was something I had not done yet, and it sounded like it might be fun.

My folks were diplomatic, though decidedly tentative, about the upcoming union. The marriage was clearly a train wreck waiting to happen; in retrospect, it might have been useful if they had been more outspoken.

Lorraine and I were married on May 8, 1954, in her home town of Eufaula, Alabama, in what was surely that city's biggest and gaudiest wedding. A friend of mine—one of ten groomsmen—described it as resembling "the finale from *Quo Vadis*."

After the nuptial festivities, we drove to Miami and then flew to Havana, when that city was at its zenith of high-quality glitz. There were not many great things about my first marriage, for me or the young lady, but one outstanding thing was that it got me to Havana—one of the great cities of all time. Every hour of the day was like New Year's Eve. We went to the races at historic old Oriental Park, saw a cockfight and jai alai, and hung around the famous Nacional Hotel, teeming with high rollers of every description. I have particularly fond memories of a restaurant called Zaragozana, but not because of the cuisine. When I ordered an "Old Granddad and water," the waiter brought a pitcher of water, a bowl of ice, and a quart of that bourbon—along with a pencil. You made a mark on the label where you started, another one when you got through, and settled up accordingly. It was a drinking man's establishment.

After the honeymoon we moved into an apartment in Atlanta, and we each went back to work. Spurred on by my new marital status, I decided it was time to find a job with an advertising agency in another city, thinking that in a new spot I could take a big step upward, leaning on a résumé that included some good stuff about prestigious accounts.

I sent résumés out to some logical agencies and soon got a call from a man named Clark Salmon, president of Bauerlein Advertising in New Orleans. They were looking for a "Radio-TV Director," one who would oversee the creative output in those media. The position would also entail purchasing radio and television time for that agency's accounts. Big job, and over my head at that stage of the game, but I flew down to talk with various people in that agency, and they hired me.

I resigned from Burke Dowling Adams. They offered me more money if I would stay, but my blood was up, and I wanted to go. Mrs. Campbell said goodbye to her film editing job, and we both headed for New Orleans. Brer Rabbit was about to be thrown into the briar patch!

Bauerlein was the third largest agency in New Orleans, heavily engaged in the city's political structure but with some decent retail accounts. Their creative work was not stressed and was pretty run-of-the-mill. Their success was due mostly to connections and very spirited client entertainment.

When I reported for work, they showed me my office, introduced me to my secretary, and then said, "Bauerlein has charge accounts with all the great restaurants: Commander's, Brennan's, Antoine's, Arnaud's, Galatoire's—you name it. We'd like you to do your share of entertaining. Get to know the clients, and take them out." I wanted to say, "You have got the right boy!" Instead, I offered a more subdued, "I'll certainly keep that in mind." Then they left me pretty much to my own devices.

Lorraine and I moved into a nice Garden District apartment being vacated by my old Sewanee friend Chuck Cheatham and his wife, who were being transferred away. Lorraine got a job as a receptionist at Touro Infirmary (where I was born, coincidentally).

It didn't take too long before we were ready to check out those Bauerlein entertainment venues. Also, I had not been in a horseracing town since my funeral home days in Miami, and we quickly became regulars at the Fair Grounds Race Course. It was the time of some splendid old campaigners, and we were there whenever Epic King, Bobby Brocato, Spur On, and Tenacious did battle in stakes races on Saturday afternoons.

Since I placed most of the radio and TV contracts for clients of the agency, I was sought out daily by time salesmen as a luncheon companion, and rarely did a day go by that I did not eat Oysters en Brochette at Brennan's, or Eggs Sardou at Galatoire's. Often several martinis preceded this, and perhaps a stroll over to the Old Absinthe House for a brandy or two followed the meal. Then, often as not, we capped off the afternoon with a trip to the Fair Grounds to catch the last three races. New Orleans mornings were murder, but the afternoons and the evenings were mighty fine.

The agency was benefiting from my presence, believe it or not. I was writing and producing all the radio and TV commercials, producing a cooking show, and activity in my department had increased to the point that I needed an assistant. The Bauerlein luminaries were quite pleased, and if they sensed that my life style was spirited, well hell, this was New Orleans, and it was almost standard procedure to "kick the gong around" pretty good.

After six or eight months of a pace that was too hot not to cool down, Lorraine and I were tending to get on each others' nerves. The foundation of the marriage had never been on firm ground, and the structure was now beginning to deteriorate. I was not easy, nor was she. At this point, I was convinced that it was not going to work, and she had an inkling. Ten months after we wed, I packed a bag, left her the car (her car it was, to be sure), caught the streetcar on St. Charles, and checked into a third-rate hotel in the French Quarter under the assumed name of Wiley C. Cranston (my initials being "WCC"), so she wouldn't know how to call me.

I think we both felt that no great harm had been done; we were quite young, no children, so let's split and get on with the rest of our lives. An attorney friend from Georgia, who was fond of us both, came down and counseled with us, while enjoying a few nights in the French Quarter. It was agreed that Lorraine would take her car and all the furniture, and I would pay her $250 per month for one year.

She left for her home in Alabama and then back to Atlanta, and I moved into an apartment right in the middle of the French Quarter—on Ursuline Street between Bourbon and Royal—and began life as a bachelor in New Orleans. Brer Rabbit was sho'nuff in the briar patch now!

One of my many non-entertainment chores was the production (in every sense of the word) of a TV cooking show. It aired at the very strange time of one p.m. on Sundays. It was sponsored by Agar Hams, Louanna Salad Oil, and Dulaney Frozen Vegetables. It was up to me to see to it that each of these products was demonstrated temptingly every Sunday from one to one-thirty. On Sunday mornings I had to devise and prepare a scrumptious culinary presentation for each product, take the dishes to the studio, and see that they were attractively displayed for the camera. The announcer who was going to enthuse over the products had to be rehearsed by me (the director), and then the show was aired. Why anyone would have watched it, I do not know, but I suppose they did.

The events of one Sunday almost brought about the unraveling of my career in the New Orleans advertising world. Actually, the causation came on the night before.

That Saturday night I had "tied one on," dividing my enthusiastic patronage among the Old Absinthe House bar, Famous Door, and Court of Two Sisters. After a very full (in every sense of the word) evening, I fell into a very deep sleep until around nine on Sunday morning.

I had a horrendous hangover. After dressing hurriedly, I gamely addressed the preparation of the featured attractions of the upcoming cooking show, now about three hours away. I made a rather anemic-looking tossed salad onto which we would later pour the "zesty Louanna French Dressing." I then cooked some of the "plump and tender" Dulaney fordhook lima beans. Finally I unwrapped the Agar Ham, scored ragged-looking diamonds into it, and ran it into my antiquated oven for ninety minutes of baking.

My hangover had not improved one whit after these exertions. I had a terrible thirst, and my mental outlook on the upcoming day was dreadfully bleak. Suddenly a wonderful thought entered my head. The ham was cooking away, and I had an adequate "window of opportunity" before heading to the nearby studio on Royal Street, so why should I not repair to one of my favorite neighborhood bars? I chose Lafitte's Blacksmith Shop and went there to have a nice bracer in the form of a Ramos Gin Fizz. This drink, made with the white of an egg, would serve as both a nutritious breakfast and, more importantly, a badly needed restorative.

My enthusiasm, moments before in such short supply, now had returned, and within minutes I was seated at Lafitte's bar having my first one. It went down easily, and before long I was working on my second. Soon other convivial souls came into the popular bar, and I found myself seated at a table with some of the pals. We were having a splendid time, reliving the events of the previous night and making plans for upcoming entertainment. The morning was now going swimmingly.

The delightful mood of the occasion was slightly altered, however, when a fire engine, its siren wide open, came careering up Bourbon Sweet. But we paid little attention. Within minutes, another big fire truck came clamoring past the bar. Now we began to be interested in the fire's location. I glanced out the window and, oh my God, it became crystal clear! Smoke could be seen billowing out of an apartment down on Ursuline Street. My apartment. The damned ham, now cooking for over two hours, was on fire!

I sprinted homeward, rushed through the courtyard, bounded up the steps (the firemen following my lead), and groped my way into the smoke-filled kitchen. I flung open the oven door, at which point a fireman unleashed his portable extinguisher onto the flaming ham. The crisis was over.

However, the ham now appeared jet-black and was severely shriveled. The Agar people would not be pleased. The firemen found it necessary to ask a few rather rude questions (they were in a most disgruntled mood when they discovered the cause of the blaze). The landlady, who had turned in the alarm, hovered nearby adding considerably to the distinctly disputatious nature of the gathering. By the time they had all dispersed, amidst serious warnings to me, airtime for the cooking show was dangerously close. And here I was with a ham that looked as if it had been nuked, a very sooty salad, and lima beans that have turned charcoal gray.

I scraped and doctored up the ham carcass as best I could, poured Coca-Cola over it (having learned that this gave it a succulent, healthy appearance on camera), and with my other dishes on a huge tray, I set off for WDSU-TV about six blocks away. I was on foot.

This took place in February, the season for Mardi Gras parades. It had slipped my mind that a big one was scheduled to begin at eleven a.m. that Sunday. It was sure to be hitting its best stride on Royal Street in the heart of the French Quarter just about now. It was.

The floats came by in close-order drill, with barricades set up on the sidewalks to hold back pedestrians. There I stood after a disastrous morning, now cruelly thwarted from reaching my destination with that which was entirely necessary to stage the cooking show.

Sweating profusely while holding my fifteen-pound tray, I pleaded with a policeman to get me across. No dice. Finally a passable gap in the parade opened, and I darted across. I arrived at the studio in just the nick of time. The smart-ass announcer who would soon gush charmingly about the ham, beans, and salad, looked warily at the foodstuffs, then at me, and said, "All of you look like you've been dragged through a keyhole!"

We went on the air, and while I sweated it, there were no repercussions. After all, who would be watching a cooking show on television at one o'clock in the afternoon during Mardi Gras?

Though there were times of pressure and tension (such as the ham episode) at this point in my life—at twenty-six years of age—I had managed to spend most of my "business life" in an atmosphere of merriment. But the merriment was taking its toll a bit more than it had at twenty-three. I did not answer the bell as easily in the morning, and I missed a day of work every so often. New Orleans was a ruinous place for me, and if earlier in life I had suspected I was an alcoholic, now I knew damned well I was, but I was going to ride it out, and I could not imagine a decent world without booze in it.

———

I did love and appreciate the personality of New Orleans. It was then one of the truly great cities of the world. The French Quarter was plenty naughty and always had been. But it was high-class naughtiness and not tawdry and cheap, which I felt it became later. I admit, though, it is hard to return to any place and find it as good as it used to be.

I adored the Dixieland music of New Orleans. Part of my job was to go down to the Poydras Street Wharf once a week and attend the festive sailing of the Delta Queen, star of the Delta Steamship Lines, a Bauerlein account. As the ship's passengers came on board they were plied with champagne, while the fabulous old New Orleans band of Papa Celestin's cut loose with "The Saints," "Marie Leveau," "Tiger Rag," and other standards.

I frequented Sharkey Bonanno's on Bourbon Street, where Wild Bill Mathews played "Didn't He Ramble" whenever I walked in the door. Down the street was the Famous Door featuring the Assunta Brothers, on their way to Dixieland Jazz stardom. This was all before the days of Al Hirt, Pete Fountain, and Preservation Hall.

The superb drinks of New Orleans favored by me were the Ramos Gin Fizz, the Sazerac, and Absinthe Frappe. Wine was not in vogue in those days and especially not in New Orleans. Happily, one did not encounter in fine restaurants studious connoisseur types peering down their noses through reading glasses and fretfully flipping pages of a wine list, while the wine steward and fellow diners gritted their teeth and waited out the big decision.

I think perhaps the greatest stripper of them all was doing business in the French Quarter of New Orleans at that time. This would have been Lilly Christine, known as the "Cat Girl." She was stupendous and easily put Gypsy Rose Lee, Anna May Wong, Blaze Starr, and all the rest in the shade. She would have been a signal contributor to the standard of excellence of sinful attractions in that city. Not that there was any paucity of such in that town.

If I were headed down the "road to ruin" when a married man in the Garden District, now as a bachelor domiciled in the French Quarter the pace was accelerating sharply.

My work at the agency was becoming erratic and lackluster. I was often late, disappeared during the day, and during one week missed several days "because of the flu." My bosses were patient, hoping I would come out of what they thought were dark days brought about by my marital upheaval. In time they would have had to fire me.

I had no chance to get straight in New Orleans. I had to leave. I decided to resign from Bauerlein and go to New York, where—I told myself—the true advertising world awaited me. There I would be stimulated, would be able to shun temptation, and would "find myself."

Oh, brother!

CHAPTER 14

BRINGING NEW YORK TO ITS KNEES

The idea of going to New York was spawned out of desperation and bravado. I couldn't stay in New Orleans, I had no other logical place to go, and the implication that New York was calling a man of my talents played well and helped me save face.

I flew to New York City and immediately went to the Manhattan YMCA, traditional stopping point for young men in the big city on the cheap (which I badly needed to be). When I looked over the dormitory setup at the "Y," I decided against it, justifying that I needed to stay at a tonier address if I were to land a job with an agency, where status was paramount. I needed to look and act the part, I told myself.

So I checked into the Algonquin Hotel, having no idea how I would pay for a week's lodging at that hotel—but I would figure that out as I went along. I reckoned, in my mixed-up way, that prosperity was just around the corner. As Roosevelt had said some time earlier, the only thing I had to fear was fear itself.

I made several half-hearted attempts to secure agency job interviews, and I got the runaround. Friends in New Orleans and Atlanta had expansively supplied the names of a few "perfect New York contacts," who would be enthusiastic about seeing, entertaining, and helping me, while I got situated. I called those names. And they weren't.

So mostly what I did in New York was sit in my room at the Algonquin, order Gin and Tonics from room service (two at a time), and stay soused.

Early in my visit I asked the cashier to cash a ten dollar check—not an ambitious amount you might say, but remember, this was 1954, and ten bucks was not to be sneezed at. In any case, the check bounced. This fact, coupled with the prodigious number of Gin and Tonics I was consuming via room service, caused that hotel to lose interest in my business. I got this message when, after an infrequent visit to the outside world, I returned to my room and could not fail to notice that a temporary bar had been bolted diagonally across my door, thus rendering my room key useless. I confronted the front desk, and they made it quite clear that it was time to say goodbye. They presented me with a bill more as a symbol of closure than anything, because I do not think they harbored any hopes of collecting it. They escorted me to the room while I packed my scant belongings and then walked me out the front door.

I went thirty yards away to the Iroquois Hotel, a third-rate establishment at that time (and one that had no knowledge of my history at their next door neighbor). I checked in there where their ignorance was my bliss.

Collect calls to the Southland, in an effort to raise money, garnered a little from a few spots, but the well was pretty close to being dry. My friend Chuck Shields, of Burke Dowling Adams days, mailed me a dollar, with instructions to spend it on spaghetti, as it was "very filling."

A helping hand was extended from an old girlfriend from Huntington. Barbara Brown was living in Forest Hills, New York, and she was flying for American Airlines. Somehow I reached her by phone. She was quite pleased to hear from me and arranged for me to team up with a friend of hers and catch the commuter train at 5:30, so that I would be steered to her apartment in what I vaguely understood was Forest Hills. We made contact and had dinner at her apartment, which she shared with three other stewardesses. She had to fly on a turn-around flight late that night, but it was agreed that I would meet her at the apartment around noon the next day. She put me on the train back to Manhattan.

I must pause here to recognize and marvel (as I write it) that this entire narrative covers many colorful, irrational escapades, misdeeds and meanderings, and they are all fueled by alcohol. Every strange turn of the road of my life to this point—and they were all crazy, or at least unorthodox—was due to drinking. The New York saga—if there is a hell on earth, it embraced that week in New York—clearly defined the downward spiral and the pronounced deterioration of my life. And it would continue for several years. My recuperative powers were lessening, I was ashamed of myself most of the time, and the only cure was to keep myself in a fog of strong drink. Every dopey move I made was launched by alcohol.

A good example occurred the day after I left Barbara. I knew she lived in Forest Hills, but I did not have her address and had lost her phone number. Still, I thought, when I catch the train today I will surely observe through the window that I am arriving in an area that looks like the neighborhood of her apartment. Then I'll get off, and I will spot her building.

My God! Those neighborhoods in Queens looked precisely the same for ten miles!

Not cognizant of the last point, I purchased a ticket to Forest Hills, leaving about four dollars to my name. I got on the train, and when I ascertained that we were nearing Forest Hills, I looked for what would be her block (or close to it). I was becoming uneasy that my plan would ever land me at her apartment, but I did get off at the Forest Hills station.

Absurdly, I began walking about the area hoping to spot her place. It was now around noon. I walked randomly for about an hour in the summer heat and decided I must have a cold beer to soothe me. I had several. Then I walked some more, realizing that I had made a horrible mistake with no idea how to recover from it. Either the elusive apartment would suddenly appear, or I would be completely stymied. I was stymied. Around two o'clock I needed more cold beer and depleted the rest of my money.

Here I was, broke except for a dime or two, befuddled by the beer (and life in general), wandering around Queens with no address, no phone number, and no chance of happening on and recognizing the apartment of Barbara Brown. I never felt more desperate, more panicky.

Finally I came to a Catholic Church and decided to ask for help. A young priest came out, earnestly listened to my plight, and quickly saw that I was in bad shape mentally and was further muddle-headed by drink. Of course, he had no solution to my thwarted quest for Barbara Brown, and it was a problem that was really not down his alley. He told me to wait while he went into a church office. He returned shortly and handed me a dollar, and said "God Bless You." It was the best he could do. I appreciate it today. Not so much then.

After about six hours of wandering, I conceived the idea of calling Barbara's home in Huntington—collect—praying that God would have her mother answer the phone. In this way, I might secure Barbara's phone number. I called; Polly Brown did answer and she accepted the call. She told me to stay in the phone booth and she or Barbara would call right back. Thank God Barbara did, and she drove to that corner—about a mile from her apartment—and picked me up. That night I slept on the sofa in the apartment of the four girls.

The next day Barbara went to the bank, got me fifty dollars in cash (a gigantic gesture), drove me to the train station, and suggested with some motherly firmness that I check out of the Iroquois, go to the Greyhound Bus station, and get the hell out of New York.

She was a great friend, very fond of me, but she must have been overjoyed to see me depart; she confessed that fact later to me.

I did settle up with the Iroquois, and then got on the next Southbound Greyhound. This was another time when that worthy conveyance was for me for me a harbinger of gloom. I will forever empathize with bus passengers—melancholy, I am sure, and seemingly headed on wretched, hopeless missions. This is absurd, of course, and is based entirely on my own forlorn experiences.

My frame of mind and my physical condition helped make the trip as horrible as I thought it would be. Also contributing strongly was the fact that on this bus were about thirty touring German adolescents, on their way to visit Atlanta. Coming off a week of steady drinking, I was as nervous as a whore in church, and their constant, harsh, excited verbal pandemonium cut through me like a knife. The bus made rest stops but never with enough time to find facilities for purchasing a pint of whiskey or at least wine. So I was dry, and consequently exceedingly jittery, all the way to Atlanta, Georgia.

From there I caught a bus to Rome. I had told my folks I was leaving New York, and they easily figured out why, though during my stay I had not communicated with them about my progress—or lack thereof; my desperate calls for money had not included them, mercifully. I arrived at their door in the middle of the night, and my story was clearly written on my death-warmed-over face. Little was said at that time.

I slept for about twelve hours while they waited patiently and anxiously for what would be a necessary but distasteful discussion. When I awakened, we did talk. They were calm and supportive, but for the first time we all alluded to and acknowledged the fact that I was undeniably an alcoholic and on the verge of even more serious grief. This talk, following my dreadful misadventure in New York, threw the fear of God into me. I promised them that there would be a change, and I meant it—as I would mean it so many times in the future. For the next three or four months I was on a relatively straight and narrow path, drinking not at all, then some, but showing restraint.

Again I was able to borrow the usual four hundred dollars. I went to Atlanta, moved in with good old Aunt Baby for a week or two, and looked for a job in advertising. In from the bullpen and to my rescue came my great friend Chuck Shields. Our working relationship at Burke Dowling Adams had actually been plenty good. I had been an asset to him and the agency in that job. So he had no compunction in recommending me to anyone. He knew I had gotten myself in a pickle in New York, but he respected my professional abilities.

Chuck knew quite well that I was short on financial resources and that time did not permit me to sit and wait on the ideal job. He knew of a radio-TV representative firm that was looking for a salesman. Headley-Reed was an outfit that represented stations around the country; they would call on advertising agencies and solicit business for those stations. I had a good background (having worked for two respected ad agencies, with the divorce giving me a good excuse for leaving the last one). I interviewed with the Atlanta office manager, and he hired me. He liked me and my credentials, and Shields' seal of approval did the trick.

It was not an exciting job, but I was thankful that I had it. Most of the day was spent reading the paper, going out for coffee twice, having lunch, or "going on an errand." Occasionally, we sold something (commercial time to an ad agency), and Headley-Reed would get a commission.

I had moved into a cheap apartment and was occasionally going out in the evening. I had a lot of friends in Atlanta and they were good about providing transportation, and most of my female companionship was selected with automobile ownership being a prerequisite.

One night a young lady and I went to a cocktail lounge and encountered and joined another couple. I knew the guy, and my date knew the girl.

The girl's name was Tubby Whitner. She was plenty good-looking, not tubby in the least, and simply had never shed one of those babyhood nicknames. The name was clearly so unsuitable that it was appealing.

This girl came from one of Atlanta's old, well-connected families, but shortly after she had graduated from the very upper-crust finishing school, Washington Seminary, her father died unexpectedly, and circumstances left the family in financial straits. Her mother took over the family insurance agency and was struggling to keep things going. Tubby could not make her debut, as planned, nor could she go to college. She got a job as a cub reporter on the *Atlanta Journal*.

I called her the next day after meeting her—and I believe she thought I would. I borrowed a car, took her out, and things clicked. For the next year and a half, she and I would have an exclusive social arrangement.

She probably liked my checkered background—the divorce had some mystique about it—and she liked the fact that I did not fit into the slot of the wealthy, provincial, young swains of Atlanta. She noted that I drank pretty enthusiastically, but then so had every other guy she'd been around.

Her mother was quite concerned that Tubby had completely withdrawn from the social circle of young Atlanta maidens. Understandably the mother was very wary of me and did everything she could to introduce roadblocks.

Tubby and I talked often about my career and the fact that I needed to get back with an advertising agency. She thought that a more stimulating occupation would be beneficial.

Presto! One day I got a call from good old Chuck Shields. He asked me to come by the agency where he worked, which was one of Atlanta's oldest and largest. I walked over to Liller, Neal & Battle, and sat down with Chuck. He told me they were looking for a Copywriter/Assistant Account Executive, and he thought I would fit the job perfectly. I was, of course, excited about the idea.

Later that day, he called again and said I should come by the agency in the morning to meet Pete Liller and Bill Neal.

I broke out the dark blue suit the next day, went over, and talked with the two principals. The plusses I had going for me were a very useful background, a plausible reason I was where I was, and the stamp of approval of the highly respected Chuck Shields. Bill Neal called me later and offered me the job at six hundred dollars per month—one hundred dollars more than I was getting and not bad for the times. I grabbed it. I gave Headley-Reed the obligatory two-week notice.

Tubby and I had considered ourselves engaged, and this gave us some justification for making it official.

It was agreed that the new job and increased salary provided a badly needed element of stability and that now might be a good time to see what Mrs. Whitner thought of the engagement idea. I called her at her office and made an appointment. She sure as hell knew I wasn't coming downtown to buy some insurance! So she was prepared.

She heard my pitch politely, then, in a very smooth but direct way, made it clear that while she acknowledged the improvement in stability, there still was not enough, and that any acceleration observed on the road to matrimony would be resisted by her. Her resistance was sound.

My alcoholism—like many diseases—was inevitably going to worsen. And I certainly did not have the right approach for curing the malady. Neither a new job with a fine advertising agency, nor the companionship and support of a young lady who would have been high on anybody's list, slowed me on my dash to destruction.

During the last part of 1956 and most all of 1957, both those relationships were slowly deteriorating. The agency looked the other way when I was late or was "sick" or did sloppy work. If they had had the hiring of Cot Campbell to do over again, it wouldn't have happened, I am sure.

While Tubby delighted in my company at first, the good times lessened steadily. I was sensitive, quarrelsome, and moody.

In the summer of 1957, with vigorous pressure from her mother, and her sister and brother-in-law in New York, she agreed to go up there for a three-week visit. This was engineered as a device to get her away from me, so she would realize that what was a questionable deal to begin with was now beyond salvaging. She would have been outraged at the suggestion of that trip six months earlier, but now it was an idea whose time had come.

Her calls back to me diminished during her visit. When she returned to Atlanta, we went out and she told me she was going to start seeing other people. She was letting me down easy, but she was letting me down for sure.

God knows she should have. We saw each other a fair amount at first, then I finally got the message, understood her resolve, and left her alone.

During the latter part of 1957, my life was bleak and getting bleaker. I was moving from apartment to apartment, I looked bad, my clothes were shabby, I owed money, and I was always broke. I steered clear of my folks. I did not want to visit Rome, and I managed to be "out of town" if they came to Atlanta for any reason.

One device to finance booze was to sell blood, which I did as often as permitted. A more imaginative one was to rent a typewriter (which oddly I could do with no money down), then pawn it. This was always good for a quick five bucks. Of course it would end up costing me about ten before it was over. But sound economics was not uppermost in my mind.

Some months earlier I had purchased a car. This was a gigantic, 1949 pink and maroon (leatherette) Packard. Not surprisingly, I was prone to losing automobiles after an evening of strong drink. Earlier I had lost the Packard when I foggily parked it behind a drug store for a month, and then I got a lovely windfall in the form of five hundred dollars in insurance money on the "stolen" auto. Unfortunately my sister and father happened to spot it during a trip to Atlanta. I could have killed them for being so "helpful" because I had to get the money back to the insurance company.

But then there came a three-day period involving the pink Packard that the *Guinness World Records* would have found uncanny.

One night while out painting the town red, I motored to one of my favorite watering holes. I parked some distance away in a spot that would accommodate my rather unwieldy Packard and strode off to the bar for a period of conviviality.

I emerged around one-thirty a.m. in a confused state of mind and was unable to recall the location of the pink Packard. It was necessary to go home in a taxi. When I awakened later that morning, the whereabouts of the vehicle still eluded me. I went to work on the bus.

At the end of a trying workday, I was badly in need of a liquid restorative. I spent an hour or two taking care of that matter, and then decided I had better find the Packard. Obviously, I needed transportation in order to be able to conduct the search. I was forced to go to Avis to rent a car. At this point I was in the Avis vehicle driving around looking for the lost car. But the search was being conducted in a leisurely way with frequent relaxation breaks for cocktails. Truthfully, the location of the Packard was not an urgent motivation for my ramblings.

Around eleven p.m. I dropped into one of my favorite haunts. And wouldn't you know! When the evening drew to a late, late close, even the location of the Avis car had slipped from my memory.

I caught a ride home, and then began the next day nervously wracking my brain about the location of both the pink Packard and the Avis car. I could come up with no answers.

About mid-morning I made it in to work, struggled through another horrible day, and determined that I simply *must* find the two cars. However, I needed yet another source of transportation to do so.

Where would I turn?

Hertz.

Soon I was cruising about the city in a sparkling new Hertz rental car, looking for both cars, and somewhat more concerned than the night before because the situation was clearly becoming critical. I had to find these cars! In those days I was not aware of a National or Budget or Enterprise, so I was really going to be stymied if the Hertz transportation was not up to the task.

So unsettling was the predicament that I felt strongly the need for a quiet drink to soothe jangled nerves. I whipped into a popular bar called Mammy's Shanty, where many of my cohorts could invariably be found. Indeed a convivial group awaited me. We ordered up several rounds while I outlined my problems and enlisted their aid in a game plan for vehicle recovery.

With a task force that included several autos, there began eager sorties into strategic neighborhoods in search of the errant automobiles. Disappointingly though, my troops soon became bored with this quest and all—save me—called it a night.

I drove on to a favorite late-night hangout called the Blue Lantern and sought solace at the bar. When the barkeep finally called "time," I teetered out onto the sidewalk in a foggy state, and—you guessed it—could not recall where I had parked the Hertz car.

Another cab home, then another dreadful, next-morning memory search that yielded nothing. Now I did have a very significant dilemma on my hands. At this point I enlisted the aid of a rather levelheaded friend who could always be called upon in emergencies. I called into my office "sick" (by no means an exaggeration!), and we meticulously sought to re-create (with no alcohol to aid us) my wanderings over the past three nights. We sought the input of some confederates and several bartenders who had been with or observed me during these periods, and we set out to locate the cars.

When the sun finally got over the yardarm that day, we had located and checked in the two rental cars, and I was in proud possession of my pink Packard.

Bringing to closure this exhausting ordeal was, of course, cause for another celebration.

CHAPTER 15

FREE AT LAST

December came, marking my first year at Liller, Neal, and Battle. I celebrated by not showing up for work two of the five days of the first week. My absence was rather critical because we were working on the sales and promotional material for the 1958 line of Hardwick Stove Company. Because of my outrageous absenteeism, the agency had to bring in a copywriter from New York to write my stuff.

I will always believe the agency would have fired me on the Monday following. But something momentous happened Saturday, December 7, 1957.

I had been drinking steadily all that week, creating within myself no pleasure and a great deal of anguish. That Saturday afternoon I spent in the bar at the Georgian Terrace Hotel; I wasn't sober, but I wasn't drunk, and I could not get myself cleanly into either category. About 6:30 I left the bar and walked out in front of the hotel. There was a fine, cold mist falling. I just stood in it and looked out onto the street for quite a time. I thought, "I am living the most horrible existence a person can have." I thought about something my father had told me a long time before. He said, "Being an alcoholic, and starting each day with a drink, leads to nothing but misery. It's like the fellow who leaves his house each morning and goes through the front gate, and when he does, a big guy jumps out from behind a bush and beats the living hell out of him. Never fails. Every day he takes that awful beating. Finally, one day, he says to himself, 'Goddamn, I can't go out that front gate again. I can't stand another beating! Today I'm going out the *back* door.'"

Suddenly my feet propelled me into the lobby. I found a phone booth and looked up the number of Alcoholics Anonymous. I dialed it, and when a gravelly voice answered, I said I was at the Georgian Terrace and had been drinking for a week and was at the end of my rope. I said, "I'm ready for some help."

"You been drinking today?"

"Yeah, but I'm not drunk, and I don't want to drink any more."

"Well, we're five blocks away from you, at 547 Peachtree Street. Why don't you come on down here? Come on now."

I did. When I found the address, there were steps leading up to a second floor, above a hearing aid sales office. I walked tentatively into a tired, worn-looking room. Nothing but some chairs, a few tables heavily tattooed with cigarette burns, AA twelve-step posters on the wall, and a very large aluminum coffee urn next to a sink. There were perhaps eight men and women sitting around.

The gravel voice got up and walked over to me. "You the fellow that just called?" he asked.

I said I was. I told him I needed help, that I had indeed been drinking that day, and that I knew from a previous failed AA venture two years before that you were supposed to be completely sober when you came to AA for help.

He looked me over and said, "Aw, come on over and sit down."

There was no awkwardness about it, no getting acquainted, breaking the ice. The place was dismal, pretty uninviting, but, God knows, the people were not. They were wonderful—so glad to see me (one of their own) and so anxious to have me be at ease with them. They wanted to help, knew how to help, and their conversation eased right into it. I told my story, which they understood completely, and each of them touched on theirs. There was an old, red-headed gal named Pearl that I particularly related to. The gravel voice belonged to a carpenter named Ned. We sat around that clubhouse smoking and drinking that strong coffee until around ten o'clock. While my blood alcohol level might have indicated inebriation, I was definitely sober and had been from the time I walked into that AA Club Room.

They told me there was a meeting at ten a.m. Sunday, and they hoped I would come. I said good night, thanked them for their understanding, and walked about a mile back to my apartment. I felt good. I mean good! For the first time I did not *want* a drink. Instead, what I wanted was to get started on the program they had told me about.

The next morning at ten, I was on hand for the AA meeting at the same clubhouse, and it was not hard to stand up and say, "Hi, I'm Cot, and I'm an alcoholic." I said it twice more that day as I went to two other meetings in the basements of churches.

Since around 6:30 p.m. on December 7, 1957, I have not consumed any form of alcohol.

Until that night I could not have considered a life without drinking. From that night on I have never considered a life *with* it. I believe if someone said I must choose between a dry martini and a shot of strychnine, I would go for the strychnine

---

I was not ready until that Saturday evening moment, standing in the soft rain in front of the Atlanta hotel, when I thought of the guy going out his front gate each day and getting a horrible beating. Thank goodness someone answered the phone at the AA Clubhouse that night. Because they did, there would never be another beating.

There was, however, widespread damage to repair, and I started on it Sunday night. After the last AA meeting of the day—my third—I called my mother, who had an apartment in an Atlanta suburb. I told her I wanted to come out and see her, that I had something important to tell her.

My mother had never wavered from being everlastingly in my corner, though I had lied to her and disappointed her hundreds of times. So there were really no fences to mend. But she was so much in need—and so deserving—of some legitimate good news about her son. There had been many talks on the subject of how my life was about to be straightened out, and she had always seemed confident that the corner was being turned. But it hadn't been turned.

"Mom," I greeted her, "I've been to three Alcoholics Anonymous meetings since last night. And I came out here to tell you that I'm sure that I'll never drink again. I'm anxious for you to know this—you deserve some decent news about me."

She could detect easily a new vibrancy in my voice. There was clearly enthusiasm on my part for not drinking, instead of half-hearted resignation that quitting was the thing to do. She locked those big brown eyes of hers into mine. They filled up, and then she started crying. She hugged me. We stayed that way for a long time. She then looked up at me intently and said, "Oh, I *know* this is it!"

We talked for a long time that night. We agreed that we would wait a day or two before telling my father and sister. Economics dictated that they live in Valdosta, Georgia. My father had a job there with a radio station.

I told my mother that I was going to give the same message to my employers at the ad agency. "Though it may be too late," I added.

Monday morning I got to Liller, Neal early, and I was plenty nervous. One thing that made me nervous was the ghastly Monday morning staff meeting, in which every account was reviewed. These convened in a too-small conference room, with us jammed shoulder to shoulder. If you had had a lot to drink Sunday night, everyone in the room could detect the fumes on Monday morning. In fact, several Mondays before, when I was quite hung over, we were all assembled for the meeting, and my friend, John Bonta, known to have a brash and reckless personality, broke the pre-meeting silence by looking over at me and, in a stage whisper, blurting out, "Let me ask you something. Did you have a drink on your way to work this morning?" Everyone in the room heard him, it was the last thing in the world I needed, and I could have cheerfully killed him.

This day's meeting was particularly painful. I had caused a problem the week before with my absence, and I felt everyone in the room was disgusted with me—and they were.

When the group disbanded, I asked Bill Neal if I could see him. I went into his office and shut the door. It was a critical moment, and I said just the right thing. He was one tough son of a bitch, Bill Neal, and this was no time for anything but very straight talk, the only kind he permitted.

"Bill, I've got a drinking problem, which I'm sure you know. I've caused this agency a lot of problems, and I imagine I'm about to be fired, and I guess I should be. But I don't want you to because I think I'm going to be straight from here on in. I can *not* drink, and I believe I never will again. I joined Alcoholics Anonymous on Saturday, and I'm enthused about it. So, I'm going to ask you to give me another chance. If you see the slightest flicker of a problem, I know I'm gone. I'm sorry for letting you down but I want you to try me again. You'll be glad you did."

Bill looked the part of a "tough son of a bitch." He was about five nine, and built like a fire plug. He had a thatch of coarse, bright red hair on top of a craggy, square-jawed face that gave him the saggy, dissipated look of a Shar-Pei dog.

His face in repose had a slightly disgusted expression, and this was particularly true when he reacted at the end of my message. He was still mad at me from the week before. On top of that, he didn't quite understand Alcoholics Anonymous and not being able to keep some sort of loose control over your drinking. Bill was a two-fisted drinker and probably could not have done without it, but he did manage to keep it from getting away from him.

"Yeah, well, you better go give Pete Liller that speech," he replied.

I knew I had gotten a reprieve. He didn't really give a damn what Liller thought. Bill was "The Man," and he had always liked me. He knew he probably should go ahead and fire me now. Without my impassioned speech, I'm sure I would have been dead meat.

I did go see Liller and told him the same thing. He acted embarrassed and mumbled that he and Bill would talk. I left and went into my office and went to work.

That afternoon, Neal looked in and said, "Aw right. No more featherbeddin' it!" He gave me a black look and left.

Did I go to work! I was like a whirling dervish from then on. All I did was work! I was the first one into the office in the mornings and the last to leave at night. At which time I went straight to an AA meeting somewhere.

I began to notice subtle changes in my fellow workers. Some who could scarcely disguise their understandable disdain for me now gave me the once-over with a hint of admiration in their glances. Word about AA had gotten around from Neal to his key people and the news had, of course, filtered down to everyone at the agency.

At the office Christmas party my conduct was observed closely, as this would have been the big acid test. Several, observing my Coca-Cola, indicated their approval and support. One of my greatest cheerleaders was the staunch Chuck Shields, who had gone to bat for me so many times but whose confidence had thus far been unrewarded.

Meanwhile, my father had long since weighed in with a heartfelt pep talk, with all sorts of reasons why I would go onward and upward from here on in (my mother would have called him the night I told her, long before I reached the bus stop). He was very proud and very moved in his sentimental way.

My friend Bonta (he of the big mouth in the Monday morning meeting) organized a subscription New Year's Eve party at the Biltmore Hotel (where I was once very much persona non grata due to the Shriner episode), and asked me to help tend bar. My pals at AA would have counseled against this, of course, but so great was my confidence, and so anxious was I to prove to myself that there would be no more serious temptation, that I agreed to do it. This was foolish, but it worked, and then the word was really out that I had turned over a new leaf.

My success in achieving sobriety was due to the fact that I had never known what it was *not* to drink. I had done it all my life. I had no idea of what it was like to be respected, to not feel guilty and, instead, to be proud that you had overcome a terrible affliction. I didn't know there was a world without drinking, that there could be social intercourse without getting stoned. Now I was being admired for turning my life around and, dramatically, I had done it just in the nick of time. I was enjoying life and liking the new me, although I sure had a lot left to do.

I owed a little money to a lot of people. I called or wrote each of my creditors. I said I did not know *when* I could pay them but that I *would* pay them. I would send something every payday. Most were surprised to hear from me. I learned that if you just let people know what you can do, they will play ball with you. Then, and later in life, I also learned that if you are in the wrong, and then own up to it and try to set it right, you'll be in a stronger position than you ever were before.

So on the 1st and the 15th when I got paychecks, I would pay the laundry $3.50, or the department store $6.00, or the doctor $4.75; every creditor got something. I had left Sewanee ten years before owing Clara's (the famous campus hangout) $126.00—a big tab for the time. I had done little about that, so I wrote Miss Clara, told her that I had straightened out my life, and said that I would be paying her off in dribs and drabs. I enclosed a $3.00 check. Over the next year, I paid her down to $48.00, whereupon she wrote me and said she was proud of me for my conscientious effort and to consider the account paid. But it was important to me to pay off the balance over the next few months, and I did. Miss Clara raved about me for years, I am told.

By the time March rolled around, a pattern was clearly being established. It looked like I was here to stay. I had not only redeemed myself with my bosses and co-workers, but I was about to make the varsity team. In the first place, I worked seven days a week, all day. I walked to and from work every day, was physically fit, and looked good; and I was constantly obsessed with making up to the world for what I had been, and done.

About this time, the agency was having a hush-hush merger talk with a Richmond, Virginia, agency, and the secret venue and time was the Liller, Neal conference room at the seemingly safe hour of eight a.m. on Sunday. Guess who was already ensconced in his own office working away when the principals started arriving for the talks? Bill Neal had no choice but to walk in my office and tell me what was happening, urging me to keep it a secret.

Of all the people who were proud of me, next to my mother and father, Neal would have led the list. I had justified his confidence in me. But I could never emphasize enough the kindness that was directed toward me from every quarter. I found out that when you're down and you're trying to get back up, people are anxious to give you a hand.

I had dinner with my mother often and talked with my father on the phone. He was always looking for a reason to be excited about his immediate family (repeat, immediate; a rather hearty mutual dislike existed between him and all other relatives). He was truly steamed up about me. Every small accomplishment was the breakthrough of the century, to hear him tell it!

At this point it was work and AA meetings. I had slowed to about four or five meetings a week, but I sure went to those, and intended to stay immersed in that program, following each of its twelve steps. I had confidence in myself, but I had even more in the AA curriculum.

While social life was impractical and low on my list of priorities at the moment, a delightful lady did provide a colorful and most interesting divertissement. One day I got a slightly surprising call from a close friend of the aforementioned Aunt Baby. This lady said that a young lady named Virginia Weinman Skakel had just moved to Atlanta and had been given a job at J.P. Allen, a stylish couture salon. She was a new member of AA, was trying to get her life straight, and this was complicated by the fact that she was divorcing her wealthy husband Jim Skakel, brother of Ethel Kennedy. Thus she was the sister-in-law of Robert Kennedy.

This matchmaker felt that Virginia and I would have a lot in common (referring to AA), and wouldn't it be nice if we could meet? I said it would, but my circumstances did not make me the ideal escort of Bobby Kennedy's sister-in-law. She made it clear that Virginia understood my situation and that she had her own auto, and ample funds, and just wanted to ease into circulation quietly. She was well-connected in the city, but because of her shakiness in the AA program, she did not want to be thrust into Atlanta's demanding social rat race.

It was agreed that I should come by the store, and Virginia and I could go have an exploratory cup of coffee at the end of the workday. I arrived just before closing time and asked for Mrs. Skakel. After a short wait, the door from a dressing room was flung open, and out came Virginia! She was clad in a full-length mink coat, with oversized, movie star, jet-black glasses, absolutely reeking of perfume, tossing her mane of tawny hair, while dramatically blowing goodbye kisses to her fellow workers. She looked like a slightly corn-fed Lauren Bacall as she advanced toward me with arm outstretched and head coquettishly tilted to one side.

We shook hands, engaged in some loud, animated conversation, then went down the street for our coffee and for what bonding there might be. She completely disrupted the coffee shop, as she would disrupt every establishment I would ever see her in. There would be loud peals of laughter, exaggerated, good natured eye-rolling shrieks of protestation about everything, always much confused interrogation about any menu—and everything bellowed out into whatever atmosphere she found herself in. To be in her presence in public was always terribly embarrassing in an entertaining way. Going into a movie with her was excruciating to the entire theater. I cannot imagine that she could have ever served satisfactorily any customer of the lofty J.P. Allen clothing establishment. I have a feeling that she was situated on the sales force because she was the store's greatest customer.

She had the means to be. She drove a spiffy Mercedes convertible, and her lodging was a suite in a fine midtown hotel. She understood my paucity of "discretionary funds" and was happy to provide transportation. When we went out every now and then, the entertainment was tailor-made to my pitiful budget, or else she gracefully financed the outing.

Virginia was an unforgettable character, a goodhearted soul, and we came into each other's lives at an advantageous time. And we had the important AA involvement in common. Mine was intense; hers not so much, and she chose to be pretty private about it. Still it was a strong bond. She did not stay in Atlanta long because she went back to her husband. They moved to Hollywood, where she would have been much less noticeable. My wife Anne and I visited with her there several years ago.

I slowly got on my feet during 1958, and my career at Liller, Neal, Battle & Lindsey (the merger went through) advanced steadily. I was made an account executive later in the year and was given some important accounts to handle. I was on the fast track thanks to my zeal in making up for lost time.

I don't suppose I've had many heroes in my life. Childishly perhaps I would list Babe Ruth, Sugar Ray Robinson, Robert E. Lee. But Bill Neal was surely a hero when maybe I needed one, and he had enormous influence on me. I do things today because of what I learned from him. He taught me that you do not have to know everything, that you can be wrong, that it is okay to make a mistake—just own up. I have heard him deliberately admit in client meetings that he did not know the answer to an important question—unheard of with ad agency types—even when it was injurious to do so. But then when he did say that he was certain about a point, you knew, by God, that you could take it to the bank.

From Bill Neal, I also learned the beauty of brevity and straight talk. And silence. He had terrific charisma, but he did not have to fill every moment with conversation.

The stereotype of the tough guy with the heart of gold was patterned after this man. What he said could be absolutely shocking, but usually what was behind it was very appealing.

I remember attending the funeral of the father of our biggest client's wife. As the graveside services concluded, Bill walked up to Beth Varner and said, "Goddamn, Beth, I'm sorry about your old man. He was a pretty good guy!" Not very charming, you say, but of all of the expressions of condolence that woman got that day, there were none that would have had the impact of that one.

A secretary at the agency went to the treasurer, Oscar Lewis, and asked about the possibility of a one hundred dollar advance on her salary. Her father was undergoing cancer treatments, and the family was struggling financially. Oscar told her he thought she could be accommodated, but that he had to clear it at the top. When Bill Neal got the request, he said, "Aw hell, we can't start doing that."

Ten minutes later, he went into Oscar's office, and said, "Oscar, why don't you give that girl five hundred dollars, and tell her to pay it back whenever she can. Goddamn it!" Oscar smiled and shook his head. He knew that would happen.

Once I brought a piece of copy into Bill's office for his approval. It dealt with a complicated subject, and I had further complicated it with a lot of words. He read it, then looked quizzically at me as if to say, "What the hell is all this?"

In defense, I said, "Bill, what I'm trying to say is 'so and so.'"

"Then just say THAT," he said. "You got all tangled up in your underwear," a favorite expression of his.

But the essence of the man is found in one of my all-time favorite stories.

The agency had for a long time handled the Cabin Crafts account. This company was a pioneer in the tufted textile industry, having sprung up as a cottage industry in North Georgia. If you've driven through the South, especially in the '40s and '50s, you've seen those bedspreads, with tufted designs of fleur-de-lis, four leaf clovers, and other patterns, displayed on the clotheslines of homes and small "Mom and Pop" stands by the side of the highway. Cabin Crafts saw an opportunity to industrialize this technique and go national with it. Liller, Neal provided the advertising and marketing know-how that resulted in national distribution for various tufted textile products. Success was so great that Cabin Crafts was merged into a huge conglomerate, and the agency unluckily lost the account. Naturally, Liller, Neal—with a good textile success story to tell—sought to gain another account in the same field.

When Celanese, a textile giant, was looking for an advertising agency for one of its related divisions, they invited five ad agencies—Liller, Neal among them—to pitch the account. Our agency was by far the smallest and quite a long shot to get the business, we feared. But we sure had to try.

The day came for our scheduled presentation at the corporate headquarters in Atlanta. We had done a lot of research and had spent a fair amount of money preparing a marketing plan, accompanied by creative work. Four men represented the agency: Bill Neal, Pete Liller, Howard Axelberg (executive VP), and me. I was there to handle the slide projector, hand out material, and little else. Celanese must have had eight execs present, including, of course, the corporate VP for advertising. And what a nasty piece of work he turned out to be.

We made our pitch, smoothly handled and effective, with Bill Neal leading the presentation. Neal concluded by saying how much this fine account would mean to us, and then he asked for any questions or comments.

At that point, the Celanese ad guru stood up, clasped his hands behind his back, paced up and down several times in silence to provide a little dramatic impact, then glared at Neal and aggressively asked, "What accomplishment in the textile field can your small agency *possibly* point to that would cause us to have confidence in your ability to handle an account of *this* magnitude?" The question was condescending and insulting.

There was a shocked silence in the room.

Then Neal stood up, his face a bright red and his eyes blazing. He understood that we had no shot to get the account, and really had had no chance when we were invited. So now he was going to have his moment.

"Accomplishment? Let me tell you something. We took the goddamn bedspreads off the goddamn clothes lines between here and Chattanooga, and put 'em in every goddamn store in America!"

The Celanese man was sputtering around trying to think of a reply, when Bill Neal said, "Thank you, gentlemen." He looked over at us, and said, "Let's go boys."

We were out of there in short order. It was one sweet moment.

CHAPTER 16

MAKING UP FOR LOST TIME

Liller, Neal had given me some accounts of my own to handle, and I was also serving as assistant account executive to George Ordway. He was an older man with fantastic family and social connections. He was not the brightest bulb on the tree but—like any of us—had to act like he was. His co-workers often had to cover for him. He had the name; others did the work.

What he did do well was write letters. That was his weapon, and it was a good one. If he encountered someone he knew while stopped at a red light, he would write him a letter and tell him what a pleasure it had been to have spent time with him, and that he hoped he reached his destination with no difficulties. Exaggerated, but not by much.

There was one ridiculous story about this man. Once a connection of George's, a rather tiresome "Colonel Milton," came to the agency for some forgotten business reason, and several of us had lunch with him. During the meal, the Colonel went on and on about his "six-year-old granddaughter." Whatever the topic, the Colonel was able to contrive a reference to his "six-year-old granddaughter." Actually we never learned her name, but the interminable meal ended when the man said he had to do something involving his "six-year-old granddaughter."

At that point, George looked at him, his eyes glazed over, and asked, "Uh, Colonel, how old *is* your six-year-old granddaughter?"

"She's six," the Colonel replied.

Life was good for me that year at Liller, Neal. Good in every way. A sure sign of my ascending stardom at the agency came in the early fall when Bill Neal invited me to accompany him and Howard Axelberg to the Greenbrier Resort in West Virginia for the annual convention of the American Association of Advertising Agencies. Bill and I roomed together. I was, of course, on my good behavior, and this was a time when he had to be. Bill had discovered a slight heart problem that scared him. He had lost fifteen pounds, thanks to less food, less booze, and the "Royal Canadian Air Force" exercises. I was never tempted to take a drink—and an advertising convention at the Greenbrier provides ample temptation. Never tempted, but still it is tiresome to stand around at cocktail parties, drinking sparkling water and hoping you can go somewhere and get something to eat fairly soon.

During the year since joining AA, I was constantly involved in a drinking environment. Drinking went with the territory in which I labored. I could not absent myself from it. But not once was it a problem or temptation for me. I think I was firmly convinced—to use my father's colorful analogy—that I must "go out the back door." Waiting outside the front door was that guy who would jump out from behind the bush and beat the hell out of me. I had seen enough of that bum. I liked my new life, but I was by no means overconfident. I attended several AA meetings each week and was quick to relate my own stories at those meetings. AA meetings are wonderful, whether you're a drunk or not. The program is simply an effective way to keep yourself grounded. The widely acclaimed theologian, Frederick Buechner, said the Alcoholics Anonymous program is the closest thing there is to the perfect church as envisioned by Jesus Christ.

I never sought to keep my alcoholism a secret. From the beginning, I would tell anyone who asked. Often I would be pressed at lunch to have a drink, or be told at a cocktail party that I didn't know what I was missing by not imbibing. My response was that I knew a great deal about that because I was a recovering alcoholic and a member of AA. The mention of AA has always embarrassed many people and irritated the hell out of the ones who were sensitive about how much they were drinking. I don't disapprove of drinking; in fact, I think it's great for those who do it gracefully. So from December 7, 1957, the day I gave it up, I have been open about the fact that it is a curse for me, and how I eliminated that curse is a story that has helped many, many people. I am proud of that.

When we got back to Atlanta from the convention, I got a call from a hospital in Columbus, Georgia, telling me that Lorraine Morgan, my ex-wife, had had an automobile accident, fractured several vertebrae, and was in rather serious shape. I went to Columbus to visit her. She was in some complicated neck braces and was going to be all right, but the accident was severe and her injuries were scary. I visited one evening and part of the next day and returned to Atlanta. We were both glad that I came to see her.

I never saw her again. Oddly, she called me on my fiftieth birthday some years later, but for some crazy reason wouldn't disclose her new name or where she lived. I heard later that she lived in Boston and had a husband and three children.

In early December—about the time (the 7th) that I was celebrating a full year of sobriety—my friend and co-worker Charlie Hull told me there was a young lady at Agnes Scott College that I should meet. I said, "Man, I'm thirty-one years old. I can't be going out to that college and dating some young girl."

"Well, at least she's a senior, and you would do well to meet her. Her name is Anne Dodd, and she's pretty sharp."

On December 16, 1958, I walked up to the sign-out desk at Main Hall at Agnes Scott College in Decatur, Georgia, and rather sheepishly asked for Anne Dodd. Sheepish I was because I doubted that it was appropriate for me to be trekking to a church-affiliated women's college in a borrowed automobile (Charlie's) to have a blind date with a person about a decade younger than me. Despite the matchmaker's glowing reviews, my heart was really not in it.

I waited uncomfortably. I was clad in rather conventional business attire: coat and tie, Harris Tweed overcoat, and a snap-brim fedora. Surrounded by Georgia Tech and Emory collegians in sweaters and windbreakers, I stood out like a sore thumb. I thought, "What the hell am I doing here?"

Then the young lady came in, waved gaily toward me—I was clearly the only one who fit the description she'd been given—and proceeded to sign out for the evening. When she came over to greet me, I quickly arrived at two conclusions: terrific smile, outstanding figure.

Off we went to the movies—an obligatory, safe, first-date activity. Spencer Tracy in *The Last Hurrah*. We were of a like mind on the movie, and everything else, as we chatted during the hamburger-and-Coke session afterward. I then took her back to Agnes Scott. She had shaken hands when we met; she shook hands when we parted. I thought that was classy. Indeed she was classy, obviously a lady, a good-looking one with a marvelous personality. I certainly wanted to see her again, and we agreed that I would call once she got back to college after Christmas break at her home in LaGrange, Georgia.

Interestingly, here's Anne's subsequent version of Charlie's inexplicable interest in making this match: "Charlie Hull was safe, sane, and very nice, but he just didn't ring my chimes, and I didn't particularly want to date him. So one day he said to me, 'All right, if you won't go out with me, I've got a friend you *will* want to go out with. He's thirty-one years old, he's divorced, and he's an alcoholic (but hasn't had a drink in a year).' I said, 'That's the one for me!'"

The highlight of a splendid year turned out to be the beginning of the Anne Dodd relationship—which, as I write this, seems headed for the span of a superb half-century.

When Anne Dodd returned after Christmas, I was soon on the phone to her, and we arranged date number two. I rented a car for the evening, and the entertainment was the boxing matches. She'd never seen a fight and ended up loving it. We were most compatible—the age difference was no problem. Anne was wise and poised beyond her years (twenty-one) and hankering to put some unconventional zest in her life. I was a viable source for this—witness an evening at the prize fights.

We began seeing each other two or three nights a week. I bought a car, slightly prematurely, to satisfy the transportation needs that went with this new and increasingly torrid romance. Soon it was time to visit her parents in LaGrange, Georgia.

John and Anne Dodd had a lovely home on a lake in that West Georgia textile town. They were popular, substantial, wonderful people. They had a son, John, who was a resident physician in Baltimore, at Johns Hopkins. The large Dodd family was the backbone of LaGrange, with the star being Anne's uncle, the highly acclaimed Southern artist Lamar Dodd, head of the art department at the University of Georgia in Athens.

On Anne's maternal side were the Choates, gifted, cultured, but chronically short on cash. Her mother, Anne Choate Dodd, had grown up in various locales in the South. When she married, she fit beautifully into the social fabric of the lovely old Southern town, which had been spared by General Sherman's chosen route to the sea. The only slight fly in the family ointment was her schizophrenic brother, Dodson Choate, who was in and out of mental institutions (and probably should never have been out). His sister was in complete denial that he was anything but a teeny bit eccentric; whereas he was potentially a very dangerous cross to bear for the rest of the family and should not have ever been on the loose. I would turn out to be one of his least favorite people, as he tended to be jealous and resentful of any normal, attractive male. Young Anne Dodd had grown up being uncomfortable about Dodson, but he was fairly well taken for granted in the community (when he was not in some institution).

The Dodds had pretty well gotten the drift that Anne and I were getting serious. This visit was by no means one in which her "hand" was to be sought, but the two of us were of a mind that such a day would come, and this trip was designed to set the stage.

My early reputation would die hard in some locales, and Rome, Georgia, was one of them. Anne's Uncle Frank lived there and felt obliged to pass on to the LaGrange branch of the family that which he had heard about my earlier days. It had to be disquieting, but to these parents any disquietude did not last long. They took to me immediately and had complete trust in me all the years I knew them. This reflected confidence in the judgment of their daughter; but also, considering the relatively straight-laced, conventional, and somewhat unworldly types they were, it indicated incredible blind trust in taking me at face value. I never forgot that, and I am proud that they were right.

During that weekend visit, I did give some consideration to a hasty departure. Anne and her mother were obliged to attend a luncheon on the Saturday, and I decided to read and take a sunbath on their dock. Dodson, the schizophrenic uncle, had been assigned the job of chopping down some small trees in that vicinity.

While ensconced in a deck chair on the sunny, lakeside dock, I instinctively kept a wary eye on Dodson, who was chopping away. However, periodically he would quit his task, walk to the edge of the dock, grimace fiercely, and make somewhat ominous gestures with the axe. The better course of action seemed to be to ignore him and to keep reading. But I must have read the same page about ten times. If worst came to worst, I figured I could jump in the lake and swim for the other shore. With the handicap of the heavy axe, I could outstroke him! It did not come to that as the mother and daughter returned soon after, and Dodson meekly redirected his efforts to the trees.

Dodson notwithstanding, the visit went well. The Dodds were truly quality human beings. John Dodd had an interest in several businesses, including an auto (Dodge-Desoto) dealership. The make of cars he sold bespoke his own personality—solid, reliable, sensible, and decidedly not flashy or colorful. He was widely respected. His one great passion, other than his celebrated artist brother, was LaGrange High School football. His son, John, had starred as a fullback and then gone on to Vanderbilt on a scholarship where he was their fine, starting fullback—while making Phi Beta Kappa in pre-med! His father doted on his every move.

My own doting was on the daughter, and on the third visit to LaGrange I sought a talk with her father. The poor man was in the hospital recovering from a minor heart attack, but he encouraged the traditional conversation. It went well, as expected. Within an hour, July 25 had been selected for the wedding date. Anne was to graduate from Agnes Scott in early June and, logically, she would spend her prenuptial days in LaGrange attending parties, learning to cook, and familiarizing herself with other domestic duties required of a young wife. She certainly attended the parties, but she did not learn to cook. I knew much more about the subject than she did when we married.

Despite my divorced status, the wedding was a big one for LaGrange—not like "the finale from *Quo Vadis*" as my first one had been, but big. The senior Dodds were not drinkers, so no alcohol was served at any of the festivities. But this did not retard the gaiety of the affair.

The only slight snag was caused by me. In the small-town South, and certainly in this situation, it would be unthinkable that the featured players of the wedding would not stay in someone's home. Too, there was a certain amount of status in being selected as a host in a wedding of this scope and significance. Snaring the groom was a major coup.

I have never been an enthusiastic house guest, and in this case I dreaded the idea of being fussed over during a special—but stressful—time. I insisted on a motel. This was looked upon as a shocking, almost insulting idiosyncrasy, and created much conversation and worried speculation in the town. My stand was resisted somewhat, but agreed to, by the Dodds. My family found the idea rather logical, but they were quite atypical when it came to mores of this nature.

My father served as best man. Predictably, he and my mother charmed the pants off the involved citizenry. My sister, then eighteen and very cute, was a bridesmaid.

All three family members were high in their enthusiasm on my choice of a bride. And vice versa.

On the wedding night, the First Baptist Church and then the Highlands Country Club were overflowing with hometown celebrants and a smattering of Atlantans. Afterwards, Anne and I were off for the Holiday Inn in Columbus, Georgia. The gala wedding trip itinerary then took us to Pascagoula, Mississippi; Mobile, Alabama; and then New Orleans—in late July. This was a masterpiece of travel planning, if sweltering, high humidity was the objective. Believe me, we had no trouble arranging reservations.

On our return, we moved into the apartment I had been inhabiting, and it was there that we discovered that the yield of the early summer cooking lessons would be meager indeed. Anne was completely baffled by her first culinary effort. She selected okra, a Southern favorite, but a rather slimy delicacy on its best day. Under Anne's untutored handling, her offering had the consistency of soup. Unfortunately she had prepared it first, and then tackled other items on the menu. Thus the okra was quite cool when served. Sadly, breakfast the next morning offered soft-boiled eggs with the same characteristics. The bride's weakness concerning food preparation—which later became a strength—was a decided irritant early on. But it was certainly the only one.

She got a job teaching school, and early each weekday she caught the bus to the other side of Atlanta. At night she was often thrust into some challenging entertainment situations. She was only twenty-one, and it was asking a lot for her to be able to hold her own with the high muckety-mucks of big companies and their sometimes disdainful wives. But she did—big time. I think the fact that she entered any social situation with gusto, determination, and charm made her all the more appealing.

Bill Neal (with all his tough swagger) and his delightful wife Charlotte were particularly sensitive to the fact that Anne had been thrown to the wolves socially. They liked her immediately and were wonderful to her. A popular entertainment package during the fall was the Piedmont Driving Club football brunches, with buses to and from the game, followed by cocktails. Anne's youth and my sobriety caused these affairs to be a trifle tedious for both of us, but one would not have known it.

Anne was an enormous asset then, and always has been.

I was becoming a major factor at Liller, Neal, Battle & Lindsey, which now had offices in Richmond, New York, and Atlanta. Early in 1960 (a little over two years since I had quit drinking, and a half-year after I married) I was making seven hundred dollars per month, decent money for the time, especially considering that I had not exactly gotten a head start.

I thought often in those days that if I ever made $12,000 a year (think of it! A thousand dollars for every month!) and became a vice president, I would consider my life a success. In the spring I was made a vice president and assigned to take over the Armour Agricultural Chemical Company account; they were makers of farm and home fertilizer. Not very glamorous, but very important at this advertising agency. Getting to my monetary goal would not be too far away.

This was fortunate, because Anne was pregnant. She would have our daughter Cary in the summer—thirteen months after we got married. We were able to buy a nice little house on Peachtree Drive. Cost: $22,500 (and a bit of a stretch to handle it).

My mother and father were living in Atlanta; my mother was a very big attraction with her Connoisseur Gallery at Rich's Department Store. Her income was enough so that my father could leave Valdosta where his work was little more than treading water financially. He was trying to write, not getting anywhere with that, but, thankfully, was in his longest-ever stretch of abstaining from strong drink. We saw my folks often and they were good friends. My sister was at the University of Georgia. Anne and I had been paying her tuition. With Anne's pregnancy and the house purchase, this had to stop. Too bad, but it really suited Sally fine. She was ready to launch her business career.

About this time, Anne's brother John and his wife Marie finished up at Hopkins and moved back to Atlanta to join a very well-established practice of internal medicine.

John Dodd was an interesting man. Absolutely brilliant but, like many near-geniuses, he was most eccentric. He was a perfectionist (which would ultimately lead to his demise) and incredibly perceptive as a medical diagnostician. John was a fine painter, carver, sculptor, writer, musician, and athlete.

While he could be a fabulous companion, sometimes he was not. Often he was off in another world. He sometimes talked interminably and interrupted others whenever he felt like it. It was irritating that he seemed never to grasp a word you said. But he absorbed it all, even when he was talking over it.

He thought well of me as a brother-in-law. I knew this but was frustrated by the fact that he was my wife's brother, we were in the same town, we would be thrown together constantly, yet when he was on one of his strange conversational tears, it was hellishly boring to be with him. What a terrible waste! If he just would not interrupt so recklessly. If we could just smooth out a few wrinkles, what a wonderful relationship we would have. I, too, am a perfectionist, and am compelled to try to fix any unsatisfactory situation.

I decided I would make an appointment and go see him at his practice (he would listen to you intently at his medical office). I would lay out for him these conversational thorns in the path of progress, and all would be well from then on.

We met. He asked me how I was feeling. I said, "Medically I'm fine, but I have another matter I want to talk to you about." He looked warily at me.

"John," I began, "you are my brother-in-law and my good friend, and I want us to have the best possible relationship we can have, and I know you'll understand if I point out a few things that can make us closer. And, I know you won't take offense. I would certainly want to change anything about myself that would make you find me a more enjoyable person."

At this point he had a sort of desperate look in his eye, as if he might flee.

"Sometimes when we're together, I find it difficult to talk with you, because you interrupt constantly. I know you're not aware of this. You don't even know you're doing it. But it's hard to get a word in edgewise, and it's not as much fun as it should be. I want you and I to have the best conceivable relationship we can. You follow me?"

He didn't, and he never would.

But John said, "Uh huh, I think so." (long pause) "But do you really *feel* okay? No physical problems? Had any more problems with that cough?" I answered in the negative.

He looked at me as if I were mentally deranged, and I may have been close to it to think that I could accomplish what I had set out to do (with his sister's blessing, by the way). He stood up, we shook hands, and I suggested that we play tennis later in the week. He nodded, took one last searching, incredulous look at me, and I left.

Nothing ever changed. But on his worst day, you would not want to do without him.

CHAPTER 17

BURTON-CAMPBELL, INC.

In the 1960s there was no greater place in America to live than Atlanta, Georgia. Today it's just another great big, crowded, generic city. In the earlier time, it had unmatched Southern charm, but it had an enlightened viewpoint that sought to eliminate segregation, thanks to the guidance and insistence of its wonderful mayor, Ivan Allen. Atlanta was a city "too busy to hate," as its slogan promised. It was sufficiently Rotarian, but increasingly hip, and there was a roaring fire in its belly. Every major league sport would soon have a team there. Atlanta was being discovered and people were hankering to live there. Now they *do* live there, and there are plenty hankering to leave.

I continued to be one of the fair-haired boys at Liller, Neal. Bill Neal had put me up for membership in the very exclusive Piedmont Driving Club (with a waiting list, and don't get your hopes up for two or three years). The agency was growing just as the city was growing. You couldn't help but succeed in Atlanta in those days. You just had to show up for work. My life was awfully good.

So good that I decided that horses could re-enter my life. As a youngster I had been champion amateur rider of Nebraska, Iowa, and Missouri, having won the "Seat and Hands" classes at their state fairs. This was while riding three—and five-gaited horses. Now I decided I should make my "comeback," but this time in the jumping discipline. Then foxhunting?

In late afternoons I took lessons, progressing to the point that the instructor made arrangements for me to borrow a horse that needed the exercise, and I would ride on my own at the farm of John and Martha Wayt. John was a prominent landowner and gentleman farmer just north of Atlanta. The Wayts were members of Shakerag Hounds, which foxhunted twice weekly. They loaned me a wonderful and reliable old horse named Deacon, a real "Christian," as the English so aptly put it. We rode together and became good friends, and one day it was deemed that I was ready to hunt with Shakerag. I secured the proper accouterments, and off we went.

Fox hunting is a rather time-consuming sport or hobby. One leaves home about six-thirty a.m., after a tedious struggle with one's outfit, in time to get to the point of origin by eight a.m., where the hounds would be cast (set loose) and the hunt would begin. The hunt would last until noon, roughly, depending on how complicated the quest for the fox might have been. Then there would be a pre-arranged hunt breakfast at the clubhouse or someone's home. The spouses (such as Anne) would be expected to provide a rather hearty fare for the hunters. During the breakfasts the poor non-combatants would be favored with a blow-by-blow account of the hunt and the performance of the hounds (" . . . American Girl was the first to give voice when we turned up toward Pauley's Gorge, and we had reason to think we were on a gray!"). Poor Anne, one of the world's great conversationalists, is, alas, so enthusiastically responsive that the most interminably excruciating bore can be energized to new heights of stimulation. So, of course, she spent hours listening to the most wearisome hunt field minutiae, equaled only by those who would tell you about their golf game or bets at the racetrack.

After the hunt breakfast it was time to van the horses back to their barns and see to their comfort. Then one went home, having blown all the daylight hours of a Saturday.

On the theory that if you cannot lick them you should join them, Anne decided to take riding lessons. She hated riding, the horses knew it, and she wisely decided that she could neither lick them nor join them.

The Wayts were intrigued with the relative depth of my knowledge of Thoroughbred racing and were keen to know more. The Campbells and the Wayts went to the races together, and they became great fans. John and I decided to form the Georgia Thoroughbred Association, with the dream that this would be the embryo that would someday bring horseracing to Georgia. We put out the word, thanks to a friendly Atlanta sports editor's column, and about twenty assorted racing enthusiasts convened at a local watering hole. Of the twenty, perhaps three could claim ownership of a racehorse. One of those was elected president, and John and I were directors. Atlanta was never a hotbed of Thoroughbred interest, nor has it ever become one. I do not believe racing will ever be legalized in Georgia. There are not enough bona fide horse people in the state to provide the impetus for such a complicated undertaking.

Meanwhile, my business life at Liller, Neal was safe and solid, but I was getting a trifle restless, wanting a bigger mountain to climb. The principals of our agency were a little complacent and not at all sensitive to changing attitudes and tastes among the public. The agency did not have much "grab-it-and-growl" about it. Our creative work had always leaned toward the old-fashioned side, it was not changing, and that reputation was quite apparent to sophisticated companies on the lookout for promotional genius. Liller, Neal felt that if you threw enough mud up against the wall, some of it would stick. The quality of the mud was not important. To the head guys at the agency, mud was mud.

Jack Burton, who had formerly been advertising manager of a large grocery chain (an LNB&L account), had been working for our agency for several years. He was a super-creative ad man and was well connected in the city. He and I had become good friends. We often bemoaned the fact that the agency's creative output was dismal. As happens with young men with ants in their pants, this itch became inflamed. We dreamed that we would have our own agency and that it would become the hottest creative agency in the South.

We did. And it would.

We were inclined to take the big step, but first there was a complicated development. In the fall of 1963, a young man with a large briefcase, named John G. Smith, called on Pete Liller. He was ad manager of a small but ambitious resort/residential home development on an island off the South Carolina coast. The name of the island was Hilton Head, and the feisty, fledgling company was Sea Pines Plantation Company, soon to become the bellwether of such developments. Smith and his boss, Charles Fraser, wanted an old, established Atlanta ad agency to take their admittedly small account. Pete confessed to the visitor that he had not heard of Sea Pines and that he was afraid the thirty thousand dollar annual advertising budget was well below our minimum. But he said the agency would consider it. He asked him to drop by the next day.

He talked to Bill Neal about it, and Neal said, "You know, Cot's been tied up for several years on the Armour account, and he might enjoy a minor diversion like this . . . get himself an occasional weekend on the beach. Let's see if he wants to fool with it."

At that point Jack and I had not finalized our plans, so when John Smith came in the next day, I had no reason not to meet with him and hear his story. Afterwards, I said I would fly down to Savannah and drive over to Hilton Head Island to indoctrinate myself, and then we would present a plan for what to do with the thirty grand—a paltry amount, even then.

I found the place stunning. The island was still primitive, but the existing development was in immaculate taste, and their plan for the future was protective of the environment, with strict regulations that would limit the growth and density of the "Plantation." Their plan insured that greed would never encroach on a partnership with nature. (It would take a while, but I'm afraid it did.)

In several weeks I returned to Hilton Head with a presentation for an annual advertising program. John Smith liked the plan and the creative work that went with it. When we had buttoned that up, I said, "Well, I've got something to tell you. I'm leaving Liller, Neal within a few days, to form a new agency called

Burton-Campbell. I don't think this account would mean a lot to them, but it would to us. I want Sea Pines to come with me."

The blood drained from John Smith's face, and he said, "Oh, my God. Charles wanted me to find an established, old-line advertising agency. And now you're telling me you want us to go with one that hasn't even opened its doors yet. This is terrible! I don't know what Charles will say."

"Well, let's ask him. Is he on the island?"

He was, and he was able to come in and see the material and be told the news—in that order. Lucky, because he often was traveling, and if I had not been able to make my pitch in person, the Sea Pines and Burton-Campbell marriage would have fallen through for lack of a blessing from the father of the bride.

Charles Fraser, a brilliant (now legendary) forward-thinking environmentalist and developer, liked the material. More importantly, he found the story that went with it deliciously intriguing. He practically squealed with delight. As it was flattering to him, he loved magnifying what he called the "chicanery" and "Mr. Campbell's machinations."

He bought the idea, and Burton-Campbell had its first account—and one that would become quite large and very high-profile. It would prove to have a major impact on the speedy growth and ascendancy of our advertising agency and my career.

Now we had to face the ghastly ordeal of breaking the news of our departure to my man Bill Neal. You know, almost every time a person leaves a company to start his own, there must be ruffled feathers. "Ruffled feathers" was hardly an apt description for the schism that the departure of Jack Burton and Cot Campbell would precipitate.

But for me there were two alternatives: remain at Liller, Neal for the rest of my business career, or accede to my ambition and leave to form my own company (and incur the wrath of some wonderful business associates and friends who had been fabulous to me). Since Bill Neal early on had been unshakeable in his confidence in me, that wrath was sure to come. I was distressed that this great friend and mentor had to be the injured party.

The night before we resigned, Jack and I had a quick supper in a nearby cafeteria to take one long, last look at a monumental undertaking, and go over some details on our new office space. Much to my horror, he indicated some shakiness on leaving. I said, "Jack, the fat's in the fire. We've got to go ahead with it. It's the only thing to do. It's going to be hard, but it's going to be good."

I remember well that he stared off toward the food line, didn't say anything for a few moments, and then turned back to me and said, "Okay." That was the way it always was with Jack. He might not lead the charge, but once he got hitched, by God, he would stay hitched.

At nine the next morning, we went to Neal's office and made our resignation speech. It would not have mattered what we said; the upshot was going to be horrible. And it was. We went through the predictable palaver about what LNB&L had meant to us, and we hoped we had contributed to its continued success, and we were sure we would all remain friends, blah, blah, blah.

Bill looked like he could bite a ten-penny nail in two. Our speech finally staggered to the finish line, with an explanation concerning the Sea Pines account, and how we knew Liller, Neal didn't want it (they wanted it now!). He said, "Well shit, you just go ahead and leave today. We don't want to slow you young gentlemen down."

So we did.

We set up shop in a new office building. There would be four employees—Burton and Campbell dragging down an annual salary of $10,000 each (with funding quite precarious), and our wives working free. After a week we added a fifth employee, and she was a doozy!

Somehow we had heard of a marvelously versatile woman named Evelyn J. Blewitt, a former major in the Women's Army Corps (WACs), and the originator of "the Blewitt System," seemingly designed to cure any and all ills that existed in the world of American commerce. We were incredulous that the mother of "the Blewitt System" would be available. Not only that, she was so convinced Burton-Campbell would flourish that she offered to work for a tiny salary and a commission on net profits at the end of the first year. This financial arrangement, along with access to the magic of the Blewitt System, made it irresistible to put her on the payroll.

She was an imposing physical type. Eve Blewitt stood about six feet two and had platinum hair arranged into twin ducktails, giving the impression of the fins on a 1960 Cadillac. She had a tendency to confront you in a stance with feet planted apart, while she sort of hitched her shoulders—or shot her cuffs—as if influenced by seeing too many James Cagney movies.

Eve had an answer for everything. This woman knew the identity of "the Unknown Soldier!" In fact, she knew the name, rank, and serial number of the Unknown Soldier! She did do a good job of buying office furniture and supplies, seeing that the telephones were installed, and taking care of other nitty gritty details necessary in setting up an office. Of course, she was quite disdainful of Anne and Virginia, amateurs who would never be able to grasp and implement the Blewitt System.

While the two wives gamely typed (slowly) and answered the phone, Eve was to handle bookkeeping and make sure that Jack and I kept our feet on the ground. She seemed very skeptical of our competence. After the first week, Eve's contributions had petered out. It took only a few more days to determine that Evelyn J. Blewitt was full of hot air, and that having access to the Blewitt System was not going to pay big dividends. The final straw came when she called Jack and me together and said she was going to establish a budget for Burton-Campbell, and to make it easy and understandable for us, we could just tell her how much we wanted our take-home pay to be; we need not struggle with the intricacies of a gross paycheck. She would take it from there.

The WAC Major was dismissed a few days later.

It didn't take much time to service the small Sea Pines account, so most of our early efforts were directed toward getting new business—a most urgent matter. We were at it night and day. The foxhunting and other forms of recreation and entertainment were on indefinite hiatus.

Soon business began trickling in. After four months we were in the black, and there were six of us on the staff. Anne and Virginia were able to go home.

A commercial real estate company for which we were doing some piddling work sold a huge piece of land to Great Southwest Corporation of Dallas, Texas. They were going to build a tremendous theme amusement park on it. It would be patterned after their original Six Flags over Texas, and it would be one of the biggest things ever to hit Atlanta. The real estate company had been asked to put together a planeload of Atlanta business leaders, politicians, the Governor, and other assorted big shots. They would be flown to Dallas and see firsthand what would be coming their way. Burton-Campbell was asked to organize the project. The visit was a great success, and successful for us in a gigantic way. The people on the plane had reason to associate the new Burton-Campbell advertising agency with a very glitzy trip and an important civic venture—Six Flags over Georgia. More importantly, the Great Southwest people liked us and decided that we should be their Atlanta advertising agency. What a breakthrough this was.

Sea Pines was already catching fire; now here came Six Flags. And Burton-Campbell, the new kid on the block, was handling both of them. *Atlanta Magazine*, a very chic, popular Chamber of Commerce publication, decided that it would do a feature story on "Young Men on the Go," and Burton and Campbell were the young men. Suddenly we were hot, and business began to flow in over the transom almost faster than we could staff up for it. But we did staff up. And we did it with the best talent. Some of the leading advertising agencies in the South today were founded by alumni of Burton-Campbell.

Hugh Wilson, Hollywood writer and producer of such films as *Police Academy, The First Wives Club, Guarding Tess*, and *WKRP in Cincinnati*; Anne Rivers Siddons, one of America's leading novelists—these are just two of the hotshot talents that were hired by us early in the game.

What was the chemistry that made us succeed? Jack and I were both creative types. Both of us were idea men, with an effective drift toward zaniness (which the Sixties was ready for). So the work we put out found its mark. The two of us had good personalities. We were popular. We presented ourselves with a good mixture of enthusiasm, aggressiveness, and cockiness. We created this impression: "We want your business, we know what to do with it, and you'll be lucky to get in on the ground floor of what is going to be a hugely successful advertising agency." We did not say it in those words but that's what we communicated.

We complemented each other in several ways. I was aggressive and impatient. He was wise, conservative, and deliberate. Thus, we kept the agency on an even keel.

In 1965—about a year and a half after we opened our door—we were able to move into much larger, schmaltzy quarters, furnished with antiques and expensive art. Jack and I started thinking about a couple of company Mercedes. We were able to get in some tennis, squash, going to the races. We were on the verge of eating high on the hog, relatively speaking—but still working hard for that status.

I thought often of the dramatic ascendancy of my life from the time, eight years earlier, when I had gone into the phone booth in the lobby of the Georgian Terrace Hotel and called the number of Alcoholics Anonymous.

I was in a wining-dining business. So was it a problem for me to keep from drinking? None whatsoever. There were certainly times when—theoretically—it would have been nice to have a belt or two to ease the pain of a bad day, but I had long since sold myself on the fact that alcohol—in any form or amount—was not an option. I have never, ever even come close to taking a drink, never given it consideration. I have always been around drinking and continue to be appreciative of the pleasure (and anguish) that it can bring others. I mix it, serve it, but don't want it for me.

A lot of significant things were happening around 1965. Our second daughter, Lila, was now part of the family. We moved into a pretty big house in the lovely Buckhead residential section. My time rolled around, and I was taken into the Piedmont Driving Club (awfully nice socially and invaluable from a business standpoint). Anne was invited to join the Junior League of Atlanta (she would in a few years be elected president of it—no small accomplishment for a girl whose early credentials were developed in LaGrange, Georgia).

I began to take an intense interest in horseracing, though it was hard to follow in Atlanta. I became president of the Georgia Thoroughbred Association, and struggled with the God-awful Georgia Legislature in an effort to enable a referendum so that the populace could vote on whether to legalize pari-mutuel wagering in the state. This was like an ant crawling up an elephant's rump with rape on his mind! We had many meetings but got nowhere. Without hefty, under-the-table payouts, the legislators had little incentive for touching this hot potato. These machinations did, however, educate me thoroughly on the inner workings, the pros and cons of the pari-mutuel wagering system that was then flourishing in thirty-five states (but only two below the Mason-Dixon Line: Florida and Louisiana).

I kept the Georgia Thoroughbred Association on the move, and its membership grew dramatically. I ran it like a dictatorship (as is my tendency). I publicized its every move to get racing in Georgia. Consequently, the Thoroughbred industry began to get overly excited about the possibility of a new racing state. I attended some national meetings representing my state and made reports on our progress, which I genuinely felt at that time was optimistic. I invited some prominent racing figures to be guest speakers at our Georgia Thoroughbred monthly meetings, and I landed a number of them. They came, and the gatherings were impressive to them as they took place at the posh Driving Club. These prominent racing figures spread the word throughout the industry that we were on the move, and the GTA president got high marks.

Each year from 1959 on, I attended the Kentucky Derby with my Atlanta friend Chuck Baldi. We left our jobs after work on Thursdays and drove through the night to Louisville. But that journey was no chore as, mile after mile, we drilled each other on every minute detail concerning the upcoming Derby. It is no great exaggeration to say that one of us would feel chagrined if he could not come up with the maiden name of Jockey Mike Manganello's wife.

The personal benefit from this racing activity was that my name was becoming known in the industry, and I did not even own a racehorse.

I felt like I owned one though. I formed a feverish attachment to a great horse of that era and tried several times each year to get away and attend his big races. His name was Kelso, and I am convinced today that he was the greatest horse that ever lived.

I first saw Kelso when he was wintering in Aiken in 1964. Anne and I drove over to that horse resort community from Atlanta with my mother and father. We had read that the great horse, then seven, would work a half-mile for the public during the Aiken Trials, a delightful exhibition day of racing. On the deep Aiken track, where a half-mile in forty-nine seconds is noteworthy, the old boy cruised in an eye-popping forty-seven.

Part of his charm to me was his looks. He didn't take your breath away; he was no matinee idol—just a plain brown wrapper. He stood a solid sixteen hands (a hand is four inches). His head was decent, a trifle too long perhaps, but Kelso's eye was the beacon of his class and quality. And from a conformation standpoint, he would have been unspectacular but awfully hard to fault.

The horse had been gelded at two, when he was on his obstreperous way to being a useless rogue. He was a poster boy for castration. Gelding him saved the day, but he never lost his impish, independent streak. This was demonstrated at the 1964 Washington, D. C., International in the fall. Each of the horses had been given a blanket emblazoned with the flag of the nation he was representing. Their connections were asked to bring the horses over from the barns properly adorned. It was part of the wonderful pageantry of that particular race.

Kelso did not care for his blanket. I can still see him, walking down the stretch, wheeling, kicking, and raising hell. Finally, before he ended up "leaving his race" on the route to the paddock, his handlers removed the blanket, and he then walked in to be saddled with complete aplomb.

That may have been the best horserace I have ever witnessed. It was Kelso's fourth attempt to win this mile-and-a-half race on the turf. The horse was now seven, and some said he was past his prime. The ingredients made for an event loaded with drama.

One of the great handicap horses of the era was the swashbuckling Gun Bow, who had taken Kelso's measure in both the Brooklyn Handicap and the Woodward Stakes earlier in the fall. Gun Bow, a four-year-old at the top of his game, was also representing America in this race.

Laurel Race Course was packed that day in 1964. Seats were long since sold out, so I tipped an usher five dollars to let me stand in the aisle behind a finish line box. I'm sure I was far more nervous than Kelso's owner, trainer, or jockey.

It was thrilling to see that fine field of racehorses, representing Russia, Ireland, France, Venezuela, Italy, Japan, and, of course, America.

In those days the International used the old-timey, walk-up start to accommodate the foreigners, and when the field broke, in a pretty orderly manner, it quickly became a two-horse race. Gun Bow powered his way to the lead under Walter Blum, and Kelso stalked a length or two behind him.

They stayed that way for six furlongs. But with the second six furlongs left, Kelso and Milo Valenzuela said, "To hell with this; let's put him to the test." Kelso ranged up and looked Gun Bow in the eye. Both horses quickened. Gun Bow was not going to relinquish the lead (and he had been running along so easily). Now Kelso had committed and was ready for a long, desperate battle.

By the time they hit the midway point on the backstretch, both great horses had been set down for the drive. What ensued was one hellacious horse race. The crowd went absolutely berserk.

Now, I have always had an unfortunate reflex that kicks in during moments of viewing thrilling physical endeavors. I scream out the oath "Goddamn!" Not admirable, I know, but if I get stirred up enough, it will happen. I was at this point stirred up.

Standing next to me was a man who felt very strongly about Gun Bow. I didn't particularly care, but just through the osmosis of standing together for several hours, I knew he was a Gun Bow believer and learned he had come down from New York especially for the race. Conversely he had to have known that I supported Kelso.

With the gauntlet having been thrown down at the three-quarters pole and both horses going at it tooth and nail, this man and I engaged in a weird sort of subconscious dialog that neither of us knew was happening.

As Gun Bow fought to repulse the relentless Kelso, the man would scream out this wishful message: "He's hooked him, but he can't handle him!"

I came back with, "Goddamn, Kelly—you got him now!"

And so it went. The two indomitable warriors locked in grim combat, neither giving an inch.

"He's hooked him. But he can't handle him!"

"Goddamn, Kelly—you got him now!"

Something had to give, and Gun Bow did. In mid-stretch, Milo asked Kelso for his life, and the old horse reached back and laid it on the line. It was as if Kelso were saying to Gun Bow, "You'd better put your heart in God . . . 'cause your ass is mine!"

Gun Bow cracked. It was Kelso's day. He exuberantly poured it on through the stretch, as if he knew this might be his greatest racing day—and perhaps last racing day.

He went on to win by four and a half lengths in a new American record time.

Both the Gun Bow man and I were exhausted, wrung out. With no words exchanged before, we were now somehow like old friends. He muttered, "Some damned horse!" We smiled at each other vaguely, stuck out our hands for a shake, and then went our separate ways.

Kelso had hooked him, but he *could* handle him.

After that, I simply had to own a horse.

My life—family, work, civic, social—was definitely in good balance, but I certainly was becoming more and more enthralled with the world of Thoroughbred racing.

CHAPTER 18

SEVERE HORSE FEVER

I could not afford much in the way of a racehorse, but I had to have one. With my budget being one thousand dollars, even that amount would have to be cut up, and I thought I knew a couple of guys who would each take a third. My agent was a Kentucky "hardboot" named L. K. Haggin, a fine horseman, an unlucky trainer, a great guy, and the flake of the world. He went to an auction sale in Maryland and spent my thousand on a yearling filly, sired by a horse called Social Climber. He called me right after the auction and told me she was "okay." Unrealistically, I was hoping for a bit more than "okay."

This was the fall of '67. We named the filly Social Asset, and believe me, she would not turn out to be one! The filly went back to Kentucky with L. K. to learn the rudiments of a racing career—which I knew would be illustrious.

Now I sought partners. The first man I went to was a fellow named Charlie Meeker, an old horseplayer and bon vivant if there ever was one. As the producer-director of the live musical shows at all the Six Flags attractions, he was in and out of Atlanta frequently, and we had become good friends.

Before I could get the pitch out of my mouth, Charlie was in, and would be fun. Charlie had had a very colorful career in show business and was the most riveting—and indefatigable—raconteur I have ever encountered, and the most skillful, entertaining, and palatable name dropper in history.

He had a most interesting preamble to telling a story. A wine connoisseur, Charlie was in his element at dinners. At just the right moment—when he was sure the waiter would not interrupt—he would clasp the hands or forearms of his two neighbors at the table, signal for silence by leaning forward and looking around the table expectantly, and then (for instance): "It's 1936. I'm in New York, and it's pouring down rain. I'm in the men's bar at the Biltmore, drinking a Sidecar with Jimmy Cannon, and we're going to the Garden to see Henry Armstrong fight for the lightweight championship. All of a sudden in comes Babe Ruth. And is he carrying a load! I yell out, 'Babe, you old son of a bitch, where have you been?' . . ." The story invariably had no significance, but the embroidery was delightful. Always the year first, then the city and, for some reason, the weather, and then a series of enthralling names, places, and events.

The other partners would be Leigh and Alyse Baier, a young couple who had met and become enamored of my father and his colorful and very charming ways.

My father would meet and captivate more new people in a week just walking around than most people would get to know in a year. He had time on his hands, and wherever he went he made an enormous hit. He was a person of authentic quality, was an interesting looking man, and had deep charm (when he was in the mood) and a scintillating wit and sense of humor. Young couples—and people generally—fell in love with him. The love affair could be short-lived, however, because Bill Campbell was demanding, and the intensity of the new friendship could eventually make one nervous.

He looked like a Kentucky Colonel should look and had credentials to qualify easily as Atlanta's resident racehorse expert.

He introduced the Baiers to racing, through me. I did not know it at the time but my father's image and credentials would often prove helpful with my future horse endeavors. Meeker, Baier, and Campbell each took a third of Social Asset, and I was calling the shots. Little did I know that she would be the first of about 1,500 racehorses whose "shots" would be called by me.

We curbed our enthusiasm during the unexciting breaking season and waited for the debut of Social Asset in the spring of the upcoming year.

The decade of the sixties was a good one in the life of the Campbell family. A fine development was the marriage of my sister to Jim Waldron, a stellar guy and an old pal of mine in the advertising business. But we were sorry when they moved to New York. Our two daughters were growing up nicely. I took both girls on separate father-daughter trips to Kentucky. My marriage was in the first phase of an idyllic union. I knew just how lucky I was, and so did Anne.

The advertising agency was going great guns. But now an unforeseen thing happened that would provide a dramatic psychological stimulus to the standing of Burton-Campbell in the Southern advertising world.

The Six Flags over Georgia advertising account had gotten very important; the gigantic theme park had enjoyed super success. But always more was needed, so they hired a hotshot marketing guy with all sorts of degrees. The expression had not been invented yet, but if ever there was an example of a man who could "talk the talk," this bird was it. Trouble was he could not "walk the walk." The first thing he decided to do was to shake up the ad agency, "get them off their asses." We suffered through a series of needless presentations, with a hell of a lot of hoops to jump through. I talked to Jack Burton about it, and we agreed that the situation was becoming intolerable and we were catching a lot of flak that we did not deserve.

One afternoon in our conference room, with about five of us and four of them (including the president of Six Flags), this marketing guru was particularly offensive. At one point he said, "I don't think you people have the capacity to grasp, or cope with, the challenges of the future. I'm not impressed with what I'm getting, and I'm getting sick of mediocrity!"

I was ready for him. I said, "We're the best advertising agency in this part of the country, and you're lucky to have us. But you don't anymore. We are herewith resigning this account."

He stammered around with, "Well, there's no need for that kind of reaction. I'm sure we can continue to work together. We just need to iron out a few wrinkles."

We did resign it. The story was in the advertising section of business news the next day. People were flabbergasted. The entire Southeastern business world knew of the enormous success of Six Flags, and they were blown away at the audacity of our having the creative integrity to dismiss a client of this magnitude. It was the talk of the Atlanta advertising community and there was considerable admiration for our guts. If our reputation was good to begin with, it was sure enough good now. The morale in the office soared because this guy had a flair for bullying everyone in any way dependent on him. I was proud of us. Most advertising agencies would have put up with it.

Anne Siddons was a copywriter on this account. Some years later after she became one of America's most popular novelists, she was recounting her early days at Burton-Campbell and said, "Cot and Jack always took care of us." I never had a compliment I liked better.

On a pleasanter note, my friend John Wayt, closely aligned to the equine jumping world, was in a sweat to start a steeplechase in Atlanta. He contacted the National Steeplechase and Hunt Association, and they were wildly enthusiastic about adding a new fixture in a big market. They sent in some of the top brass to talk it over with John, another equine enthusiast named George Chase, and me, and to survey the proposed course to be built on a lovely piece of land John owned just north of Atlanta. This was in the fall of 1965.

It was agreed that the first one would take place the next March, and the fixture would kick off the hunt meet circuit that would move northward each weekend, ending up at Belmont Park in New York in June.

John asked me to be co-chairman, but he was the one with the time and enthusiasm for the effort and did not need a co-anything. It was agreed that I would undertake the public relations and would call the races. Many helped, but John Wayt was the father of the Atlanta Steeplechase, which became one of the most successful in the country. Like most of them it was great fun, good sport, but a knockdown-drag-out drinking jamboree, complete one year with streakers and every year with various other forms of public misbehavior.

John Wayt did a marvelous job pulling together this big endeavor, one that was fraught with difficulty in many aspects. John had been known at the University of Virginia as "Fog," and he lived up to that appellation. He always maintained a slightly jittery, distracted, preoccupied demeanor, but was quite effective as a leader. Selling tickets, traffic control, construction of the course, recruiting horses, and security were the primary areas of concern.

Strange as it may seem, he and I hit it off beautifully. He stayed in a nervous mode most of the time, and, indeed, once stated that he enjoyed being nervous. I can see his point in a way.

Our handling of security was interesting. We arranged for the services of both the Highway Patrol and the Sheriff's department to help with traffic and drunks. But we bolstered the concern for the latter by hiring "Unit 16 of the Dixie Alert." If you think this sounds like an offshoot of the Ku Klux Klan, you are absolutely right. Unit 16 consisted of a ragtag (but uniformed) group of vigilantes from relatively primitive Forsyth County, resembling some of the cast of *Deliverance*. Somehow they were legal to carry weapons and arrest people. That very thought boggles the mind today.

The unquestioned leader of Unit 16 was Eugene Jackson, a man whose day job was being superintendent in Burton-Campbell's office building, a sheer coincidence but a relationship that put me in a position of considerable prominence—with Eugene Jackson, at least.

Eugene was a dead ringer for Don Knotts ("Barney") of *The Andy Griffith Show*. And he had many of his mannerisms and his misguided enthusiasm for upholding the law.

The first Atlanta Steeplechase took place on a hot, dry Sunday in March 1966. Nine thousand people came out to enjoy the first rites of spring and to see the horses run for a total of seven thousand dollars in purse money. I called the races, shakily at first but pretty well after that.

The inaugural steeplechase was lucky, because a disaster was narrowly averted. Drought conditions prevailed, and there were many tailgaters cooking away on outdoor grills. Predictably, the grass caught on fire, and it began to spread rapidly. The Roswell, Georgia, Fire Department had furnished one of its vehicles for just such an emergency. It was parked off the course under some trees. When we signaled and screamed frantically over the loudspeaker, the crew did leap gamely into action, but the truck had a flat tire, and this slowed the rescue alarmingly. Finally it came lumbering (at about four miles an hour on the flat tire) into the troubled zone and managed to halt the blaze before it got under someone's car and blew us all to smithereens. The drunks all applauded, while Eugene Jackson and the men of Unit 16 rushed about like the "Keystone Cops." It was after this performance that John Wayt took to referring to Mr. Jackson—certainly not to his face—as "Jackoff Jackson." Because of the formality of our relationship at our building, he was always "Mr. Jackson" to me, despite our close working relationship at the Steeplechase course.

As race caller I was positioned at the top of a three-level tower. On the ground beneath me, arrayed in a loose semi-circle of protection, stood the men of Unit 16—ready to put down any uprising. In fact they were more than ready, spoiling for a fight like true Confederates. If a nearby patron with a can of beer in his hand so much as raised his voice, Mr. Jackson, wildly brandishing his nightstick, would scream up to me, "Mr. Campbell, you want me to take him downtown?"—meaning did I want him arrested and taken to jail. I must admit it was a heady position to be in, but I exercised tolerance and restraint most of the time,

The Atlanta Steeplechase became extremely popular, but it has been forced to move four times in the forty years it has existed, and is now virtually the Rome (Georgia) Steeplechase, as it takes place ridiculously far from Atlanta. The last time I was there was 1988. Dogwood Stable owned the North American Champion Steeplechaser. His name was Inlander, and he came out for his first race of 1988 at Atlanta. He broke his shoulder going over a jump right in front of the stands and had to be euthanized.

All eyes in Thoroughbred racing turned to Louisville and the Kentucky Derby that spring. But not the eyes of the Campbells. They turned to Cincinnati, Ohio, and to River Downs Racetrack. It was there that Social Asset would make her debut in a five thousand dollar claiming race (meaning that she could be claimed, or bought, for five thousand dollars by anyone racing horses at that meeting—cheap company).

In order to be on hand for this long-awaited event, I left work about three o'clock the previous day. Anne and I drove straight through from Atlanta to Cincinnati, arriving about midnight. After checking into a downtown hotel, I rushed out to get the early "bulldog" edition of the morning newspaper—just to see the words "Social Asset" in print. What a thrill! She was certainly not picked nor written about in any meaningful way, but her name was set in print along with other entries in this modest group of twelve maidens contesting a six-furlong race. And I wanted to gaze upon it.

The next morning moved with excruciating slowness. We arrived at the racetrack just as the gates opened for the first early birds. We had an interminable lunch. Thank God the filly was in an early race or we would never have survived the wait.

Under the guidance of a rather untidy looking groom in an alarmingly soiled undershirt, Social Asset warily made her appearance in the paddock. An encouraging sign was that she was slightly less nervous than her owners—who, incidentally, were easily the best dressed couple in all of River Downs.

I am sure I have repressed much of the rest of the afternoon. Suffice it to say that the filly ran horribly, as would be her custom during much of her career. She beat two horses (thank goodness!). As the poor, mud-caked thing was being unsaddled, Anne and I hovered about to get some encouraging comment from her jockey. I remember that he muttered something about her being "green," and we all quickly agreed that *of course* she was *bound* to be green. What the hell! We did not address the fact that nine other green ones had finished ahead of us.

The return drive to Atlanta, I recall, seemed much longer than the drive up. However, much of it was spent analyzing the race, and by the time Anne and I had gotten home, the consensus was that Social Asset was an enormously talented filly who had shown incredible grit and determination. With that effort and education under her belt—and with a better ride from a different and more appreciative jockey—who knew what the future might hold. The other partners luckily did not make the journey, but agreed readily with our assessment.

Social Asset ran four or five more times in similar five thousand dollar maiden claiming races, and perhaps finished ahead of an aggregate of three or four horses. Pitiful!

Charlie Meeker kept the faith and decided he was going to go see her race. I cautioned, "Charlie, you don't want to make that trip just to see her get nothing but hot and dirty." No, he was determined to go see her. I opted not to go.

He did fly to Cincinnati and went out to River Downs. Social Asset was in the first race on the card. Being the gambler that he was, he had to bet on her, futile though it clearly was. He "wheeled" (combined) her number with every horse in the second race, hoping for a big payoff on the daily double. He then bet twenty dollars across the board on her. Money down the drain.

In her race, when the field turned for home she was in mid-pack, preparing for her patented retreat to the rear of the field. Social Asset was being ridden that day by a battle-scarred old veteran given to riding 50-1 shots, a jockey named Bob Noble. He said later, "By God, I decided when she started to quit I was going to terrify her and see if I couldn't keep her going." Old Bobby showered down on her and did, indeed, terrify the hell out of her. The upshot was that she got herself into contention in mid-stretch. Bobby kept "encouraging" her, and in the last jump she got up to win in a four-horse photo.

She paid $132.50 to a two-dollar ticket. The daily double was the largest in the history of the state of Ohio, paying $2,138 for a two-dollar ticket. Meeker walked out of River Downs needing a satchel to carry the money. He called me in Atlanta that night, nonchalantly saying, "Hell, I knew she would win."

I could just hear him later, presiding at dinner at some steak house in New York, "It's 1966, I'm in Cincinnati at River Downs to see my filly run, and it's hotter than the hinges of hell . . ."

Social Asset never won again. We dropped her into even cheaper company, and someone finally claimed her for $1,500. We said goodbye to Social Asset—who had clearly not been a social asset.

*　　*　　*

It was during this time that the fun and success of life bumped up against another of its realities. Not long after we returned, my mother went into the hospital for treatment of a minor illness. I called her room one morning, and she reported that she had fallen during the night and hit her head on a table but that she was fine. She was always "fine." But she wasn't, and she never would be again. She imagined that she had hit her head. She had a stroke. She seemed quite lucid at first, but deteriorated over the next few days—surprising because nowadays one hears that strokes can be minimized if treated quickly. This lady was already in the hospital when she had hers.

My father wanted to care for her at home. His heart was in the right place, but the emotional chemistry, logistics, and facilities made this a disastrous idea. It became clear after a week that we would have to find a nursing home for her. We found one. In fact we found one after another. All of these turned out to be horrible, though we had sought the best. No matter who ran the place, the care of my mother was dependent on what, at these places, were for the most part lazy and unkind women.

An avid reader all her life and a TV viewer, my mother lost her eyesight, and all she had for diversion was a radio and visits from us. Her fumbling with the radio would inevitably get it off the station she wanted, and with her lack of dexterity she could not reset the dial. Rarely could she get a nursing home attendant to do it for her.

My father came to see her every day and called her all day long. Anne was there often. I was there every day I was in town. I would pick her up, carry her out to the car, and we would go for a drive. She got benefit out of it, I suppose, but she spent the entire time worrying about something. On weekends we would bring her to our house with my father, but I can't imagine she was able to enjoy that. She wanted to die, and it would have been wonderful if she could have. But she did not for six more years.

She was a splendid human being and deserved more pleasure than her life gave her. Or that is what I think.

First equine exposure—San Francisco, 1933.

Author with friend Edward, Rome, Georgia, 1932.

U.S. Navy at 17.

William T. Campbell, Armistice Day, 1918. He had just broken the
world's loop record (151) in this Curtiss Jenny.

Lila Cothran (Campbell) as Queen of Osiris Mardi Gras Ball in
New Orleans.

Author's grandfather and sister, Dick Cothran and Sally Campbell.

Lila and Bill Campbell in later years in Paris.

One of many early festive occasions. This one in Huntington,
West Virginia, 1951.

Advertising executive Cot Campbell.

Wedding Day of Anne Dodd and author, La Grange, Georgia, 1959.

Campbell and Jack Burton, February 1, 1965 in Atlanta, when they started their ad agency (Burton-Campbell, Inc.)

Mrs. Cornwallis wins prestigious Alcibiades Stakes at Keeneland in 1971, a career-changing event.

Young Campbell family at Dogwood Farm in 1973.
Cot, Anne, Lila and Cary.

Saudi royalty at Dogwood: Princess Asiya, Lila Campbell,
Prince Faisal, Anne

Dogwood's Million Dollar Dance, Piedmont Driving Club, 1983.

Dogwood hero Dominion after a victory in 1978.

Southjet wins the Canadian Championship defeating the
Aga Khan's Shardari in 1986.

Campbell and Sheikh Bin Had, up to no good.

Town and Country spread when Dogwood moved to Aiken in 1987.

Relief and joy on the faces of Dogwood celebrants Don Weir, Paul Oreffice (front left), Cot, and Michael Morphy after stewards confirmed Summer Squall's win in 1989 Hopeful Stakes at Saratoga.

Summer Squall in a crowd after Preakness win—1990.

Body language says Summer Squall has just won another big one.

Dogwood set on Aiken Training Track.

Dogwood barn in Aiken.

Aiken—a picturesque town

Campbell walks the "Derby Walk" at Churchill Downs.

Dogwood staff (Back row: Jack Sadler, Bill Victor, Cot Campbell, Suzanne Davila, Mary Jane Howell. In front: Darby Copeland, Missy Poe) and office in Aiken.

Umhau family (L to R) Carter, Andrew, Cary (Campbell),
Lila and Charlie, in Turkey

Tindall Family (L to R) Cot Tindall, Campbell Glenn, Lila
(Campbell), Brady and Tommy Tindall.

What's next?

CHAPTER 19

AN IDEA WHOSE TIME CAME

Predictably there would be other horses. Each one played a role in moving me toward my destiny of centering my life around the seemingly ridiculous quest for large, one-thousand-pound animals that could run fast. That might have been the steak, but the sizzle was elsewhere. I loved the life, the gamble, the atmosphere, the tradition, and the madness of the other people who also pursued the same quest.

My next horse was a filly selected and bought by me for nine hundred dollars at the Keeneland Sale in Lexington. We named her for our wonderful housekeeper, who was a little blasé about it all. Mattie Burson was very fast, and very unsound, but did finish second in a semi-important stakes race at Tropical Park in Miami. She was sold as a broodmare early in the game because of physical infirmities. But she gave the Campbells and two other couples a taste of a headier atmosphere.

Next I bought a filly we named Speckled Hen. She was little, cute, and slow.

I thought I would try a colt next. My friend L. K. Haggin found me a big, fat slob of a two-year-old gelding owned by an old man in Georgetown, Kentucky. We went to this old fellow's sea-of-mud backyard and inspected him. He had been named Memphis Lou, for the grandson of the owner.

During the inspection I reached down and felt his ankle, as if I were worried about some filling I had discerned. I did not know what I was doing but felt that I should demonstrate some expertise. It was such a dumb, obviously phony thing to do. Haggin pulled me up short when he asked, "That ankle feel all right to you, Cot?" He knew what I was doing, and he knew that I knew that he knew!

I bought Memphis for two thousand dollars. I marked him up and offered three other guys a share in him. One of them wanted to know what I had paid for him. Stupidly, I would not tell him, and he would not buy the share.

I learned two things from the Memphis Lou experience. One, do not pretend to know things that you do not know (and in time I would know plenty). Two, go out of your way to be transparent concerning any financial transactions.

If I had not already fallen head over heels in love with horseracing, Memphis Lou would have done the trick. He was the soul of honesty, never failing to try like hell. Though he was a horse of mediocre talent, he would give you what he had every time. He just asked that you not overmatch him.

I wanted Haggin to train him, but he was going to Narragansett in New England with a string of horses, and this was not convenient for us. We turned the horse over to a crafty, gambling trainer named Bill Gateman.

Bill had not so much made his living winning purses, as he had in cashing bets on horses that looked to other bettors like they were not ready for the upcoming assignment. Nothing immoral or illegal about that; you are simply in possession of facts that other bettors are not. Bill would hit the betting windows pretty good when he thought the spot and the price were right. And he had done well. He adored engineering a gamble. And so do I. Later at Churchill Downs we would set up a lollapalooza—involving Memphis Lou.

While he was close-mouthed by nature and necessity, he did love playing the role of the mystery gambler—lots of shifty-eyed, meaningful looks, finger to the lips indicating that silence was called for, furtive glances over his shoulders (even if he was about to enquire as to the time of day). I got a kick out of him, and he knew it.

Bill Gateman, Memphis Lou, and the rest of Bill's string headed to New Orleans and Fair Grounds for the winter racing season. I was in touch with him every other day and knew that Memphis was training quite well and would be ready to run the first week of December. Bill talked me into running him in a $7,500 claiming race, meaning, of course, that any horse in the race could be claimed (or bought) for $7,500. Being green at the time, I was fearful that he would be claimed, but Bill practically guaranteed me that no one would take him, based on less-than-spectacular published training works, a modest pedigree, his being a first-time starter, and his uninspiring connections (translated to mean owner and trainer prestige.). Bill spotted a race on December 14, six furlongs for maidens at the $7,500 claiming level. Gateman engaged the services of a journeyman jockey, one Jimmy York. I am sure that Bill planned to have a hefty wager on Memphis Lou.

From about Thanksgiving on I was on tenterhooks. I told the other partners about the race date, and eight of us—four partners and wives—made flight reservations to New Orleans. The day came, and we caught a morning flight. I was so jittery that I could not remain in the general vicinity of the group and their understandably excited chatter. I moved to the back of the plane.

When we got to the Fair Grounds, we all had lunch before Memphis Lou was to run in the third race on the card. I had a few dollops of gumbo and then went by myself to the paddock to get away from my noisy companions, all of whom had had a few drinks by now and were having a wonderful time. Anne and the others strolled down to the paddock when Memphis Lou arrived there from the barn.

Gateman came stealthily over to meet everyone, winking, looking furtively over his shoulder, and indicating that this was no time for frivolity. The rider appeared in our green and yellow silks, and this hit me like a ton of bricks. At this point my nervousness peaked; I could easily have thrown up. But Memphis Lou was quite composed and looked like the 5-2 favorite that he was, despite being a first-time starter.

The field went out onto the racetrack for the post parade. We, along with Gateman, positioned ourselves on the concrete viewing steps in front of the finish line; I stood alone twenty paces right flank rear, thinking, "Whoever said that horseracing was fun?"

The horses went into the gate for the start, and my heart was doing loop-the-loops. There was the eerie silence as the horses stilled themselves just before the break, and then the clang of the break—doors opening, the bell ringing, and six tons of racehorses exploding out and on their way.

Memphis Lou lay third, about four lengths behind two dueling leaders. Around the turn they went in that order, and when they came spinning out of the turn into the stretch, Jimmy York asked Memphis Lou the question. He delivered the answer, bounding to the lead within a sixteenth of a mile. I had never known such a feeling before. I screamed "Memphis!" and "Goddamn!" about fifty times, as the black horse widened out to win by five lengths. Gateman looked at me as if I were bonkers. And I was. Winning that race with that horse was easily the greatest thrill I had ever known. Sheer maniacal exhilaration! I don't even remember how we got to the winners' circle. I was so beside myself that I forgot to be worried about whether he was claimed or not. He was not.

I was so grateful to that horse for providing me with that unsurpassable moment. It has been said by the most jaded, sophisticated people that no experience can compare with seeing your horse, carrying your colors, win a horserace. If the likes of the Queen of England, Winston Churchill, and the Aga Khan can find it so, there must be something to it.

On the flight back to Atlanta, I was much more companionable, being quite agreeable to sharing my analysis of the race five or six times.

God gave Memphis only limited ability but endowed him with an indomitable, workmanlike spirit. What a human being he would have been!

He campaigned as a solid $10,000 claimer in the early Seventies. We adored him, and luckily he was never claimed from Dogwood. We were careful not to let him drop into a claiming neighborhood in which he would be irresistibly tempting. On the other hand, if we raised him much above $12,000, he would begin to struggle, but never quit trying.

Midway in his life with Dogwood, a paralyzed vocal chord caused wind problems. He underwent surgery to correct this, and then we turned him out on the farm for six months.

When the old boy returned, he was as good as ever.

Because he had thrown in a couple of inferior races when his breathing was not good, because of his hiatus from competition, because he was getting sharp as hell, and because you could stake your life on him when he was right—here was a lovely betting opportunity.

I have always appreciated this sort of "special" wagering situation.

We got old Memphis ready right on the farm and then we shipped him to Churchill Downs. We worked him once there, before the sun was up, and he sizzled five furlongs in fifty-nine seconds flat. Memphis Lou was as sharp as jailhouse coffee. But that knowledge was confined to our small group.

We still needed an "edge," so we entered him in a $3,500 claiming race—significantly below his usual level of competition. On paper, this horse, coming off a long layoff necessitated by physical problems, did not look good. Were we trying to tempt someone to claim him, so we could dump a crippled horse, stuff him down someone's throat? The typical crafty claiming trainer was going to watch him run once before taking him.

We had engaged the services of the ideal jockey: Weston J. "Buddy" Soirez, hardly a household name but a good, capable rider.

Memphis was in the fifth race at Churchill, $3,500 claimers going six furlongs; and, by design, the day of the week was Saturday, a heavy-crowd day at the storied Louisville track. A hefty bet by us would not shake the sizeable pari-mutuel pool.

We bet money with the bookmakers in New Orleans, Atlanta, St. Louis, and Pawtucket, Rhode Island. We then flew to Louisville to lay more through the windows.

Our contingent went to the windows in shifts, keeping a close eye on the fluctuating odds. Thankfully, there was a "sure thing" in the race, a 4-5 shot that was dropping down from an easy win at the $5,000 claiming level. The fact that Memphis was going to the post with all the verve of an old milk cow, his customary pre-race demeanor, did not cause a stampede to the windows. There was just no visible reason for anyone but us to bet on him!

Memphis Lou opened at 5-1, at one point shortened to 5-2, but then drifted up to close to 9-2, a price we were glad to settle for.

Post time.

The starter sprang the latch, and the field started down the backstretch. Memphis Lou was laying fourth, about five off the lead, and Soirez had a "half-nelson" on the old boy. Looked like this gun was loaded: all we had to do was pull the trigger!

Through the turn they proceeded in that manner. When they hit the quarter pole, Soirez wheeled Memphis out for the drive and had a clear path ahead. At the three-sixteenths pole, he clucked twice, shook the reins at him, and it was "Good-bye, baby, so long!"

Memphis Lou took off like a scalded dog, collared the favorite at the sixteenth pole, and went past him like he was tied to a tree. Our horse won by four lengths.

How very sweet it was. He paid $11.40. It was the right move, with the right horse, on the right day.

After the race and the boisterous winner's circle ceremony, we went back to a TV monitor in the clubhouse to watch the replay of the race.

I noticed a wily old racetrack clocker named Indian Charlie standing nearby. He laughed, shook his head, and said, "That's the greatest robbery since the days of Jesse James!"

Memphis Lou had gotten the attention of a good many sporting types around Atlanta, and others were indicating interest in owning part of a racehorse. So I went to Florida to the Hialeah two-year-old training sale, ready to move up a notch in the Thoroughbred talent chain.

Late in the evening, when most of the bigger buyers had struck and gone off to the bar, a little, crooked-legged filly came into the ring. She was sired by Yorktown, and her dam was Evening Out. She had a marvelous pedigree—one of the finest families in the Stud Book. I bought her for five thousand dollars.

I turned her over to a trainer named Harry Shillick. Shillick had been a good jockey and was well-respected as a trainer. He had a touch of class about him, along with a sour disposition.

Our very clever daughter Cary looked at the filly's lineage and suggested the name "Mrs. Cornwallis." If you are any kind of historian you can figure it out. Cornwallis was a major player at the Battle of Yorktown. Evening Out hinted at the distaff side.

I bought her in January 1971. Harry Shillick took her and had her ready to run in April at Gulfstream Park. Typically horse trainers do not like to suggest any trace of optimism, and Shillick genuinely warned that she was not quite tight enough to win her first start.

She almost did. She missed by a length and a half. My father and I had flown down in the new Burton-Campbell plane. Two weeks later she came back in her second race, and so did we. This time she won easily, in fast time. One thing was crystal clear about Mrs. Cornwallis: she could run a hole in the wind!

A new racetrack in Florida came into being that year. It was Calder Race Course, built by the McKnight family of Minnesota Mining and Manufacturing (3M) fame, for the purpose of showcasing their new synthetic "Tartan" all-weather surface. We ran our filly there next. She won a stakes race, and then came back and won the next one. There were clearly no two-year-old fillies in Florida that could warm her up. Those stakes races had the absurdly small purses of five thousand dollars. But, hey, this was 1971.

Hoping that Mrs. Cornwallis could hold her own with the best fillies in America, we next vanned her up to Delaware Park to run in a celebrated fixture at that racetrack known as "The Blue Hen Stakes."

Dogwood, Shillick, the Florida filly, and her Panamanian jockey Gerardo Mora were looked on askance at that historic old blue-blood track, founded by the DuPonts. But Mrs. Cornwallis did not grasp her impertinence. She scared the daylights out of them, finishing a very close second with a few excuses. Now she and Dogwood, a true Cinderella team, were beginning to be noticed in the racing trade press. Even the financial publications were beginning to take note of this up-to-now unheard-of limited partnership approach to owning a racehorse. The fact that this upstart horse, with upstart owners, was competing with the aristocrats of racing was a rather salty story.

We decided after Delaware to run her in what was then the most prestigious two-year-old filly race in the land. This would be the Alcibiades Stakes at Keeneland Race Course in the heart of the Bluegrass. So, again, she took a long van ride from Miami to Lexington for this important race, to be contested at a distance just short of a mile.

This partnership had six partners, some of whom had read earlier about me in the Atlanta papers and then asked about participating. Therefore, some of the partners I knew only slightly. They were all in Lexington for the big event, and I had to struggle mightily to get seats for so many and, more to the point, so many unknowns.

When we were all ensconced in our box seats at Keeneland, Harry Shillick, his countenance even more lugubrious than usual, said he needed a word with me. He told me that there was a problem at the barn. The filly's groom, Scotty, whose only drawback was that about once every year he would go on a drunk, had selected this day in Lexington, Kentucky, to go on one. Great news. But Harry said he was checking the barn periodically and everything would be okay.

When race time neared and the horses were called to the saddling paddock, Mrs. Cornwallis did appear, but she was more nearly escorting Scotty, and not the other way around. Scotty, listing badly to starboard, had a pleasant, amiable demeanor, demonstrated by his insistence on shaking hands with everyone in the immediate vicinity. Shillick, quite a small man, needed more help than he got saddling her, but finally the tack was on and Gerardo Mora, a jockey completely unknown to Keeneland, was thrown up on her.

Again, Mrs. Cornwallis, listed at 6-1 on the tote board, did not concern herself with the daunting nature of her competition, nor was she troubled by Scotty's sudden ineptness in her preparation. She launched her attack as the field turned for home and, with Gerardo riding like a man with his pants on fire, she won that great race by two lengths. We were escorted into the infield for the trophy presentation and were photographed and made over, with the amiable Scotty hanging on Mrs. Cornwallis and loudly congratulating one and all while recounting the highlights of the race.

The horse and groom, accompanied by Shillick thankfully, went back to the barn, while the Dogwood ownership group repaired to the charming, oak-paneled Trustees Room to be saluted and to drink champagne. The affair was a trifle short of trustees that day because we were nobodies, but we had a big time.

I remember distinctly the hospitable efforts of one trustee, a distinguished Kentucky horseman from a storied old Bluegrass family. This was Duval Headley, who was slightly bewildered by both the size of our ownership group and the stunning win by this unheralded invader. He came over to me and said, "Mr. Campbell, I do not believe I am familiar with your nom de course." Somehow that did not surprise me.

Keeneland, and the rest of the racing world, would in the not-too-distant future become quite familiar with the nom de course, "Dogwood Stable."

I truly loved the advertising business, but it was clear that horses were pushing it to a back burner. The accomplishments of Mrs. Cornwallis, which continued through 1971 and 1972, brought more and more exposure both in Atlanta and throughout the racing world to the Dogwood concept of group ownership of a racehorse. It was certainly an idea whose time had come, and why no one had put it into play previously, I do not know.

Mrs. Cornwallis, flawed in conformation but long on family and with a game and genuine nature, became one of the top three fillies of her generation, and in so doing really put me into the horse business, changed my life. One of the great charms of the horse business is that a beautiful, four-legged animal can—through its class, desire, and talent—shape the world of the people with whom it is connected.

My great partner and friend, Jack Burton, saw where my heart wanted to take me, and one day he said to me, "Man, you've really stumbled onto an idea that is catching on. If you want to leave the agency business, I would understand. I would hate it, but I would understand."

I suppose the idea of being full-time in the horse business was beginning to take hold. And my wife Anne, never one to be apprehensive, encouraged it. She was plenty caught up in it herself. But at the outset, I never dreamed that my horse ventures would override my advertising career. Far from it. I adored the advertising business.

The reputation of Burton-Campbell was a matter of supreme pleasure for me. I was very proud of our agency and the people that worked there. An advertising agency is customarily staffed with a lot of versatile, street-smart types, many of whom have a slight bit of madness about them. They are creative people, and creative people are different, maybe not easy to regiment but usually entertaining and delightful companions.

But there is creative and there's *creative*. Just as an opera singer couldn't do a very good rendition of "Chattanooga Choo Choo" or "YMCA," some creative types can't get themselves down to the level of communicating with the unwashed public.

One that fell into that category was the celebrated—nay, renowned—poet/novelist James Dickey (who did throttle himself down to the level of writing the superb book and movie *Deliverance*). I must go back a few years and deal with this unusual man.

He was hired as a copywriter at Liller, Neal (during a dry spell in his career, I guess). I worked closely with him for about six months, and he was absolutely useless. He clearly felt that writing advertising copy was beneath him and was intent on keeping that fact established. It was beneath him perhaps, but his efforts were beneath what any cub copywriter could have delivered. It is not flattering to me that I never understood any of his poetry. But no one understood any of his output at the advertising agency.

Most of his days were spent in his tiny office with his feet on the desk, playing "My Wild Irish Rose" on the harmonica. It was cute, colorful, but slightly disruptive to the workday.

We had the Bowater Paper Company account at the time, and I was handling it under the account supervision of Bill Neal. Dickey was assigned to write the copy on this large industrial account. So the three of us drove up to Rock Hill, South Carolina, to meet with the Bowater people and learn about the company. We had dinner with their communications director. Neal had a fair amount to drink, and Dickey had a great deal.

After dinner on the way back to the motel, our host detoured through the sprawling manufacturing facilities, which were operating full blast during the night shift. He was explaining what was happening in each building.

Suddenly Dickey, the famed Poet Laureate, began a sort of weird murmuring and then (in a loud voice full of drama and crescendo) cut loose with something like, "The crashing tumult of the seething furnace wrenches the heart from my breast and casts it down midst the seed of my issue, . . ." followed by three more uninterrupted minutes of the same unintelligible material.

When he finally wound down there was a long, embarrassed silence, and the host lamely sought to pick up where he had left off.

When we got back to Atlanta, Neal told Dickey that he thought his talent and advertising were not a good fit.

But he was a splendid poet.

During my advertising career, I worked with some colorful, interesting situations and people. Included were two gubernatorial campaigns, a special, secret assignment on a presidential campaign, and goofy projects involving the hilarious double-talk comedian Al Kelly and Eddie Mayehoff, co-star with Jerry Lewis in a long-running TV comedy. I did a lot of radio and television work with the great country singer Eddy Arnold, who was an absolute delight to work with.

However, on the other side of the spectrum were somewhat more challenging recording work sessions with film star Joan Fontaine. This was in the twilight of her career, when she was no longer suitable for leading lady roles. Still, she had her magnificent speaking voice, which literally dripped with elegance and all that went with gracious living, and that was what we wanted for the Sea Pines account (Hilton Head Island). I contracted with her to do a batch of radio commercials twice a year for us.

The pattern was that I would fly to New York and meet her at a recording studio I had rented. I wanted to schedule the sessions in the morning but found that she did not do much work before lunch. Problem was that she liked to have a few pops for lunch, and you could tell it when she did go to "work." I would always send the radio copy to her about two weeks before the recording session so she could become familiar with it. If the recording session was set for two-thirty, to give her ample time for her midday meal, she would invariably float in about three, chortling and tossing her hair about. And that was when she became familiar with it! I never knew her to have the copy with her. Still, after several hours (and many telephone call breaks), we would have done six sixty-second commercials, and they would be splendid.

I learned two valuable things in my advertising career: restraint and brevity. Restraint—often a whisper is stronger than a scream. Brevity—I was taught brevity by the king of brevity: Bill Neal. Never use words just to use words. Ernest Hemingway, who was known for brevity, also had disdain for complicated words and thoughts. At a boozy lunch in New York with some other literary types, the subject of brevity came up. Someone asked him if he could write a short story in ten words. He thought for a moment, and said, "I can write one in six words: 'For sale: baby shoes, never worn.'" Your imagination can flesh that out more poignantly than six pages of copy could ever do.

As covered earlier, we had an all-star team working for us, and we had a wonderful, diverse roster of accounts. The agency did fine work, and we had been approached a few times by big agencies seeking to merge.

We had a flair for everything but politics; we stunk in that department. We tried five or six times and didn't get anyone elected. Our most ignominious failure came in the gubernatorial election of 1968. We were offered—and quickly accepted—the advertising account for the campaign of the popular ex-governor Carl Sanders, considered a shoo-in to beat anybody. And he was running against a nobody from South Georgia named Jimmy Carter. How could we miss? Little did we know at the time that we were running against a vote-getting son of a gun.

If our man had a chink in his armor, it was that he was a trifle slick in image. He was known as "Cufflinks Carl." Being suave, urbane, and soigné did not play well with the good old boys in South Georgia—maybe in Atlanta, but not in Vidalia. We made a horrible mistake in one of our TV commercials that played all over the state. To depict Carl as young, vigorous, and pure, we had a good bit of footage of him jogging through Piedmont Park in early morning. But jogging was not the activity of choice in the rural precincts.

Carl Sanders lost to Jimmy. Had we known Carter would go on to be President of the entire United States, the defeat would have gone down more easily. We learned that creativity did not necessarily equate to success in politics.

Jack and I agreed that I would leave the agency within a year, but he asked me to continue to maintain my Dogwood office—and a presence—within the Burton-Campbell organization. This turned out to be a mistake. When you're going to leave a place, go on and leave. It's fairer for everyone involved.

To prepare for my departure, Burton-Campbell did purchase a small boutique ad agency in New York—one that did some work for Cartier and Gucci. The principal was Austin Kelley, who could assume some of the business I was handling—primarily Sea Pines Plantation. We became Burton-Campbell & Kelley.

I was excited about my new horse venture, but I knew I would miss the zany, delightful, stimulating people in advertising.

I still do.

CHAPTER 20

DOGWOOD FARM, INC.

For about a year and a half, I had been imposing on a horse sage named John A. Bell. Each time I went to Lexington I sought his advice on different racing/breeding business scenarios that would blend with my existing partnership activities and make for a viable game plan for making a living in the horse business. John Bell is a noted industry leader, a breeder, and a practical, no-nonsense sort of a guy. He had an insurance agency, and my excuse for taking his time was that he insured the relatively few horses Dogwood had.

He did the responsible thing and discouraged me—consistently—after hearing one hair-brained scheme after another. What he did not crank into the equation was that I was becoming determined to go into the horse business, that I had really stumbled into a legitimate entree with my partnerships, and that energy and enthusiasm could often overcome stupidity and bad judgment.

These factors caused me to burn my bridges at Burton-Campbell and take the plunge. A little bit of my paternal breeding may have been demonstrating itself.

For some time, Anne and I had discussed the "plunge." She would be vital to its success. Her superb judgment has served us both well through the years; she has both guts and optimism, and she has always had confidence in me. Her enthusiasm for this undertaking was as great as mine.

The blueprint that emerged was that a new corporation would own a farm in West Central Georgia. It would be the promotional headquarters for forming the partnerships, the backbone of the enterprise. But another profit center would be Dogwood Farm as a major training center for breaking and rehabilitating horses, attracting clientele from northern areas where such activities are hampered by cold weather and frozen racetracks.

Anne and I owned 422 acres of farmland in Greenville, Georgia, near LaGrange. We decided that we would donate this to the Dogwood Corporation, for forty percent ownership. The plan then was to sell nine other units in the venture at thirty-five thousand dollars apiece. This would fund the construction of facilities that would house many people and one hundred horses. Today I marvel that a project of this scope could be accomplished for less than half a million. But this was 1973.

The nine people who bought into the corporation were some of the leading lights of Atlanta. Names like Harvey Mathis, George Mathews, Michael Rich, Virginia Crawford, William Rooker, Harper Gaston, Ed Loughlin, John Wayt, and Doug Elam would have gotten the attention of any knowledgeable Georgian in that era. Happily, the banks in Atlanta found that to be the case.

These investors obviously liked me, liked land—a popular commodity in fast-growing Atlanta—and liked the fact that there then seemed to be a good shot to legalize pari-mutuel racing in Georgia. And, too, Dogwood Farm and racehorses were a very sexy venture. Good fodder for cocktail party talk.

Through the years, eight of these players would be bought out by me and Dr. Harper Gaston, a supportive but silent partner who owns a minority interest.

My departure from the advertising business into the absolutely unorthodox Dogwood Farm racing world generated a great deal of shocked speculation. It was a very revolutionary undertaking in a city that was quite provincial, and not in the least "horsey."

Long established, well-heeled, "true" Atlantans are very clannish, and despite the existence of wealth, do not tend to stray very far from established patterns of living. They attend high school at private institutions in Atlanta such as Westminister, Lovett, or Pace Academy, and the males go on to college at the University of Georgia, Emory, or Georgia Tech. Maybe the odd maverick will go to the University of Virginia. They marry meticulously coiffed, adorably garbed, honey-toned Atlanta cuties, educated at Sweetbriar, Randolph-Macon, and, of course, Georgia. They go to Sea Island or Ponte Vedra on their honeymoons and vacations for the rest of their lives. Mountainous Highlands, North Carolina, is also quite acceptable. For the more adventurous, there's maybe a trip to New York, Paris, or London every other year. The accepted vocations are lawyers or doctors or stockbrokers; not too many embrace horseracing as their life's work.

If Atlanta was buzzing over the creation of Dogwood Farm, then you may be sure the tiny town of Greenville was in a frenzy of excitement. The site of "the Dogwood racehorse farm" was two miles outside the town square, and rumors were flying.

It was full speed ahead to launch Dogwood Farm. Based on the volume of the previous year, I figured I could form enough partnerships to account for perhaps seventy percent of the nut. And hopefully, I could draw enough non-Dogwood horses to break and rehabilitate to take care of the rest of the expenses and start making some money.

The construction project included a six-furlong racetrack (I don't ever want to build another one), two training barns with twenty-six stalls in each, four houses for key employees, a dormitory for young girl riders and grooms, a recreation building, miles of black fences, and an office. On property that was adjacent to the training area, we built two barns for lay-ups (rehabilitation) and a guest house. Oh, it was first class! You could have picked it up and moved it to Old Frankfort Pike in Lexington and it would have fit in perfectly.

In my enthusiasm—and greenness—I had constructed and outfitted a kitchen in the dormitory that could have serviced the needs of a Ritz-Carlton Hotel. Anne and I recruited the leading old-time, down-home Southern cook in that part of Georgia. I had envisioned companionable meals with the happy Dogwood family munching away on fried chicken, hoe cakes, cornbread, etc., while reliving thrilling races of Dogwood stock at various points around the nation on that day. I did not reckon with the point that most of the riders would be trying to hold their weight, and the kitchen and magnificent culinary fare were counterproductive to this objective.

When we first started the construction program, in a rainy period in the dead of winter, a friend of mine from Lexington, Jimmy Drymon (who had for many years managed the famous Domino Stud), was visiting his daughter in Atlanta. I invited Jimmy to ride down to the site near Greenville, Georgia, and let me show him around. In a steady drizzle, we drove through the muddy fields and I proudly pointed out that the racetrack would go here, and the two barns would go there, and that I planned to do this and that. We got stuck in the mud a couple of times, and all in all it was not a terribly stimulating day for a visiting farm manager, who was probably anxious to get away from farms and horses for a few days.

At the end of the tour, I eagerly looked over at my passenger and asked, "Well, what do you think, Jimmy?" I was brimming with excitement over what I knew would be an encouraging verdict.

Jimmy blew his nose, looked over at me, and muttered, "I think you ought to start the car; let's get out of this mud hole and get the hell back to Atlanta."

Well anyway, it did look good the following fall. In September when I got ready to go to the Keeneland Fall yearling sale, which is like a national convention in the racehorse business, Dogwood had a population of two horses—both unsyndicated yearlings I had bought at the Keeneland July sale—and about twenty-five employees waiting expectantly for action.

During Dogwood's corporate history we had four farm managers. The last two were wonderful. The first two were not, although all four have been superb horsemen.

At this juncture, the first one was in place. He was a rather irascible, older man who had been one of England's greatest jockeys. While he was known to be a gifted breaker of yearlings and an all-around fine horseman, his career had not exactly taken off—perhaps because he was "bad to drink whiskey," a problem I quite well understood but did not need in an employee, especially at this crucial stage of the fledgling farm's life. His name was George Archibald.

Among my ideas about a Thoroughbred training center were these: that most of the workers should be girls, there would be no dogs on the farm, and I thought it was very bush league to have radios blaring away throughout the barns. Archibald agreed with me about the girls and the radios, but not about the dogs (in his particular case, that is). George really had as his only two friends in life two very active, feisty Jack Russell Terriers. If they were not welcome, he could not come. Because he was a highly regarded horseman (with a following, I thought) I agreed to make his two dogs an exception.

Both George and the dogs quickly began driving me crazy. George had a vague, out-to-lunch demeanor about him, never seeming to be tuned in to what was going on. Nor was he aware of any mischief or unsuitable activities the two dogs might be pursuing.

At the time, I had a sporty Lincoln Mark IV with black, vinyl seat covers. Georgia is noted for its red clay, and during the construction on the farm, this clay was often soft and wet. Invariably when I asked George to get in my car so we could go check out some area that needed discussion, he would invite the two dogs. They would—within seconds—efficiently cover every square inch of front and back seat with red paw prints, while George looked on, oblivious and adoring.

In early fall, when most of the construction had been completed, George Archibald and I set off for Lexington, seeking to make known that Dogwood was in existence and that we were ready to accept horses to break, train, and/or rehabilitate. Our pitch was to be that we offered the finest facilities and personnel, a climate milder than Kentucky and not as hot as Florida, and a location right on the main transportation routes between New Orleans and New York, and Chicago and Florida. Furthermore, we would be mighty anxious to please.

I don't know that this message was received with much excitement at the fall sale. But try we did—especially me; I don't think George's heart was in it.

As we made the rounds, buttonholing every yearling buyer who would give us a brief audience, the first score came. I'll never forget it, and God bless the kind man who provided us with this accomplishment.

Brereton C. Jones, later to become governor of Kentucky, was a very young man who had a farm in Woodford County, Kentucky, and he too was trying to get started in the horse business. He and I had become friendly. Brerry came up to me at the sale (while I was standing around trying to look busy, accompanied by the preoccupied George), and he asked, "Do you think you might have room for two yearling fillies at your farm?" I started to scream out, "ARE YOU KIDDING!"

Instead, I suavely struck a thoughtful pose and, looking as if he had created a terrible problem for me, I said, "I don't know . . . we're awful full! But for you I think we could handle a couple more," and looked over at George as if for affirmation.

Whereupon George glared at Brerry and blurted out, "Well, I hope they've been vaccinated for equine encephalitis, because, by God, we've got a hell of a lot of it in Georgia!"

We got the horses, but at that point I think it was clear that George's days were numbered.

We got a few more clients out of that sale, but it was tough sledding. I had brochures extolling the virtues of Dogwood, and of course I was very proud of them and wanted everyone in Central Kentucky to read and relish every word. At the sale I would make sure that an adequate supply was available in neat little stacks at strategic points throughout the Keeneland sales pavilion. Furthermore, leaving no stone unturned, I visited the leading hostelries of the city (the Campbell House, Springs Motel, and others) and asked permission to leave a supply on registration desks. I would revisit these sites periodically, optimistically counting the remaining ones to determine the demand for this literature. Occasionally I would find that the brochures had been thoughtlessly swept off the counters and onto the floor. This hurt my feelings.

Dogwood bought several horses at the sale for syndication, and some other benevolent souls sent two or three young horses down for breaking. When we got back to Georgia, other young horses from the area began filtering into our training barn.

One we could have done without came following a phone call from a "Mr. House" from some little town in Alabama. He was a good old country boy, and he informed me in his call that he had a five-year-old stallion that had never had a saddle on his back and—if he could get him on the trailer—he wanted to bring him to Dogwood to be broken and trained for racing. This did not sound like a very promising prospect. I had a feeling we were going to more than earn our thirty-five dollar per diem, but I said, "Wonderful, bring him on."

"By the way, this is one of the fastest horses I've ever seen in my life," Mr. House announced.

"How can you tell if he's never been broken?" I asked.

"Well, hell, I sic the dog on him and he'll run him for three miles, and he can fly!"

This was our clientele.

That fall we had enough horses to fill up one twenty-six-stall barn, so cosmetically we were looking pretty good to visitors. We did a lot of entertaining at the farm, and as I expected, just having a good-looking, first-class Thoroughbred horse farm in the Atlanta area was quite a boon in moving shares in our partnerships.

We had what were called "Breezing Parties," where we would invite fifty or sixty visitors to the farm and expose them to our wares. The guests would arrive about two o'clock on a Sunday. We would walk them around for a while; then with liquid refreshments in ample supply, we would bring out the young horses we were seeking to syndicate. Armed with a bullhorn to help me hold their attention, I would enumerate the attractive features of the horses and cover the partnership details. It worked quite well, and afterward when we repaired to the guest house for more liquid refreshments and serious (it was hoped) discussions about participation, we usually did some business.

The term "breezing party" was sometimes confused with "breeding party," and this may have accounted for the good turnouts that we had. Although people began to understand that the term "breeze" meant a sharp speed drill of a racehorse in training, word did spread through Atlanta and environs that this was a pretty pleasant way to spend a Sunday afternoon.

At this point one crystal clear truism was established: If Dogwood was going to make it—and it looked increasingly promising—it was probably because we were in Atlanta and *not* in Kentucky. Putting a Thoroughbred horse farm in this non-horse, but populous and very affluent, Southern city really made a lot of sense. We were *the* horse operation in that part of the country. Had we started Dogwood in Lexington, teeming with long-established, famous old farms, we would have been a "lost ball in the high weeds."

Things were looking up, but we still needed more outside (non-Dogwood) clients for training. The following summer the big breakthrough came . . . but not without its price.

One of the leading trainers in North America was a man named Frank Merrill. He had a lot of horses, and he campaigned in Canada in the summer and went to Florida in the winter. He had been sending his young horses every fall to a farm in Ocala for breaking and early training, before he took them over for campaigning. I had targeted Frank as an ideal client for Dogwood—lots of horses controlled by only one man, and potentially top-class racehorses that could cast a nice reflection on Dogwood if they turned out to be high-profile stars.

For some time I had been talking to Frank about giving us his business. I knew he liked the idea, but he was reluctant to leave his Ocala connection. I thought we were making headway, however, and it was a project that was heavy on my mind.

One day in July 1974, I was due to fly to England to look at a couple of older horses in training that I was thinking of buying. I was at our Dogwood business office in Atlanta, had my bags with me, and was set to fly out on a late afternoon plane to London. I got a phone call that morning; it was Frank Merrill. He said he wanted to talk to me about the training arrangement, so would it be possible for me to fly up to Canada that day and have dinner and discuss the matter? The timing was not convenient, but I absolutely had to go.

I quickly rearranged my plans. My secretary booked me on a flight to Buffalo, leaving later that morning. Frank said I should fly to Buffalo because the current Canadian race meeting was at Ft. Erie, right across the border, and we would spend the night at his cottage near Ft. Erie. Fine. I made arrangements to fly to England the next day from up there.

It was a hot day when all this developed, but since I was going to England where the weather is usually cool, I had on a fairly heavy suit. And since I was going to be in England a week, I had packed a big bag and a garment bag and had my briefcase with me. I also had no time to go to the bank. I only had twenty-one dollars on me, but I knew Frank would meet me and I could cash a check through him in Canada.

I arrived in Buffalo at 2:30 p.m., but I didn't see Frank or any emissary. My bags came up, but Frank did not. I hung around until about 3:00 p.m., and then I thought I'd better call his place in Toronto. I got his wife, and she said she was sure he must be on the way. "Be patient. You know Frank, he's always late (heh heh!)," she offered helpfully. At 3:30 I called again. Frank's wife told me to catch a cab to the cottage. She promised he'd either be there or would arrive shortly after I did.

So I lugged my bags to the curbside, hailed a cab, and asked the driver how much it would be to take me to 532 Dalton Road in Ft. Erie. Eighteen dollars. Close, but that was okay. Off we trekked to Frank's cottage. I gave the driver twenty bucks, since he helped haul the baggage up to the door (and it was hotter in Canada than it was in Atlanta). I had one dollar left . . . and was a long way from home.

I had no choice but to sit down on the steps in the hot sunshine and hope and pray that Frank showed. I was sweltering and dejected at this point, and I'm sure I looked the part, sweating heavily in my cavalry twill suit.

In the yard next to his small house, four small children were playing rather noisily. They noticed me, of course, and they observed, I am sure, that I was in a foul mood. After awhile it dawned on them that I might somehow fit into the afternoon's recreational activities.

Soon a rock came whistling over my way! With all four crouched behind bushes in the yard, a rock barrage then started in earnest. This was definitely too much!

Summoning up my sternest demeanor, I warned, "Now, see here, you children, this is going to have to stop. We're not going to have any rock throwing!" Like hell we're not. Now it was like the barrage at Omaha Beach.

At this juncture, one of them yelled out, "Hi there, old Poo Poo Man," a term which seemed to capture the fancy of all the combatants.

Picture this. Here I am on a sizzling hot day, burdened by some very heavy baggage, one dollar in my pocket, no transportation, no idea where any acquaintances are, in a strange land, with four tiny children throwing rocks and screaming "Poo Poo Man" at me.

This may have been the low ebb of my life.

I decided to seek a less hostile atmosphere. I picked up my bags and struggled up the street, to what destination I did not know. After about a block I was ringing wet. A pickup truck came by, and when I dropped my bags and began waving frantically, he stopped. I told him I was looking for a motel, and he said he was going by one about a mile away—the best news I had heard all day long. He took me there, I checked in with my credit card, and things began to look up, relatively speaking.

After numerous phone calls to his connections, I finally talked to Frank later that night. He seemed only vaguely aware that he had caused me some slight degree of inconvenience. Showing remarkable restraint, I pleasantly made arrangements to meet him at his barn in the morning. We talked then and, perhaps in a fit of remorse (although I doubt it), he agreed to send me twenty horses to train.

He continued to send me horses for some years after that. But I *did* pay a price.

So many diverse new experiences were happening in my life all of a sudden. All because I had chanced onto a very logical, viable idea, while pursuing what started as a minor hobby. This simple idea was group ownership—so elementary, so obvious. Instead of buying the entire horse, you own a piece. You'll feel like you own all of him. But if the horse can't run fast or gets hurt, you'll be thankful that you own only a piece.

It would be important that one person manage the horse and that that point be clearly established. No committees in my concept; that dog won't hunt! The manager would need to be a person who knew what he was doing and was one in whom you could put your trust. Me, presumably; strong in the second part, and improving rapidly in the first.

A key to success would be to communicate with the partners before they find it necessary to hunt you down. You don't have to cover every little niggling problem, but if there is a big one, the sooner that information is moved to the partners, thoroughly and with no punches pulled, the better.

During all my years in the horse business, I have been flabbergasted that the Thoroughbred racing industry did not embrace my new idea. But it did not. Part of the charm of racing is its tradition, but tradition is also a stumbling block to changing with the times, and Lord knows racing has been slow to do that. Most of the ills with which the racing game struggles today can be traced to the complacency of a blue-blooded, old boy network.

How appalling that is. The future of racing was formulated through the planning and maneuverings of an all-star team of "Captains of Industry." New

York Racing Association (owning Belmont Park, Aqueduct Race Track, and Saratoga Race Course) has always been the bellwether of the sport. And it has been singularly effective in shunning every golden opportunity that came its way: control of television coverage of the sport, the right to operate the invaluable off-track betting facilities in New York state, the establishment of a central control point in racing (a la commissioners of major league baseball, basketball, football, golf, hockey). How could names synonymous with the growth and development of this country—Phipps, Widener, Olin, Hanes, Dreyfus, Vanderbilt, Guggenheim, Whitney, Chenery, et al—not have foretold some of the ills that were coming to racing? How could they not have seized opportunities and not done more strategic planning?

At any rate, it was this sort of complacency and lack of foresight that caused many of the old guard in racing to look askance at our Dogwood partnerships. All we were doing was bringing new money into racing—money that would not have been there had it not been for this logical partnership concept. Unbelievably, the horse breeders of Kentucky (the cradle of the industry) were also petrified of the idea. They should have dropped to their knees and thanked their Maker when they saw me coming, laden with serious money to buy horses they bred for the market—again, money that would not have been there had it not been for Dogwood.

They finally caught on. In 2004 I was named Honor Guest of the Thoroughbred Club of America, at a Lexington fete that recognized my contributions to the industry. This was the thrill of my life.

CHAPTER 21

DOWN ON THE FARM

In 1974, Dogwood Farm was pulsating with all of the intrigue, jealousy, and passion of the neighborhood of "Desperate Housewives"—and then some.

We had a dormitory full of young, female riders and grooms, many of them quite attractive, and some more than a little adventurous. There were three or four married couples in houses on the farm and several single male exercise riders bunking together. And all of this explosive mix was under the supervision of George Archibald, who was not exactly ruling with an iron hand.

George's modus operandi was to train the horses in the morning—and he did this painstakingly, with admirable military precision. That done (when I was not on the farm), he would retire to his small apartment and drink beer ad infinitum. Every now and then during the rest of the day he would sally forth serenely to make an "inspection" tour of the barn.

Fortunately, we had hired a pretty conscientious assistant trainer/exercise rider from Ocala, and he kept the afternoon equine chores on course.

In the very beginning I was much too wrapped up with the people on the farm. If "energy and enthusiasm were overcoming stupidity and bad judgment," as suggested earlier, then those ingredients were also causing too much involvement on my part in hearing the varied complaints of the entire work force. Part of this was my desire to generate esprit de corps, and part of it was necessity—as I began to see the unsuitability of the man in the farm manager's job. He could train horses. But he could not manage himself (or his two dogs), much less a large Thoroughbred training farm.

It got so that when I drove in from Atlanta and got out of my car, the employees would be lined up with their problems. Soon I would hear the dreaded question, "Mr. Campbell, can I have a word with you?"

I needed a strong farm manager, more of the girls living off the farm, and less intense involvement on my part.

One day, four months after George had come to work, I learned that a quartet of visitors had come to Dogwood one afternoon and started to walk through the main training barn. George had spied them, groggily burst forth from his abode, and run them off, saying that no one could come into the barns in the afternoons because "the horses are sleeping."

I let George go.

I have always been known to be quick on the trigger. This time I had gone on a month or two longer than I should have. However, I had known the time was coming, and I had begun to scout out a replacement.

The assistant trainer took over for the time being while I concluded negotiations with one Barry McGillivray. He was a tall string-bean of a guy with a nice, almost obsequious, personality and a superb reputation as a horseman, having worked at some of the best farms in Ocala. There had been hints that he did not mind taking a drink, but several references thought that "he has gotten that under control." When he called me around midnight on New Year's Eve to accept the job, I should have surmised that maybe total control had not yet been achieved.

Barry hit Dogwood several days later, and he came on like a whirling dervish. Never have I seen a human with more nervous energy. He was like a man on Dexedrine. He was everywhere, doing everything, and instilled a lot of hustle in the entire staff. Barry would wake a horse up and get him on his feet so he could massage his tendons. He had to be doing something every minute of the day. I began to breathe a sigh of relief. Managerial matters at Dogwood Farm seemed to be shaping up.

My pattern had been to work in the Dogwood Atlanta office and drive down to Dogwood, sixty miles away, three or four days a week. Sometimes I spent the night in the guest house, but I preferred going home. In the early days, time on the farm was associated too much with hearing and solving personnel problems.

I still had some responsibilities at Burton-Campbell. Jack Burton counted on me to lend my presence occasionally for an agency new-business pitch or in some client entertainment activity. But my last days within the agency were coming to an end, and I was looking for Dogwood offices elsewhere.

I had hired an executive assistant/secretary named Susan Dillon. She was smart, innovative, creative, and as energetic as Barry McGillivray, and would be invaluable for a number of years.

Susan and I moved into an office building in downtown Atlanta and spent most of our time on the marketing of the partnerships. This was vital, and the sale of shares in horses was going well. I was relieved that the organizational tumult on Dogwood Farm had subsided and did not seem to require my constant supervision.

It was in the early days of starting Dogwood that my mother died. We were all thankful that the wretched final years of her existence came to an end. She was certainly tired of living, and she was in no way scared of dying.

Her death was imminent for a month or two, and we were all more than prepared. From the time she had had her stroke years earlier, my father had spent time with her every day, talked with her on the phone five or six times each day, and thought about her constantly. I am sure he castigated himself that he had let her down in their life together—through drinking and some ill-advised and selfish decisions and acts. But through her last years he had been the Rock of Gibraltar. It was now clear that she would die soon and that she did not depend on him for succor.

So he responded by going on a bender. I can't say I blamed him.

When we buried my mother, my father was drinking alone in his tiny apartment. He was in such bad shape that he could not attend the graveside service. On paper this seems reprehensible. But I don't think it was. During their marriage, he had been perhaps twenty-five percent lacking; but he had been seventy-five percent magnificent, and Lila Campbell was always convinced that she could not have lived without him. On balance, theirs was probably a fine married life, uneven but better than plenty. When my father could no longer help my mother, he gave way. None of his family blamed him for this.

Nearing the mid-mark of the 1970s, Dogwood was getting on firm footing. We were attracting a number of horses to train, and I was syndicating horses at a clip that put the farm on profitable footing. It was a good thing, because I was in for a rude shock.

My stock purchase agreement with Burton-Campbell had been set up to give me a cushion until the farm really got rolling. I would be paid over a period of seven years. After the first two years—with five payments left—I got a disturbing call from Jack Burton.

After I left the agency, Jack had brought in a couple of hotshot advertising boy wonders. Once they were aboard, I think he relaxed a little, and let them run with it. They did run with it. Very quickly, they ingratiated themselves with the major clients, as Jack may have let the fire in his belly simmer down. In a short time these guys controlled most of the significant business at Burton-Campbell. They did not know me, had had no part in negotiating the buy-out of my stock, and, though it was grossly unfair, they had little interest in paying me my annual stipend.

They told Jack one day, in effect, "Look, pal, we're working our asses off in this agency; it's our sweat that's making it go, we're the ones the clients are looking to. So, we have no intention of honoring the agreement that this corporation made with Cot Campbell.

"If you don't like it, we'll leave with the business we control and start our own agency. And if Campbell doesn't like it, he can sue the corporation, but there won't be anything left to sue for. His other choice is to drop the racehorses, and try to come back into the advertising agency business and regain control. We don't think he's going to try that."

I settled for ten cents on the dollar of what was owed me, and spent little time brooding about the injustice of it. Sure it was outrageous, but I had launched an exciting new business, and there was little point in losing sleep over some dirty dealing in the previous one. I never liked the people who engineered the deal. Maybe Jack should have stayed on top of it better, but he didn't, and he felt badly about it. He was still my good friend, and has remained so.

It was about this time that Bill Neal returned to his agency from lunch at the Driving Club, and stopped by the office of one of his account executives. He sat down in a chair, started to say, "I want to go over those . . . ," and he died.

When I heard about it, it took the wind out of my sails. He was so important in my life, had done do much for me, and much of who I am came from him. We had been great friends, but in the years since I had left, we had been semi-estranged. Any effort to speak to Bill when we bumped into each other brought only a cold look and a curt nod. The only thing that could have avoided that unhappy schism would have been for me to stay at Liller, Neal, Battle & Lindsey. Looking back through the years, that would never have been an option. My life would not have had the quality, the pizzazz, or the zest that it has had.

I'll tell you one thing: Old Bill would have gotten a kick out of my getting rooked out of my stock at Burton-Campbell!

*   *   *

The Dogwood racing stable, made up of about twenty-five horses at that time, could not boast of any stars since the 1971 accomplishments of Mrs. Cornwallis, but we were winning races and establishing the name, and the innovative Dogwood group ownership concept was in the eye of the industry.

Most of the horses then were being trained and campaigned by a good old Kentuckian named Elwood McCann, who has been associated with Dogwood in one way or another since 1971 (he trained Memphis Lou in his final days with us). Elwood still trains a small division in Kentucky. We were beginning to spread our horses out with other trainers; Steve DiMauro, a big time New York trainer, and Larry Jennings, in New Jersey, both had some for us.

The arrangement with such public trainers is that they are paid a per diem (sixty to ninety dollars per day, depending on the locale in which they are operating). They receive ten percent of the gross income from purses earned.

I traveled constantly in those days and thought nothing of doing it. Every May I covered the Kentucky Derby for three Southeastern newspapers: Augusta, Savannah, and Athens, Georgia. This arrangement was probably of little use to the Morris Newspaper chain, but it was wonderful for me. It put me in the press box of Churchill Downs for one of the most thrilling, drama-packed days in the history of sport. There I typed away in my little space, down the line from Red Smith, Jimmy Cannon, Joe Hirsch, Furman Bisher, Jim Murray, and every other major sportswriter of the time.

Like many Americans, I have had a long, intense love affair with the Kentucky Derby. I saw my first one in 1942. My father and I drove up from our ill-fated farm in Tennessee. In fact, we ran a two-year-old filly during our stay in Louisville. Shut Out won the Derby that year, the great jockey Eddie Arcaro having opted for his stable-mate Devil Diver.

From the late Sixties to the present time I have not missed many Derbies, as a spectator, sportswriter, or participant. There is magic, an indescribable electricity about the event, that is unmatched in any other sporting event, I do believe.

I am absolutely flabbergasted when I think back that Dogwood has run seven horses in six Derbies. We have been second, third, and fourth. We have not won it, but we're not through trying, and our record of participation stamps a gigantic "A" on the report card of Dogwood Stable. It is not easy to get a horse to the Kentucky Derby.

I have so many dream-like memories of it. Walking over from the barn to the paddock with the co-favorite, Summer Squall, one of the most popular horses ever to run in the Derby—that was the greatest. Seeing our Dogwood entry in 2000, Trippi and Impeachment, lead the parade onto the track while 150,000 sang "My Old Kentucky Home." What a thrill! But there is another indelible memory from way back in 1971.

It starts in 1969, when I went to the Keeneland Fall Sale to buy some young horses. Armed with my marked catalog, I went through the barn area and stopped at Barn 21, where I asked for Lot Number 128 to be brought out. This big bay colt looked impressive, until I asked that he be walked straight toward me. It was clear then that he had a crooked right front ankle, so obvious when he winged it out to the side as he advanced. I told the boy to put him up. He was damaged goods. I couldn't use him.

I watched him sell that night, remembering it only because when the big pavilion doors opened and he was led into the auction ring, you could easily see him tossing that right front leg to the side as he approached. I watched while some idiot paid $1,200 for him—peanuts for a racing prospect, but this colt would never stand training, I was sure, and he would require thousands more to be spent on his futile preparation. I congratulated myself on my good eye, enabling me to avoid such a disaster.

Never thought about him again.

Then, in 1971 I was in Louisville to cover the running of the Ninety-seventh Kentucky Derby. It was a tremendous field that year—twenty horses. When the horses broke and came by the stands the first time, it resembled a cavalry charge.

Eastern Fleet, the Calumet speedster, was showing the way, trying to slow the pace and lead every step of the race. Into the backstretch they went. Now Bold and Able had taken over, with Going Straight, Jim French, and Eastern Fleet stalking the pace. Then it was into that far turn, where the front runners started to shorten stride and the stretch runners began to make their moves.

Bold and Able and Eastern Fleet were fighting for the lead. But in the back of the pack I saw a big colt launching his bid, and he was passing horses like they were tied to a tree. I didn't know who he was, but I knew he would have something to say about the finish of the Kentucky Derby! The boy on that colt wheeled him six wide into the stretch, sought a clear path, and asked him for his life. Man, he was picking 'em up and laying 'em down!

In mid-stretch Jim French gained the lead, Unconscious was making a furious bid on the rail, but in the middle of the racetrack, the big colt I'd been watching swept relentlessly into contention—like a tidal wave. He hit the front at the sixteenth pole and began to draw away.

Suddenly, I noticed a funny thing. He was throwing that old right leg out to the side! You guessed it. That was the yearling colt I had smugly rejected two years earlier. He won the Kentucky Derby, went on to win the Preakness in track record time, and was later sold to King Ranch for $1,000,000.

And I am the genius who turned down Canonero II for $1,200.

During the early years—despite headaches with farm managers—I did love to go to the farm and to take visitors there. It was a knockout-looking place, and Anne and I were very proud of it. And go to it we did, especially in spring and fall.

The spring was better than the fall, because those Saturdays and Sundays did not have to compete with football; and with the Kentucky Derby in the offing, spring was a time when it was not difficult to turn people's thoughts toward the horse.

Exactly what is the anatomy of a "Breezing Party"? About three weeks ahead of an upcoming Sunday, say, invitations go out to around eighty people, mostly within the environs of Atlanta. We hope sixty will accept. Twenty regret; ten more will not show; but ten more will appear out of nowhere at the last minute.

The guests start driving into Dogwood at two-thirty; they are greeted by us and then ushered to the nearby bar, where a white-coated bartender awaits smilingly.

People stroll through the barn, making more noise than we wish they would. If there's a horse in the barn that will bite the hell out of you, somehow most of the crowd will manage to congregate around that animal's stall.

The guests have a tendency to regale you with many horse stories about swift ponies ridden with wild abandon in earlier days.

Around three o'clock, when latecomers have arrived (we've been checking the guest list to make sure there are no live ones still on the road), we summon all the guests up to the racetrack for the start of the afternoon's "program."

With Anne, my daughters, and Susan Dillon herding the guests from the barn to the grassy slope by the racetrack, I and my beloved bullhorn are loudly suggesting that they take a seat on the grass or the benches and that "We're gonna show you some exciting racehorses." When all are settled and quiet (I glare at the ones who are slow to cut the chitchat!), I tell about Dogwood—our wonderful concept of group ownership, along with some favorable information about the racing stable's successes. Then I introduce the first "set" of horses. Three horses, with green-and-yellow-bedecked riders astride, make their way up the gravel path from the barn a hundred yards away. Each horse is attended by two grooms on foot, creating the impression that there could be equine mayhem at any moment.

The horses come onto our beautifully engineered, carefully harrowed, three-quarter mile racetrack. The three turn and face the audience and stand, while I extol the virtues of their bloodlines. The less quietly they stand, the better impression they make (people love the idea of unruly horses; horsemen do not). If only one of them were to rear up and strike at his attendant, the shares in him are assuredly sold. Obstreperous behavior equates to money in the bank.

The horses then jog off counter-clockwise; they break into a canter, then a gallop, and just before they disappear behind an unusual infield hill for a sixteenth of a mile, they go into their "breeze" (or sprint). When they come out from behind that hill, they are hauling ass! The crowd can hear them coming before they see them, and I am helping it along on the bullhorn. They come by us at full tilt, really providing quite a thrill! There is nothing more exciting than being close to three one-thousand-pound, gorgeous racehorses, moving at forty miles an hour. It will guarantee the goose pimples.

The horses are gradually brought to a stop. They then jog back to us (rapidly, I hope, before the magic spell wears off), turn, and face us. I tell how fast they breezed that three-eighths of a mile, cover their attributes briefly, and tell how much a share in each would cost.

While the riders were not instructed to do anything other than to work the horses, I did have one rider who sold more shares during those years than all the rest of us put together. His named was Jimmy Grizzard (accent on the "Griz"). He was an old quarter horse rider, and he could ride the hair off a horse. And he was a natural-born showman.

His "schtick" was to take off his helmet and mop his brow; then when I paused, he would shake his head, and say, "Whooeee, Mr. Campbell, I ain't never been on no horse could move that fast!" That would bring out the checkbooks.

We would show a couple of other sets. I would then suggest that we all caravan down the road to our very attractive guest house. There the bar would have been reestablished, and there would ensue a couple of hours of "cocktailing" and consumption of comestibles supplied by Anne. These would have included, of course, her reliable spinach dip—the quantity of which, over the years, would have taxed the capacity of a tank car.

A giant bowl of strawberries and powdered sugar was a popular standard for these occasions. It was with this delicacy that the crown prince of Saudi Arabia, Prince Faisal—a fairly frequent, free-loading guest at the farm—made a name for himself.

Faisal, who in many ways was barely housebroken, would pull a chair up to the table, remove his sandals, rear back, and start dipping the strawberries into the sugar, while alternately massaging his toes. You could see the other guests shrinking from the table.

Around dark, the guests would be headed home. The Dogwood insiders would "postmortem" the day, count the shares sold, and speculate on the people who would come around when called Monday or Tuesday. Anne and I—and daughters Cary and Lila when they attended—would load up what food was left (always plenty of strawberries!) and head home. It would have been a long day, but most were productive.

Despite the showmanship and the salesmanship involved, the shares in Dogwood horses were presented for what they were: highly speculative investment ventures, suitable only for discretionary funds.

When asked if I thought this or that partnership would make money, the answer was always a resounding "NO." I often said, "This is a three-pronged proposition: 1) It could make money—and it could make enormous money—but chances are it won't make any. 2) If it loses, you can take a meaningful tax write-off. And, 3) most importantly, it should put a little excitement, zest, and adventure in your life. If that third ingredient doesn't appeal to you, and if you can't afford to lose the money, don't touch it with a ten-foot pole."

I rubbed people's noses in the risky nature of horseracing. And that's one reason we have been so successful. Another reason is that I always made it seem as if we did not particularly care if they bought the share or not. There was always the unspoken implication of a phantom waiting list to get involved with us. I understood snob appeal and I knew how to exploit it. I knew how to sell "the sizzle and not the steak." I understood whispering, not screaming. I understood restraint. Admittedly, in the early days of Dogwood we were certainly whistling as we walked past the graveyard. And soon the graveyard was in the rearview mirror. But we kept on whistling.

CHAPTER 22

THEY DON'T LAY EGGS, AND THEY DON'T GIVE MILK, BUT . . .

The case of mistaken identity, known as "The Wiggolinski Affair," was the ruination of Barry McGillivray.

Old Barry was a likeable, companionable son of a gun—so companionable, in fact, that he had imported some old friends from Canada who were seeking warm shelter for the winter season. These were a couple of amiable, rough-hewn types who did not bring much class to the Dogwood staff, but they were effective drinking companions for Barry.

For a while I had noticed in a few evening phone conversations that Barry had a tendency to slur his words, and a few times when I was on the farm he preferred to be where I was not.

Barry had brought a new bride with him to the farm, and he was now having some complicated marital travails. He would take a drink with little or no provocation, and given provocation, he would really get serious. His "better half" was furnishing ample provocation. He was a gifted liar and, when confronted, would have all sorts of plausible excuses for any indications of drinking on the job. I wanted to believe him, because it was more convenient to give him another chance.

Barry ingratiated himself to me that Christmas when he proudly gave me a two-week-old pit bulldog. We named him Dempsey. This dog was bred by Ocala's dean of bulldog fighting men, a legendary horseman—and fighting man per se—one Clayton O'Quinn. More about Dempsey, a provocative sort, later on.

In early spring we were beginning to ship freshly turned two-year-olds to the races—our own and those of our clients. One load had four Dogwood horses going to two of our trainers, two to Frank Alexander at Belmont Park in New

York, and two to Larry Jennings at Monmouth Park in New Jersey. Another bleakly endowed, two-year-old filly belonged to a Maryland client named Morris Wiggolinski, and his horse (Mamma's Moolah) was to go to a trainer at Suffolk Downs in Boston.

Mr. Wiggolinski was a nervous type, harboring high hopes for his horse, and had required considerable hand-holding during the winter.

Barry and his helpers got the five horses ready, and late one night the van pulled out for the East.

One of the horses going to Frank Alexander at Belmont Park was a racy, attractive bay filly named for my sister, Sally Waldron. The aforementioned Mamma's Moolah was also bay, but a dumpy, lazy little thing.

Several weeks later, in a conversation with Frank Alexander, I asked about Sally Waldron's progress.

"Well, she's okay, I guess. I breezed her, and she went pretty slow. She's kinda' deadheaded," Frank reported.

"Deadheaded? That filly's pretty flighty, wound up tight," I said.

"She's not too wound up here," Frank came back.

In a week or two, I got a call from Wiggolinski: "The horse identifier at Suffolk Downs came by my trainer's barn to lip tattoo Mamma's Moolah, and he said the Jockey Club papers don't match the horse. My trainer called your farm manager, and he said not to worry about it. Are you sure we've got the right horse?"

I briskly suggested the horse identifier try again.

Two more weeks went by with more calls from the agitated Wiggolinski, who still couldn't get his filly tattooed so she could race. Then I got a call from Frank Alexander, saying our filly had bucked her shins, though she really hadn't gone fast enough to do it. "I'm going to ship her back to you because she'll needed pin-firing," Frank reported.

Several days later Sally Waldron was led off a horse van at Dogwood. But, it was NOT Sally Waldron. Instead we were welcoming good old Mamma's Moolah. Barry's face turned a deep shade of red.

I surmised—and found out from other sources—that Barry and the boys were in the midst of a rather festive party the night the horses were prepared for shipping, and the halters identifying Mamma's Moolah and Sally Waldron were switched.

We called Wiggolinski and gave him the great news that we had indeed shipped the wrong horse—as he had been insisting to deaf ears. And, on top of that, his beloved Mamma's Moolah had bucked her shins while in the care of the wrong trainer. This put him in a contentious frame of mind. Contentious enough that his attorney called, and we soon agreed to send him a check for five thousand dollars, rehab the filly, and then ship her back to his trainer at no cost.

At my strong suggestion, Barry sought employment elsewhere.

Barry's replacement was on the farm within a week, and I knew he could be. I had kept in touch with my old friend and trainer Elwood McCann, and knew that he had taken a farm manager's job in Virginia. As boozing was taking its toll on Barry, I had queried Elwood about his availability. I knew that he would come to Dogwood when I pulled the trigger.

All of the travails of Dogwood Farm and the horse business don't sound like a funfest. But, despite that, I was having the time of my life in my new career. Racehorses and horseracing—and all that has gone with them for close to forty years now—have put me right where I want to be in my life. I adore the ups, and I can handle the downs; and there are plenty of the latter. It has been said, "It is not a game for boys in short pants."

If you wanted to go through life on an even keel, not straying from the middle of the road, then racing horses—any aspect of it—would drive you nutty. A predisposition toward post mortems, brooding about what could have been, or dwelling on disasters—these tendencies would make being in racing a miserable existence. When I see a person heartbroken because his horse ran second, I think how hopeless it is that they are engaging in a business or pastime where they are demanding a window of satisfaction that is infinitesimal. A racing man or woman must gain satisfaction from a good effort—not necessarily a win (which, if you are *lucky*, will occur about twenty percent of the time).

And there must be a keen appreciation of class, and enjoyment of the quest for it. What exactly is "class"? Is it courage, poise, guts, determination, quality? It's all of those things. It's just *class*. And what an awe-inspiring thing it is when you encounter it in man or beast. When you really see it, you'll know it. It certainly could never be confused with what we know in racing as "cheap speed." The horse with cheap speed is one with ability who comes roaring out of the gate, opens up a five-length lead, and looks invincible. But if another horse can look him in the eye, he will quit. He throws in the towel. That's cheap speed. Have we not encountered it in our fellow men?

A perfect example of being confident in a horse's class occurred in the running of the 1989 Preakness, with the splendid rivalry of two indomitable horses, Easy Goer and Sunday Silence. With Sunday Silence on the lead and Easy Goer engaging him from the outside, they hit the sixteenth pole, and neither fine horse would blink. Easy Goer simply could not get past Sunday Silence. So his marvelous jockey, Pat Day, steered the big horse right up against Sunday Silence and turned his face toward the other horse as if to say, "Now look him in the eye, and put him away. Dominate him!" Pat knew he had "class" to call on, and it was a logical move. Easy Goer got on even terms but lost to his rival by the bob of a head at the wire.

I got in the horse business, and am still in it today, for one reason and one reason only: I am beguiled by all horses. But I truly adore—repeat, adore—a class horse.

What created this obsession with horses, and particularly racehorses?

As I have said before, it started with my grandfather in New Orleans. Dick Cothran was the definition of a gentleman. And he was a gambler. He was a big time cotton speculator, and in his suite of offices he had a special room in which he had ensconced a professional horseracing handicapper with telegraph and telephone hook-ups to every major racetrack in the country.

Dick Cothran bet the horses—through bookmakers—every day of his business life. I remember well as a child the absolute enchantment of visiting this wonderfully exciting room, tended to by a pale, chain-smoking, nervous character named Edmund.

My grandfather would leave the floor of the exchange periodically during the day and scurry up to the "race room," where he and Edmund would confer over a page from the popular racing paper of the day, *The Morning Telegraph*. There would be some brief, serious murmuring, and then Edmund would nod his head with whatever degree of approval my grandfather's final decision had evinced. He would then call in a bet, usually just a few minutes before post time.

Often, when we came downtown to pick up my grandfather in late afternoon, I was permitted to go in and visit the "race room." Maybe, if the timing was right, I would get to listen through the headphones to a race call of, say, the eighth at Belmont Park. I can recall even today the excitement, mystery, and the tension of that room. It had exquisite allure and charisma compared to today's off-track betting parlors, simulcast centers, or the race books in Las Vegas or Atlantic City.

There was no television then. There were no betting windows, no plethora of races running within minutes of each other, no cocktail waitresses in scanty garb, no glitz. There was just old Edmund; the magical earphones; the clacking ticker tape; old-time, stand-up telephone instruments; the alert demeanor of these gambling men; and their quiet, terse phone conversations.

The idea that this exercise revolved around gorgeous horses trying to out-race each other in glamorous, far-off places set me on fire.

And I think often of the delicious thrill of that wonderful May day in 1934 when I put the big earphones on and heard the electrifying call of Cavalcade's Kentucky Derby victory, made so much sweeter by Papa's having given me two dollars to wager on this special occasion.

Alas, Dick Cothran was wiped out in 1935—not by the horses, but by the nosedive taken by the cotton market.

Readers with a gambling bent will be delighted that he partially solved his downturn by—of all things—buying a book on how to play poker. Though he had never played poker, he read and completely absorbed this book, memorized the percentages, and in no time could tell you the exact mathematical likelihood of drawing to an inside straight or turning two pair into a full house.

In the middle of the 1930s, he supported his family by playing poker three times a week at the better social clubs of New Orleans. When cotton made a comeback, he resumed trading. But thank God for poker in the meantime. He did much better with poker than he did with the horses, but he never quit trying because he did love a racehorse and a horse race.

The next influence came through my father's interest in show horses. I rode and showed them with great success, becoming champion amateur rider of three states. I groomed them, lived with them, got to know something about a horse, and loved the animals.

My father—who liked any kind of horse—and I visited Kentucky in the '30s and spent our days going to see Man o'War, Twenty Grand, Exterminator, Equipoise, and—later—Whirlaway, Citation, and other special horses. Man o'War fractured me. I can still see him, posing with his head up high, his ears pricked, gazing out at the horizon. Perhaps he was reliving his battles with John P. Grier, Sir Barton, Upset, and other cracks of his day. His famous groom, Will Harbut, stood at his head, jiggling his lead shank and carrying on about "the mostest hoss."

But perhaps it was the simple, understated grave of a racehorse that did the most to light the fire. In a small plot of ground, surrounded by a charming old Kentucky stone wall and a grove of trees, was the burial site of the legendary Domino. The stone marker, still there today, reads:

"Here lies the fleetest runner the American Turf has ever known. And the gamest and most generous of horses."

That stark epitaph speaks volumes to the imagination . . . or at least it did to mine.

Then toss into this mix listening to the great races of the day on the radio, called dramatically by the driving, gravelly voice of Clem McCarthy.

I was primed to love the Thoroughbred racehorse, and the characters that surrounded him.

Wonderful racehorses have always had the power to move the public. At the turn of the century, when Dan Patch, the great harness horse, would travel by rail to his engagements around the country, literally thousands of fans would line the roadbed just to watch the superlative pacer roll by in his boxcar.

Man o'War was—and still is—a household name. The magical sound of those words, along with Red Grange, Jack Dempsey, and Babe Ruth, are synonymous with an exciting era in our history.

People in all walks of life still talk about that magnificent, golden chestnut running machine, Secretariat, and his winning the Belmont Stakes in 1973 by thirty-one widening lengths. All the people who claimed to have been there would fill up the state of New Hampshire!

I often think about when I was eleven years old and saw the legendary trotting horse, Greyhound, when he went for the world record, by himself and working only against the clock.

This was at an old-timey state fair in Sedalia, Missouri, with a ragtag crowd of about a thousand looking on from a grassy bank—and it was a scene straight out of the movie *Paper Moon*. When the fabulous grey streak came spinning out of the turn at about a forty-five degree angle, his driver asked him the question, and Greyhound gave him the answer! As he swept past us with his furious rush, a black man in overalls, seated to my left, slowly got to his feet, almost in shock and wonderment. He grabbed the tattered felt hat off his head, crushed it in his hand and screamed out, "Gawd a mighty DAMN!" He took the words right out of my mouth.

Rudyard Kipling wrote, "Four things greater than all things are—Women and Horses and Power and War."

God only knows what the common ingredients are that have caused Queen Elizabeth II, the Aga Khan, Sheikh Mohammed, Winston Churchill, Bernard Baruch, Sam Shepard, Jake Delhomme, Rick Pitino, Paul Mellon, Burt Bacharach, Gary Player, on down the scale of diversity to Suzie Glutz and Joe Schmo to be engrossed with the capability of a large, four-legged animal to get from Point A to Point B sooner than some other large, four-legged animals.

What could those factors be? I wouldn't be able to get my arms around them. But I do believe this: When a person owns a horse, breeds a horse, works around a horse, bets on a horse, or, for any reason, just pulls for a horse, that beautiful, intriguing animal becomes an extension of one's own persona. And it makes a successful shot to the moon seem possible. It is *hope*—always a wonderful commodity.

Several years ago, my wife Anne and I were killing time in our box at Saratoga as a thirty-five thousand dollar claiming race was about to be run. It was a very modest event by Saratoga standards, and since I am an infrequent bettor, definitely of minor interest to me.

Several minutes before the horses loaded in the gate for the mile and one-sixteenth race, three men rushed into the adjacent, empty box. It was not their box; they were just taking advantage of a spot from which to watch a race in which they obviously had particular interest. They were pleasant-looking, middle-aged fellows, dressed casually, and a couple of them were drinking beer. But there was an intensity about them that indicated they were on a mission.

One of them muttered as the horses approached the gate, "Awright, Edgar, now don't screw it up!"

The situation aroused my interest. My detective instincts told me they had a horse in the race, and Edgar Prado must be the jockey. I looked on the program and deduced that the "seven horse" was theirs. She was a six-year-old gray mare, owned by the "Jersey Boys Stable." A quick look at the *Daily Racing Form* told me that Polar Princess was one of those honest, hard-knocking, old campaigners that didn't have a lot of talent but consistently tried like hell. She was 12-1 on the tote board.

The boys remained standing in the box as the horses loaded in front of the stands thirty yards down to our left.

The break came, and as they went through the first turn, the gray Polar Princess was tucked in about eighth in the full field. She was nine lengths from the lead.

The gray-haired man in the windbreaker and floppy golf hat standing nearest us had his glasses trained on the mare, and he murmured, "That's the way, Momma!"

Down the backstretch the horses went in that same order. "Come on, Momma!" I heard him say.

Now I'm getting wrapped up in this race.

They're into the far turn now, and "Momma" is starting to pick it up a little. She's six lengths out of it, Edgar has her in the clear, and she's got running on her mind!

"Come on, Momma!" A little louder and more insistent this time.

They're at the eighth pole now, and this gray mare is driving! She's three lengths out of it and closing like a freight train.

They're all yelling now. "*Come on, Momma!*"

At the sixteenth pole, this horse is head and head for the lead, and she's going to get there!

At this point a blood-curdling scream: "GODDAMN, MOMMA! ONE TIME FOR THE BOYS!"

One time for the boys. That's what it's all about.

My enthusiasm has always been there; it has never faltered (well, maybe for a minute or two every now and then) and it continues unabated to this day.

But good horses would need to come along and fan the flames for Dogwood. And they would. One in particular would come in 1976—at a propitious time. He would strike a mighty, and a lasting, blow for the cause. Never has a day passed since that I have not thought about him.

His name was Dominion.

CHAPTER 23

FOREIGN AFFAIRS AND FAMILY MUSINGS

Anne and I had vacationed in England for the first time in the early '70s and loved it. While in London we had been put in touch with Dick Francis, the famous English steeplechase rider who became the world's leading mystery writer (with the strong right arm of his wife Mary). We had gone racing with Dick, and they had entertained us in their home in Didcot. Our trip was cut short with sad news that Anne's father had died of a heart attack. We hurried back to LaGrange, Georgia.

Our visit inspired me to return many times over the next decade. I learned that for around $150,000 one could buy a sound, stakes-caliber racehorse, often with already established minor residual value for stud duty. Racing people in this country had not yet "discovered" England, Ireland, and France. I often flew the wonderful supersonic Concorde (justified by the need to get there quickly to see and buy a certain horse that had just gone on the market).

I loved the country and admired the racing—where the people lined up ten-deep outside the paddock, referring to horses' names and not numbers ("Ooh, just look at Ganimede! Isn't he a picture!"). I became well known in the British racing industry. Anne often went with me on those visits, and we made many friends and had fun there.

Arguably, Dogwood would go on to import more racehorses than any other outfit in the history of American racing. The mid-Seventies to mid-Eighties was a good time to do it. Later, American racehorse buyers got the hang of it, and by 1985 the High Street in Newmarket resembled Rodeo Drive, teeming (mostly) with Californians looking for racehorses.

I got started with a bloodstock agent named Michael Motion, an energetic, well-connected, gentlemanly sort of fellow. I bought several nice horses at public auction through Michael, and we combed the yards of the leading trainers for established racing prospects.

The first significant horse I bought was Western Jewel, a speedy chestnut filly. She could fly—fly for five-eighths of a mile—but only on grass, not on dirt. Thus the window of opportunity in this country (where there are virtually no turf sprints) was about the size of a peephole. We were forced to run her in middle distance grass races. Her tactic—her only tactic—was to go as far and as fast as she could. She ran on the straight in England, but had to negotiate turns on our race tracks. Her fruitless pattern then was to break on top, roar into the first turn with a gigantic lead, where centrifugal force would cause her to end up in the parking lot. I learned a lot about English importations from Western Jewel.

On one of our tours, Michael and I had gone by the facilities of a trainer named Arthur Budgett, and we were shown a promising three-year-old. He was not for sale but might be later. His name was Dominion, and he was being readied to run in the Two Thousand Guineas, one of the English classics, comparable to our Preakness Stakes.

I fell in love with the horse. I went into the stall to examine him. A wee lad was nervously holding this muscular bay colt. When I walked up to him and put my hand on his shoulder to gauge his size, he made an indelible impression on me. He quickly cocked his head around and looked me straight in the eye as if to say, "What the hell do you think you're doing?" Man, did he have charisma. He was a smallish horse, with a fine head. He had a luminous eye about the size of your fist and was muscled to his eyebrows. Talk about the look of class! I loved it that he immediately reminded me of Spencer Tracy.

He was third in the Guineas, then ran respectably in the Epsom Derby, and then went to Germany and won a big race. He knocked off one in France early the next year. And then his owner died.

Michael Motion called me right after the last rites were administered. He suggested that he try to buy the horse, bypassing the trainer (who might have had a tendency to knock the deal because he wanted to keep the horse in his care), and go straight to the widow and offer £90,000 ($130,000 then). Michael gritted his teeth impatiently for a barely decent interval after the funeral. He made his offer and succeeded in securing the horse. Best day's work he ever did, from my standpoint.

The horse came to the States, and never has one horse done more for one outfit than Dominion did for Dogwood Stable. He was our first major racehorse. And he danced every dance. He ran in the big races from Saratoga to New Orleans and from Chicago to Miami. He didn't care what town he was in; he came to race. You had *him* to beat. Our green and yellow silks were popping up in the glamour races on many Saturday afternoons at five o'clock.

Dogwood needed to prove that we could compete in the major leagues. Dominion led the charge and pressed the attack for several years.

Rarely in life is there that one, well-defined moment when you know that a mighty blow has been struck for the cause. That moment clearly came for me and my outfit one August afternoon in Saratoga Springs, New York. It was the running of the Bernard Baruch Handicap, a very prestigious race at a renowned racetrack.

A large, contentious field was assembled that day, and the racing glitterati were out to watch. When the field of eleven came down the turf course past the stands for the first time, Dominion was tucked in around fifth in the early running, riding the hedge and biding his time. He edged a little closer as the field went into the final turn, with about a half-mile left to run. And when they swung into the stretch, Dominion didn't have to be asked. He knew the drill. It was time to go to work. He launched his bid; and as they quickened through the stretch, five of them were spread out across the course. In the middle was the tenacious Dominion. With his ears flat on his neck and his "belly on the ground," inch-by-inch he fought his way through that long stretch and won by a hotly contested three-quarters of a length.

I had to struggle not to make a complete ass of myself. As we made our way through the box section, glorified by such as Lillian Russell, Diamond Jim Brady, and John L. Sullivan, you could really feel the thaw: "Maybe this Dogwood outfit is okay after all. They sure threw a quality horse at us today." It was a great moment, and the applause for the victory had significance, I do believe. The trophy was presented by Bernard Baruch's daughter (who looked like old Bernard himself, with a wig on).

There was certainly never a conspiracy among the fat cats to squelch Dogwood, but the racing establishment has always been somewhat of an "Old Boys Club." It has never maintained a "Welcome Wagon" for new wrinkles, and the original idea of a partnership owning a racehorse seemed a little gauche. The traditional old racing stables definitely were not enchanted at that time with the Dogwood group ownership concept.

It was that same suspicious demeanor that greeted me when I went up to Kentucky a year or so before for what was called "A Day In Kentucky," a seminar hosted by the Kentucky Thoroughbred Breeders' Association, designed to attract new people to the horse business. That translates: designed to get new money.

In a lovely setting at one of the storied old farms, around one hundred visitors gathered to hear from some of the area's most respected commercial Thoroughbred breeders. I paid my fee and went. There had been a fair amount written in the financial and trade publications about my new concept which facilitated entry into the game, so many of the attending guests had heard of me and Dogwood. The truth is that what Dogwood could offer was the ideal way for many of them to enter the sport. So, logically, during the question and answer session, one of them asked, "What about this racing partnership idea that Dogwood Stable thought up?" Someone else suggested, "I think Mr. Campbell is here. Could he tell us a little about it?"

Well, several of the organizers became very uneasy. Finally, with great reluctance, one said, "Cot, would you want to give us a *very brief* rundown on what you do?" This was incredibly shortsighted, because—as stated earlier—we were the conduit by which new money could be brought into the horse industry.

Today, some of those same people who looked down their noses at our approach are partners in Dogwood horses. Much of horse racing currently is driven by partnerships patterned after ours, and originally conceived by us.

But it is true that after winning the Bernard Baruch with that wonderful horse, there was discernible defrosting. Penny Chenery (owner of Secretariat and a longtime booster of the Dogwood concept) was having a cocktail party that afternoon, and so many of the Old Guard were there; Anne and I sensed that they were genuinely appreciative of that horse's performance and accepting of our participation in the sport. Adding fuel to our small victory bonfire was the fact that within half an hour of Dominion's win, we got the wonderful news that Delta Flag had splashed through the mud to win the $100,000 Monmouth Invitational at that Jersey shore racetrack. What a hell of an important day!

Within months, Nizon, Pessu, and Practitioner would all win stakes and push the stable to a high spot on the national list of winning owners. But Dominion was the guy that got it going. It was his impetus that created a gigantic step forward.

When Dominion's racing days were over in 1978, we sold him back to England for stud duty. Predictably, he turned out a steady stream of hard-knocking, honest horses. He was five times champion sire of England. I went to see him whenever I was in England. And when I would walk up to him and pat him on the shoulder, he would quickly turn and look at me, as if to say, "What the hell do you think you're doing? Don't take any liberties with me, big boy!" just as he did years earlier when he was a promising young racehorse.

For me, Dominion was "one of the ones."

So you see, my importation program was a significant contributing factor to the Dogwood success story—and personally pleasurable to me, Anne, and our daughters Cary and Lila. We attended Royal Ascot as a family. These four June days of tip-top racing, with the crowd dripping with tails-and-top-hatted elegance and haute couture bedazzlement, are unmatched anywhere for glamour. It is also the greatest concentration of fops in the universe.

During an Ascot visit, our family visited Sandringham, the Queen's Stud. This great experience came through our friendship with Sir Michael and Lady Angela Oswald. He was manager of the Queen's Stud (translated to mean one of her landed estates, and a very large Thoroughbred breeding farm), and Lady Angela was Lady-In-Waiting to the Queen Mother, another avid racing enthusiast. We spent several days with the Oswalds. Later, they and their children visited us several times in Atlanta.

Understandably, this English involvement led to Lila working in London for an equine insurance concern. And what a fabulous experience for a young girl that was.

I continued to pop over to London and/or Paris at the drop of a hat in those days. I knew the horses and the players and moved easily around the nearby Thoroughbred training environs. Most of my horse hunting during that productive decade of importation was done with a wonderful fellow named James Wigan, who replaced Michael Motion when that man and his family moved to the States. James became a close friend of Anne and mine.

When half the horse world began converging on Newmarket, Lambourne, and Chantilly, buying horses at decent prices became impossible, and I was sad when I had to quit that market. We stay in touch with James and see him when he comes over here to the American sales.

*   *   *

One would assume that I lived and breathed the horse business, which can easily consume a person. But I had no intention of being consumed. I always kept a good balance in my life when in the advertising business, and I did the same when in the horse business.

I'm sure I have many undesirable characteristics—and I pointed out in vivid detail quite a few of them earlier in this saga. But one of my desirable ones is that I am organized; I am a planner; I'm looking over the next hill to see what might be coming. I have got Plan A, B, and C (a worst case scenario). Consequently, never in my business career have I found it necessary to work all night to develop a report, or stay until midnight to prepare tomorrow's presentation. I am way ahead of the game.

I arranged to have ample time for my family and for normal outside activities: Rotary Club, tennis, squash, movies, theater, bridge, spectator sports, vacations at the beach, friends, you name it. I may have gone into an unorthodox livelihood by Atlanta standards, but I meant to keep participating in the normal pattern of life there.

Not that I needed it, but the woman I married would have helped me maintain that healthy equilibrium.

Perhaps it does her an injustice for me to attempt to describe Anne Campbell. My powers of portrayal are not adequate. I will say that she has been the ideal wife. She has a wonderful personality, fabulous sense of humor, delightful enthusiasm, and a remarkable disposition.

She is strong, has guts aplenty, but is anxious to please and does not want to cause trouble or inconvenience to anyone. In fact, the last characteristic is best demonstrated by the fact that when she was a child, she was once being transported with other children in the back seat of a 1948 Ford V8. This two-door model featured front seats that tilted forward to enable passengers to gain admittance to the back seat. Somehow the seat was tilted forward and then released—released on Anne's foot. She did not want to bother the driver so she did not bring this dilemma to her attention. The destination was not a distant one, fortunately.

Throw in that she's a good mother, smart, a snappy tap dancer, and is enormously interested in me and anything that involves me. And she's plenty good-looking!

She is certainly the best friend I have ever had and a world-class companion. So I would not want to do much that did not include her.

A lot of the horse business has involved her. But neither of us ever had any intention of Dogwood Farm/Stable being a "Mom and Pop" operation. She has been a vital part of everything I have ever done. She has no job with Dogwood, yet she has a job description:

1. Travel with the president, when possible
2. Provide counsel to the president, when requested (often)
3. Exude charm

She has performed these services unfailingly and, thus, has played a major role in the successes of Dogwood Farm, Inc.; Burton-Campbell, Inc., before that; and, most importantly, W. Cothran Campbell.

So Anne always maintained her own life. She was a factor in the civic sphere of Atlanta life. She was the co-founder of Village Atlanta, Inc., a haven for down-and-out battered women; she was the first woman to serve on the Board of United Appeal; and she was president of the Atlanta Junior League, the largest Junior League in America. The latter was a remarkable achievement, because she came to Atlanta as an adult and had no family or social connections to aid her in her election to that post. In addition, for twenty-six years she has taught a very popular Bible Study.

Anne loves the racing stable, loves the races, and loves the horses—but does not desire any physical contact with the animals. And they pick up on that fact. Amusingly, she may be asked by a client who thinks Dogwood *is* a "Mom and Pop" organization, "How's my filly doing? When do you think she might run?" She has no idea who the filly is, or how she is doing—and says that.

The quality of Campbell "family life" (to use a Norman Rockwellian term) was heightened further for me by the fact that Anne and I produced two mighty fine daughters, Cary and Lila, foals of 1960 and 1963, respectively. They were both superb young girls and grew up free of any dire, residual adolescent miscues.

Cary grew up with a buttoned-up, conscientious approach to life, went to both private and public schools, tried hard to do the right thing and did it. She worked on Dogwood Farm in the early days, and later—after graduation from Davidson College—served ably as editor of the *Dogwood Newsletter*. She has a strong literary bent. She is a gifted editor.

She rode horses and showed a little bit when she was young, but we were delighted when she abandoned what is a complicated activity. Cary always had a keen understanding of the nuances of horse racing, and not many big moments for Dogwood came without her being present. Her first introduction came at age six when I took her to Lexington. We visited the racetrack and many farms, and I spent most of my time combing her hair and arranging the barrette.

She was a good companion then and has become a warm, engaging, witty woman, with a great flair for conversation and for making people feel comfortable and important.

She married a fine man named Andrew Umhau, today a popular doctor in Washington, D. C., and they have three intriguing children. We are all very good friends.

Her oldest child is Lila. She did not inherit her grandfather's lack of appreciation for educational opportunities. She is twenty years old and is a super-bright student at the University of Chicago. She speaks Russian. She is attracted to the downtrodden. You couldn't pay her to go to St. Bart's, but she'd head for Rwanda or Somalia in a heartbeat.

Carter is a seventeen-year-old daughter, and she, too, has a heavy concentration of the milk of human kindness, having made numerous humanitarian trips to Katrina-ravaged Biloxi, as well as needy Central American countries. She is tall, striking in appearance, and has much mystique.

The third offspring is Charlie, fifteen and a character. He is big into Civil War re-enacting but, alas, wages war on the side of the Yankees. He has thus far not indicated that he is as studious as his older sisters, but he is plenty bright and is likely to have much style.

He certainly had it when he came to visit us in Saratoga when he was eleven. He got off the plane in a very smart, tan, poplin suit, with sharp shirt and tie. And on his head was a jauntily angled sailor-style straw boater. An hour later, he was the sensation of the Saratoga Racetrack. People were clustered around our box (because of Charlie) like bees around honey.

Our younger daughter is Lila, equally as wonderful as Cary, but one who matured with an early appetite for the adventurous and an inclination to make questionable moves—not disastrous moves, but often ones that caused complications. She has three children also and has had three husbands. The present one—Tommy Tindall, permanent I am sure—is ideal; and the previous two were good guys. And they're all friends now, a neat accomplishment.

She, too, went with me to Kentucky when she was quite young. Lila was not a gabby child and could be withdrawn, shy, and preoccupied. Nothing significant, she just was. She grew out of that as a teenager.

How well Anne and I remember being in Louisville for the Kentucky Derby and staying with friends who had laid on a pretty big dinner party in our honor. Just as the first guests were arriving, our hosts called us to the phone. It was a long distance call from Lila. In a voice taut with emotion and remorse, she advised that she and other fifteen-year-olds were picked up by the authorities for drinking beer in one of Atlanta's public parks. It all got straightened out, but it was most disconcerting at the time.

Saratoga always brought out the festive side of Lila's nature. One of our trainers, Frank Alexander, was staying in a basement apartment in our rented house, and we all laugh today that when Frank was headed out to the barn at dawn, he once encountered Lila coming in.

Was she headed toward being a chip off the old block? No, not by a longshot. Today, she—like Cary—is deeply religious. She is unrelenting in her desire to do the right thing and has an urge to right every wrong she runs across. She is a superb mother and has an overabundance of compassion and empathy galore.

Lila also went to both public and private high schools in Atlanta, and then went to Hollins College and the University of Georgia. She accomplished nothing at either place, and her mother and I suggested she quit and go to work. She did and made a fine employee. Most of Lila's learning came from being out in the world. Later on, she too served as *Dogwood Newsletter* editor. Like Cary, she can write.

She has an eighteen-year-old daughter, Campbell Glenn; a seven-year-old boy, Brady Tindall; and a five-year-old son named Cot Tindall.

Anne and I had a strong role in the raising of Campbell, who was quite young when her mother and father divorced—quite harmoniously. She grew up in Aiken.

She was a star from the time she was born. I am not one who automatically thinks every relative I have is outstanding, but I know this one is. She is pretty and petite, but her personality is gigantic.

I also made the Kentucky trip with Campbell when she was five. She was a great companion then, as she is now.

On our trip, which included the races (and a win), I asked her where she would like to have dinner, suggesting a variety of places. She selected the Waffle House. When we settled in there, she wanted to play the jukebox (standard equipment at Waffle Houses), but only one selection appealed to her, and we played it over and over. Campbell and I dined at the Waffle House while listening interminably to "The Star Spangled Banner."

Brady is a spectacularly handsome child, athletic and super-energetic. He is sweet, witty, and conscientious, but "all boy."

His younger brother is burdened with the name Cot, a point of great pride to his grandfather. He is an adorable-looking boy with a profusion of blonde curls. Cot has a beguiling personality, augmented by a deep, fog-horn voice which he uses with great gusto.

Sons-in-law are dicey propositions, and I am a finicky father-in-law, possessed of a perfectionist nature. That said, I state that my two sons-in-law—Andrew and Tommy—are true stars. I credit luck and the superb taste of my daughters. Both guys are successful, fine men, good fathers, and among my small coterie of best friends.

The aforementioned lack of application to educational opportunities is something the mother, Lila, came by naturally, I am afraid. I certainly never had much education. When it was there for me, I was not ready to absorb it. This was not due to any shortcomings of the various institutions. But my own situation—and observations of the college scene generally—has caused me to believe that not every human being needs to go to college. Are you keen to be an aeronautical engineer, or an orthodontist, or a lawyer? Then it wouldn't be a bad idea to go to college. But if a kid has no idea what he's going to do, rather than major in Greek or basket weaving or modern dance, and lay around and raise hell, he or she would be better off going to work. You can goof off completely in college, but you can't if someone is paying you a salary to do something. I learned more in two years on newspapers than I did in my entire educational career.

Learning sometimes comes the hard way, which describes perfectly the process by which I educated myself on the selection of a compatible "pet" for a family of city dwellers.

This has to do with Dempsey, the wonderful pit bull given to me by an earlier farm manager. Appealing though he was, Dempsey did not blend easily into a congenial residential neighborhood. Perhaps this was predictable.

Dempsey was bred in Ocala by the renowned Clayton O'Quinn, a major breeder of fighting dogs and a man interested in all aspects of fighting. Clayton owned Dempsey's sire, Bully, a legendary dog who campaigned in Chicago and went through the ranks of fighting dogs there and elsewhere like Grant took Richmond. Dempsey's mother died producing his litter, and he was sent up to Dogwood on a horse van when he was two weeks old.

The sweet, pitiful little puppy was fed with an eye dropper until he began to thrive. Anne, the girls, and I were all enthused about Dempsey, although we already had a little dachshund-type, mixed-breed female named Nell. We were sure that despite Dempsey's heritage of bellicosity, if raised in a home of harmony and love, he would become a sweet-natured, affable pet.

Dempsey soon got off the milk bottle and developed rapidly. He grew to stand about twenty-four inches tall, and he was brindle in color, had a massive chest, and was muscled up like our horse, Dominion. He had an awesome head and jaw, and his eyes were sort of a supernatural yellow, rather like a cat. He would get your attention, old Dempsey!

Let me quickly point out here that I do not espouse dog fighting. I did not want Dempsey to fight any dog or human and hoped that he would not. But (and this may have a connection with my love of courageous racehorses) I was intrigued with the fact that a pit bull would fight until he died. I did not want to see or encourage that, but I liked knowing that he would. I did!

The first year of Dempsey's life was harmonious, and he had an almost timorous, obsequious way about him. When his play irritated the tiny Nell, she would growl or snap at him, and Dempsey would flinch fearfully into a corner. He was anxious to stay on the good side of Nell. And so he was with all humans. Dempsey could not have been more affable or affectionate with people.

One day when he was a year old I was walking him on a leash through the neighborhood. We unwisely passed a house on a hill where two Rottweilers dwelled. They spied Dempsey and me strolling by. Enraged at our temerity, they came charging ferociously down the drive, snarling and almost in a frenzy. They scared the living hell out of me, and I thought, "Oh Lord, they're going to kill my dog, and probably me in the process."

When they got within twenty feet of us, and I was bracing for the onslaught, Dempsey turned and stared at them, beaming those yellow eyes into theirs. I don't know what the message was, but it was effective. Those two big dogs slammed on the brakes, came skidding to a halt, looked at us for a moment, then put their tails between their legs and trotted back up the driveway.

Dempsey seemed to have reached that point in life when he knew that his time had arrived. He was a man.

A few days later, Anne and I were sunning ourselves in the backyard. Dempsey and Nell lay nearby—just a pleasant, relaxing weekend interlude. Anne had strongly suggested that we keep Dempsey tied up, but I insisted that he should be permitted to roam freely.

Our next-door neighbor was a widow with whom we had had some minor disagreements. She was a tad neurotic, slightly on the prickly side, with a marked inclination toward the dramatic. She owned a little white dog with a startling profusion of hair. This was "Fluff."

As we dozed in the sun on this pleasant spring afternoon, suddenly we heard shrill canine shrieks from next door. We looked up and saw that Dempsey was missing. I called him, then went next door to investigate. There in a bed of ivy crouched Dempsey, with white tufts of Fluff surfacing occasionally through the ivy, as he struggled to get away from Dempsey's chokehold. Fluff was screaming; his owner understandably was frenzied and was demonstrating it by bellowing, "Oh, my God!" She was half-collapsed against a tree, with the back of her hand pressed to her forehead, and looking skyward as if seeking divine intervention.

I plunged into the ivy, took off my tennis shoe, and smote Dempsey about twenty times on his head. Finally, he relaxed his hold on Fluff. Fluff was fine, it turned out, but if nature had been allowed to take its course, he surely would not have been. We apologized profusely and promised that Dempsey would never be permitted to return.

But it was becoming clear that Dempsey—as devoted to us as he was—might not be a pet ideally suited for our situation.

I got a formidable-looking muzzle for the dog and equipped him with that when we walked. He looked like a canine Hannibal Lecter. I took him once to an art show in Piedmont Park. It was swarming with browsers, and when I strolled through there with Dempsey, muzzled and fearsome with his demeanor and yellow eyes, it was like Moses parting the Red Sea.

It broke my heart, but I had to give Dempsey away. Dogwood's blacksmith, who lived near the farm, was overjoyed to have him. He kept us up-to-date on Dempsey, faithfully recounting details of this pit bulldog.

One involved the time Dempsey broke his leg. The blacksmith was driving down the highway in his pickup; Dempsey was in the back, guarding his equipment. Dempsey saw a large dog on the side of the road. Traveling at sixty miles an hour, over the side he went, broke his leg, then attacked the dog. When Smokey the farrier backed up he found him with the broken leg, preparing to put the finishing touches on the poor dog.

Dempsey, sad to say, had a short life. Shortly afterward, he was kicked in the head by a bull he had attacked.

In the final analysis, Nell and the bull were the only animals that could handle him.

CHAPTER 24

THE ANATOMY OF PARTNERSHIPS

A round the late Seventies, I developed a sixth sense for spotting, when they called on the phone, would-be syndicators wanting to "go to school" on Dogwood. First sign would be considerable reticence about the background of the caller ("What is my business? Oh, I'm into different investments . . ."). Then, there would not be much interest in details of what horse or horses were involved. The payoff was the request that we send the legal agreement ("So I can see what I'm getting into. Heh Heh").

There were beginning to be many individuals hankering to form partnerships. And brokerage houses, always subject to fads (oil and gas tax shelter deals, leases on barges and railroad cars, cattle breeding and feeding schemes), decided to tackle horses. Legg Mason, Prudential, Merrill Lynch, and lots of other biggies got into racing and breeding offerings. Some were well conceived. Others had irresponsible projections ("We'll buy twenty mares, breed them, sell the yearlings in the Summer Sale . . . let's see, last year's yearling average was $400,000, so twenty times $400,000? . . . Presto! Eight million a year!").

The chink in the armor of a horse deal is that to present it properly you must warn the investor that if he is going into this to make money, he's probably going to be disappointed. If he doesn't love horses it doesn't make sense. Investment counselors would choke over such a pitch.

No brokerage firm ever did any good with any horse deal, and some of them got the hell sued out of them.

Practically every horse partnership in existence today—and there are plenty of them—got started (directly or indirectly) with a Dogwood legal agreement. Imitation may indeed by the sincerest form of flattery, but if you have to educate the imitator—who intends to be your competitor—you could do without the

---

flattery. For a while, the time Dogwood wasted on these wild goose chases drove me up the wall. Then I got used to it.

Perhaps I am a slow learner, but it took me a few years to figure out two things about what I was doing for a living. The first had to do with the format of the partnerships. Early on we did every kind of thing. One horse, five partners; six horses, forty partners; two horses, eight partners. We sometimes combined broodmares and race horses in the same partnerships. We bred horses for the yearling market. We bought yearlings for pinhooking (reselling as two-year-olds). Part of this was because I liked the dealing, the auction scene. I just liked action! But we were doing a lot of different things . . . fairly well. Finally, it dawned on me that I should do what I knew how to do best.

In 1990 we started doing individual partnerships with one horse (yearlings or two-year-olds), with Dogwood retaining five percent and four partners each with 23.75 percent.

The second thing was a monumental change that freed us of one of the most onerous burdens ever known to the commercial world. But first, here's the background.

One day in 1980 our fine lawyer, Kimbrough Taylor—who has made numerous contributions to my success—said, "I hate to tell you this, but because you are selling Limited Partnerships, in which you serve as General Partner with the passive investors entirely dependent on your management, you are technically selling a security. And you don't have a license to do that. If you continue, you're going to have to become a licensed member of the National Association of Securities Dealers."

"Suppose I don't want to?"

"The Securities and Exchange Commission could make you give a complaining investor his money back."

"What after that?"

"You could end up in the penitentiary."

"Okay!"

I decided that the key people with Dogwood should become "Broker Dealers" with the National Association of Securities Dealers (NASD). I would just as soon have become a member of the Nazi Party. Or the ACLU.

Four of us studied for the test, under the direction of a guy whose job it was to crash-prepare us for a passing grade—70. One of us flunked, two did all right, and the Dogwood president squeaked by with a lucky 71.

Next it behooved us to prepare an "Offering Memorandum" for each partnership—a tome about the size of the Chicago Yellow Pages.

Easily ninety-five percent of it was designed to tell the reader why he should not have anything to do with this proposition, or the people presenting it.

On top of that, if a guy from Denver, Colorado, say, wanted to consider buying a share in a Dogwood horse, the Offering Memorandum (known affectionately as "the O. M.") had to be first submitted to the Attorney General of Colorado for his approval.

This necessitated an increase in our Dogwood staff in Atlanta from eight to thirteen, just to handle the extra paperwork.

After following this ghastly procedure for several years, I determined that life was too short for this. I had gotten into the racehorse business because I loved horses and the racing of them. Suddenly I was spending all my time with lawyers, regulatory types, and bankers.

That's the background; the solution was to start doing General Partnerships. A General Partnership is simply a group of people who get together and decide to invest in something, with each of them permitted an equal say, and the majority ruling. No NASD or Offering Memoranda, praise God! The downside was that technically I could be outvoted by people who didn't know what they were doing.

But I knew my clientele well, and I had strong rapport with my partners. So I was convinced that with me serving as Racing Manager, making the day-to-day decisions, the chances for mutiny were negligible. Indeed, I would have welcomed mutiny rather than continue with the dreaded NASD.

At this stage, the complexion of the Dogwood clientele was evolving rapidly into a more sophisticated, upscale roster of investors, much more national in scope.

Some interesting observations could be made about geography and occupations and the variance of the level of comfort with the idea of plunking down, say, forty thousand dollars to buy a piece of a racehorse, while faced with strong odds against making any money on the deal.

I can't explain all the geographical patterns, but some are obvious. First, the best place in the world for selling shares in racehorses is between 50th and 90th Streets, between Lexington and Fifth Avenues in Manhattan. There you'll find sporting blood, sophistication, and heavy brass. And the people don't dilly dally.

New Jersey is good state for such ventures as racehorse ownership; so are Pennsylvania, Connecticut, and Massachusetts.

Maryland is interested in the subject but wants to do it on the cheap. Oddly enough, Florida is disappointing. Lots of enquiries, but little action. Great backswing, but no follow-through. Too much con, and a lot of tire-kicking seniors.

Atlanta was vital in the early days, but when the price of racing (with Dogwood) went up with the purchase of higher-priced stock, provincialism took its toll.

The rest of the South is anemic until you get to Texas, and that's a productive area for what we offer.

Kentucky is, of course, a hotbed of Thoroughbred racing fervor, but so is it a hotbed of established horse people with deals to sell.

In the Midwest, there is a certain amount of interest in Chicago. And there could be more if we maintained the presence there that we have in New York.

———

But West and North of there? Forget it. Wisconsin, Minnesota, Nebraska, Iowa, Kansas. Nothing doing—much too conservative.

An enquiry about racehorses from Missouri or Ohio is to be treated hopefully, but not with wild optimism.

Surprisingly, California, Oregon, and Washington make up a significant portion of our client base, even though we don't race on the West Coast. Those people like living out there, but they maintain keen interest in Eastern action.

Small towns are not good. Everyone knows everyone else's business, so there is strong fear of looking like a sucker and being talked about for not doing the solid, sensible, defensible thing.

How about the small, wealthy, sophisticated resort horse towns? The same is true. Saratoga Springs, New York; Middleburg, Virginia; Camden and Aiken, South Carolina; Pinehurst and Tryon, North Carolina—the spirit's willing but the flesh is weak.

There are, of course, exceptions to all of these patterns, but the trends do hold true.

Occupation-wise, the easiest sell and the smoothest to deal with are stockbrokers, money managers, financial types; if they're interested, they're interested. And they will make a decision. Doctors are the worst. They get excited, then diverted; they disappear and can't be reached. They are tough to do business with. We have some pronounced exceptions, but mostly doctors are tough. They also tend to want to "learn about it" before they do it. That's going to take a long time, and they'll never get around to it anyway.

An unexpected pocket of racehorse passion developed at a meaningful time in our existence. This was in an especially affluent zip code on Long Island, and it happened through our association with a man named George Howard.

George was a likeable, handsome man who had gone to the right schools, knew all the right people, and, in general, was to the manor born. He had not deviated from the prescribed route: married a well-connected young lady with the proper pedigree, joined the appropriate clubs, and had embarked on a career with an old-line brokerage firm. He was somewhat retiring, but he had done passably.

Later in his life, when the equine auction firm of Fasig-Tipton, Inc., needed a man to head up their newly-formed financing division, they hired George, who had followed the horses some and had the right ingredients for the job. I first knew him there.

Later he left Fasig and was at loose ends. When I was in the midst of my NASD tribulations, with a larger staff and struggling to feed that monster, George had a good suggestion. He pointed out that he lived in the midst of a nest of very rich people in Locust Valley, Glen Cove, Oyster Bay, and environs, and they were hard-pressed for amusing things to do. He thought many of them would get a kick out of being involved with racehorses, affording them excuses to while away afternoons at Belmont Park and Saratoga.

He wanted to try to deliver some of these folks, with a five percent commission (all kosher with NASD practices) going to him.

George Howard became our "Northeastern Regional Manager." He also became a good friend. He was considerable help in the marketing of shares in Dogwood racehorses. George knew the "territory" and worked it sensitively, presenting the venture exactly for what it was.

A lot of the prospects were friends of prominent people in racing—Alfred Vanderbilt, Tom and Billy Bancroft, and Martha Gerry, for example—and those people spoke kindly of Dogwood.

Many shares were sold, and getting in with Dogwood became sort of a popular fad in that densely populated lair of the super-rich. There was a lot of camaraderie about it, and some wonderful horses—like Summer Squall, South Jet, Nassipour, British Banker—were owned by some of these types. George and his energetic wife Gloria handled a lot of the day-to-day communication and arranged for outings to the race track, and on a number of occasions brought Long Islanders down to Dogwood to our guest house, which they found a unique adventure.

George Howard died in 2004. He was a great guy, the epitome of a gentleman. Like me, he was an alcoholic, and for the last twenty-five or thirty years of his life, he was successfully on the AA Program. George had a good sense of humor, so I'm sure he would not mind my telling this story about a very colorful peccadillo from his wild days.

George liked horseback riding and kept a couple of horses on his property in Locust Valley. One day, when very much in his cups, he decided that he would go riding.

This happened to be a day when his wife, Gloria, was having a rather large ladies' bridge luncheon. George decided that he could contribute to making the function one of the most memorable occasions on the Locust Valley social calendar.

Just as the ladies were seated and dealing the cards for the first rubber, George and his obedient horse came bursting through the open French windows and sashayed among the tables in the living room. This act in itself was colorful enough, but what really created a sensation was the fact that George sat astride his mount completely in the nude!

George did eventually regain his social standing in the community, but it was an uphill struggle for a while.

Not withstanding this earlier act of indecorum, George was most effective for Dogwood. But the partnership participation was too hot not to cool down. Once the Long Islanders had all done their number two or three times, many wandered off to other diversions. Some stayed with us for a long time. But overall it was a terrific stimulus to business at a time when we needed it.

Most of the men in that set belonged to Piping Rock Club, or Meadowbrook, or the Links, Leash, or Athletic Club in the city. Many of the women were members of the Colony or the Cosmopolitan clubs in Manhattan.

They tended to migrate to Hobe Sound in Florida, or Palm Beach, but the latter had become a trifle pushy. Miami would have been comparable to a visit to Harlem. Many even found it distasteful to go as far south as Gulfstream Park when we were running a horse there during the winter.

I was quite fond of many acquaintances made through George, and some are still good friends. I do find it fascinating that they all tended to be cut from the same cloth, and I made many observations on their habits and mores.

So, here are some affectionate—and insignificant—findings. The old-moneyed, super-rich of Long Island:

- Do not have telephone answering devices.
- Like to employ non-English speaking domestics to confound phone messages.
- Do not wear socks much of the time.
- Do not bother much with introductions (the theory being that if the people are worth knowing they must already know each other.)
- Are more comfortable eating dinner at a home.
- Frequently go about with exotic dogs on leashes, sometimes to unsuitable places.
- Refer to their parents as "Mummy" and "The Old Man."
- Do not go to movies.
- Tend to be thin.
- Forgive practically anything as long as the offender is "one of ours." But loyalty to one's pals would not necessarily include extra-marital affairs.
- Are taught—when quite young, and by professionals—to dance, golf, ride, shoot, and play racquet sports.
- Play bridge and backgammon quite well.
- Do not like to be hugged, but kiss fleetingly on both cheeks.
- Would not drive a Cadillac.
- Wear their clothes forever.
- Are made most uncomfortable by the subject of religion.
- Smoke cigarettes whenever and wherever they want.
- Enter a public place with no curiosity as to the identity of anyone else who might be there.

Dogwood partners have included some of the most fascinating people in existence. At the head of that list is one of the all-time great delights. This would be the inimitable Mickey Rooney.

Sir Laurence Olivier stated that Mickey Rooney was the single best actor ever produced in America. I don't know about that, but in the late Thirties and early Forties he was the biggest box office attraction in the world. He had an affair with Lana Turner and married Ava Gardner. Those are noteworthy accomplishments.

I did, and do, think he's wonderful. Some years ago I wanted to name a horse for him. A mutual friend told Mickey of my wish, and he was delighted. Mickey and I talked, and he gave me permission for the name "Mickey Rooney" to be registered for a handsome bay colt by Nashua. Mickey and I got to be friends, and he bought a share in that colt.

Mickey Rooney, star of *National Velvet, The Black Stallion,* and other racing pictures, is no dummy about racehorses. Mickey has spent a lot of time at racetracks, was a stockholder in Santa Anita, and had owned horses before his Dogwood ventures. He told me he had once been aboard Seabiscuit in a five-eighths mile training drill.

At the time of Mickey's equine adventures with us, he was appearing on Broadway in the wonderful burlesque review *Sugar Babies.* While our friendship and business relationship existed primarily on the phone, his equine involvements quickly expanded, and within a few months he owned shares in five horses.

Mickey did not sweat the small stuff, and the small stuff often included funding his purchases. Referring to the young horses by their sires, he would say, "I'll take a share of that Vaguely Noble colt, and let me get a piece of that Nijinsky filly. Just tell Otis (his business manager) to take care of it."

The problem was *he* did not tell Otis to take care of it. Otis knew nothing about it and did not wish to hear about it. He had heard about enough already. Consequently, it was tough to get paid for the horses Mickey "bought." Some of them almost died of old age before Mickey and his business manager got on the same page. This, of course, presented me with some fierce fiscal challenges, and finally Dogwood and Mickey got a divorce.

At the outset of our relationship, Mickey (an avid gambler) instructed me to "bet five hundred dollars every time a Dogwood horse runs." I knew this was an insane idea and told him, "Mickey, if my own dear, departed mother gave me such instructions, I would decline to follow them. I love you dearly, but I can't bet for you."

In those days when I went to New York, I would always make arrangements to stop by the Broadhurst Theater and call on Mickey. I wanted to bring him up to date on his horses and, hopefully, discuss his always alarmingly delinquent account.

Business sessions with Mickey were experiences you would never forget.

The only time he could see me was just prior to his going on in *Sugar Babies.* Curtain was at eight. So Mickey would say, "Meet me in my dressing room at 7:45." This impressed me as rather tight scheduling, so I would invariably arrive early, at 7:30. Mickey would invariably arrive at 7:55. The system suited me fine, because when the meeting was over I would hustle into the theater and see the delightful show for the umpteenth time—having bought a ticket, you may be sure.

His dressing room was a ramshackle, disreputable hovel. Mickey had his favorite chair, in which he would hold court (for the brief time you got to see him). It was a huge, overstuffed chair that looked as if it might have been bought secondhand from the immigrants' lounge on Ellis Island. Much of the original cotton stuffing that held it together was now strewn around Mickey's dressing room.

Just before eight, Mickey would breeze in, strip down to his Jockey underwear, and plop into his chair. He would quickly run through the opening pleasantries and then recite a litany of projects he was going to undertake, most of which were creative, promising, and fascinating. If you ever complimented him or asked him about some accomplishment in the past, he would quickly brush you off and move into the future. (ME: "Mickey, your performance in *Bill* was absolutely incredible. You've got to win an Emmy for that." ROONEY: "Yeah, but lemme tell you—Martha Raye and I are going to do a musical based on the comic strip *Maggie and Jiggs!*").

Now it would be 8:05. I could hear the overture strike up. As it finished, Mickey would be enthusing over another project. I could hear audience laughter and applause as Ann Miller, his co-star, finished her first number. With one nude leg thrown over the arm of the battle-worn chair, Mickey would be explaining his ten rules for a happy life. I would offer, "Now, Mickey, I know I'm taking too much of your time, but let me talk to you about that last filly you bought a piece of . . ."

"Aw, don't worry. Did you hear about the commercial I'm doing for the Animal Rights Foundation . . . they're going to . . ."

My watch read 8:20. The musical has now been going on for twenty minutes, and the star is still in his underwear! A barely audible knocking signal comes at the door. Still Mickey is talking, now discoursing on his religious conversion. I can hear two comics on stage, and their routine is bringing down the house. Still he talks; I listen.

Suddenly, as if an electric impulse has surged through his short, chunky body, he is out of the chair. He grabs a clown suit off the coat rack, leaps into it, zips up the front, grabs my hand, pumps it once, and goes flying out the door. As I walk down the rickety stairs, I can hear him on stage, belting out lyrics.

"If you knew Susie, like I know Susie, oh, oh, what a girl . . . !"

CHAPTER 25

STONE CRABS,
PIPEDREAMS, AND ROWDY DOGS

Dogwood's racing silks are a green jacket with gold dots, and gold sleeves with two green bands. After about ten years, some prominent stakes winners and some lesser lights had helped establish those colors, and Dogwood Stable was becoming a major presence on the American Turf.

Dominion, Practitioner, Dana Calqui, Pipedreamer, Proctor, Delta Flag, Domynsky, Sea Chimes, and Anne Campbell—they were all important campaigners for Dogwood in the late Seventies and early Eighties.

"Anne Campbell," did you say? Absolutely. I bought a well-bred, two-year-old filly from the renowned Claiborne Farm at the Keeneland January Sale. She was a handsome filly, though possessing some minor flaws. I named her for Anne; she was thrilled, and the filly turned out like you would want her to. She won stakes, and then we sold her as a broodmare to our friend Brereton Jones. Through the years she produced some super racehorses, and she changed hands several times at public auctions for millions of bucks. Ultimately she was owned by the famed Kentucky horseman Arthur Hancock, and was named Broodmare of the Year.

While the Dogwood name was gaining esteem in the racing world, so was its president becoming quite well-known. Of course, the press was titillated by the Dogwood story; I was good copy and knew—from my previous life—how to exploit opportunities for publicity.

Also, I was in some demand as a speaker. One of my few gifts would be as a public speaker, thanks essentially to two things. One was the confidence I got at Cypress Gardens when I volunteered to replace the bingeing master of ceremonies of the water ski shows. I learned then that I could hold an audience. Second, I

---

had spent much of my time in the advertising agency days writing radio copy and directing radio shows. I understood the nuances of the spoken word. I knew how it should sound.

I have spoken at conventions of practically every major racing state in America and numerous national racing seminars, have hit more civic clubs than I care to remember, addressed the British Thoroughbred Breeders Association and Canadian Thoroughbred Breeders, have been invited to speak in Australia (didn't go; too far!), and have done many television and radio interviews. All this is logical, considering the unique Dogwood story.

Speechmaking is appealing to me for several reasons. One, you are in no danger of being interrupted. No one will screw up the story by deciding to pass the pigs-in-a-blanket or the egg rolls while you're on a roll. No waiter arrives to take your order.

Another has to do with the fear of boredom. Thankfully, I believe I am not inclined to be boring, because for one thing I am petrified of ever letting it happen. During a good speech, you can scan the audience and easily determine whether or not you are clicking. My ideal form of communication would be to make a speech to five hundred people, knock them dead, then leave by the back door, and later receive numerous letters telling me how the wonderful speech—and the magnificent speaker—had changed their lives!

You see, the truth about me is that I really don't want to converse very long to anyone. I really don't.

I am a spirited conversationalist when I need to be, and in draggy situations I can and will grab the ball and run with it. I'm like a good prizefighter. I will stand toe-to-toe and slug it out during that three-minute round. But then I want the bell to ring so I can go back to my corner and sit down on my stool. Preferably, I'd like to get a knockout, so I can go on home.

I've gotten picky about where I make speeches. I've found that an engagement for next June sounds like fun in January, but when the time rolls around, I wish I hadn't signed up for it.

Recently, I got a call from a lady, and she said, "I heard that you were a pretty good speaker, and I wondered if you wanted to come talk to our Lions Club." I knew immediately that I did not.

First I asked, "When did you want me?" Whenever she said, I was going to be tied up, out of town, or something.

"Oh, the first or third Monday in any month."

I was just getting ready to tell her that I had some other projects and couldn't take on any speaking engagements. Then in the background, I heard this strange, guttural sound, like a voice box. It went on and on. She didn't say anything, and I didn't say anything.

Finally, she said, "I'm sorry, that's my voice computer. You see, I'm blind, and I can't get the darned thing to do what I want it to do."

Blind. I thought, "Oh, hell. There's no way in the world I can say no to this blind lady." So, we arrived at a date. "How many do you expect?" I enquired. "Fifteen," she told me. "What time do you meet, and where?" "Seven o'clock in the evening," and the venue was to be Shoney's Restaurant. At this point, I thought, "Why, oh why, did this lady have to be blind? I'm going to blow an entire evening doing something I really don't want to do."

The evening rolled around, and I arrived at Shoney's—the only one in a coat and tie. In a small, semi-private room I found nine men, two women, and a dog (Seeing Eye). I surmised that one of the ladies was my contact, although she did not introduce herself—or even speak to me. Nor were any of the Lions anxious to engage me in dinner conversation.

After a cafeteria-style dinner, during which we all traipsed back and forth to the buffet with salads, entrees, and desserts, some Lions Club business was discussed at great length, and then the president (I think) resignedly said, "Well, I don't know anything about the speaker, but I guess Sarah does. Do you want to introduce Mr. Campbell?"

"Well," she said, "I don't really know him. I heard he was a pretty good speaker, but I heard it from Tom Simmons. And he didn't even show up tonight!"

With that great send-off, a baby crying audibly in the next room, and the canned music playing too loudly in the room occupied by the Lions and me, I introduced myself and launched my address.

It was a good exercise in humility, if nothing else.

When the decade of the Eighties rolled around, another farm manager had to be replaced, and a very satisfactory new one came in.

As this is written, I have maintained a relationship with Elwood McCann for thirty-five years, and we both intend to keep it up. He is a friend, and was a high class farm manager.

When Elwood came to Dogwood he was in a long-term marriage that was just going through the motions. So it did not come as a great shock several years later when rumors developed that he had discovered a young lady employee who interested him romantically. I empathized with this, but it was a potentially disruptive situation.

Sadly, after a time both Elwood and I understood that he needed to leave. He returned to Kentucky; Elwood and his wife got a divorce. That lady died quite unexpectedly several months later and, later on, Elwood married Suzanne.

In time, the two of them had a son, and I'm delighted to say they have had the happiest sort of life together. I'm very fond of both of them. Indicating my esteem for Elwood, I once named a very good horse "McCann."

Within weeks of his Elwood's decision to leave, I had hired Ron Stevens. He, his wife Julie, and two little girls, Lesley and Nikki, showed up on the first day with T-shirts on which were emblazoned the words, "I Luv Dogwood." It was a nice sentiment with which to launch a relationship.

Elwood was perfect for Dogwood, but Ron was just as perfect. He was a college graduate from Kansas State, and had had an intense relationship with quarter horses and Thoroughbreds since he was a child. Ron was a fine-looking, clean-cut fellow with a sharp personality and was a very good horseman—an ideal combination for our operation. He has certainly made his share of contributions to the success of the outfit. We have gotten along beautifully for a quarter of a century.

At the racetrack, I had made the decision that I wanted a private trainer. I had some horses with Frank Alexander. That relationship had been good, so I hired Frank on an exclusive basis. He had been big in the show-jumping world and later worked as assistant trainer to some high profile Thoroughbred trainers, and then served as farm manager for Alfred Vanderbilt. He had gone back to the racetrack as a public trainer and was doing well. He, too, was an attractive fellow, ideal for an outfit with partners showing up in the paddock to see horses run. Chatting up partners would not have been his favorite part of the job, but he did it with sufficient verve. Frank's wife, Linda, could charm the birds out of the trees and was an enormous help.

So the entire Dogwood racing stable occupied a full barn at New Jersey's Monmouth Park in warm weather and at Hialeah Racetrack in Miami in the winter. The horses, barns, and employees were all decked out smartly in Dogwood colors.

This arrangement lasted for several years until we grew to the point that it was essential to spread the horses around. With the entire outfit in one location we found some runners were getting in each other's way; sometimes there would be three or four horses eligible for the same type of race. We split with Frank for a while, and then got back together with him as one of several public trainers. We still have horses with him.

Dogwood enjoyed success with Frank with horses like Timely Counsel, Dancing Master, Sea Chimes, Proctor, Faisana, Ice Cool, McCann, Wallenda, Windsor Castle—and, last but not least, Pipedreamer.

I have known well over one thousand horses. Some I quickly forgot, and they deserved forgetting. You remember well the great ones, and you think of them often. You appreciate their vital role in the development of your career. There were others that were not necessarily great, nor even close to it, but they were characters, with charm or personality or goofiness. Some were really not very good horses—but refused to believe it! These are the ones that touch your heart and make the game so wonderful.

We had one that was the character of characters. He was the quintessence of goofiness. He thought he was invincible . . . though he was not. His name was Pipedreamer, and he was nutty as a fruitcake!

Most of us in business have, on occasion, let our hearts rule our heads. In racing, if our hearts were not influential factors in our make-ups, we would probably be pursuing some other enterprise.

248

That's what happened when I bought Pipedreamer in England. I saw him first at Royal Ascot, where he was one of twenty-eight horses in the Britannia Stakes. With a crowd of sixty thousand—including Queen Elizabeth—cheering him on, this tiny black horse, his tongue lolling out of the side of his mouth crazily, shot of out the pack about thirty yards from home—like a seed popping out of a grape—and won by two lengths. I fell in love with him, as one would be smitten by a three-legged dog, perhaps.

A few days later, when he had been returned to his home stable at Lambourne, I drove there to inspect him. What a disaster he was. Physically, he was most unattractive; and from a soundness standpoint, he was quite ill-suited to be a racehorse. He was a little fellow and seemed frail. He might have weighed as much as eight hundred pounds. He made a terrible wheezing sound when he ran and had a rather strange-looking growth on one ankle. He had one testicle to his name (and future prospects of using that one in a stud career were not very bright!). He was plagued with a heart murmur. His demeanor was eccentric, to be charitable. I should have beaten a hasty retreat.

That fall he was put in a public auction, and I bought him for thirty-two thousand dollars.

Someone asked me why I would pay anything at all for such a wreck. I said, "Because I have seen him run. And he's a running son of a bitch!"

I sent him to Florida to the racing stable at Hialeah, and we decided to run him in the Appleton Handicap at Gulfstream on opening day in January. We gave the ride to the stylish French jockey Jean Cruguet.

As the race unfolded, Cruguet sensed a slow pace up front, and with a half-mile left, he let out a notch on Pipedreamer. Wham! Suddenly Pipedreamer was six on top! And he never looked back. He cruised home with two and a half lengths to spare, and what a sight he was. I can see old "Pipes" now, running with his head up in the air like a goose, roaring down that grassy stretch at Gulfstream. His long tongue was flapping in the breeze, and his eyes were about to pop out of his head. What a wonderful day!

Pipes campaigned up and down the Eastern Seaboard, never intimidated, never in doubt, and whipping many a good horse.

When his racing days were over, we were even able to find a place where this little shrimp could stand at stud—Kansas!

Hell, it didn't matter to Pipedreamer. Kansas, Royal Ascot, Gulfstream . . . they were all the same to him. He was just a little working guy . . . with one testicle to his name.

The character of the horses is the true fascination of the sport and industry. I am certain by now that it is quite apparent that I am obsessed with getting my arms around the elusive explanation of the allure of racing horses. I want to quash the notion that the game consists of large animals running around in a circle. It is their quirks and personality traits that have so much to do with the intrigue of horseracing.

I have always found that good horses, the high quality competitors, have about them a slightly aloof manner, an independent air. They do not want much babying. If there are peppermints or carrots involved, they will condone some petting; otherwise, they can be a little on the edgy side. And the closer they are to a race, the edgier they are likely to be, and the quirks may become more prevalent.

Sea Chimes was a handsome, rangy chestnut, and a stakes winner of the highest category in England. He had a darkness about him that manifested itself in a strange way. He savaged (bit) himself. He would suddenly go into a whirling maneuver while biting himself on the stifle (where the back leg joins the stomach). Blankets, leather shields, cradles on his neck, foul-tasting unguents—Sea Chimes could beat them all. He would not be denied. When he was at Dogwood Farm and there would be a Breezing Party, if a guest lingered outside his stall, the horse went into his act. Immediately, every other guest would be attracted, of course, and soon a throng was clustered around his stall, causing the poor horse to step up the tempo. One of us would find Sea Chimes in a virtual blur of motion, with visitors squealing with delight over this cute trick. We would have to ask them to move on and leave him alone.

He could be quieted by turning the radio on to a country music station, the more rural the better. But God forbid that a gospel number slip into the programming. He absolutely could not abide gospel music. Old Sea Chimes was good, but complicated.

Dominion also liked music, but any kind. He would nod his head up and down to the beat, shifting from one foot to another. Otherwise, he was plenty aloof. Spencer Tracy, I have said.

Cinteelo was a talented racehorse, closely inbred to a fiery horse, Nasrullah, so he came by eccentricities naturally. When he went to stud and was turned out each afternoon, he would circle his paddock endlessly. At day's end, he refused to let anyone catch him unless that person was wearing a cowboy hat!

Practitioner was wild about airplanes. When hearing one, he would scan the skies to find its location and then stare at it until it disappeared. Since Calder racetrack, where he was stabled, was on the flight pattern for Ft. Lauderdale International, his trips from the barn to the racetrack for morning workouts could be quite time-consuming. He refused to move forward until the sky was clear. A toy plane was hung on the stall door, and he found that mildly engaging. But he preferred authenticity—the big jets.

I find it enthralling that these large animals, through their power and their derring-do, can change one's life, as Mrs. Cornwallis did mine. They can create undreamed-of elation; but they can also bring about a disrupting obsession and unhealthy imbalance in one's life.

MEMOIRS OF A LONGSHOT

Racing historians (and gossips) can point to most superstar racehorses and cite examples of divorces, estrangements, family feuds, and chronic unrest spawned by their celebrity.

When a horse gets good, the intensity of his connections increases in direct proportion to his renown. People who are completely bumfuzzled by the proper course of action in managing a moderate horse become instant experts when a horse achieves stardom.

I have always been enamored of animals that work. Their reliability and earnestness are inspiring. They do it because they are convinced that is what they ought to do. And then they pass on that inclination to their progeny.

If someone were to tell me that I could behold the greatest coon dog in the world if I were up to a two-mile walk through the woods, I would want to make the trek, although I'm not particularly avid about coon hunting. But I would like to look into the countenance and the eyes of the greatest anything, especially in the animal kingdom.

I go ape on the subject of Balto, the famous Alaskan sled dog of the Twenties. With a diphtheria epidemic raging out of control in Nome, the team of dogs and driver, led by the indefatigable Balto, did double duty in the race against time to deliver the precious serum in a relay journey across Alaska from Fairbanks to Nome.

We have a photo of the burly husky in our den, and when Anne and I are in New York we go into Central Park to see the magnificent statue of Balto, which commemorates the feat that deservedly captured the imagination of the entire world.

I love to watch a fine birddog work, to see the concentration and the discipline that will see him stand frozen in point over a covey of quail.

How could one not be fascinated with carrier pigeons, finding their way to their home loft from hundreds of miles away? How dramatic are the tales of their flying vital messages over enemy lines in World War I?

How could one not be touched by the sight of a Seeing Eye dog standing beside his blind master on a street corner? It is not my imagination, I am sure, that they have worried looks on their faces as they prepare to take responsibility for getting their charges across busy intersections at the right time.

Retrievers, bloodhounds, fox hounds, camels, draft horses, falcons—they're all fascinating.

But there was once a Russian wolfhound who created a situation that was unappealing to one gentleman, exceedingly amusing to many others, but unforgettable to all concerned. This dog—and not a horse—was the star of the 1984 Washington, D. C., International.

This race was run for many years at Laurel Park racetrack and was one of the great races of its day. Conceived by John Schapiro, Laurel's owner, the invitational grass race at a mile and a half attracted the stellar turf runners of every major racing nation.

Dogwood ran in it in 1984 with Nassipour, and the night before the event a screamingly funny situation occurred at the Canadian Embassy.

John Schapiro glamorized his race marvelously by surrounding it with glittering parties. It was a highlight of Washington's fall social season. Usually one of the major embassies hosted a beautiful dinner. In 1984 Canada did the honors. Washington was seriously cold that weekend, unfortunate because the party's large size necessitated the erection of a tent for the dinner portion of the party. Cocktails were served inside in the lovely embassy foyer.

Anne and I and our Dogwood partners were bowled over by the gorgeous party and its extremely elegant setting. And we were charmed when we observed the ambassador's family dog, a tremendous Russian wolfhound, wandering amiably among the distinguished guests during cocktail hour.

This was a very appealing, "down home" touch to what otherwise could have been a rather stuffy affair.

Ambassadors whose countries had entrants in the race were all present. That year, Russia—despite the chilly Cold War relationship with the United States—was represented with a horse in the International. That country's envoy was present, and he definitely looked the part. He was tall and spare, with prominent features supporting a huge, but very patrician, nose. He had a luxuriant head of wiry gray hair that swept back in wild profusion from a high, pallid, blue-veined forehead. He looked like a mad scientist or a symphony conductor.

The dinner hour was announced, and we filed apprehensively into the uncomfortable climate of the tent (we are talking cold!). Space heaters blew hot air throughout the spacious tent, and the embassy staff actually handed out thermal socks—to put over our shoes—as we went in.

Our table for ten happened to be adjacent to the Russian ambassador's, and we watched with interest as this stork of a man stalked somberly past us. He was clad in a dramatic, floor-length fur coat, ideal for Russian winters and not a bad idea for this night in Washington. After removing and draping the coat over the back of the chair, he seated himself.

The congenial family dog had also strolled in with the other guests. Undaunted by the frigid conditions, he had reclined between the two tables to await the evening's proceedings.

The meal was served, the wine replenished generously, and the party was going nicely, considering the temperature.

After dessert and coffee, the Canadian ambassador rose to toast the fine horses that would face the starter on the morrow. He then remarked on the great, healing significance of friendly competition at the International at a time in Cold War history when relations between many nations were tenuous.

The Russian ambassador decided at this juncture that he was cold, and he shrugged himself into his great fur coat.

With that, the huge dog, dozing several feet away, jolted to attention. He jumped up and stood riveted by this heretofore unobserved large, hairy object. His head was lowered like that of a bull before a charge.

Inexplicably, this animal (who stood a good six feet when on his back legs) leapt onto the back of the unsuspecting diplomat, planted his front legs on the man's shoulders, and began—with astounding enthusiasm—to make love to this irresistibly attractive, furry creature.

Thrusting rhythmically and vigorously, with a seriously rapt demeanor about him, this dog now completely stole the attention of the entire party. The host began to falter slightly in his remarks, but could hardly stop and scream at his "pet." He had no choice but to continue gamely.

But the "mother of all dilemmas" lay with the Russian ambassador; never would his skills of diplomacy be so severely tested.

First he looked around with some understandable surprise to ascertain the nature of the attack. When he had assessed the situation, he addressed the problem by shrugging his shoulders discouragingly and glaring menacingly at the beast, while uttering a sharp but well-modulated command. It did not work.

The huge wolfhound picked up the tempo, if anything.

What a problem! The ambassador must bring closure to this unseemly episode. The speaker was by now just going through the motions; the audience was tittering audibly, and some members were in stitches! Everyone in the tent was aware of this humiliating spectacle.

The ambassador had several choices, none of them promising.

He could get up and walk out. But this was fraught with risk. He couldn't be sure just what the response of the Russian wolfhound might be. Would this stimulate him further? How would it play that a high-ranking diplomat was vanquished from the field by the amorous attentions of a large dog!

He could turn and smite the dog forcefully, sending a signal that this activity was not at all suitable for this occasion. But we're talking here about a very, very large dog, in a most intense frame of mind. Would this be a judicious course of action? Of considerably less significance at this point, the animal was the house pet of the host (who would have cheerfully slit the animal's throat right about then).

Third, he could try removing the garment that triggered all this misery in the first place.

The Russian did take off the coat, struggling mightily and trying not to stand up and attract further attention while he did so. He then tossed the troublesome garment several feet away between the tables. This did the trick.

The dog reluctantly dismounted and looked completely crestfallen. He stared first at the now inanimate fur coat, then at the seething ambassador. Had he been able to shrug his shoulders as if to say, "Well, it was nice while it lasted," he would have done so. He then lay down to resume his nap.

By this time the party was in complete chaos. Amidst audible giggling, the host lamely finished his lofty remarks. We clapped politely, adjourned, and headed for valet parking, with the Russian ambassador leading the way.

Nassipour ran fourth in the International. After the Russian wolfhound's spectacular antics of the previous night, the race itself was a bit of anti-climax. But what an honor it was for Dogwood to have been invited to represent our country in this splendid international race.

Overall, the progress of Dogwood Farm was inch by inch, but steady. There were some big leaps, such as when Dominion won the Barnard Baruch in Saratoga, but, like most things, progress came from keeping at it. And keeping at it was fun. There were the trying days when we were saddled with horrible NASD regulatory hoops to jump through. But the horror of that was mostly in retrospect. I could have corrected that problem sooner; and I should have.

By the early Eighties, the original ten owners of the Dogwood Farm Corporation had been winnowed down to three, as some of the original members lost interest when it became clear that pari-mutuel racing was not going to be legalized in the state of Georgia.

Finally, Dogwood, the corporation, would be owned by Dr. Harper Gaston and my own majority.

At that time, I was often at the racetracks because we were training and running there, and because partners were attending those races. With two daughters in their teens, Anne, understandably, could not often go with me.

In the summer, I left my black Lincoln Mark IV at the Newark Airport, so I could jump in it and head for the Jersey Shore and Monmouth Park racetrack. Anne and I bought an apartment on Collins Avenue in Bal Harbour (on Miami Beach) and the black Lincoln resided there in the wintertime, as did the two of us from time to time.

So between Miami, New Jersey, the farm, Europe, and Atlanta, I was rushing around like a blind dog in a meat market.

I have always had a love-hate relationship with Miami. After being in the city for a few days one can quickly figure out the basis for the "hate" aspect. The atmosphere can be mean, hateful, smart-ass. In the words of the old Dixieland tune, "Ace in the Hole," "In this town there are some guys who think they're mighty wise, just because they know a thing or two!"

But I have much history there from the days of parking cars at Copa City night club and driving the ambulance for the funeral home. A still-open chapter of that history began the night after a friend and I saw the great horse Kelso go down to defeat at the hands of Beau Purple at Hialeah Racetrack in 1963. When we were leaving the track, my pal said, "Let's go over to the beach to Joe's."

"Joe's what?" I asked.

We went to Joe's Stone Crabs on the very south end of Miami Beach. I discovered what must surely be the greatest restaurant in all the world. Or it is to me.

That night we ate the ice cold, succulent stone crabs, dunked in hot melted butter, served with coleslaw and French fried sweet potatoes, and finished off with key lime pie, served on cold pewter plates.

That was forty-three years ago, as I write this. Never has a winter gone by since that I did not hit Joe's at least fifteen times. Talk about history! Much of my life has been played out during evenings at this fabulous restaurant with 1930s atmosphere.

I love the raucous atmosphere and the wonderful waiters, many of them avid horseplayers who spend their summers working at Saratoga, or even take cruises on the money they've raked in at Joe's. The quality of both food and service has never once been compromised at Joe's. It is an eating man's joint. Nothing drizzled onto a bed of wild saffron rice . . . No reductions. No bull ____! Well, you know what I mean.

I admit that I love being able to stroll into Joe's through throngs waiting two hours for a table, never break stride, and go right to a table. I've paid my dues, but transcending that is the fact that Anne and I have also made some great friends with the boys there. Roy, Dennis, Bryan, Billy, Eddie, Calvin, Bones, Steve, Greg, Don (the names sound like something out of the finale to *Hello, Dolly!*). We keep up with a lot of them. They follow Dogwood. And on evenings when we might have won a big race—or even lost a tough one—dinner at Joe's has sometimes been on the house.

Oddly, I am sort of fond of going there by myself. And, after dinner, when I'm full and content I sit and look around that restaurant and think back on all the nights there when big events were celebrated, downers became unimportant, or good pals (many of them gone) were enjoyed. I can become very sentimental.

Silly as it may be, Joe's Stone Crabs is more than a place to get something to eat—to me. It remains one of the good reasons for going to Miami.

CHAPTER 26

THE SHEIKHS OF ARABY

In the Eighties, the great Arabian potentates discovered—with resounding impact—the American Thoroughbred racehorse. Major players were the "Dubai Brothers" from United Arab Emirates: Mohammed, Maktoum, and Hamdan Maktoum; there was Prince Khalid Abdullah, a Saudi; and another non-titled, but royally-connected, Mahmoud Fustok.

Arabs definitely had the horse world all atwitter—one way or another. The Arabs flew into Lexington in 747s and took over entire floors of various hotels. The Thoroughbred auction sales companies provided private rooms in which the sheikhs and their British bloodstock advisors—old, crusty types usually bearing military titles of "Major" or "Colonel"—could do their auction bidding. They did not request much they did not get—a situation that usually exists with shoppers of that magnitude.

They moved through the sales grounds in large, grim-visaged entourages, with a clearly defined pecking order. It was great fun to observe them in action. When a consignor spied them moving in the direction of his barn he would practically wet his pants. Enthusiasm for a yearling, when demonstrated by an Arab, could make a market breeder's year, and then some!

My niche in the horse business and their modus operandi were hardly compatible, so I had little truck with them. They were not ones to hang around the track kitchen, or go to any of the parties given by consignors before and after sales sessions.

The first horse ever bought in this country by Mahmoud Fustok was a two-year-old sold at public auction by Dogwood. He paid twenty-five thousand dollars for a colt named "T. Harvey." The bidding was done by a good-old-boy trainer in Florida who had somehow hooked up with Fustok shortly before the sale. Fustok decided a few days later that he needed a more stylish trainer. He gave the original man ten grand in cash for his trouble and said goodbye.

Khalid Abdullah's reserved seats in the Keeneland sales pavilion were right in front of Dogwood's. I never met him, but he was intriguing to observe. The name "Khalid Abdullah" conjures up an image of a fierce Arab warrior, mounted on a pure white Arabian steed and brandishing a scimitar, slashing through hordes of Berber tribesmen. This man was far from it. He was a quietly important-looking gentleman—elegant, intellectual, sensitive, and most unassuming. He rarely spoke or was spoken to. He just chain-smoked cigarettes, and our whole section was enveloped in a fog bank of Parliament smoke. When he wanted to buy a horse, his agents bid for him from another location in the sales pavilion so as to not tip off anyone.

I had no dealings with any of the Maktoums. However, in later years, Anne and I were invited to spend a week in Dubai at the portal-to-portal expense of Sheikh Mohammed. It was a nice compliment and a wonderful opportunity. We were treated royally, although the Sheikh himself and the Campbells were not involved in too much direct social intercourse. When we got off his United Arab Emirates airliner in Dubai, he was not waiting at the gate with a sign saying "Welcome Cot and Anne." But his emissaries took great care of us, and there were several sheikh sightings during a fantastic trip.

If Abdullah is effete in appearance, Mohammed exudes strength and vigor and is a fierce-looking customer, though he is obviously a visionary genius and a popular ruler. You *can* see him attacking the Berbers!

I am an Arab admirer. They are bred to be horse lovers, and they truly are. The Arabs adore racehorses and racing competition. They understand the charms of the sport per se and are not in the game so they can go to parties. Collectively they must have poured over a billion bucks into the auction market. Arabs have bought farms in Kentucky, England, and France; employed many people; and have single-handedly shored up the international Thoroughbred racing industry. Bravo for Arabs.

But the great thing about racing is that the old boy with three horses at Oaklawn Park in Hot Springs gets as much thrill out of winning a ten thousand dollar claiming race as does Sheikh Mohammed when he wins the Epsom Derby. It is all relative.

I was determined to have some kind of Arab in the Dogwood camp. I told earlier of Prince Faisal attending our breezing parties, and tossing hygiene to the wind when dunking strawberries while intermittently playing with his sandal-shod toes. Faisal liked horses for sure, but the Dogwood relationship might have gotten off to a rocky start with his first visit.

He and his entourage were invited to come see the horses train and then have lunch. Faisal, his wife Princess Asiya, and various spear carriers and court jesters arrived in a special motor coach late one morning. We trained several sets of horses for them, and then repaired to our guest house for just the right luncheon one would lay on for visiting Arab royalty.

One hitch: the Arabs do not eat pork (which our research did not reveal). Because of our ignorance on Arabic culinary traditions, the meal—consisting of Kentucky ham, Kentucky Burgoo (a regional delicacy riddled with pork), and a lovely salad adorned with plentiful bits of bacon—did not exactly score a bulls eye!

One of his advisors hit the buffet line first and attempted to save the day by exclaiming, "Oh, how nice. We're having corned beef."

Anne briskly straightened him out, "Oh, no! That's Kentucky *ham!*"

After that the meal tended to head downhill. In an effort to salvage the situation, Anne rushed into the dining room with some piping hot (I mean steaming!) cheese biscuits, and offered them first to Princess Asiya.

Now the princess was a generously endowed young woman, staggeringly buxom, and was wearing that day a blouse that amply demonstrated her décolletage.

Just as Anne proffered the earthenware dish, it inexplicably broke in half, and a couple of the hot cheese biscuits fell into that cavity housing the plump bosom of the Arabian princess.

It was one of those days that was so bad it was almost good. In fact, when the royal motor coach departed through the Dogwood gates, the prince good-naturedly bid us goodbye on his public address system, "Anne . . . next . . . time . . . give . . . me . . . CORNED BEEF!"

Did he buy any shares in horses? No.

Arabs were certainly in vogue in the horses business. But, disappointingly, there were none in the life of Dogwood. That is, until the emergence of "the Desert Mouse," the mysterious Sheikh Bin Had.

The American horse industry's feeding frenzy for Arab money struck a chord in my whimsy.

I should interject here that I have always been a sucker for a midget. I love midgets. I think there is no situation that can't be enlivened by the judicious involvement of a midget. This may have all started years before, when I covered a wrestling match in Florida where there was featured a spirited tag team match billed as "*colored, midget, women wrestlers.*"

When I was chairman of Burton-Campbell, we hired a midget, dressed him as a Western Union delivery boy (an unheard-of occupation today), and had him deliver an oversized telegram to a prospective client we were pitching. It didn't work, but it was no fault of the midget's.

Now in a very fanciful spoof designed to do nothing but entertain ourselves—and, hopefully, a lot of other people in the horse world—we created "Sheikh Bin Had" (Bin Had, get it?).

The role of sheikh was played by a midget—in real life an undersized bellman employed by the Hilton Hotel in Atlanta. Through a talent agency, we hired this gentleman (he stood all of four feet), fitted him in loose-flowing Arabic garb with burnoose, and set up a photo session at Dogwood.

We arranged a stretch limousine, and the Sheikh motored to the farm, in costume, of course. He was driven there by his bodyguard-driver "Punjab."

Dogwood farm manager Ron Stevens and I were there to greet Bin Had, and the cameras started clicking. We brought horses out on our racetrack for training; the Sheikh inspected them, and we looked others over in the paddock. After several hours we had photographically captured everything a visiting potentate might logically do on a Thoroughbred horse farm.

We then fashioned a news story for our Dogwood Farm quarterly newsletter. The gist of it was that Sheikh Bin Had had come to America to buy shares in horses from Dogwood.

The front page bannered this headline: "Arab Potentate goes wild on Christmas Shopping Spree! DOGWOOD HORSE INVENTORY DEPLETED!"

The body copy read: "Dogwood Farm, one of the few commercial thoroughbred operations in America without a tie to Arabic petrodollars, has now catapulted to the top of the heap following an epic equine Christmas shopping spree by Sheikh Bin Had.

"Sheikh Bin Had, known as 'the Desert Mouse,' visited Dogwood in his never-ending quest to acquire unique gifts to please his twenty-seven wives. Lest any of his wives take exception should one horse do better than another, twenty-seven horses were packaged into a limited partnership of twenty-seven shares—one for each wife . . ."

The spoof was goofy enough to capture your attention and straight enough to make you wonder . . . briefly. However, an astonishing number of pretty sophisticated people gobbled it up. We got calls from all over: "Is the Sheikh on the level?"

One local social-climbing type beseeched us to let her have a cocktail party for him the next time he came to town. We were having so much fun with it that we decided to perpetuate it, milk it for all it was worth.

Different sheikh-like scenarios were played out for three or four years, and the delighted character playing Bin Had was making more money from "acting" than from hustling tips at the Hilton.

When Dogwood Stable hit the one million dollar mark for the first year, in 1983, we threw a big dance at the Piedmont Driving Club in Atlanta. An honored guest, of course, was the Sheikh.

And when our daughter Lila got married, her reception was held there and, unbeknownst to her, Anne and I invited Sheikh Bin Had (in costume). When he entered the ballroom, just as the featured couple was having their wedding dance, it was like Moses parting the Red Sea. The guests did not know how to handle the Sheikh.

The midget "Arab" Sheikh Bin Had delighted ninety percent of those who encountered or read about him. I admit Bin Had was a product of my admittedly zany nature.

Since we could not drum up any but legitimate business with an Arab potentate, we set a more realistic target, deciding that Dogwood should invade California, where we had never raced nor done much business.

Enter Michael Morphy, a dashing, highly successful businessman from California and a nut about horseracing. He had tried in years past to form a racing syndicate. He had met with moderate success; then interest on the West Coast petered out.

Morphy had heard about Dogwood. And he was part of the old boy network that included our man on Long Island, George Howard. Michael looked me up when on a business trip to Atlanta; we stayed in touch and became very close friends. He sold me on the idea of sending a division of horses to California, bolstered by forming a Dogwood West Coast "Advisory Board," made up of influential types who obviously put their stamp of approval on the Dogwood outfit.

Thanks to Morphy (and our good reputation), the Advisory Board was truly blue ribbon, including a distinguished international horseman, Rollin Baugh; Morphy, of course; socially prominent Frank McGinnis; a well-known plastic surgeon named Max Pegram; Eddie Gregson, a highly popular trainer who would condition the horses; and the splendid actor John Forsythe, an avid racing enthusiast.

There were a series of cocktail parties to introduce the project, and there was much interest in the idea. Some shares were sold. We would have done well had I been able to send some effective horses out there. But the stock we sent just sputtered along, and I was wearing myself out running out there. We met a lot of great people, had some good times, but we folded that venture after several years, and I stuck to racing east of the Mississippi River. Many of the California clients continued to do business with us for years to come.

We were tearing 'em up on the racetrack in the late Eighties and, as is usually the case, thought it would never stop. We had not yet had any Derby runners, nor anything very close to it, but we had some wonderful older horses who were among the best turf runners around, including Nassipour, Southjet, Domynsky, and Crazy Moon. We were invited to represent the United States twice in the Washington, D. C., International, twice in the Japan Cup, and twice in the Canadian International at Woodbine Racetrack in Toronto. To boot, we campaigned the North American champion steeplechaser, Inlander.

Meanwhile, the American horse breeders were having a field day as the cost of young bloodstock had gone plumb crazy, thanks to a great extent to the influx of Arab buyers.

While I had been buying yearlings and two-year-olds in the neighborhood of $150,000 to $200,000, I even got caught up in the madness, and once paid as much as $500,000 for a colt sired by the great Nijinsky.

But, folks, that was petty cash. In what was to be a world record for a yearling colt, and one that would stand for twenty years, a son of Seattle Slew sold at Keeneland in 1985 for $13,100,000. The consignor was pretty confident that he would bring that kind of money because he asked me to bid up to $8,000,000, strictly as a means of achieving the reserve that had been set (a perfectly ethical practice). He must have asked quite a few guys to bid. I raised my hand around $6,000,000, and the action blew past me up into the wild blue yonder!

When the seller asked me to be what is called a "by bidder" on the sensationally bred and conformed colt, I asked, "If I get him, what name shall I sign?" A good question.

The confident consignor said, "You *won't* get him."

But success does not come in direct proportion to the amount of money invested in young bloodstock. Thank goodness for that. And here is a lovely example!

We won the Canadian Championship in 1985 with Nassipour, a horse I had bought off the Aga Khan for eighty thousand dollars. He was a three-year-old then and was being culled by that vaunted stable, powered by untold funds supplied to the titular ruler, the Aga Khan, by the entire Muslim world. Nassipour was thought by his connections to be just another horse.

Ironically, he beat the Aga Khan's champion, Sumayr, in Toronto and then went on to win close to a million dollars.

The next year we came back with Southjet in the same race and won back-to-back Canadian Internationals. Our good horse came charging out of the pack and overhauled another horse of the Aga Khan's. This was the celebrated Shardari, an overwhelming favorite who supposedly had only to go through the motions. Shardari led into the stretch while under a stranglehold by his French jockey. But midway down that stretch that rider heard a sudden roar from the crowd. He looked over his shoulder and beheld the white-blazed, chestnut head of Southjet in a furious charge. I will never forget that rider on Shardari and his immediate transformation from supreme confidence to sheer panic. Flailing away on the European horse, the jockey looked back over his right shoulder every other stride and prayed for the wire to come up. But Southjet had him measured, pulled alongside, looked him in the eye, and said, "Not today, baby!"

I'm sure the Aga had no trouble surviving the disappointment. But what a sweet, wonderful day it was for our team.

The next year we came back again with Southjet to try for a third straight Canadian Championship for Dogwood (and back-to-back victories for Southjet). There had been much written about Dogwood's quest for three straight, and there was enormous respect for Southjet among the fans and the horsemen. We experienced a moving emotional jolt early one morning before the race.

Southjet was stabled in the "stake barn" where visiting runners were housed. It was perhaps a quarter mile from the racetrack, and to reach the track a horse had to walk down a lovely, tree-lined path with other barns, housing other stables, situated on either side. Our horse, having flown in the day before, was going out for an easy, leg-stretching gallop just after dawn. Steve DiMauro (the trainer), Southjet (with exercise rider and assistant trainer Carmela Gadler on him), and I headed down that path.

As if a signal bell had tolled, while we were making our way down the lane, grooms, riders, and trainers stopped their work and came popping out of the barns on either side. They watched in admiration as we walked by, the big horse on his toes, prancing, sensing that he was "The Man." From all around us came shouts: "Good luck, big boy!"; "Do it again, Southjet!"; "We're with you, big fellow!" The three of us were nodding and waving back. Pretty heady stuff, and an example of the hospitable spirit I have always found in Canada.

Southjet did not win a third race, but he tried hard, as he always did.

Dogwood was a steady factor in the racing world, always ranked in the top twenty. And because this was so, the farm in Georgia was becoming less essential. We had needed it in the early days because it was a quality place, and its Kentucky look gave us an aura of credibility. Now our reputation on the racetrack was carrying us, and it didn't make much difference where our horses were based. This was especially true because Georgia and Atlanta were no longer vital to us. Our client base was national.

On top of that was the fact that it looked to me that Georgia was never going to legalize pari-mutuel wagering. All things considered, the need for a farm in Georgia was not necessary. Indeed, the need for a farm anywhere was not necessary.

I have always been blessed with the world's greatest equine CPA. We got together when we were both green in the game, and we're together still—thirty-five years later, when he is known as the dean of American horse accountants. This man, Nelson Radwan, has never given any advice yet that was not right on the money. He's an easygoing old boy from the coal mining section of Western Kentucky, and is the most non-accountant accountant I have ever known. Nelson—God bless him—not only identifies the problem, he provides the solution. I have found in encountering life's problems that there are many eager identifiers, but we're woefully short on solvers.

Radwan had been telling me, "You don't need that farm. It's expensive. The pride of ownership is not a big deal anymore. It's become a drag driving down there and showing it to people. Move the operation to some horse town and rent some facilities. Streamline your life. Sell the son of a bitch!"

This seemed unthinkable at first, but the more I thought about it, the more it was an idea whose time had come. But a lot of thought and planning went into making it happen.

First, where would we train the horses? The nearest training centers that made sense were Aiken and Camden, South Carolina; and Ocala, Florida. How would we sell the property? It was a horse farm, so a public auction conducted by a well-known Kentucky real estate auction firm seemed logical.

What about the office in Atlanta? It would stay in Atlanta. Certainly Anne and I would continue to live in Atlanta. To entertain any change on that score would be ludicrous!

How would the farm staff handle this? Ideally, we would want to take at least half of them with us. With kids in school, family, and roots in Georgia, the idea of moving to another state might go over like a lead balloon with some of them.

Anne and I had been to Aiken the year before for the Aiken Trials, as guests of Dogwood partners Allan and Nubbins McKelvie, and loved the town and the ambiance. We had some pals that wintered in that traditional old horse town. There was the great trainer Mack Miller and his wife Martha. A wonderful friend and Dogwood booster was Whitney Tower, president of the National Museum of Racing in Saratoga Springs, New York. Also we had known Mike Freeman, president of the Aiken Training Track, very pleasantly.

I visited Mike and Mack and found that the horse community was keen on having us move the outfit into Aiken, where we could rent a barn and pay a per-horse annual fee to use the community training track, one of the greatest in the world and a site where close to forty champions had trained.

We decided that Aiken was perfect for us. The welcome was there, the facilities were first rate, and the atmosphere was in keeping with the grandest tradition of racing.

I then arranged for Walt Robertson, a well-known Lexington auctioneer of livestock and horse farms, to come to Greenville, Georgia, see the property, put a price estimate on it, and discuss the logistics of a gala auction to sell it. After his inspection, he was confident that it ought to bring close to a million and a half. That would be quite nice for the late spring of 1986, representing a fine profit for property we had held and used for thirteen years. But, he pointed out, you must offer fairly liberal terms.

So I pushed the button. The staff was informed first. A contract was signed with the Aiken Training Track, an announcement was made in the national and local press that we were moving from Georgia to South Carolina, and a May date was set for the auction.

The farm staff was not overjoyed. Ron Stevens and Jack Sadler, farm manager/trainer and assistant trainer, respectively, were dubious at first, a little scared by it all, but they soon warmed to the idea—especially after they had visited

Aiken. Predictably, many of the farm staff—grooms, exercise riders, foremen, maintenance workers—decided not to go to Aiken. The horse citizenry of Georgia (and especially the population around the farm) were not at all flattered by the announcement. Many interpreted the move as a protest over the bleak outlook for pari-mutuel legalization in the state—accurate in a minor way.

The day of the auction arrived and, oh, how very exciting and festive it all was! Auctioneers, spotters, clerical types, caterers, and a very fine organist (and his organ, of course) were on hand. Barns and farm buildings were strewn with bunting, and a good, jolly crowd was buzzing about (several eagle-eyed bankers included). We offered barbecue and all the fixings, and there was certainly an open bar to relax and mellow everyone out a bit.

After the organist favored us with some renditions such as "Georgia on my Mind," "Beer Barrel Polka," and, of course, that grand old farm-auction favorite (I learned later) "Bill Bailey," the auctioneer took over. He dealt with some housekeeping details. Then he auctioned off the property. The hammer came down at $1,350,000.

The buyer was a pretty slick-looking character I had noticed earlier when he wheeled up to the barn in a white Mercedes. His trappings were turtleneck sweater, leather coat, and silver gray pompadour with a lot of stickum on it. And with him was a pretty flashy blonde lady—in jodhpurs!

I learned this about selling a horse farm at public auction in Georgia: They are easy to sell. Collecting the money is the hard part. We sold this farm three times over the next several years!

The silver pompadour—whose name I have repressed, else I would display it in bold face type—put up a check for $50,000 as "earnest money." He signed agreements, notes, and security interest instruments. There was much handshaking, toasting the future of the new farm venture, and picture-taking. The blonde—having hit the open bar several times—kissed auctioneers, the organist, and me repeatedly. There was much joie de vivre. But, alas, there was to be a severely disappointing shortage of money forthcoming.

The $50,000 checked bounced and was re-deposited several times, while we waited on a "transfer of funds." The auction company finally collected it, but there were no further remittances.

Six months later we tried again. There was another auction, a little lighter on the amenities this time, to be sure. That buyer bought it for $1,100,000, paid in about $300,000, and then he went belly up.

A bank later bought Dogwood Farm for $800,000. We ultimately got close to what we originally thought we would get, but it took several years and some hustling around on the part of the auction company to get it done. There was much anguish on our part because we could have put that sale money to good use.

Meanwhile, the horses and equipment were long gone for Aiken.

CHAPTER 27

AIKEN

Of course we could have used the money from the sale of the farm. Cash flow for Dogwood had always been tricky. During the long period when we were under the burdensome restrictions of the National Association of Security Dealers, we required a big staff, jumping through expensive hoops. We had to form partnerships hand over fist to feed the monster we had been forced to create.

In the early days, Dogwood Stable was headquartered in the fiftieth most non-horsey state in the Union, and Georgia banks had no reason to be sophisticated on commerce involving racehorses. Consequently, they were quite queasy about providing a really adequate line of credit for the purpose of buying horses.

Necessity being the mother of invention, I had to solve that problem, and I did it in a very innovative manner. You see, when I went to a horse sale, the "necessity" was that I had to spend several millions of dollars. I had to buy the inventory . . . so I could form the partnerships . . . so I could make the profit that would enable us to stay in business. I might have flunked out of college, but I did understand those simple economic principles.

The "invention" was buying horses at public auction—on terms! It was a revolutionary idea—completely unheard of. But as I said earlier, I was no stranger to unorthodoxy.

The scheme embraced the buying of a commodity that had no established residual value and was highly perishable—and taking a year to pay for it, with no legal recourse for the seller. It was a pretty dicey exercise for the consignor (one that mandated enormous trust on his part). That I was ever able to arrange this was flattering to my reputation—and even more flattering to the guts of the willing consignors.

Predictably, there were two different outfits that agreed to try this out. One was Leslie and (son) Brownell Combs of the world famous Spendthrift Farm, wheelers and dealers of the first order. The other was Lee Eaton, the most resourceful and out-on-the-cutting-edge auction purveyor of horse flesh in the history of the game.

I went to each of them originally and made this pitch: "You know me, and you know my word is good. So I want to ask you to let me buy your horses on terms. If the auctioneer knocks the horse down to me—if I am the successful bidder on any of your horses—I want to know that I will be permitted to pay for that horse over a period of a year. I will pay one third immediately, the second payment in six months, and the final payment six months later, with interest at one and a half points over prime. I'll probably pay off the balance well before that, but I don't have to. You will be the loss-payee on the life insurance of the horse, but you will turn over the foal registration papers to me right away. After I buy the horse, I will send you a letter of agreement covering all this, but I will not be signing any security interest agreement or any other documents. How's that sound?"

It sounded fine to both Spendthrift and Lee Eaton, for several reasons: they knew I would pay the money; they surmised my discomfort with a line of credit in Georgia; they understood that I would pass those terms on to my investors, making a Dogwood partnership more attractive; and they knew—all else being close to equal—I would want to buy a horse from them. Finally, Spendthrift and Eaton cannily figured that I probably would not end up with the horse. But providing terms to me would put another bold bidder in the fray to bolster the price of the horse.

The auction companies were all for it. They got their commission out of the first payment, which came in to them. And the letter of agreement absolved them of any future collection responsibilities.

Word got around, and ultimately I could buy horses on terms from practically any major horse consignor in America, and some in England and France. Some small breeders or consignors simply could not play ball because they had to have their money right away. No one ever got a late payment from Dogwood, and most were paid off early. The system gave me leverage in buying horses—important, because from the time I spent, say, two million dollars at the sale, to when I got the funds from the sale of the partnership shares, several months would have gone by. Instead of having to come up with two million dollars right after the sale, I took down $666,000 (one third) from my bank line of credit.

The need for terms would be eliminated in future lush years. But it was a lifesaver early in the game.

Moving day to Aiken rolled around on a hot June day in 1986. It has now been twenty years since three big horse vans rolled into Aiken, loaded with Dogwood horses and equipment. When they were unloading at the Aiken Training Track, I was in the midst of a speech to the Aiken Rotary Club.

Aiken is a famous horse town, and some of the greatest horses in the history of the American Turf have called it their home town. Whether this is "the chicken or the egg," I don't know. It's both, I guess. Good horses, good horse people, and successful stables attract others of the same ilk.

The Aiken Training Track is a mile in size and is one of the best in the country. The track is owned by the Whitney Trust, and we who use it pay six hundred dollars per horse per year for that privilege. Barns—and houses—are scattered around its environs in an easy, attractive manner. One of the most delightful attributes of Aiken horse training, and a cherished tourist attraction, is the "Track Kitchen." An ex-groom named James "Pockets" Carter and his wife Carol run this delightfully ramshackle establishment. The food is outstanding, the service relaxed, and the ambiance warm and helter-skelter. Pockets also operates a morning food service for busy grooms and riders at the various barns. This he does in a dilapidated old panel truck, on whose sides are emblazoned the words, "Pig Coffin." As you may guess, barbecue is a feature of the Track Kitchen and its catering service.

During much of the last century Aiken has also been the winter playground for a cadre of very rich, stylish northern families known as "the Winter Colony." Remarkably, there was a time when the railroads ran special trains out of New York to Aiken on Thursdays and Fridays to accommodate the captains of industry keen to join their families and friends for equine-oriented weekend frolic. Names like Whitney, Grace, Knox, Bostwick, Ruckelshaus, Goodyear, Hitchcock, Rutherfurd, McCormack, Clark, Von Stade, and many more from *The Social Register* were on those trains. And when they got to Aiken there was an unwritten rule that one had to participate in three different sports each day. Choices could have been riding, fox hunting, polo, golf, tennis, court tennis, and shooting. The nights were filled with all sorts of gaiety. But these functions were pretty clannish; they did not necessarily include the year-round residents of "the village."

As Florida (Del Ray, Hobe Sound, Boca Grande, Gulfstream) flourished as a recreational destination for the wealthy, Aiken became somewhat less in vogue, but it always kept its patina of laid-back, slightly shabby elegance that appealed to a certain, unflashy type. I think it is a compliment to the authenticity of Aiken when I say never would one boil down a choice for a winter home to Aiken or Palm Beach. They are apples and kumquats.

When we arrived in Aiken, the days of the special trains were long since gone, and the Winter Colony had shrunk considerably. There was beginning to be a healthy blend of all types in the community, but there was a trace of malaise in the economic structure of the little town. More and more racing outfits were wintering their stock in Ocala or in South Florida, near the racetracks that were in operation during the winter.

Aiken was small, still great, but its re-discovery was still a few years in the future.

Because things were a little slow horse-wise, our arrival in town was received with some enthusiasm. Mack Miller, Whitney Tower, and the McKelvies had put their social stamps of approval on Anne and me, and Dogwood Stable (no longer "Farm") was known quite well by racing people, of whom there were many in Aiken. Still, we were a large outfit with a little flash about us, such as our riders being bedecked in stable colors, and we were not unfamiliar with the value of publicity, so resentment among our new neighbors was certainly a reaction waiting to happen. We were wisely sensitive to this point. The fact that Ron Stevens first made a nice impression and blended into the community smoothly was a big factor in our acceptance.

We were delighted with the Aiken move. I drove over often and spent the night. Anne came with me frequently, as there were social activities in which we were anxious to participate. But, since it was a three-hour drive from Atlanta, we decided to look for a weekend cottage (cottages can run pretty big in Aiken). We looked at quite a few and finally saw one that was great, but considerably bigger than what we had in mind.

Then—like a bolt out of the blue—an idea: "Why don't we just move to Aiken?"

We had never entertained the idea of leaving Atlanta, as we were an integral part of the community. It had been good to us, and we had played small but enthusiastic roles in its development. Anne and I had been in Atlanta for twenty-eight years. But the town had changed. From the exciting, progressive, but strongly Southern-flavored city on the go, suddenly much of its personality had got up and gone! Atlanta had become a big, important, generic city. If you had known it in the great days of the Fifties and Sixties, you had to be a little sad about it in 1987.

Then too, our daughters, Cary and Lila, were grown and married. And, curiously, maybe it was at a time in our lives when the journey needed a jolt, though we certainly were unaware of it. I believe it is healthy to have an upheaval (non-catastrophic, of course) and readjust your sights every so often. The lives of Anne and Cot Campbell could not have been happier, but we were receptive to a new adventure.

We embarked on one rather matter-of-factly. The Campbells would move to Aiken; and I would move the Dogwood Stable, Inc., office to Aiken.

The office staff in Atlanta were, for the most part, not horse people, and none of them wished to move. With the Atlanta job market being very advantageous, most would take their chances relocating there. I was hoping our treasurer, Bill Griffin—well-versed in the regulatory requirements of the NASD—would come. And I was disappointed that Margaret Layton, our communications director, elected to return to Kentucky. Both of them did come to Aiken several times during the transition period to help locate a new office and to recruit staff from

Aiken and nearby Augusta, Georgia. They found a wonderful old Victorian home, which we bought and converted into office space. Dogwood operates out of that house today, and it is a knockout and a joy.

We staffed up nicely; we had a few bumps in the road, but very few.

It was entirely coincidental, but our dramatic (and really rather surprising) relocation to Aiken ushered in a four-year era in the life of Dogwood, and in the personal life of Anne and me, that could best be described as tumultuous.

Never was the stable as strong as in the beginning of 1988. Dogwood came out of 1987 with a North American Champion, the fine steeplechaser Inlander; the stakes-winning Southjet, with $1,105,000 in earnings; and three other major stakes winners: Law Court, Atlas, and Dana Calqui. And there was good depth on the fifty-horse bench.

Within a six-week period in March and April, Inlander and Southjet were gone. Law Court got sick and was taken out of the line-up for a long time.

Inlander broke a shoulder when he got careless going into a jump in the one hundred thousand dollar feature at the Atlanta Steeplechase. He took off early, struck the jump, and somersaulted over it. An eerie, collective gasp rose up from the tremendous crowd. When I got to where he lay helpless, I immediately authorized his destruction.

Two weeks later Southjet, hero of the Canadian International, was making a brilliant move in the two hundred thousand dollar Pan American Handicap at Gulfstream Park when he took a bad step and was quickly pulled up by his jockey Jean Luc Samyn. He had torn badly the support ligaments in his ankle. He was removed from the course in a horse ambulance. In his stable that night a worried team saw him through a critical post-injury period. It looked as if he could be saved for stud duty.

However, the blood supply system in the injured ankle was so badly damaged that he soon took a turn for the worse. In several days, he had deteriorated considerably and was in great discomfort. Then Southjet was gone.

Three days later I got an early morning call (never a good sign) from a trainer in Hot Springs, Arkansas (Oaklawn Park). A panicked, riderless horse on the training track had struck into our colt, Buckhead, while he was galloping. All concerned were banged up significantly.

So, to quote an old racetrack expression: "Chicken one day; feathers the next."

I am first and foremost a horseman, and you can't imagine the emotional trauma of losing quality performers and individuals who mean so much to your life. You're losing great friends who have done a great deal for you. Certainly, when it happens, when you're making the long trek down the racetrack to where the distressed animal is, you rise to the occasion. You don't weep and wail and rend your garments and gnash your teeth. You quietly deal with the situation, discuss what needs to be discussed, and then try to move on without a lot of useless post mortems. A defense mechanism kicks into place. You show no emotion. In fact, you go to great lengths not to. You go on about your business and activities outwardly unaffected and you do not discuss it. Believe me, this is the only way to handle it; for *me* to handle it, at least.

But when you wake up at three o'clock in the morning, the tragedy and the significance of it engulfs you. Two weeks later you may have an illogical, weird reaction to some completely unrelated situation. You're surprised at yourself, but you know the reason.

Because you don't demonstrate emotion does not mean you don't feel as much pain. But my business is a business of a few incredible highs and frequent lows of varying degrees—some very deep and pronounced. For your sanity, you must try to move on away from the dreadful disappointments and occurrences as rapidly and efficiently as possible. Maybe it's part of "professionalism."

If the doctor who tells his young patient he has a terminal disease then spends the next two days anguishing over that situation, he's done a terrible disservice to his other patients, his family, and himself. He *cares* though.

After being a horseman, I am next a businessman. Good news stimulates the sale of shares in Dogwood partnerships. Bad news creates a bear market. And in the spring of 1988, we had on our hands "the Mother of all Bears"!

There was really nothing but bad luck to blame for this disastrous spring. We were providing the best of care for our horses. They had been developed conservatively, and certainly none of them had shown any forewarnings of the injuries or maladies that struck. But when 1,100-pound animals, with 115-pound jockeys on them, run at top speed in large groups, accidents happen—just as they do in any field of athletic endeavor. Accidents are infrequent, but loaded with impact. What had happened to us was that we had been hit by a decade's quota of gloom in a period of six weeks.

Our racing stable was like, say, the Notre Dame football team that won the division championship in 1987; then when the team reported for the 1988 season, a freak accident wiped out the starting backfield, in which there had been several All-Americans.

Nothing seemed to go right. If there was a photo finish, we lost. If a young horse had shown promise during the winter in Aiken, when he got to the races that spring he failed to deliver. An unimportant but time-consuming virus hit several racetracks where we had divisions, and it zeroed in on the Dogwood horses of course. As the old country song complained, "If it weren't for bad luck, I'd have no luck at all."

I think all of us in racing understand luck—or at least we understand that we *don't* understand it. We sure believe in it. When it's running badly, all you can do is keep on truckin', doing what you're doing, and hang on tight. It will change when it changes; you can't make it happen. But when your luck turns and the good streak starts—and there are streaks—then take your shots, and, like a hot crapshooter, crowd your luck.

July came and Dogwood was still floundering. I was faced with a dilemma: the Keeneland Summer Yearling Sale.

Among many Thoroughbred auction sales around the nation, the granddaddy of them all in those days was Keeneland Summer. It later lost its luster; it was deemed an anachronism in 2003 and was consolidated into Keeneland's more practical Fall Sale. In its day, around three hundred of the crème de la crème of yearlings were at Keeneland in July. They represented the finest of physical specimens and the very choicest bloodlines. This sale was surely one of the most exciting and glamorous "happenings" in the world. The richest and most influential racehorse fanciers flocked to Lexington for a week of wining and dining, gossiping and horse buying. In four sales sessions on Monday and Tuesday afternoons and evenings, many of the equine stars of tomorrow were sold.

For days before any sale, young horses are brought out of sales barns and posed and paraded for buyers and pretend-to-be buyers. They are poked at, felt, walked, x-rayed, scoped, and scrutinized in every way prior to the bidding. The average sale price per animal at that time was close to four hundred thousand dollars, and the gross amount spent—with Keeneland taking out five percent—would hit over one hundred million. An important economic exercise!

I was on my way then to becoming one of the country's most significant buyers of Thoroughbred bloodstock, but I was definitely a "boy among men" when compared to the truly top international players in action at that time, such as the Arab sheikhs, the Japanese consortiums, Stavros Niarchos, Allen Paulson, William T. Young, Robert Sangster and John Magnier, D. Wayne Lukas, and other deep-pocketed enthusiasts.

The sales are exhilarating, exhausting, tedious, nerve-wracking, fascinating, boring, and depressing. The procedure is analogous to recruiting a professional football team from a bunch of ten-year-old kids. My job is to buy young horses about which I am genuinely enthusiastic, because I'm the one who has to sell them. They must be sound (structurally correct). They must be athletes, so great attention must be paid to how they move. Since they've never had a saddle on their backs, I put great store in the way they walk. And their pedigrees must appeal to my clients (through the years there has been sheer magic in such sire names as Northern Dancer, Secretariat, Mr. Prospector, Nijinsky, Danzig, Alydar, Storm Cat, A. P. Indy, etc.). The other criterion for me is that they must escape the lust of the strongest suitors.

I have enormous optimism or I wouldn't be in the horse business, but I did not arrive in Lexington that Wednesday before the sale with an air of invincibility; nor, indeed, was one warranted. Whether I knew it or not, the year thus far had taken a bit of a toll on my confidence. And why not? Horses were not running well, and the phone was not exactly ringing off the hook with clients calling to chat about the upcoming Keeneland Sale. Each year I've been able to sense and measure the electricity among my clients. In 1988, the voltage was low. And, believe me, I did not want to buy too many young horses if there was a bleak market for their syndication. The idea of launching my own personal racing stable with several millions of dollars worth of young horses did not seem appealing. But I have always felt that when your back is against the wall, the best plan is to charge. And I did.

By Sunday afternoon before the first sale session, Ron Stevens and I had seen every horse we wanted to see and had culled the possibilities down to about twenty-five. We had inspected this short list at least three times. In the hot sun of July, this is exhausting work. Among three or four thousand people on the grounds, perhaps eight hundred are legitimately engaged in the commerce of the sale. The rest of them are there just trying to rub elbows with someone for some reason, or they're tourists observing a scene they've read or heard about. Certainly the very presence of the fun-seekers slows down the laborious looking and culling process for the buyers.

I like to buy horses alone. I am not interested in a lot of opinions. However, Ron Stevens is the exception. He is quiet, sharp, and a good horseman, and he and I work well together at the sale. Sometimes I am asked by others if I mind if they tag along at the sale to see how I go about selecting these yearlings. The answer is that I really do mind. It is disconcerting to be looking at horses while answering questions, chattering, introducing people, and worrying that someone is going to get run over or kicked by a horse. This is crucial work for me, deadly serious when I'm preparing to commit hundreds of thousands of dollars in a split second. Many laymen think we travel to Kentucky, get all dressed up, ensconce ourselves in a comfortable seat in a cocktail party atmosphere, and occasionally say, "Ooh, isn't that horse pretty. Let's bid on him."

I had spent a good bit of time at Will Farish's barn at the sale. He had three or four that I was keen on. Farish is a wealthy Texan (Humble Oil) who has a marvelous farm, Lane's End, just outside of Lexington; and while he did not exactly have to claw his way up from the bottom, he has done well racing and breeding and has become one of the most respected men in the Thoroughbred horse business. Incidentally, he is one of George Bush's best friends, and the Queen of England stays with the Farishes when she comes to Kentucky to indulge herself in the pursuit of her first love—racehorses. He also served as Ambassador to the Court of St. James. But, more importantly to me, Will breeds and raises good horses.

I was quite keen on an elegant looking filly he had. She was from the first crop of Kentucky Derby winner Spend a Buck.

There was a Danzig colt that I liked. He was a little on the dumpy side, but I thought there was a lot of improvement in him. Often buyers will penalize a young horse for something that time will cure. I thought the Arabs and Japanese would pass him up.

Finally there was another colt, by Storm Bird and the first foal from the fine race mare Weekend Surprise, a daughter of Secretariat. Thus this individual offered the effective genetic cross of Northern Dancer on top with Secretariat on the bottom.

I loved that, and I fancied the colt, though with reservations. He was average-sized, nicely balanced, had good bone, and was a little crooked in his left front ankle (which I could live with). But, he also had a way about him. He definitely got my attention. In fact that was also my main objection. When I first asked for him to be brought out of the stall, he was exceedingly obstreperous, dragging his poor showman all over the viewing area. And he was quite studdish; he definitely had his mind on the fillies in the nearby walking rings. Much to the embarrassment of the Lane's End people, he came out of the stall with, and maintained steadfastly, a huge erection. No amount of slaps with the shank or cold water from the sponges aimed at the strategic area could correct this situation. Overall he was not presenting himself well. However, on return visits to see him, he improved markedly as the newness and excitement of the sales grounds at Keeneland wore off. Another thing worried me a little. He did not have a good walk—and this is the only demonstration one gets of athleticism at this early stage of the game. I remember writing on the catalog page—along with other comments—"walks like a Chinaman."

There were eight or nine other horses at other consignments that I was going to take a shot at. And by now I was sufficiently caught up in the spirit of the sale so that my mind and judgment had been cleared of the cobwebs of gloom.

At one o'clock Monday, the seats in the pavilion were almost full. The auctioneer's insistent gavel established some semblance of order. The announcer made the obligatory opening announcements about establishing credit "if you have not done so previously," and about soundness, bidding procedures, moving your purchased horses, etc. The sale began when Hip Number 1 was led into the small, tanbark-filled ring in front of the auctioneer's stand with about two thousand seats fanned out in amphitheatre configuration.

A lot of buying horses at sales is waiting. I did because my first horse was going to be Hip Number 46, due in the ring about 3:00 or 3:30. I bought that horse, a big, solid bay colt by Nijinsky, for $110,000.

No more action until the evening session. The fifth horse in the ring was a sharp, chestnut colt by Blushing Groom. I went to $300,000, but the bidding blew past me and the colt sold to Wayne Lukas for $625,000.

Hip Number 110 was the Spend a Buck filly from Will Farish's barn. I was delighted to get her for $250,000.

In the middle of the evening session, Hip Number 130 came into the ring. This was the feisty Storm Bird-Weekend Surprise colt. This time, perhaps mesmerized by the bright lights, auctioneer's gavel, and the murmuring crowd, his conduct was quite exemplary. No erection.

He opened at $50,000, bumped along in $25,000 increments and at $175,000, when the bidding slowed, I jumped in and bid $200,000. I thought I had him, but a young English agent, representing one of the lesser Arab sheikhs, bid $210,000. We see-sawed back and forth, with me bidding quickly to show strength and resolve. I bid $300,000 and bought him.

When the sale ended the next night around eleven o'clock, I had bought six for $1,600,000. Buying young horses stimulates optimism for me; thus the dismal black cloud that hung over the Dogwood operation was, for the time being at least, obscured.

We arranged shipping to Aiken and we headed home. We would have to wait a year at least to determine whether or not we had bought wisely. But how nice in the meantime to dream of what immortals might be among the new six.

An Alydar colt we bought was named Autocracy. The Spend a Buck filly became Pinch Penny; the Nijinsky colt was Hitchcock Woods; the Danzig colt was Zig Zag Zig; the Raise a Native colt, Malagueta.

The Storm Bird colt was named Summer Squall.

And he would turn out to be "faster than the Word of God!"

CHAPTER 28

ANNUS HORRIBILIS

There were major domestic developments in 1988, and the scale tilted to the negative side.

My father died. He was ninety-three. He had continued to live in his small apartment in Atlanta until he was almost ninety, when my sister Sally took on the difficult task of getting him to move into an "assisted living" facility.

For some time, Sally and I had been supporting him to whatever degree was necessary. He had not had a source of steady income since he left the Coca Cola Bottling Company in Des Moines, Iowa, in 1940, forty-eight years earlier. When I was in the advertising business, I arranged a job for him as traveling goodwill ambassador for a sizeable tourist attraction in Florida. This was a "History of Aviation Museum." This was perfect for a distinguished, colorful, charming old aviator, but it didn't last forever. I was able to manufacture some minor income-producing assignments from Dogwood. He sold off some of the paintings that my mother had bought on her buying trips to Europe for Rich's Connoisseur Gallery. And he became close with a very lovely, and very rich, widow in Atlanta. This was a wonderful arrangement for them both, encouraged by both families.

When Anne and I moved to Aiken, it was upsetting to him. We stayed in touch as closely as possible, but my sister bore the brunt of trying to keep him happy, and this—as always—was not an easy assignment.

He said it was time for him to die. And it probably was. He had always said that when he could no longer occupy his unwavering, compelling persona (my words, not his), he would kill himself. I thought he would. But that time had come and gone several years earlier, and he never considered it.

He was a handful, Bill Campbell! He was a wild assortment of wonderful and very difficult qualities. Whenever I smell Bay Rum after-shave, I think of my father. I think of him anyway. Certainly much of what I am came from him—with some tinkering and tempering on my part. To use a hackneyed, but most apt, expression: "When they made Bill Campbell they broke the mold."

The true tragedy of that dark year had to do with Anne's brother, John Dodd. This man was one of Atlanta's most respected doctors, and people. John was a truly gifted, versatile—and eccentric—Renaissance Man. He was an absolute perfectionist, sometimes to an alarming degree. John agonized over every diagnosis, and was determined to bring to successful conclusion every medical problem he ever faced. If he didn't, it drove him crazy. He was a man whose day could be ruined by the simplest, most inconsequential annoyance. If someone cut in front of him on his way to work, if his stock went down two points, or if the morning newspaper got rained on, the irritation from this could and would fester all day long.

During much of his life, he seemed to have some anguish simmering in his soul. His relief from the cares of the world seemed to come when he could have a drink, or when he painted or played his guitar or piano into the wee hours of the morning. He liked the idea of playing tennis and squash, but his missed shots and bad bounces drove him up the wall.

His achievements, which were many, were taken for granted and were never enough. He derived little satisfaction from them. The hiccups, rare or minor though they might be, were devastating to him.

We saw John, Marie, and their three children often; and looking back on the early part of 1988, nothing seemed amiss. He was the same old John. But one day Anne got a call from her mother, who said she was concerned that John seemed quite "depressed." Anne was very disturbed, of course, and arranged to talk to her brother the next day. He admitted that he was depressed, but they had a long and satisfactory talk, and afterwards he had a better outlook on life. In fact, he called her back the next morning (at dawn, oddly) and said he felt much better, referring to the fact that the bird now singing outside his window sounded sweet, whereas last week he wished "that goddamned bird would shut the hell up." He also told her that a close psychiatrist friend had urged him to visit a facility in Dallas, Texas, for several weeks of treatment, and he had agreed to go.

Everything sounded so much better. The day for his trip came. He had an afternoon flight to Dallas, and Anne and I had coincidentally flown to New York that morning.

We flew into La Guardia, rented a car, and drove into the city, checking into the Plaza Athenee Hotel. We had just walked into our room, and the bellman had delivered the bags and was going out the door, when the phone rang. I answered. It was our son-in-law, Lawson Glenn, calling from Atlanta.

He said, "Cot, John Dodd is dead. About a half hour ago, John shot and killed himself."

With his mother and his daughter in the house, he had dressed for his flight and was sitting on the bed waiting to be driven to the airport. He could go on no longer. He put a gun in his mouth and ended it.

Life was simply too difficult for John Dodd to bear.

A gigantic crowd came to the Atlanta funeral service for this beloved man. The family then took him back to LaGrange, Georgia, where he was buried.

This year then was a time when there was a need for a new hope and new beginning, and that had come a month before this tragedy with the birth of a little girl to Lila and Lawson Glenn. Campbell Dupree Glenn was born in Aiken, her parents having moved from Atlanta when Lawson went to work for Dogwood, leaving a post with Bank of America.

Campbell was a welcome diversion in a bleak time.

She lived in Aiken for nine years. Her mother and Lawson, a fine fellow, decided their marriage was unsuccessful, and they divorced amicably. Sadly, under the circumstances it was untenable for Lawson to continue to work for Dogwood, and he left and went back to Atlanta. Several years later, Lila married another guy we liked a lot. She and Campbell lived with him for two years, and they then divorced. Lila and her daughter moved to Atlanta, and she married Tommy Tindall. This time she got it right. The family lives happily in Atlanta.

I liked the fact that Lila believed in Holy Matrimony. She was just a little quick on the trigger. She married good people, but when the union turned out to be less than perfect, she felt she owed it to all concerned not to settle for it, and called it a day. Amazingly, she was able to part on good terms and then remain friends.

During Lila's stay in Aiken, it followed that Anne and I would play a major role in parenting Campbell, and what a great joy that was. Consequently, we have an understandably unusually close relationship with her. She is an "old soul."

Aiken turned out to be the best of all worlds for the Campbells.

The only unattractive thing about the city of Aiken is the hideous experience of driving into it. One encounters a pageantry of junk automobiles, derelict shacks, and scrubby land and vegetation. But once in the city, it is a knockout, and rarely is there a visitor who does not fall in love with its very distinct personality.

Aiken has more than its share of beautiful, tasteful homes, and often you see a large, stately old home next to a small, modest cottage. As I said earlier, Palm Beach it is not. Many of the houses have high, ivy-covered brick walls surrounding them, and an astounding number have small stables on the property. All the streets are boulevards, with lush parkways laid out between one-way streets. There is luxuriant growth with an abundance of tropical palmettos and canopies of live oaks over some of the streets. Many of the streets in Aiken are still dirt, to accommodate the horses. Equestrians are everywhere, and it is no surprise to see a four-in-hand carriage, with top-hatted driver and passengers, going up the main drag.

In the middle of Aiken—repeat, in the middle—are two thousand acres of protected woods. Hitchcock Woods is open only to equestrians and pedestrians. Developers have licked their chops over this land, but it can never be touched, thanks to the airtight trust established for the city by the Hitchcock family.

For that matter, the Aiken Training Track is in the middle of the city. The mile track, along with a nearby five-eighths-mile track, several polo fields, and the ancillary barns clustered about in the pines and the oak trees, must occupy a hundred acres. The tracks and many of the other facilities are owned by the Whitney Trust.

Aiken is a small town, with a population of unusually sophisticated people. There is a blend here of the old South, Northern retirees, egghead intellectual types associated with the Savannah River Plant (titanium and other mysterious chemicals), and a harmonious relationship of blacks and whites. And it all works and makes for a pleasant, stimulating, and charming community. Believe me, Aiken is not just another little country town in South Carolina. This is precisely what our friends in Atlanta wanted to think when we injured their civic pride and left that city.

Living in Aiken did usher in interesting new developments in our lives. Anne and I certainly flung ourselves into the offerings of the new environment. If there was a community activity, we took part in it, even going so far as to attend what was known as "the Chitlin Strut," an annual jamboree of rednecks that took place in the nearby down-at-the-heels town of Wagener, South Carolina. The "Strut" is a community function that was founded and is sustained by the popularity of the chitterling, or chitlin, surely one of the vilest forms of culinary output in the food chain. Chitlins are the intestines of the hog, cleaned (not thoroughly, I firmly believe) and then fried. When one enters the environs of Wagener, one's olfactory glands can verify that this is the right place if the Chitlin Strut is the destination. So great was our desire to partake of all that which South Carolina offered, that I actually put chitlins in my mouth—for about six seconds.

Chitlins aside, we discovered that South Carolina was an under-appreciated state, abounding with tradition of the highest authenticity and quality.

I had hunted as a youngster and took up quail hunting again. I also became a court tennis player.

In Aiken there exists one of nine court tennis courts in America. Court tennis, also known as "real tennis" in England, is a racquet sport originated around eight centuries ago in the courtyards of monasteries in France. Hampton Court in England has a court tennis court. The Jeu de Paume museum in Paris was originally a site for court tennis. It is a game that is a combination of tennis, squash, and jai alai, and takes a graduate of MIT to learn how to understand and score it. It is very elitist, and most participants take the position that it would be best if the proletariat be kept in the dark about its existence.

I would be ranked among the top five hundred court tennis players in America. It is a minor detail, of course, but I will point out that there are only five hundred players in America, and no one would be rated behind me.

Still I love it, and I hated to abandon it this year when a knee replacement forced the issue. My doubles partner was a friend of mine in Aiken, Harry Shealy, and we billed our team as "the Fighting Grandfathers."

Part of being a good new citizen included support of the South Carolina Thoroughbred brotherhood. So, when shortly after Dogwood's establishment in Aiken I was asked to address the South Carolina Thoroughbred Association at its upcoming annual dinner meeting in Camden, I accepted and looked forward to fomenting a fraternal bond with my fellow horsemen.

I was soon to make South Carolina Thoroughbred history at that event.

First, Anne and I (and our daughter and son-in-law, Lila and Lawson Glenn) drove the sixty miles to the dinner meeting at a Holiday Inn. There was a lengthy cocktail hour (of no value to me), and about eight o'clock we went in for our repast. Anne and I were seated at the head table of what was a U-shaped configuration.

The meal did not proceed swiftly, but finally when the banana cream pie had been consumed, the president rose and started the agenda. First he wanted to recap what had transpired at a previous meeting some months earlier. Then there were some awards for "Best South Carolina Breeder," "Best South Carolina Two Year Old," etc., etc, ad infinitum. Each recipient had remarks dealing with his accomplishment. Next, there were details of an upcoming Association picnic to take place several months in the offing.

It was now well past nine o'clock, and there had been no reference yet to the fact that I might speak. I thought surely my time had come. I glanced at my notes, straightened the folds of my coat, and edged forward in my chair. At that point, the president said, "We're mighty lucky tonight because two members of the House Ways and Means Committee have joined us, and I am hopeful they will share their ideas of what components should be included in a racing bill, and what the outlook might be for legalizing pari-mutuel racing in South Carolina."

The first of the two legislators decided that he would indeed share a few thoughts with us. He droned on for about ten minutes. I looked at my watch and it was nine-thirty. I knew the second Representative was going to want equal time with the first guy.

I looked at Anne and said, "Let's get the hell out of here!" I gave the high sign to Lila and Lawson, and we rose and made our way out. I heard the president stage whisper, "Cot, you're not leaving . . . ?" I waved toward him vaguely, and thought of an old line from a blues song that my father was fond of quoting: "If you don't believe I'm leaving, just count the days I'm gone."

The impact of my actual role in the evening's program was more memorable than any speech could have been. But the "snafued" occasion was typical of the nature of 1988. But to be fair to 1988, there *was* a most exciting development.

We got word that the fine New York publishing house, Viking-Penguin, wished to publish a coffee table book that would cover a year in the life of a Thoroughbred racing stable, and they would like Dogwood to be the stable.

This windfall came about through the good offices of Helen Brann, a distinguished literary agent in New York and a Dogwood partner and dear friend. Fortuitously, the project hit a most responsive chord with Viking editor Amanda Vail, a keen racing enthusiast.

Viking contracted with Robert Parker, one of the world's most commercial and best-selling authors. Bob would write the book with his wife Joan. He created the "Spenser" mysteries and the subsequent TV series, "Spenser: For Hire." Since then he has branched out into many other literary projects, all wildly successful. Neither Bob nor Joan professed to know anything about racehorses, and their unfettered outlook on the game was to be a refreshing slant for a racing book. The book—to be titled *A Year at the Races*—was to be photographed by the Pulitzer Prize-winning Bill Strode of Louisville.

The idea was to cover every annual activity and cycle of a racing stable: first the yearling sales, then the fall breaking season in Aiken, action at the racetracks, steeplechase racing, rehabbing injured horses, parties, client entertainment, the "beautiful people," the glamour of Saratoga, Lexington, the winter season at the Miami tracks—and anything else that was schmaltzy and made good copy.

The astounding stroke of sheer, fabulous luck came with the fact that the future star, Summer Squall, was bought in 1988. He would be trained in that crop of yearlings and then introduced to racing, with all of it chronicled in this book.

The sequence of *A Year at the Races* was to begin with the yearling sales in 1988, and with Helen Brann serving as badly needed mother hen, the Parkers and Strode were herded into Saratoga for that happening. There they could kill two birds with one stone: observe the Saratoga yearling sales, and cover older Dogwood horses training and running at the concurrent race meeting.

I always thought Joan Parker was fine, and today I am a staunch friend of Bob's; and he and his work have no greater admirer than me. But Bob Parker and I did not get off to a good start.

Bob is a big, beefy Irishman, a meat and potatoes type guy, and proud of it. A Bostonian, his idea of a super evening would be beer and hot dogs behind third base at a Red Sox game, where he would be smartly turned out in a T-shirt and blue jeans. To put it mildly, he is not one with a hankering for social intercourse with the swells.

So, when he got to Saratoga—which he had pre-determined was a hoity-toity playground for the rich, the snooty and the frivolous—he had a chip on his shoulder about the size of a Frisbee. And he had about halfway poisoned the well with Joan. Bob had not yet met me, but he had decided that I was going to be a rich fop, even though he had gotten good reviews from his trusted friend and agent Helen. I think he had just planned to show the world of Thoroughbred racing that he was not impressed.

After we met and had dinner at Saratoga, I went out of my way to win him over, and I certainly tried to tell him a few things about what this game was all about. But he seemed singularly uninterested; he was intent on establishing his boredom. Clearly he seemed not to like me. Consequently, I was not enchanted with him.

When it was explained that the agenda for the next day included being at the barn on the backstretch of Saratoga Racetrack at 6:30 a.m., he was clearly disgruntled. But, he, Joan, and Helen showed up at the appointed hour, amidst much grousing over the hour, the lack of breakfast, and what a pain in the ass all this was generally.

Most of Bob's remarks and witticisms—in plentiful supply—were directed toward impressing his wife, whom he adores. Joan is a pretty good-looking old gal, quite clever, and her offhand, blasé way with him sets him ablaze. And he does not care who knows it. He does idolize her.

Quite interestingly, they have a long-term marriage, though there were once a few potholes in the road. These have been reckoned with, partially by the very creative arrangement of having separate living quarters but in the same house. At one point, they each went their separate ways much of the time, but met periodically for meals, dates, and connubial bliss, one surmises. It has worked. They are, in their way, a devoted couple.

Our happy little group attended the races that afternoon after a sporty lunch at the Saratoga Reading Rooms, a private club in a delightful old Victorian mansion. Bob was loaned a tie.

All of this time the delightful Bill Strode was shooting away in his unobtrusive, Pulitzer Prize manner.

That night it was off to the Humphrey Finney Sales Pavilion for the select yearling sales. While I can see that anyone might eventually tire of one yearling after another selling for hundreds of thousands and sometimes millions of dollars, it would have to be enthralling for at least awhile to the most sophisticated type. Apparently, not Bob; he yawned and made a point of signaling his disdain for it all.

But! As bored and preoccupied as he seemed at Saratoga, I learned later that he did not fail to grasp, retain, and catalog every utterance and nuance that he encountered during his visit. He was uncanny. What a mind! He wouldn't have admitted it, but he was beginning to dig it.

The next step, after the Saratoga visit mercifully ended, was to visit Aiken in early Fall for the breaking of the yearlings, the training barn routine generally, and—again killing more birds with more stones—we would have a Winter Colony-type dinner party with some of Aiken's notable names attending. This was one of the aspects of *A Year at the Races* that was likely to be least appealing to Bob, but it was part of the deal, and we had to expose the writers and let Strode photograph it.

At this point, Bob clearly did like Anne (how could he not?), and he was warming slightly to me (baseball lore having played a part, I think). So he came into the entertainment phase of Aiken life with a trace of a more forgiving attitude. Helen—who loved any excuse to come to Aiken—had long since decided that if this project was ever to see the light of day, she was going to have to serve as a catalyst at all educational stops along the way. To help matters along in Aiken, which she knew was going to be tough sledding, she had brought along two women who were quite lively and were known and liked by the Parkers.

Anne broke out all the crystal, the fine china, the good silverware, an overabundance of candles, and considerably more flambeau than were used at the Twelve Oaks barbecue in *Gone with the Wind*. We had a group of around twenty for dinner. Bob wore a tie, an enormous concession, and was relatively affable, though he was sweating profusely and grimacing wildly because of the constriction of a tie and buttoned collar.

Anne seated Bob, the guest of honor, next to a grande dame of Aiken, Joan Tower—a pretty lively old girl, and one elegantly suited for Bill Strode's photographic objectives.

I watched anxiously as Mrs. Tower sought to draw Mr. Parker out. But she was in heavy weather. Probably we had made a mistake, as Bob spent the evening either sullenly glaring at his plate as he shoveled in the quail hash, or peering fretfully toward *his* Joan.

The dinner limped toward a close, Mrs. Tower extricated herself from Mr. Parker, there was a bit of brandy afterwards in the living room, and we adjourned early, with Bob Parker eagerly anticipating the early morning routine of more horse training.

The next day Joan Tower called Anne to thank her for the "lovely evening." But after some digging by Anne, she did say, "That man you sat me next to was the rudest person!"

There were more colorful chapters in the saga of *A Year at the Races*, but they must unfold as does the career of Summer Squall.

CHAPTER 29

SUMMER SQUALL

I have learned that you cannot draw too many conclusions about the future quality of young racehorses. They will fool you. The early flashes are often "in the pan." And sometimes the unwatched pots are the ones that suddenly boil. In the sophomore high school class, the charming, bright, fireball fifteen-year-old may be then at the very pinnacle of his existence, but may never develop beyond that level and may end up working in a convenience store. Conversely, the gawking, dull-eyed klutz, stumbling about with his mouth open, may become the Wizard of Wall Street.

As soon as Summer Squall arrived in Aiken from the Keeneland Summer Sale, he not only *looked* like the Wizard of Wall Street, he *became* the Wizard of Wall Street!

As Ron Stevens started breaking the young horses to saddle, this bay colt began demonstrating his intelligence and his class. He learned everything quickly, was afraid of nothing, and found life in general for him to be a piece of cake. We had assembled some pretty nice stock in the yearling class of '88, but he was the unquestioned leader. When the young horses and their riders went out to the big, sometimes terrifying, racetrack for the first time, he blithely led the way. When asked later to confront the starting gate, he walked in that formidable green monster as if he owned it.

His randomly assigned rider was a pretty little girl named Julie Stewart, and she adored the colt and jealously guarded her affinity with the budding star. But through the fall, the miles of galloping replaced baby fat with tough, hard muscle and grit, and Summer Squall was about to become too much for Julie. One day he ran off with her. Though he was still a far piece from having the condition for it, he grabbed the bit in his teeth and took off. He galloped full tilt around that mile track with Julie, her feet in the dashboard and leaning back, frantically trying to pull him up. Finally he tired of the game and let her ease him up.

I thought, "Oh, my God! He'll come back to us with a bowed tendon, or wrenched ankle, or bleeding from the lungs. No telling. He'll be ruined!"

By the time Julie walked him back to us, he would not have blown out a match. Nor was he stirred up mentally by the excessive workout for which he was physically unprepared. Julie was in tears, very embarrassed, and frightened about letting him get away. She was afraid she would be replaced by our stronger, more experienced ace rider, Kim Baker; and that girl, by God, could hold an elephant away from a bale of hay!

Ron talked it over with Julie, because we absolutely could not let that happen again. She was determined that he would never get away from her again, and Ron helped by putting some different equipment on Squall. His exuberance was kept under control for the rest of his time in Aiken.

He had been put in training in September, and along about February 1989, we began to ask the more precocious youngsters for some easy speed. Boy, did he have it, and it did come easy.

He could cruise down the stretch for a quarter-mile in twenty-five seconds, under a stranglehold, while his contemporaries were all out and floundering in his wake. We had to know that he was something special.

What was he like? Average size; he matured to be sixteen hands but was about two inches short of that then. He was a lightly-made horse, which later caused the press to relegate his size to somewhere between a Shetland pony and a yak. This made for good copy, but when he was a three-year-old actually he was average in size. As a two-year-old, perhaps he was a little under average. Squall would never be a good walker, but that fact became quite academic.

He had a quality head, but not a real pretty one. He had a slight roman nose, and a nice, wide, interesting, crooked stripe meandered down his bay head. His eye was most arresting—sort of a cat eye, hooded, with a bit of an evil look about him. And indeed he was a little tough.

He didn't want to be played with, unless you had a peppermint to give him. His groom started with the peppermints, and I picked it up with great delight. Somehow he learned to signal for more peppermints by picking up his front leg. He learned the sound of my voice, and he certainly knew the sound of cellophane being unwrapped from a peppermint. Even today I can visit his paddock in Lexington, where he stood at stud for so many years. I will get out of the car, and if he is in the far corner of the paddock and hears me yell out, "Hey, Pops!" he'll look up abruptly, then break into a gallop, screech to halt where I'm standing by the fence, and jerk that front leg up abruptly.

Summer Squall was precocious, to put it mildly. So we decided he was an ideal candidate to run in the Aiken Trials. The Aiken Trials is an exhibition day of racing, offering quarter-mile races for two-year-olds and longer races for older horses. It is held on a Saturday in mid-March and is educational for the babies, in that they experience the excitement of the competition in front of a crowd of six thousand to seven thousand people. It is close to what they will experience when they get to Keeneland or Belmont. The older horses benefit from a nice tune-up after being in winter quarters in Aiken. Dogwood usually runs four or five horses. It is great fun for all concerned.

We decided to run Squall, with the idea that he would ship out to Keeneland and have a nice understanding of racetrack demeanor when he got up there for the April meeting.

Who would ride him—Julie or our regular Trials rider, Kim Baker? Our hearts held sway over our judgment. We decided that it would break Julie's heart not to ride him, and we figured he was so much the best, she could make a mistake or two and he would still win. And, after all, it was just a fun day of exhibition racing. Did it really matter if he got beat? Ha! Any time you race a horse, it matters.

Four two-year-olds were in his race. Squall, with his formidable reputation around Aiken, drew a big crowd in the paddock. He handled himself well, was very interested in the proceedings, but certainly was in no way intimidated. The post parade went smoothly, although Ron Stevens was alongside on the "nursemaid" stable pony, just for good measure. The four colts loaded into the gate reasonably well. It was positioned at the top of the long homestretch. Just before the starter pushed his button and the doors crashed open with the bell ringing, Summer Squall turned his head to look at the noisy crowds in the infield. He got left flatfooted. Not a good thing in any race, but certainly not in a quarter-mile dash to the wire. He left the gate about two lengths behind the other babies. When they hit the wire, he was flying—but had run out of ground and ran third, beaten a half-length by the winner. Three strides beyond the wire, he had engulfed the other two and was on top by a full length. But the race was not a quarter of a mile *and three strides*.

When he jogged back to be unsaddled (with Julie looking like she would commit hari-kari) it was as if a light had been switched on in his brain. He was thinking, "I won't let that happen again!" It didn't.

I shipped him up to Lexington about a week later to the barn of Neil Howard, the private trainer for Will Farish, from whom I had bought Summer Squall. Since Dogwood trainers were not going to be in Lexington for the spring meet at Keeneland, Will was just doing me a favor to offer Neil's services. As it would turn out, he was doing his farm and his trainer a gigantic favor also.

Neil, a wonderful horseman and person, worked the colt a half-mile out of the gate, and then we picked out a race on April 20. A fine rider named Randy Romero rode him that day. He went off as a strong favorite. Word was out all over the racetrack that "Dogwood has a good one in the third race."

He didn't miss the break that day. After three jumps, Randy shook the reins at him and he opened up daylight, then widened out to win by eleven lengths in very fast time. Neil Howard laughingly observed, "He was a baked cake; all I had to do was take him out of the oven!"

As I walked jubilantly down to the winner's circle, I went past a well-known clocker-gambler-character, a colorful fixture around Kentucky racetracks. This was Indian Charlie. If he wasn't a bona fide Indian, he certainly had the mystique of one. He gave me a sly grin, cocked his thumb at the colt, now galloping back to be unsaddled, and said, "That's the one you been waitin' on, Cot."

The colt was never beaten again as a two-year-old. He moved over to Churchill Downs and won two big stakes. The redoubtable Pat Day replaced Randy, who gave up the mount when he went to Europe; Pat Day would ride him for the rest of his career.

We shipped to Saratoga, where every great two-year-old in America would converge. And where immortals Man o' War, Secretariat, and Citation had put the luster on their reputations. Squall had whipped everything in the Midwest, but he had not yet tackled the stars of the East and the West, and they would be in Saratoga. Summer Squall hit town as a star. But there is much validity in the saying: "There are bigger fish in the sea than have ever been caught."

We went first for the Saratoga Special, and our colt handled the assignment with great ease. We decided to skip the Sanford, situated in the middle of the meeting, and wait for the Hopeful, a Grade One blockbuster on closing weekend. This is a race that has often, in the past, crowned the two-year-old champion.

I have described Summer Squall's career as "an agonizing ecstasy." And that it was. With a good horse, every time the phone rings—in the morning especially—you jump out of your skin. If a trainer calls you about another matter, he knows to lead off with, "Everything's okay. I just . . ."

Summer Squall was one of the last of the old-style partnerships we were doing in those days—five horses, owned by forty shares. In this case, twenty-eight people had bought the forty shares. Thank God there were not forty, but twenty-eight owners—and their connections—is a tough number to take care of on a big day at a very popular racetrack. Of course they all wanted to come to the Hopeful, so the arrangements for seating were horrendous. Dogwood has meticulously avoided getting involved with travel arrangements—hotels, air travel, restaurants. Perish the thought! But we did owe our partners a place to sit down. In the past, it had been no problem because we always figured correctly that eighty percent of them would not be there. But with the enormity of this race, they would want to attend, many with the legitimate plea: "I've never seen him run before, but now I've got to!" Some of the shareholders were established racing people and they had their own arrangements at Saratoga (Will Farish had wisely bought into the partnership, after the colt won at Keeneland).

Some of the partners indicated they didn't need any help, and we sure did not argue with them.

The day of the race, I was as nervous as a long-tailed cat in a room full of rocking chairs. This horse was undefeated—except for the unimportant, unofficial Trials fiasco—and a lot depended on him staying that way at least for the rest of the day.

Five o'clock finally rolled around, and we all headed down to the paddock, where there were the usual lame observations and questions: "Well, he sure looks good," "How do you think he'll do?" or "What does the trainer think?" One does have to say something.

Summer Squall was the strong favorite in the field of eight, the size of which was diminished because of his accomplishments. Neil Howard arrived in the paddock looking as if he might get sick any moment. So did I, and I made no effort whatsoever to do any introducing or chatting up of visiting partners. The colt's wonderful groom, Willie Woods, and the horse were the only ones that seemed easy with the upcoming assignment. But so too did Pat Day, who came sauntering in the paddock, popping his whip against his booted calf, composed and automatically giving tongue to the usual banter required of a jockey, even one of the world's greatest. The Paddock Judge sang out, "Riders Up!" Neil gave Pat a leg up, amidst shouts of "Good luck!" and "See ya in the winner's circle!" And the outrider led the fine field of young horses onto the track. We humans scampered back through the big crowd to our assigned box seats.

The field started near the end of the backstretch in this six-and-a-half furlong race. They got off nicely, and Pat took Summer Squall back off the pace, dropping into fifth position. He had no intention of making an early lead, for he had supreme confidence in this horse and in his own sensationally cool ability to find an opening at just the right time, and then produce him and win the race. Pat was a great rider because he never asked a horse for more than he needed, nor would he ask him the question sooner than necessary.

This day it did not look like it would work.

When the field turned into the stretch, Squall was still fifth, and you could have thrown a blanket over the four fanned out ahead of him. Our colt was crying for a place to run, the four in front still had plenty of steam left in them, and the race would be over in a quarter-mile.

There was no room on the rail. Going outside of the four would have necessitated a pretty sharp right oblique movement and the loss of a lot of ground. Pat didn't want that, and it was his style to wait—and count on heavenly intervention, if all else failed.

At the eighth pole, heaven did intervene—a little bit! The pair of Carson City and Bite the Bullet edged inward, while Adjudicating and Sir Richard Lewis, shoulder to shoulder, drifted out slightly. Now! There was sufficient space between the two pairs for a horse to go through. Wham! Summer Squall saw the opportunity and grabbed it.

Craig Perret, the fine jockey on Bite the Bullet, saw what was happening and he moved quickly to "shut the gate." But he was too late. Our colt had seized the space to which he was entitled. The result was a chain reaction "Pier Six brawl" with five horses—ours in the very middle—bouncing off one another. It was so rough that Summer Squall would have gone down—if he'd had any place to go. For about three strides it was like a rugby scrum, and then the Dogwood colt, mad as hell now, shouldered his way through there, popped into the lead, and went on to win the race by a length and a half.

It is a race still talked about today. Mack Miller, one of the greatest trainers in the history of the American Turf, said he had never seen a braver performance than that of Summer Squall. Pat Day said, when he got off the colt, that he was the most courageous horse he had ever been on.

Not surprisingly, when the field crossed the finish line, the Stewards flashed the "Inquiry" sign. Without seeing the head-on view, it was impossible to determine who was at fault. Was the outcome compromised by a foul committed by one of the horses?

For eighteen minutes the three Stewards reviewed the films while our group stood down on the racetrack, near the winner's circle, watching our number "4" blinking on the tote board, hoping and praying that it would cease blinking so the announcer could intone, "Ladies and Gentlemen, the Stewards, after reviewing the films of the race, have concluded that the order of finish will stand . . ."

Wayne Lukas, the renowned trainer, walked by me to unsaddle his horse, one of the ones in the melee, and cracked devilishly, "Man, I'm glad I'm not you, standing down here and watching that light blink." Not very reassuring about the outcome, but I don't think he meant it to be.

There must have been twenty-five photographers standing fifteen feet in front of us with their cameras at the ready, some with power drives whirring. They knew that there could be some prize-winning expressions—anguished or jubilant—when the final judgment on the disqualification came.

Then we erupted! The light had frozen on the board. The number 4 held firmly in the top slot. The head-on views of the race were shown on all TV monitors, and it clearly proved that for five or six seconds the foursome on the lead parted, leaving space for a horse if he could move faster than that hole was moving. Summer Squall could and did.

Summer Squall had won the Hopeful.

That night we celebrated with Bob and Joan Parker and Helen Brann. Here's what Bob Parker wrote about a snippet of dinner conversation between Joan and me:

"'What did you do,' Joan asks, 'after the decision, and the champagne in the directors' room? On the greatest triumph of your life.'"

"He paused a moment while the waitress passed out a platter of sliced tomatoes and the tinny piano in the bar played 'Sweet Rosie O'Grady,' and he looked at his wife.

"'We went to see the horse,' he said. 'At a time like that the best thing to do is to go and look at the horse.'"

Summer Squall shipped from there to Chicago. We planned to run him in the Arlington Futurity in September, and then win the Breeders' Cup Juvenile race at the end of October, in Florida at Gulfstream Park.

Feeling pretty full of myself, I issued a challenge in the press for a special three-horse race—with Arlington to put up $100,000 and the connections of the three top two-year-olds to each put up $100,000. Winner take all—$400,000. There would be the good Phipps two-year-old, Rhythm; Mrs. Harry Lunger's filly, Go For Wand; and Summer Squall. Dick Duchossois, owner of Arlington Park, jumped all over it, but the other owners did not, and the idea died for lack of support.

It would not have happened anyway. I got one of those early morning calls from Neil soon after he arrived at Arlington. He said Summer Squall was slightly lame, and he was being x-rayed at that moment. The films revealed a hairline fracture in his cannon bone. This was something that would heal in a few months, but his undefeated two-year-old campaign was over, and there would be no Breeders' Cup. But we could count on a Triple Crown campaign in the spring.

The only treatment for the hairline—which obviously occurred in the donnybrook at mid-stretch in the Hopeful—was time, and it would knit perfectly. The colt shipped to Aiken, which had gone wild over his wonderful, undefeated freshman campaign.

We wanted the community to be able to see him, but we did not want people wandering into the barn all day long. So the *Aiken Standard* published a story saying that the horse would be shown daily from 1:00 p.m. to 1:30 p.m., Monday through Saturday. Each day around 12:45, cars would start rolling into the parking lot at our barn. Folks would walk up to the board fence overlooking a grassy area in front of the stalls. Ron Stevens would bring Squall out, and he would eat grass while the people in this horse town looked on reverently and adoringly. Occasionally, the colt would cut up a little bit, then snort and look dramatically out at the horizon. The forty or fifty on hand would ooh and aah but would refrain from clapping. I got a kick out of it and went out most days and talked about him, much to the delight of the audience.

We thought that with his high-quality, undefeated year, he would be Two-Year-Old Champion. However, he suffered from the "out of sight, out of mind" syndrome. Rhythm won the Breeders' Cup in late fall, and he was named Champion.

We put Summer Squall back in training in December, put the fitness foundation back on him, and then sent him down to Gulfstream Park in Florida where Neil Howard had the Farish horses. The colt was not too far away from his first start in a seven-furlong sprint in February, when I got another of those dreaded early morning phone calls from Neil: "Mr. Campbell, I worked him this morning, and when he came back to the barn, he bled significantly from his nostrils."

Terrible news. This meant we would have to give him a month of easy work to heal the ruptured blood vessels in his lungs and then he would have to run on the anti-bleeding medication Lasix—basically a diuretic that was legal in some states but not yet in New York and a few other important states. It was not an earth-shattering problem; it could be controlled. But it was worrisome; it set us back time-wise on our Kentucky Derby campaign.

Summer Squall did make his 1990 debut on March 17 in the seven-furlong Swale Stakes, a less-than-ideal assignment as Housebuster, on his way to becoming one of the best sprinters of that era, was at his peak and was deservedly the strong favorite. Our colt, off since the previous August, made a marvelous showing to be a respectably close second. It was a fine effort, he did not bleed, and, for a non-winning day, it was a beautiful result.

We then went to Kentucky and won the Jim Beam on a muddy track at Turfway. Then it was down to Lexington where Summer Squall was a strong favorite for the Bluegrass Stakes at Keeneland. He won that race by a length and a half, with his future rival, Unbridled, third.

On to Louisville then, where he would be co-favored for the Kentucky Derby, the Holy Grail of racing. Easily the most important race in America. In the words of Cole Porter, "You're sublime, you're a turkey dinner. You're the time of the Derby winner!"

Derby Week is unbelievable! Especially if you are running the favorite (though Mister Frisky, an undefeated Californian, technically went off at infinitesimally lower odds.) There are parties all week long, civic events to be attended, and there are constant interviews from the hordes of press people on hand. It is fun, it is hectic, but surely running in the Derby is the most exhilarating experience a human being can have.

Most Derby horses ship in for the race and are, therefore, stabled in one of several special Derby barns. Neil was a fixture at Churchill and had his own regular barn, so we were located off the beaten path. That did not keep droves of the Fourth Estate from coming by each morning. The TV cameramen were constantly scuttling around the outside of the barn. There were security people stationed at barn entrances to keep the press at bay, and they had their hands full. In addition, tourists and human beings we hardly knew suddenly became long-lost buddies and wanted to come by and see the horse. We were very protective of the colt. He came out to train in the morning and looked like the Pied Piper of

Hamelin as writers and photographers scurried along in his wake to and from the track. In the afternoon, Willie, his groom, took him out to a grassy patch so he could graze. An immediate but respectful circle would form around him and take photographs while he chomped on grass.

The highlight of 1990 Derby Week for us was the party on Derby Eve given by Will and Sarah Farish at their gorgeous Lane's End Farm in Versailles, Kentucky. We supplied the Farishes with a list of partners to invite, they had some of their own friends, and the party convened at the stallion barn for cocktails on a lovely spring evening. It was so very dramatic, as winners of previous Kentucky Derbies were brought out and paraded. Then there was a motorcade along the farm roads to the big house for dinner. On the way, Lane's End employees were stationed at every turn in the road, pointing the way, and yelling "Go Summer Squall," "Go get 'em, Squall." The dinner was delightful, and the entire dining room table was arrayed with desserts done by the Farishes' chef.

Will had had a special Summer Squall film produced, and every invitee got one, along with some other nice mementoes. While he did own a share, of keener interest to Will was the prestigious fact that the Derby favorite was bred by Lane's End. And the fact that Summer Squall had already established himself as a stellar stallion attraction of the future had not escaped Will's notice.

Surely it was one of the great evenings of all time for all of us.

On Derby Day, around noon, we zipped from the house we had rented on the grounds of the Louisville Country Club right into our barn on the backstretch of Churchill Downs—in about nine minutes. How did this happen? Our Official Derby Host (volunteers are assigned by Churchill Downs to help make life easier for the connections of Derby runners) was the Louisville Chief of Police, and he offered us a police escort to the Downs. What fun!

We walked on the racetrack from the barn over to our box in the prime third floor Clubhouse section beneath the storied old Twin Spires of Churchill Downs. And the afternoon slowly—I do mean slowly—ticked away. Most of our time in the very prominent box provided by the racetrack was spent receiving well-wishers. It was very heady stuff.

About 3:30 I slipped away and walked back to the barn. The barn was where I wanted to be, although no place was going to be easy on the nerves. I had about two hours to kill. A few press members were already staked out at the barn, having gotten permission to walk over to the paddock with Summer Squall and his entourage. I talked to them for a bit, then went and sat on a bale of hay outside Summer Squall's stall, while Neil, his assistant trainer, the exercise rider, and groom walked up and down the shedrow and looked miserable. They tried to think of things to do to the horse without driving him crazy in the process.

The race was at 5:45, and around 5:00 the tension, already almost touchable, cranked up several notches. Oddly, everyone was speaking in lower tones than usual to demonstrate coolness.

Pretty soon, on the P. A. system came, "Attention in the barn area. Horsemen, bring your horses to the paddock for the ninth race, the Kentucky Derby!" We suddenly responded like the Notre Dame locker room after one of Knute Rockne's half-time speeches. We all shook hands; Willie put the shank on the horse, already bridled; and our little caravan made our way through the barn area to the gap at the three-quarter pole, the staging area for the walk-over to the paddock. As we approached the gap to the racetrack, there must have been two thousand backstretch workers and families lined up in a genuinely appreciative gauntlet through which we walked.

Ours was a popular team. The horse was bred in Kentucky, and he was a battle-hardened, honest-to-God Thoroughbred racing machine. He had demonstrated a heart of pure hickory while overcoming adversity—the bleeding. His breeder was Kentucky, his trainer was Kentucky, and Pat Day was a beloved Kentucky rider. Dogwood was well known in Kentucky, and we had paid our dues. There was nothing not to like about our team. No horse ever went into the Kentucky Derby more popular than Summer Squall.

And you sure could tell it, as the horse and five men made their way over to the paddock. We happened to lead the way along the outer rail of the racetrack, with the other fine horses and their connections in line behind us. Appreciatively, we saluted the shouting crowd and looked up in reverence at the Twin Spires, one of the most notable landmarks in all of sport. Our own special wave of noise followed us along that half-mile walk to where we turned into the tunnel that would take us under the grandstand and into the fabled Churchill Downs saddling enclosure, or paddock.

This had to be one of the most thrilling moments of my life. The hair on the back of my neck stands up as I think about it now. I have walked that Derby walk six times now. But nothing compares to that first wonderful time. My career in racing seemed to be kaleidoscoped in that brief, but splendid, span of time.

"The Walkover," as it is known today, has become a very popular thing, but in 1990 I don't think the idea of walking with your horse to the paddock had dawned on many people. Nowadays there are blacksmiths, van drivers, policemen, scads of the press, owners, and their friends and relatives, and it looks like the start of the Boston Marathon. And it is a standard pre-race television feature.

Anne and my children stayed in their seats in the box so they could see me walk by with Summer Squall, our first Derby runner. They loved it. I wish my old man could have seen it. He would have loved it.

CHAPTER 30

NOT THE DERBY . . . BUT THE PREAKNESS

A lot of people thought it was a foregone conclusion that Summer Squall would win the Derby. We had beaten many in the field already, and done it pretty easily. Mister Frisky, the California entry, had compiled a lot of his flashy record in Puerto Rico—and seemed to be a sprinter anyway.

I knew we were good enough to win the Derby, but I had no confidence that we would. Victories of that sort are mighty hard to come by. They're mostly too good to come true. But for about twenty seconds that afternoon, I thought we had it won.

Summer Squall was the ideal type to win the Derby. He had both speed and endurance and he was very handy, not a big ox of a horse that would have trouble regaining his momentum if he got stopped in the cumbersome field of fifteen. He wouldn't be unnerved by all of the Derby hullabaloo. And he loved to mix it up. The worst mistake in a race with that horse was to rough him up. That was like poking a stick in a hornet's nest.

The moment of truth arrived.

As always, he broke sharply. When he came past us the first time, Pat had gradually eased over from his thirteenth post position and was sixth and on the rail by himself. Perfect. Down the backside they stayed pretty much that way. Mister Frisky was up on the pace, and Unbridled, highly regarded because of his distance-loving proclivities, was in the back of the pack. In the middle of the final turn, at the three-eighths pole when the real running begins, the pace was telling on the front runners. Pat gave Squall a bit of nudge, as if to say, "It won't be long now, my man."

At the five-sixteenths, just before turning for home, we inherited the lead—a little sooner than we really wanted it because we had that long heart-breaking stretch in front of us. Still, he was running easy.

293

Summer Squall wheeled out of the turn on the lead, and the announcer bawled out, "They're in the stretch now, and it's Summer Squall who hits the front!"

At that point our colt thought he'd done his work, and his blood was not up as it would be in a furious stretch drive. Then he heard the roar of the multitude responding to a big move by the favorite. It didn't startle Summer Squall, but it did get his attention. You could see him cock his head toward the stands. Meanwhile, Craig Perret had put Unbridled into a drive. He was coming like a runaway freight train, and he blindsided us. He went by, and opened up three lengths before we could get back in the game and fight back. They stayed that way through that long stretch. Unbridled, an awfully good horse, won the 119th Kentucky Derby, and Summer Squall was a decisively beaten second.

Perhaps you will remember that this was the race that furnished that dramatic jewel of TV sports coverage, in the form of Unbridled's nonagenarian owner, Mrs. Frances Genter, having the race described to her by her trainer, Carl Nafzger, with a protective arm around her. This sweet old lady had a cute little pillbox hat on her head and an expression on her face like a five-year-old girl experiencing the Christmas tree.

"He's gonna win, Mrs. Genter! He's gonna win! Oh, Mrs. Genter, I love you!" Carl called out very accurately. It was a magic moment in television, and I have seen it now about six hundred times. With gritted teeth.

After the race, Anne and I were not devastated, taking the position that if someone had told us a year earlier that we would run second in the Kentucky Derby, we would have been ecstatic. We were proud of our horse.

Still we began hearing immediately that God was looking down on the elderly Mrs. Genter, and how appropriate that this was cut out to be her Derby, and how could anyone not be overjoyed that she had finally experienced that rapture. "All well and good, Mrs. Genter, but don't count on any rapture in Baltimore. You've had your day," I thought.

Earlier the Viking-Penguin Publishing firm had been faced with a minor dilemma: when should *A Year at the Races* be concluded and printed? A logical time might have been after the Hopeful victory, coming as it did at the end of a year. But could they stop when Summer Squall was seemingly a big factor in the Triple Crown races of 1990? They decided that the book would end with the Hopeful, but that printing would be held until after the Preakness, at which time a prologue would be added. This made sense.

Dogwood had committed to bypassing the Belmont Stakes because our superb colt had had a very intense spring campaign, and we could not use the anti-bleeding medication Lasix in New York State. It would not be fair to ask him to run without it, because, like a lot of horses before and since, exertion could cause capillaries in the lungs to rupture, and a tiny flake of blood could seriously impair a horse's breathing. I had announced after our run in the Derby that no matter what happened at Pimlico, "We will not run in the Belmont! That is etched in stone." At which point, our friendly rival, Carl Nafzger (Unbridled) snorted, "Yeah, it may be etched in stone, but that's what they make chisels for!" Not withstanding that skeptic, the publishers could count on a logical stopping point after the running of the Preakness at Pimlico Race Track in Baltimore, on Saturday, May 19.

We shipped to Baltimore a week before the race. So did most of the other runners, now winnowed down to nine from fifteen. Most of the key players among the press came in with the horses. The stable area of Pimlico was teeming

The stabling was much cozier at Pimlico. All of us were in one long barn, with the Derby winner traditionally assigned to stall number 40. Near the barn was a strip of grass about thirty feet wide.

Just after dawn on Thursday, Summer Squall was given a good brisk gallop, but he was on the muscle and it was all his exercise rider, Robert Vickers, could do to keep him from running off. He was as "sharp as jailhouse coffee." But a problem came when he came back from the gallop. He had his bath, cooled out, and then went out to graze, with about twenty reporters looking on.

Eagle-eyed Jennie Rees of Louisville's *Courier-Journal* spied a trickle of blood coming from his nostril. So did his groom, Willie, and he immediately took him back in his stall. But it was too late. A headline was created: "Favorite for Preakness Bleeds Two Days before Race."

Jennie and several of her cohorts rushed over to me. "Didn't Summer Squall bleed just now when he dropped his head to graze?" Knowing full well what the answer was, I acted surprised at first—which was dumb. Then I went in the stall with the horse as if to check it out, came out, and said, "Yeah, he did bleed. But he had an awful strong gallop. He almost breezed a mile, and he wasn't treated with Lasix. When he runs with Lasix on Saturday, there won't be any bleeding."

The post position breakfast was set for 10:30. This would be attended by all the owners and trainers in town, and certainly all the press would be there to ask questions about the post positions. I knew, therefore, what the major topic of the breakfast would be, and I had to play it just as I had with Jennie.

Neil did not go, press relations not being his favorite thing. There were many questions, of course, and I answered just as I had with Jenny, very casual and matter of fact. However, one jerk—who later apologized—sought to stir things up by saying, "There's a ruling in this jurisdiction that if a Steward observes a horse bleed within seventy-two hours before a race, that horse must be scratched. Where does that put Summer Squall?"

"Which Steward was it that recorded that bleeding episode, Bill?" I asked. None had, and that was the end of it.

The night before the Preakness, the Maryland Jockey Club threw an exquisite party at the fabulous National Aquarium on Baltimore's Inner Harbor. The food and drinks were overwhelming, and there was dancing to the delightful Doc Scantlin and His Imperial Palms Orchestra. In the shank of the evening, a barge was pulled into position fifty yards away in the harbor, and a stupendous fireworks extravaganza commenced. Even people on the backstretch at Pimlico, fifteen miles away, delighted in it.

We remarked at the time how ironic it was that we were experiencing this superlative occasion of a lifetime, and it was all due to the courage, ability, and class of a four-legged animal, dozing in a dark stall on the grounds of a storied old racetrack in a bad section of Baltimore, Maryland. But, who knows? Perhaps Summer Squall was looking out over the webbing on his stall door, marveling at the fireworks. His personal pyrotechnics would come at 5:30 the next afternoon when about ten million people would watch him go after victory in one of America's greatest sporting fixtures.

Summer Squall was the pre-race favorite and would remain so through post time. The theory was that the shorter (one-sixteenth mile) distance would benefit him, and his shiftiness would adapt well to the "tight turns" of Pimlico (actually they're no tighter than Churchill Downs turns).

I slipped away from the box section about four o'clock on Preakness afternoon and went to the barn. The ABC Television producer had asked to "mike" me during the running of the race so that the audience could hear my comments (screams, that is). Dave Johnson, the great race caller, was also going to do a pre-race interview with me at the barn for use in a feature during the telecast.

We did the interview, and of course the bleeding episode was a major topic. I remember saying, "Believe me, the Lasix will hold him, and he will run a bang-up race!"

Finally, around 5:10, we got the call to bring the horses over to the paddock. Actually, they would be saddled picturesquely on the turf course in front of the stands.

There ensued an amusing display of gamesmanship between Carl Nafzger, who would saddle the Derby winner, and Laz Barrera, the brilliant and crafty California trainer who had Mister Frisky. Laz liked to be late into the paddock, keeping everyone cooling their heels. Carl was determined to wait until Laz and his entourage had left the barn. They each capitulated, and we all went over pretty much on schedule.

Race time, and Anne, Neil, and I were seated together in a box, with a hand-held ABC TV camera staring up at us. I checked my ear piece, in place so that the TV anchorman could ask me a question should the happy occasion arise. The audio mike was in place to record my extemporaneous, candid commentary.

A silence fell over the crowd. The starter sprung the latch, and the race was on.

An outsider named Fighting Notion set the pace, with Mister Frisky stalking him. Summer Squall was in fourth spot and on the rail, where Pat liked to be.

The late-running Unbridled was three or four lengths behind us in the field of nine horses.

Leaving the backstretch, Pat pushed Squall a mite, and he easily slipped closer, still hugging the rail. It's funny how some sound bite, completely illogical and inconsequential to the import of the event, will be the emblematic one that sticks in your memory. So it was in the Preakness. As the horses turned into the stretch, with Summer Squall now moving on the inside and Unbridled rolling hard on the outside, Dave Johnson sang out, "And Fighting Notion leads 'em into the stretch in the Preakness!" It was really a meaningless utterance, but for some reason those words conjure up the Preakness for me.

But Fighting Notion's moment was soon over. Tiring, he drifted out a bit, and Summer Squall—waiting again for divine intervention—had room. He (on the inside) and Unbridled (on the outside) swept past the laboring frontrunner and looked each other in the eye. Johnson screamed his signature line, "AND DOWN THE STRETCH THEY COME! Summer Squall on the inside. Unbridled on the outside." This time Summer Squall was ready for him. They went at it in a ding-dong battle for an eighth of a mile, but then Unbridled blinked. Summer Squall had made him crack. The next memorable sound bite was, "It's Summer Squall by two lengths. Second in the Kentucky Derby, he's gonna WIN the Preakness!"

The rest is like a dream. Hugging, kissing, whooping, with the ushers trying to get our sizeable group collected and moving down the steps and across the track, so that I could lead the colt into the winner's circle and the TV-formatted presentation could take place.

Where were those post-race questions from the TV people? I found they had given up when, during the furious stretch battle, I had resorted to my unfortunate reflex of screaming out, "Goddamn!" About fifty times. This was an exclamation high in drama certainly, but not exactly what the network was looking for.

It was Pat Day's first Preakness, and it was one of the fastest ever run. Unbridled finished second and Mister Frisky third, but the outcome was without excuses, and Summer Squall had clearly carried the day.

For Dogwood and the Campbells it was monumental. Winning the Preakness was like taking the report card of my life and stamping it with a gigantic, indelible "A+," and then erecting a billboard in Times Square to display it. It was like throwing a stone into a pool and watching the ripples emanate from it. Those ripples would slow through the years, but they have never stopped coming, nor will they ever. In the big scheme of life, winning one of the Triple Crown races will not rank with finding a cure for cancer, but given this career—and the life I had once led—it was a gargantuan accomplishment.

I led the horse in, amidst much clapping and furor, and then made my way up onto the presentation stand, where TV luminaries Jim McKay and Jack

Whittaker, the president of the Maryland Jockey Club, and the Governor of Maryland awaited. Anne was with me, of course, and so was my long-time partner and wonderful friend, Paul Oreffice.

My remarks reiterated that there would be no Belmont. I managed to get in a plug for the great horse town of Aiken, and I referred to the fact that Summer Squall had "the heart of a Capetown Lion." This was an expression that had struck my fancy years earlier for some strange reason. But it was one that hardly anyone else ever understood. In fact, many who saw the telecast thought I was attempting to strike a blow against apartheid in South Africa.

The logical rubber match would have been the Belmont Stakes, of course. We had declared out, even though whichever horse finished best in that race would receive a one million dollar bonus. Unbridled, also a bleeder, did run in the Belmont, finishing fourth. So he backed into big dough. (I always kidded Carl Nafzger that he should have given Dogwood a ten percent commission.)

We rested until September, won the Pennsylvania Derby, and then headed for Bossier City, Louisiana, for the $1,000,000 Super Derby. Unbridled had the same race on his dance card. Here, then, was your rubber match.

The race at Louisiana Downs was set for a Sunday. I arrived in Shreveport on Friday afternoon, drove to Bossier City, and, of course, went straight to the barn. When I pulled in, I noticed Neil and two veterinarians at the door of the horse's stall. As I approached, several sportswriters stopped me. While I talked to them, I glanced over at Neil who impatiently motioned me over. I did not like the looks of that. I excused myself and sauntered casually over to the stall.

Neil announced, "Horse has got a temperature. Not much. Took it an hour ago, and it was 102 and change. It may not amount to anything. Might have gotten stirred up . . . or something."

We waited fifteen minutes and took it again. Going down—101:4. In another hour, it was normal. Whew! We were okay. The next day he galloped like a champ and had no temperature.

At noon I went to the airport to pick up Anne and our friend and partner, Helen Brann. Lots of other owners were arriving and so were press representatives coming in. No wonder, because the Super Derby was shaping up as the race of the year, with the two big contenders vying for the divisional championship.

The racetrack had promoted the daylights out of the race, and there wasn't a hotel room available within fifty miles. Louisiana Downs had sold out of reserved seats. It figured to be the biggest and most important day in the track's history.

The three of us had lunch and then went back to the motel. As Anne and I walked into our room, I noticed the dreaded red light on the phone blinking away. The message center told me to "call Mr. Howard at the barn." Oh Lord. "Better come on out here," Neil suggested.

When I got to the barn, a forlorn little cluster had assembled outside the stall: two vets, Neil Howard, and Willie. Sportswriters were hovering like vultures about thirty yards away, so we all went into the stall with the horse.

"One hundred and two," Neil said, rolling his eyes. "We've come a long way. But I know one thing. It's not like him to carry a temperature of 102, and he's shown us that twice in two days."

"Aw, hell, we've got no choice but to scratch him," I told Neil. He breathed a sigh of relief.

"It's going to destroy the race of the year, and this racetrack is going to lose hundreds of thousands of dollars. Plus all the owners are going to be crushed, but we've got to scratch. But don't breathe a word of it until I talk to Edward DeBartolo (owner of the racetrack). They've got this big party tonight, and I want to find out how he wants to handle this."

I called the Racing Secretary and told him we had to see the big boss. DeBartolo was in his suite in his skybox, hanging out until the party started. He jumped to his feet when we came in, gave me a big grin, shook hands, and said cheerily, "Hello, Cot, my good man. Whatever can I do for you? Are we treating you right?" He thought maybe I needed some more seats or something.

"I've got to scratch Summer Squall. He's sick."

"Oh, shit!" said DeBartolo.

"Oh, shit!" echoed the Racing Secretary.

DeBartolo gazed out the window for a moment and said, "Okay, here's what you gotta do for me. The deadline for the Sunday papers is eight tonight. I don't want this to get out until the papers have gone to bed, and I'd really like to keep it under wraps until it's too late for TV news at ten. Please. Can you keep it quiet until then?"

What ensued was about the toughest three hours of my life. We did go to the party—as late as we could. By the time we got there certain members of the press were beginning to smell a rat. I did have to tell my partners about the scratch. Otherwise I played along with the party line, and should have been nominated for an Academy Award for the "best performance by an actor whose heart was not in it." I'm sure some of the partners spilled the beans later in the evening, because the Dallas paper the next day did have Summer Squall's scratch. None of the other papers had it though.

Damn Louisiana—our horse had a virus all fall. He wasn't right until after we had given him another winter in Aiken.

Unbridled ran second in the Super Derby, and then went on and won the Breeders' Cup.

The two rivals met six times. Summer Squall finished in front of Unbridled four times and lost to him twice. Yet Unbridled ended up winning more than twice as much money as our horse ($4,489,475 versus $1,844,282). Unbridled won the Kentucky Derby and the Breeders' Cup Classic. He was named Champion in 1990, and he deserved it.

Summer Squall was surely one of the top racehorses of his time, and he then went on to be a wonderful stallion. He produced a Horse of the Year, a Derby winner, and several Champions—one being the Dogwood filly, Storm Song. He got wonderful fillies, and versatile racehorses generally. He was not terribly fertile, and this worsened as he grew older. For several years now—as this is written—he has been out of service and pensioned at Lane's End. He is quite content in his paddock, which is far removed from the titillating activity of the breeding shed in the springtime. He loved his job in earlier years but does not fret about the absence of love life now.

Lane's End Farm (Will Farish) bought twenty-five percent of Summer Squall from our partnership for two million dollars, about the time of the Preakness. After his four-year-old campaign, the partnership sold another fifty percent to various breeders, and we kept the remaining twenty-five percent. This entitled us to ten breeding rights. We could either breed a more on each, or sell each for the going stud fee. We did the latter, and the stud fees ranged from $25,000 to $50,000 during his years in service.

While Summer Squall had a fine four-year-old campaign, it did not have the wallop of his great sequence of races when he was three. His feet were not his strongest feature, and he was plagued with quarter cracks much of that year. This is a split in the hoof, which acts like a severe hangnail would on a human. The cracked hoof can be patched with plastic, but the hoof of a horse is vital to that 1,000 pound animal, and unless it is perfect, the horse's performance is not likely to be. When he's running against the very best at forty miles an hour, an infinitesimal defect can tell.

I also think we might have gotten a little too careful with him when he was completely sound. He was never better than in the spring of this three-year-old year when we were behind the eight ball and playing catch-up to get to the Derby. We were jamming it to him, and he was thriving. I think, in retrospect, he loved work. If we were too conservative, I take the blame. I managed his campaign.

How about his trainer? When you combine horsemanship, integrity, intelligence, and congeniality, Neil Howard has few equals and no superiors. He has no greater fan that me.

In that ghastly year of 1988, when I purchased a yearling by Storm Bird out of Weekend Surprise, how comforting it would have been to have known what a source of joy, thrills, and recompense that animal would be.

CHAPTER 31

YOU BETTER BE LUCKY...
IF YOU'RE GOING TO KENTUCKY

As we moved into the Nineties, I made three weighty decisions. Two improved the quality of my life. The third was embarrassing, but it made me *appreciate* the quality of my life.

The Summer Squall saga, involving twenty-eight people owning the forty shares in him and five other horses, caused me to arrive at the conclusion that that was a hell of a lot of people to deal with. And life was too short to try. I decided right after he was retired that we would do each partnership individually from that point on. Dogwood would keep five percent of each horse and sell four shares of 23.75 percent interest.

Furthermore, with small partnerships, this would be a practical time to do away with the dreadful NASD and all the regulatory hoopla that came with Limited partnerships.

From now on, four people in every horse, and General partnerships—not Limited. This was a splendid move, greatly streamlining my life and business.

The second streamlining move came with my decision to ask Ron Stevens to leave the Dogwood payroll and set up his own independent training operation, with the understanding that Dogwood would be his "soup bone" account. We would turn over our tack and equipment for him to use. In other words, he could be set up in his own business with practically no outlay on his part.

This was a slight shock to him and others but was quickly seen as a logical and beneficial move for Ron. We asked that the barn continue to have the Dogwood look, with our colors on everything, including the riders when they went out in the morning.

The third move was that I decided that I did not want a big outfit with sixty to sixty-five horses—too much work and responsibility, too many headaches. I would enjoy life much more if I cut the size of the stable down to forty horses. Thus I would buy and manage one-third fewer racehorses.

I made a big "to-do" about the "cutback," as we referred to it. Dogwood sent out a news release; we notified our clients, and blabbed it around generally. There was only one thing wrong with this plan, and it took me about ten days to figure it out. When I did, I never forgot it.

The last thing in the world Cot Campbell wanted to do was less of what he was doing. I adored my life. I loved buying the horses, managing their training and their racing campaigns. So the cutback idea was the bomb of the world. And the announcement concerning it made me look like an imbecile.

I realized I like what I do and the way that I do it. What could I possibly do instead that would give me as much pleasure? Nothing. So, I will work until I cannot work anymore.

The Nineties were a great, in-the-groove time of my life. I had gotten it right. I was in my sixties and early seventies, healthy, with an adequate amount of youthfulness (using the term recklessly, perhaps), enough money, with my children happy and doing well. I was a major figure in racing, with much recognition for my "contributions" to the game. I was enjoying the fruits of my labors.

I have always been intrigued with asking people the question, "What has been the best time of your life?" No matter the age of the person, the answer is usually "Now." Occasionally someone will answer, "Oh, when I was in high school (or college)!" or, "When my babies were coming up." But most say "Now," even if they're ninety years old. My own answer has certainly always been a resounding "right now."

By the start of the Nineties, Dogwood had emerged as one of America's prominent racing stables. Our size and the caliber of the racing stock we carried would indicate that we should crank out $1.5 or $2 million a year in earnings, and we were doing it.

The luster of the decade was increased considerably by Dogwood's five trips to the Kentucky Derby—1990, 1993, 1994, 1997, and 2000. Another one came in 2004, and more are on the way, I hope. In all, we have taken seven horses to six Kentucky Derbies. We have run in nine Triple Crown races, with a win, a second, two thirds, and a fourth to show for it.

Just running in the Derby is a magnificent accomplishment in racing. Many of the great stables, and plenty of distinguished trainers, have never entered a horse in the Kentucky Derby. This puts it in perspective: There are close to forty thousand foals born each year. Three years hence, around fifteen or sixteen of them, on the average, will be good enough to run in the Kentucky Derby. It is not easy. And to place in the Derby? Well as the hardboots say, "You better be lucky . . . if you're going to Kentucky!"

To make a horse eligible for the Derby, you put up six hundred dollars in February. But then the price of the game goes up. To enter, three days before the race, you put up twenty-five thousand. And then when you actually run, you are charged another twenty-five thousand. This fifty grand total is meant to retard the entry of unsuitable horses, but it does not always accomplish this.

Admittedly, we have been guilty in a few of our Derbies of sending "a boy out to do a man's job." But the Derby (and the Preakness and the Belmont) are the brass rings on this merry-go-round. And reach you must.

In 1993, we had a three-year-old colt with the intriguing name of Smilin Singin Sam, possessing that moniker when I bought him for twenty-eight thousand dollars at a two-year-old sale. We turned him over to an irrepressible Irish trainer named Niall O'Callaghan. He trained him and exercised him. This gray colt was sort of what his name implied—a loopy, free-spirited, lanky drink of water, who could run like hell and liked to demonstrate it from the start of the race. "Catch me if you can" was his natural philosophy, and we did not tamper with it. We sent him out to Oklahoma in April, and he romped off with the Remington Park Derby. We decided that we must try the Kentucky Derby, and we did, retaining the same, capable rider we had been using through his entire campaign, a likable Cajun named Larry Melancon. Larry was a second echelon rider and one who was accustomed to being replaced when his mounts reached truly big-race status. We decided to "dance with the guy who brung us." Larry rode him in the Derby and has always been grateful for our sticking with him.

Old Sam got shuffled back at the break and could not make the lead, which was the name of his game. However, down the backstretch he had ranged up to be fourth, and Larry decided, "What the hell, let's enjoy fifteen seconds (not minutes) of fame." He gunned Sam into the lead, and we all got to scream a little. He led into the turn, and that was about it. All he got in the Derby was hot and dirty!

He ran a good third later in the Ohio Derby, and then one day when Niall was galloping him at Churchill Downs, Sam stumbled and collapsed on the racetrack. He got up quickly and just stood there while Niall got his bearings. Very scary. We did some treadmill tests on him at a vet clinic in Lexington and found out that he had a serious heart murmur. Who would have dreamed there was a weakness in Sam's wonderful old heart! We retired him.

In the year that Sam ran in the Derby, I went to another two-year-old sale and bought a strong, masculine, dark bay colt. He was sired by Gulch and out of a good Argentine mare named So Glad. He had a big, ugly blemish on his ankle, so I only had to pay forty-three thousand dollars for him.

We named him Wallenda. Do you remember the famous daredevil, high-wire-walking Wallenda family? Eight of them took a horrible spill while performing for Ringling Brothers, Barnum and Bailey Circus in Detroit. Karl Wallenda was the patriarch, and he once walked across Tallulah Gorge, a sickeningly fearsome gash in the earth in North Georgia. It is a deep gorge, a quarter-mile across and seven hundred feet down, cut out of the Appalachian Mountains. Thirty five thousand came out to see this scrawny, sixty-five-year-old geezer, with his thirty-six-pound balancing pole, creep agonizingly across that horrible gorge, in a gusting wind, on a quivering, gleaming silver wire. He paused in the middle—resisting the inclination to look down—then stood on his head twice.

It was courage, hovering on insanity.

So why did we name our horse Wallenda? The colt was sired by Gulch (a gorge?) and out of So Glad. Old Karl walked across that damned "Gulch" like he owned it, but when he got to the other side, we figured he was "So Glad!"

The famous circus family got caught up in the name and his Derby quest, and there was much conversation back and forth about the progress of the equine Wallenda. We got to be pals with the Wallendas. It was a delightful experience. Sadly, but not surprisingly, Karl Wallenda was killed several years later, at age seventy-three, when a gust of wind blew him off a high wire stretched between two tall buildings in San Juan, Puerto Rico.

Wallenda was a splendid racehorse and made well over one million dollars in his career. He won a nice two-year-old stake in New York in the fall of 1993. Then he came out as a three-year-old and ran third in the Florida Derby and then second in the Bluegrass in Kentucky. Pat Day was available in the Derby, and we nailed him for the big race.

Frank Alexander, our trainer with whom we've had a number of good horses, had a tall, pretty exercise rider named Darlene LaFollette (with one eye of brown and one eye of blue, incidentally!). She was a take-charge gal who traveled with the horse when he went out of town to run in stakes. She was smart and had a good sense of humor. Darlene decided that Derby participation called for the creation of a special dance to be named "the Wally Walk." The routine involved a prancing, cake-walking, foot-in-front-of-foot motion with the arms outstretched as if balancing. It did not become a national craze, but we all enjoyed doing "the Wally Walk," and it got considerable television coverage

Wallenda did not cotton to the Churchill Downs racetrack surface, and indicated this to Pat Day with a pre-Derby work. He was never a factor in his Derby race. But he was of a caliber that belonged in the Derby.

Wallenda's Derby performance was quite like our journey from our rented house on the grounds of the Louisville Country Club to Churchill Downs.

You will remember in 1990 that our Derby host, Louisville's Chief of Police, provided a police escort to the racetrack.

Well, when Wallenda came to the Derby in 1994, the Governor of Kentucky was our close friend, Brereton (Brerry) C. Jones. He was, and is, one of Kentucky's most prominent horsemen. He was delighted that we were coming back to run in Kentucky's great Classic while he was Governor. Brerry called to ask what he could do for us while we were in his state. Remembering the wonderful police escort earlier, I said, "Well, in 1990 we had a police escort to the track on Derby Day. Is there any way you could handle that?"

"Done," he said.

Several weeks before the Derby, I got a call from Governor Jones' secretary, and we arranged that a Highway Patrolman would meet us at the entrance to the Louisville Country Club at eleven a.m. on Derby Day. Oh boy. Now our transportation worries were over.

The day came. Anne, two daughters, their husbands, and I piled into our car. At the appointed spot, there he was, reading the paper in his patrol car. We greeted one another, and he got out of the car and inquired, "Well now, where're we headed?" A slightly unnerving question.

"Why, we're going to Churchill Downs," I replied.

"Churchill Downs. Hmm, Churchill Downs. Well, do you know where it's at?"

"Sure! I know. Don't you?"

"No sir," he said, "But if you'll lead the way, I'll be right behind you."

Now this "escort" had turned into an impairment. Believe it or not, we started out, and he was *behind* us. No siren. No lights flashing. We're creeping along the interstate, bumper-to-bumper traffic, and I am going crazy with this ridiculous caravan in heavy Derby traffic.

Finally, while we were at a standstill, I told one of the boys to take the wheel, and I got out. I went back and slipped in the front seat beside the patrolman. He smiled pleasantly, happy to have the company.

I said, "Put your siren on. Now put your flashing light on. Pull ahead of my car." We started making headway, cars ahead of us were scattering to the sides, and in ten minutes our little motorcade glided into the stable area at Churchill Downs.

I thanked the patrolman, who looked around and replied affably, "So this is Churchill Downs. You know—this is my very first trip to Louisville. I'm based in Hopkinsville."

It was funny when it was over, but I never had the heart to tell the Governor. He might not have been amused.

Our Wallenda won many a good race. He put $1,125,638 beside his name, but he did not raise any hell in Louisville. However, he did elsewhere in 1994.

He helped Dogwood get the "Leading Owner" award at the Saratoga meeting that year, and we finished the year with earnings that put us in the top ten of over twenty thousand racing entities in this country.

In 1997, we came back to Louisville with a showy-looking, big horse named Jack Flash, trained by the popular, adopted-by-Louisville Nick Zito. Jack Flash would take your breath away with his looks—a strapping mahogany bay horse, with just enough white on him to provide some elegance. Craig Perret was his jockey.

The '97 Derby was fun (if that is ever really the word), thrilling but, for some reason, not quite the blockbuster experience of some other Derbies.

Jack Flash was always knocking at the door, but he never came in! Referring to the three Triple Crown races, Craig Perret announced before the running of the 126th Derby, "One of these races has his name on it." Seemed possible, but none did. He ran seventh in the Derby, closing, as always, from out of the clouds. But he was always a little late.

He looked and acted like a developing Classic winner should look and act, but he just kept "developing." We decided against running him in the Preakness or the Belmont. When unsoundness reared its ugly head later, we made a steeplechaser out of him, and there again he was terribly promising.

We finally retired him—with a bowed tendon—and turned him over to a lovely, young lady in Florida. He became a show horse, and then finally a very high-class stable pony.

Jack Flash was in the same barn with Dogwood's Storm Song, two-year-old Champion. She was clearly the best juvenile filly in America in 1996, and after she won the Breeders' Cup in Toronto, we gave her a nice vacation, bringing her to Aiken for several months of doing nothing. Great idea, but a mistake it turned out. She was like a working girl who took an extended vacation to the Caribbean. She said, "Where has this been all my life?" When it was time to go back to work, the enthusiasm was not there. Storm Song was never very good at three. She was at Churchill Downs to run in the Kentucky Oaks, the female counterpart to the Derby. She was a very distant third, after a couple of earlier prep duds. We retired her then, and sold her at public auction in the fall for $1.4 million as a broodmare

We came again to the Derby in 2000, this time with two horses—Trippi and Impeachment, both trained by Todd Pletcher.

Pletcher, at this writing, probably dominates American racing as no other trainer in history has come close to doing. He and I got together in the winter of 1996 when I sent him five horses (he only had seven or eight total at the time). After serving a pretty long apprenticeship with Wayne Lukas, one of the great trainers in the history of racing, he had decided at age twenty-eight to go on his own.

He was awfully glad to receive those Dogwood horses when they got off the van down at Hialeah. While Todd is by no means the demonstrative type, he has never ceased being grateful for my confidence in him at that time.

He is highly intelligent, honest, driven, possesses a flair for communicating with a horse, is incredibly organized, and has an astonishingly keen memory. He trains so many horses nowadays that it can make you uneasy. But the bottom line is that he knows everything you would want him to know about your horses—including, most impressively, the ones that are proving to be of no account. On top of all this, he's a dedicated family man.

Todd first danced into the national spotlight when he brought four horses to run in the 2000 Kentucky Derby, unequalled except for when his old boss had saddled that many a few years before. Two of Pletcher's charges were ours. And what admirable horses they were.

Trippi was sired by End Sweep, so when the time came to name him I remembered, from my youth, one of the great practitioners of football's end sweep: the great University of Georgia All-American, Charley Trippi. Thanks to the efforts of my good friend Loran Smith, venerable Georgia Athletic Department guru, Charley gave his rather disinterested permission. But he got pretty keen on his namesake when the colt got good. In fact, when Trippi went to stud, Charley wrote, "I feel discriminated (sic) at this time. After playing football for nineteen years, I didn't have the luxury of being put out for stud." Always one with a keen interest in coin of the realm, Charley was subconsciously nettled by the fact that the equine Trippi was being paid for his stud services.

The horse blossomed in January 2000 and won race after race with his blinding speed, carrying it a mile and one-eighth in April when he won the Flamingo Stakes in Florida, thus punching his ticket for the Kentucky Derby a month later. His character could be seen in his lovely head and big generous eye. Trippi was not what you would call a good mover. In fact, he moved like Quasimodo, "the Hunchback of Notre Dame," as he lurched along in an ambling, sidling, hippity-hop gait. But could he ever scorch the earth! In his races, he would break a half-length behind the field. But the next three strides would find him two lengths on top, and chances are he would never look back.

His more abrasive stablemate was Impeachment. He was sired by Deputy Minister out of a mare named Misconduct. The colt was bought in the fall 1998, when President Bill Clinton was engaged in his indiscretions with Monica Lewinsky, and impeachment proceedings had begun in the House and Senate. When we took Impeachment the horse to Hot Springs, Arkansas, to run in the Arkansas Derby, the significance of the name was by no means lost on the Arkansans.

Impeachment was a late bloomer also, but unlike Trippi, he had a running style in which he dropped so far back he was almost out of the line of vision until the field hit the far turn; then he would come flying. Man, was he fun to watch! You knew he was coming. He might not get there in time, but he had running on his mind. He was very masculine, muscular and chunky in appearance. When he was sharp and in racing trim, he would delight in biting a hunk out of your arm if you got too close to his stall. Trippi was a gentleman; Impeachment—as his name implied—was not.

Their running styles complemented each other: Trippi on the pace, Impeachment dawdling in the rear of the pack. In the Derby, Trippi—with "Chop Chop" Chavez aboard—made the running with another speedster named Hal's Hope, inevitably tiring after a fast mile but hanging on courageously to finish mid-pack in a route that was beyond his range. Impeachment got the signal from our old friend Craig Perret at the half-mile pole, and he came storming up the stretch to be third, behind the celebrated Fusaichi Pegasus.

One of the proudest moments of my life was in that 2000 Derby. It came when the two Dogwood horses, in our sparkling gold and green silks, led the field out onto the racetrack for the post parade, with the gigantic crowd singing "My Old Kentucky Home."

It had been a thrill for me and my partner, Paul Oreffice, to walk over from the barn with the two horses, but this post parade was almost too much. There was not a dry eye in the Dogwood boxes.

Our most recent Derby runner was a horse whose photograph should be in Webster's Dictionary next to the term "Thoroughbred Racehorse." Limehouse ran a gallant fourth of seventeen in the 2004 Derby. Limehouse ran in twenty-one races, and he fully intended to win every one of them. He did win $1,100,433 and seven races. He "broke his maiden" at first asking, and then proceeded to run in nothing but stakes races for the rest of his career, and seventeen of them were graded stakes. We called him our "Road Warrior" because he ran at ten different tracks from California to Saratoga, distances from four-and-a-half furlongs to nine furlongs, turf and dirt, at ages two, three, and four.

Limehouse was named for the Dixieland tune "Limehouse Blues." You see, his momma was Dixieland Blues.

When his racing days were over, we sold Limehouse for stud duty for six million dollars.

The old boy is enjoying life now, having served his first season at stud in 2006. He was bred to 140 mares, and he handled that "chore" as he did everything else—with great efficiency and class. He has an active career ahead of him, and it could not happen to a more deserving guy.

*   *   *

And *this* old boy is enjoying life now. The twilight years, as they are euphemistically known, are supposed to be easy, with the hardships behind you and nice things happening. Believe me, it was that way in the '90s. It is that way now.

Though "the shadows may be lengthening on the lawn," this time of my life would be hard to beat. I have worked hard, and I love working, and I never want to stop. I thrive on action. And I'd rather struggle with (minor) trouble than deal with boredom. I am proud of my outfit and my people. Pound for pound, the Dogwood staff is the best there is. Dogwood Stable is highly respected. I am highly respected. Immodest of me to say that, I am sure, but when you were the prohibitive longshot that I was in my turbulent years, perhaps I can be cut some slack for my lack of restraint.

Within my industry, there have been many tangible indications of appreciation for Dogwood and me, most of them coming in the last fifteen years. There's nothing more tiresome than reporting a long litany of accolades, and I promise to whip through those that must be mentioned.

In 1992 I was the recipient of the John W. Galbreath Award for "entrepreneurial excellence" from the University of Louisville. Clearly this recognized the successful Dogwood concept of group ownership. Around that time, I was the keynote speaker at the National Museum of Racing Hall of Fame Induction ceremonies, one of racing's annual highlights. A few years back, I was presented with the Clay Puett Award by the University of Arizona's Race Track Industry Program. This was for "outstanding contributions to the racing industry." I will refrain from the boards, trusteeships, executive committees, chairman stuff. I do have the biggie of biggies, but I will save that for the last chapter.

But one very exciting bit of recognition of a very sporty nature was the selection of Dogwood colors to be on one of the jockeys that line the wrought iron balcony in front of the legendary New York watering hole "21." First established in 1920 as a speakeasy, 21 Club has since reigned as one of the most famous and popular restaurants in the world. It is their tradition that the greatest racing stables in history have their colors at "21". You may be sure we tend to dine there when in New York! But we must also dine at the great old New York hangout for sports and entertainment stars and "wannabes." Gallagher's Steak House now features a giant mural depicting 73 men and women from Irving Berlin, Jack Kennedy, and Marilyn Monroe, on down to Cot Campbell. The mural was done in 2006 by the superb French caricaturist, Pierre Bellocq ("PEB").

Dogwood started its own tradition in 1993, and I am very proud of it. This was the year that wonderful old Dominion died in England after an illustrious career at stud, where he sired one hard-knocking, blue-collar racehorse after another—with a good smattering of top-quality runners thrown in. As a fine compliment to Dominion and his genuine spirit, the British Breeders Association had earlier established an annual "Industry Award" to salute a behind-the-scenes worker who had contributed to making the racing world better. The recipient received a lovely bronze of the horse, Dominion.

When the old guy died (while serving a mare!), we decided to bring the award across the ocean. We started the Dogwood Dominion Award, offering five thousand dollars and a bronze of Dominion to an unsung hero in American racing.

Judges for this award, through the years, have been racing luminaries Pat Day, Mack Miller, Jerry Bailey, Penny Chenery, Jay Hovdey, and Anne Campbell. The latter three are currently serving. These people have an agonizing assignment, because each year around thirty wonderful men and women from all across America are nominated. Picking one is absolute murder.

The presentation of the Dogwood Dominion Award is made at a gala luncheon at the Saratoga Reading Rooms during the race meeting each August, with about seventy-five on hand. We have just completed our fourteenth, as I write this.

From a business standpoint, we have been in an enviable position for fifteen years, with the demand exceeding the supply. We carry a stable of sixty horses, and we buy about twenty-eight to thirty yearlings or two-year-olds each year, to replace those that are annually culled or retired. At four separate times of the year—August, October, March, and May—we make an offering of about seven horses. The first two offerings are yearlings that I purchase at sales in Lexington and Saratoga Springs, New York. The March and May horses come from two-year-old sales in Miami and Lexington.

The drill is to buy the young horses at public auction, bring them back to Aiken, and photograph them. Glowing descriptions of the horses and their pedigrees are then blended with the photos. The sales material is sent out to our clients and prospective clients. Happily enough, within ten days the horses are usually sold out. We are by no means complacent about the ease of this sales effort and we keep running scared, but the main problem we have had for quite awhile now is to avoid irritating those people who got the sales material, acted on it rather promptly, and then were told that the horse they wanted a share in was no longer available. Very annoying. A problem for us . . . but a nice problem to have!

Taking some of the pressure off us is the fact that ever since 1992, one man, Paul Oreffice (ex-chairman of Dow Chemical Company), has automatically taken a share in every horse Dogwood has offered. So when we come out with an offering of seven horses, each to be owned by Dogwood (5%) and four (23.75%) shareholders, instead of having twenty-eight shares to sell, we have twenty-one. I think it is a fine arrangement for us both.

Paul is a major league sportsman and an avid horseman—and a very knowledgeable one. He realizes racing is an inexact science, and he is not a second guesser.

I think he and I have played important roles in the lives of each other. Anne and I are fast friends with Paul and JoAnn. I have known Paul for close to twenty years, and each year my fondness for him increases. He is a strong man with spectacular class.

Paul Oreffice is the poster boy for a client roster of the highest quality, one that has included the heads of such companies as Delta Airlines, Prudential Financial, Ralston Purina, Marsh & McLennan, Leggett & Platt, Textron, and Visa USA. Thirty percent of Dogwood clients are chairmen or presidents of companies, or own their own businesses. The client roster has also included many in the worlds of show business and sports.

One unforgettable honor for me came in 1999, following the death of a long-time client and friend. This was Flora Roberts, one of the most celebrated theatrical agents in the history of the New York stage. Flora came into the Dogwood fold with her close friend Helen Brann when we were introduced to them by Tommy Valando, a well-known music publisher and producer (*Fiddler on the Roof, Company, Sweeney Todd, Merrily We Roll Along*).

I was asked to speak at the memorial service for Flora, an artful production master-minded by Helen Brann, the aforementioned noted literary agent. It was held at the famous Broadhurst Theater on Broadway. This program included Hal Prince, Cameron Mackintosh, Stephen Sondheim, Robert Parker, John Kander and Fred Ebb, Wendy Wasserstein, Maury Yeston, Barbara Carroll—so many heavies of show business. I spoke about our days with Flora at Saratoga, told about a horse we had named "The Great Flora," spoke of her love of racing (and slight lack of understanding), and . . . just about Flora. I said that while she was undeniably brilliant, she was prone to wander off on conversational tangents that were hard to follow, and "sometimes I didn't know what the hell she was talking about." This brought the house down, because all her friends had been in the same boat.

What a great honor for me to be included; it was one of life's most unforgettable experiences.

I performed on Broadway.

CHAPTER 32

A RIPROARIOUS LIFE

I love Aiken, and am lucky to live in it. But my heart wanders often to Saratoga Springs, New York. I have gone there consistently since 1971, and heard tell of it long, long before. By now I am an old Saratoga hand. I was even once paid the great compliment of being asked to be the keynote speaker at the Saratoga Springs Chamber of Commerce dinner. Unfortunately it was in sub-zero February!

Saratoga is that sporty town in upstate New York where such diverse types as Diamond Jim Brady, Lillian Russell, John L. Sullivan, Al Capone, Jock Whitney, Alfred Vanderbilt, Colonel E.R.Bradley, Arnold Rothstein, and Estes Kefauver cavorted and/or did their own brand of big deeds.

There's a great old Dixieland song ("Ace in the Hole") offering these lyrics:

"In this town there are some guys/ who think they're mighty wise/ just because they know a thing or two.

You can see them every day/ strolling up and down Broadway/ telling of the things that they can do!"

There's just enough of that in Saratoga.

The fictitious character Elwood P. Dowd (played by Jimmy Stewart) in the play *Harvey*—a production about a pleasant but consistent boozer and his imaginary companion, a six-foot-tall rabbit named Harvey—sagely proclaimed, "No one ever brings anything unimportant into a bar." So do I say, nothing unimportant ever happens in Saratoga in August.

I am a lucky man who leads an interesting, colorful, delightful life. I spend a lot of time each year in New York City, Lexington, Louisville, New Orleans, and Miami, but no period of my superb year can touch the six weeks Anne and I spend in Saratoga. It is intermittently exhausting, stressful, exhilarating, joyful, and disappointing. But I'll take a miserable day at Saratoga before any other kind, in any other place.

I really can't describe it; you must experience it. First, the six-week race meeting brings together the greatest concentration of quality racehorses in the world. Inexplicably, the atmosphere in this lovely old town is charged with marvelous good will and warmth. The citizenry is as excited as we who visit. Everywhere there are flowers, food, drink, parties, and celebrities, with the undisputed grande dame of the town, Marylou Whitney, dispensing glamour like a fairy godmother.

Interestingly, people instantly become more attractive, more likable when they enter the city limits of Saratoga. Someone who might vaguely nod at you at Belmont, Gulfstream, or Keeneland will practically squeal with glee and clutch you to his bosom when encountering you at "the Spa."

Wherever you go there is music for every taste. There is a great Dixieland band called "Reggies's Red Hot Feetwarmers" playing around the town and the racetrack, and they add much zest to our life there. When we enter the racetrack on opening day, they beam with delight, and break into "Carolina in The Morning" ("Nothing Could Be Finer than to Be . . ."). "The boys," as we refer to them, have played for two Tea Dances we've had up there, and we've brought them to Aiken for dances at the Green Boundary Club.

If dancing is your game, there is no shortage of opportunity in Saratoga. One of the big affairs is the Museum Ball, attended faithfully by Anne and me, as I am vice president of the National Museum of Racing and Anne has twice been Ball Chairman. Lester Lanin played for the Ball for years and now Bob Hardwick is a fixture.

There is plenty of glitz and glamour at this function. One year, Ginger Rogers (one of the greatest musical comedy dancers of all time) attended. Ginger was getting a little long in the tooth then, and was carrying considerably more poundage than when she was Fred Astaire's partner. Still, every guy in the place wanted to dance with her, just so they could say they had.

One old gay blade suavely cut in and announced, rather boringly, "Now, I'm not any Fred Astaire."

Ginger gave him a weary look and shot back, "Well, honey, these days, I'm not any Ginger Rogers!"

It's a rich atmosphere—Saratoga. Imagine taking a year of your social, economic, and entertainment life and cramming it into one six-week period. That's why Anne and I have learned to set a sensible pace, and why we take off every two weeks and spend a few days in Vermont, being anonymous.

While at Saratoga in 2004, I got a call from the Director of Keeneland's Auction Sales and the executive director of the Thoroughbred Owners and Breeders Association. They said that a "blue ribbon" committee of twenty leaders in the horse industry had been formed for the purpose of developing a Code of Ethics regulating conduct and procedures at horse sales in America. This venture was to be called the Sales Integrity Task Force, and they thought I would be well suited as chairman. It was a nice compliment, but a hellacious undertaking.

The idea of such a committee was a wonderful idea, and it came into being because of the insistence of one Satish Sanan, an Indian whirling dervish from the computer world and a fairly new player in Thoroughbred racing and breeding. Mr. Sanan was convinced that some serious skullduggery had attended his entrance into our somewhat complicated game, that he had sunk a lot of money in to buying horses—primarily at public auction—and a damned good portion of it unnecessarily. And his blood was up.

The Thoroughbred world is as honest as any industry, but—as in any other field of endeavor—there are some unscrupulous players who would steal the pennies off a dead man's eyes. At auction sales, it can be tempting for an agent, hired by a well-heeled newcomer to advise him on the purchase of racing or breeding stock, to pull some shenanigans. This could be in the form of an under-the-table kickback from a consignor, or buying for his client a horse in which he had secret ownership, with a few other wrinkles here and there.

Our committee, made up of leading owners (including Satish Sanan), sales company executives, veterinarians, breeders, agents, consignors, and trainers, met for three months. We addressed dual agency, improper veterinary practices, and full disclosure. We issued our Code of Ethics, which was adapted in varying degrees of enthusiasm by the leading North American Thoroughbred sales companies, and which has now been implemented as wholeheartedly as possible in an industry that has no central governing body, like the NFL or Major League Baseball.

I have never had a tougher assignment. How did I do? Here's what Ray Paulick, Editor in Chief of *The Blood Horse*, our leading trade publication, wrote:

"Campbell's stewardship of this most difficult issue was inspiring, and his phone soon should be ringing off the hook with inquiries and job offers from scores of failed committees, task forces, and do-nothing organizations within the Thoroughbred world and beyond. The master of Dogwood Stable did the impossible. He herded cats, and did so in world-record time.

". . . Put Campbell in charge of Amtrak and the trains will run on time."

*   *   *

That fall was a momentous time for me. While in California to make a speech to the California Thoroughbred Breeders Association, I got a call one morning from Bennie Bell, president of the Thoroughbred Club of America. She said I had been chosen to be the 2004 Honor Guest of this fine organization, and the seventy-third testimonial banquet in Lexington on November 5 would honor "one who has rendered distinguished service to the sport of racing." Would I accept? I told her I thought I would!

I was positively thrilled. This was the accolade of accolades, and the nicest honor that I could ever receive. This meant I would follow in the footsteps of such as William Woodward, Samuel D. Riddle, Alfred Vanderbilt, John W. Galbreath, Col. E.R. Bradley, William T. Young, Ted Bassett, Paul Mellon, Mack Miller, and sixty-four other giants that I have long admired.

I thought I would certainly qualify as the Honor Guest who had been in jail the most times. That's sort of funny. But I did think about those early days quite a bit in connection with this award, which has been compared to the highest honor that can be paid in the entertainment world—the Academy Awards' Lifetime Achievement Award.

At the dinner, attended by several hundred, I was introduced by the ideal person—my wife. She stole the show, with some commentary about my early days, along with a lot of very serious stuff.

In my talk, which tried to include some weighty industry topics, I started by sincerely stating, "No one has ever stood up here in the past, nor will anyone ever stand up here in the future, who will appreciate this honor more than this boy here tonight."

I knew how delicious this honor was when it happened, and I think of it often. I have a sure antidote should I get down on myself; I can look at the framed scroll on my office wall.

If you do anything for thirty-five years—if you just keep going to work—you will become an expert. That is why in 1999 I was offered a contract by the book publishing arm of *The Blood Horse* to write a book that would "demystify the intricacies of the Thoroughbred Racing Industry." The challenge was quite intriguing. I enjoyed writing *Lightning in a Jar*. I should have called it *Lightning in a BOTTLE*, that expression being more readily used. Whatever, it sold well—around ten thousand copies. Subsequently, I was asked to write a compilation of amusing anecdotes and stories about my life in the horse business and the characters I have known. It was published in 2002 with the title *Rascals and Racehorses*. It did fine, although not as well as *Lightning*; the latter was a "how to" book, which helped it commercially.

I guess maybe I am an expert, generally. I am not a trainer, breeder, farrier, veterinarian, acupuncturist . . . certainly not a jockey. But I am a horseman, with a good overview of all of them, and have watched the maturation of their practices—and my own—for around four decades.

I doubt that anyone has bought more horses at public auction than we have—around 1,100, I would think. Dogwood has probably imported as many horses from England, Ireland, France, and Argentina as any outfit in history.

Certainly no one in our sport has brought more people into participation in Thoroughbred racing. Not all of those people were glad of it, but not one of them was misled.

The Dogwood name and our silks of gold and green are recognized and respected in the racing world. We are one of few outfits to win both a Breeders' Cup race and a Classic (Preakness). In taking nine shots at Triple Crown races, Dogwood has a win, a second, two thirds, and a fourth to show for it. The total of our stakes-winning horses is seventy-one at this point. We have had two North American Champions, and on six occasions have represented this country in international racing competition, in Japan, Canada, and this country. In 2005 (the most current year, at this writing), Dogwood Stable grossed $2,688,782, and we were ranked seventh in North America by the compilations of *Thoroughbred Times*.

As I write this, I am a year away from fifty years without a drink. Anne and I will have been married for half a century in 2009. I have a good bit of age on me, and she has ten years less on her. But we look and seem—relatively—young, especially Anne, who has good genes and an exuberant, joyful nature. We both keep fit. Anne is a splendid tap dancer and has the figure to prove it.

No one ever had better insights into age than the indefatigable Satchel Paige, who pitched big time baseball into his sixties at least (no one, including him, was ever sure how old he was). He asked rhetorically, "How old would you be if you didn't know how old you were?" He also advised, "Don't look back; something might be gaining on you."

If happiness is the goal of life, then I have had a superlative existence. I have been successful in achieving a happy state of mind. Though the early years were turbulent, by my own doing, and there were a few times when I thought I would be better off dead, much good came out of those stormy days. Because of them, I became a better person than I was cut out to be. Those times taught me about what is important. I went into my sober thirties knowing that no matter what manner of adversity came up, I could handle it because I would have my wits about me, and I would have my self respect.

You know, I have dealt with my alcoholism in a light manner for the most part, stressing the funny, outrageous aspects of that blight. But it is a blight, a terrible one, and I pull hard for those out there who are struggling to gain control of it. God bless you.

On the subject of happiness, I have the knack of knowing how to be happy. I have no trouble identifying those things that will or will not make me content. I also know that the true definition of happiness is the avoidance of *unhappiness*. Happiness does not necessarily mean that one is in a prolonged state of ecstasy . . . capering about, beaming and giggling like the village idiot.

I have been successful in business, an important method of keeping score. I have started two businesses. My advertising agency—Burton-Campbell, Inc.—was started from nothing, and grew to be one of the South's most successful. It was boldly creative, strong in integrity, fiercely independent, and greatly emulated and admired.

Dogwood Stable—like its founder earlier on—was a laughable longshot to come out of the starting gate, much less finish, and—much, much less—win. But it did win. Big time.

The successes have come from a variety of reasons, a little of it luck, of course. But the major factors are two things.

One, I have good instincts. I am like a good bird dog with an unerring nose for determining the presence of quail. If he went on point on the runway at O'Hare Airport, improbable though it may be, you could bet there were quail in the immediate vicinity. I think I have a sixth sense in detecting the genuine or phony nature of a person, and the longer I have lived, the more I have relied on it. After almost eight decades, I can tell instantaneously the difference between chicken salad and chicken . . . you know what.

Second, I know what I know, what I'm good at. I understand what my strengths are and have enormous confidence in those strengths. More importantly perhaps, I have a complete understanding of my weaknesses. And I am confident enough of my strong points not to be embarrassed by my weak ones.

For instance, I am not good at reading a balance sheet, but I can hire a good accountant or treasurer and let him be the technician that he knows how to be. What I can do while he prepares and interprets the balance sheet is to see to it that more money comes in than goes out. That's the name of the game! So I do what I know how to do, and I don't try to fake it. In concert with this philosophy is the fact that I have no trouble saying "I don't know," and "I'm sorry."

I like money and have a fair amount of it; but I am no slave to it. I spend it. Grab more checks than I have to, tip too much. I certainly could have amassed more money. But if I had three times as much I don't know what I would do differently. You could say, "Leave it to your descendants." And I could, and would. But that's no guarantee of happiness for them—quite the contrary. I have never understood my well-to-do friends who stay in cheap hotels, travel in steerage, ride the subways, and worry about picking up the tab in a restaurant, all so they can squirrel away a little more for their children to inherit. It doesn't make a damned bit of difference whether your son inherits $10,000,000 or whether he has to make do with $9,800,000 (or—on a lesser level—whether he gets $900,000 or tries to struggle by on $800,000). He might be better off with nothing.

All this comes from one who during his lifetime inherited only one thing: old maid Great Aunt Isabel Gammon, Society Editor of the Rome *News-Tribune*, bequeathed to me a steel engraving of Stonewall Jackson and Robert E. Lee conversing stealthily on horseback (which I adore!). Still, I've gotten along just fine. Sometimes I think I was blessed by the fact that my father lost everything when I was fourteen years old.

My two daughters will do quite well from Anne and me, but in the meantime we are going to use some dough to make life easier for the old home team, and have as much fun as possible in the process. We have invested money in a Broadway play (introduced unsuccessfully on Broadway the very week that war with Iraq broke out). We put money in a few prizefighters, who either could not fight or did not wish to. I've made a few sizeable bets on the "right" opportunities through the years. And we would be game for more zestful financial adventures in the future.

I am not afraid of money; it is to be used and enjoyed. In fact, I am probably not fearful of many things. As I said earlier, I am afraid of being bored, and I am more afraid of being boring. I want to be dead sure that if I say something it is directed to a person who is truly interested in hearing it. My conversational gambits are not likely to be categorized as "pearls," but, such as they are, I want to make sure they are not cast before "swine." If something is important to me it would be a desecration to force that topic conversationally on one who did not appreciate it.

As a conversationalist, I might be described as "cautious." I love to talk about certain things to certain people, and, when put to the task, I can hang in there with the best of them. I will do my part and then some. But I do not want to go longer than is absolutely necessary. In fact, there can come a time when an inane conversation simply must be terminated. I remember that in my younger days there was an admittedly extreme example of this. I had a date with a dreadfully stultifying, name-dropping, shallow young woman. The evening was a disaster. We were part of a large group, partying at a nightclub. The girl and I were dancing, and she was babbling interminably. Suddenly I thought, I cannot continue this. In mid-step on a crowded dance floor, I stopped and said, "Excuse me, please." I walked off the floor, went out the front door, and left in a taxicab. Abominable behavior, admittedly.

I have found that one's innermost and most precious thoughts are probably best left thought about and not talked about. With the exception of immediate family members, seeking audiences for one's weighty ponderings—poignant observations in life that bring tears to your eyes or make the goose pimples appear—is a serious mistake.

Some of my most satisfactory conversations have been with myself.

Cocktail parties. Contrary to Elwood P. Dowd's observation that no one ever brought anything unimportant into a bar, let me assert that few utterances of true importance are brought into cocktail parties.

For a variety of good reasons I am not fond of cocktail parties. I look upon them now as a necessary evil, though I am grateful to be invited. Of course, in my early drinking days I was the last man standing.

My tried and true modus operandi is to whip through the party like a fast-moving tornado. With almost frightening animation, while I ooze charm from every pore, I circle the room, heartily engaging every group, pausing to pump every available male hand and enthusiastically embracing and kissing (both cheeks) every female with whom I am even faintly acquainted. Within twenty minutes, I have encountered and made my presence known to every human being on the premises. Then I have a flare for surreptitiously fading out into the front yard and departing. My wife, Anne, is more conscientious than me, and would wish to remain for a "proper" period of time.

Two conversational topics that I abhor—at cocktail parties or any other time—are politics and religion.

My theory on politics is that after fancifully determining whether or not I have properly categorized a new acquaintance as to his broad political persuasion, I have no interest whatsoever in pursuing his or her theories about global warming, immigration, abortion, or anything else of that nature. If we are inclined toward edification on those subjects, we have immediate access in various forms of the media to the opinions of the world's most informed pundits. My neighbor's other-than-superficial views are a matter of supreme indifference to me. My theory on all matters, national and international, is the same I apply to all problems: if I can help fix it, lead me to it. If I cannot fix it, I don't want to stew about it. This may be part of the formula for happiness that I have alluded to.

A subject to be avoided even more assiduously is religion. One's relationship with his Maker is a most private matter to me, and a simple matter to me.

The religious principle that fills the bill best for me is: Do the best you can. Be kind. Be a good friend.

I do believe that reading the Bible is a rich experience. But as a guide for my conduct, I do not need the clarification of what Paul had in mind when he wrote one of his (many) letters to the Thessalonians. Generally, I know what is right and what is wrong.

A good friend of Anne's and mine is Frederick W. Buechner, one of the world's most respected theologians. Freddie says that Alcoholics Anonymous is more of what Jesus Christ meant the church to be than most present-day churches. This man is a preacher's preacher, one of the most enthralling speakers I have ever heard, and a delightful companion in every sense of the word. Interestingly, he does not belong to any church.

I like the wholesome experience of going to church. I like to observe the other people, and I like to hear and sing some of the hymns. But the denomination of the church does not matter to me.

Anne is very religious and is an avid seeker of religious enlightenment. She is a wonderfully popular and effective teacher of her own weekly Bible Class. I have great respect for this aspect of her life and applaud her quest. She and I understand each other perfectly on this subject. We are both walking the same walk, without talking the same talk.

* * *

During my life I have been no stranger to unorthodoxy. I have marched to my own beat. I have praised individualism, and I have probably gone out of my way to do things in a way that others do not. I like that which is not in style. I would not have been a likely candidate for a Nehru Jacket or a Leisure Suit when they were in style. My sideburns would not have been lengthened some years back, nor have I contemplated a goatee. I have dressed as an individual, my business life has been most unconventional, and I have avoided any tinge of provincialism.

Anne and I have a nephew of whom I am quite fond. Technically, he is Anne's nephew, but he is a high-quality guy, so I also claim him. He finds me interesting, and some years ago he asked me to list for him those qualities "that have made you successful." I protested that such an exercise would be exceedingly presumptuous of me. He persevered, and I did make the list. I wanted it to be useful, and I spent a lot of thought and time on it. Here is that list, but there is an interesting postscript to it:

Success

1. My alcoholism created many terrible complications for me up to age thirty, but my conquering the problem gave me added strength for the future, as I developed a keen understanding of whether problems were or were not truly important.
2. I have an innate optimism about the future. However, I look ahead and plan meticulously for every conceivable bump in the road.
3. I do not talk too much. And I waste little time.
4. I am afraid of very little, except boring someone, or being bored.
5. Years ago—by accident—I was thrust into a situation where I had to speak in public. I discovered I had a flair for it and this talent has been a major factor.
6. I know what I am good at and where I am weak, and I don't fool myself about either. And I don't mind acknowledging either.
7. I have the ability to determine genuineness in human beings. When I am convinced of a person's quality, I put complete trust in that person; and I employ and rely on those persons to guide me in the aforementioned areas of weakness.
8. I am almost in a frenzy to face up to and try to correct troublesome problems. I do not want trouble, am on the lookout for it constantly, and

go out of my way to avoid it. But if it is inevitable, I want to deal with it as quickly and thoroughly as possible, and put it behind me.

9. I believe in cordial, thoughtful business relationships, but I do not let my personal life become entangled unless it is entirely natural. And I have always treasured and maintained my own private integrity—and that of my organization. I have terminated profitable business relationships—sometimes to the shock of onlookers—because of a lack of consideration or respectful demeanor. On occasions this has paid enormous dividends in the image of respect it has helped create.

10. I *never* look back. Sometimes, in an extreme case, I may brood as long as two minutes about what might have been. But then I move on optimistically.

11. I have enormous self-confidence and self-esteem and I have no trouble admitting my mistakes. And it is no problem for me to apologize.

12. I like almost everyone, but "fall in love" with only a handful, and maintain a healthy and benign cynicism toward human relations. I hate no one and could easily forgive almost anything. I never hold a grudge.

13. Last and most important, in 1959, I was lucky enough—and smart enough—to marry a wonderful woman, who has encouraged me, understood me, and tempered me, all in very skillful proportions.

I sent this list to my nephew. Weeks went by and there was no reaction from him, not even a confirmation that he had received it. Having gone to considerable trouble, this was annoying. So, I sent him the following:

"Dear John:

"Before Christmas you requested several times that I provide you with a list of factors which have contributed to my 'success' in life. I was glad to do this for a person of whom I think quite highly and wish well. There was a list of 13, and now I provide number 14, and suggest that it may be the most important of all for you to absorb:

14. I understood the value of communication. And, when someone went to a little trouble on my behalf, I promptly acknowledged it with a word of thanks or appreciation.

With very best wishes, I am . . ."

He never forgot Number 14.

*　　*　　*

During the almost fifty years Anne and I have been married, we have had only a handful of arguments, and I'm sure ninety percent of those disagreements were caused by me. We are known to be a devoted couple.

During one spirited argumentative exchange, she said, "I just want you to be my best friend!" That sentence cut like a knife. It brought tears to my eyes and a very quick end to the argument. I will never forget those words. We have always been, and will always be, the best friends of each other.

Much of this book should be about Anne. There would be no book without her.

I have touched on many aspects of her wonderful self during the chapters I have written. I really should wind this book up properly with a summation of her great qualities.

But Anne is so very fine that it would be a desecration for me to try.

I am a strong believer in the power of brevity, so I will simply say: she is the best human being I ever knew, or ever heard of.

I do love her so very much. And I thank her for her major role in my wonderful life.

ACKNOWLEDGEMENTS

My wife, Anne, has lived the best part of the life herewith chronicled. She read these chapters as I wrote them, and offered sharp suggestions while enthusing encouragingly over the material. Her contributions are numerous and pervasive. Some are covered in the book.

My great friend Ed Bowen—a superb writer and editor—read and liked the stuff, though was often shocked at some of the revelations. His memory and intelligence served me well.

Cary Campbell Umhau, my daughter, did copy editing on *Longshot* and organized the hell out of her changes, and suggested improvements. She has always been a "go-to person."

* * *

The Dogwood office in Aiken—touted by me as "pound for pound" the finest organization in the country—has been a vital part of the creation of the book:

Darby Wallace Copeland is my strong right arm. As such, she has logically paved the way for 139,740 words to be written. She is the "mother of all problem solvers." To Darby I am beholden big time!

Jack Sadler, now Executive Vice President of Dogwood, has contributed more from helping to create the history (and success) than in any other way. He has been with Dogwood for thirty years. He makes the Rock of Gibraltar seem like a bowl of Jell-o.

Bill Victor is our Treasurer. He nurses every nickel, but understands going first class, and spending money to make money. Armed with the facts of a sticky situation, Bill can provide positive solutions.

Mary Jane Howell is our P. R. Director, and a cheerleader, spark plug, and general joy to have around. She understands books, and has sure helped with all three of mine, glorying in weird literary research assignments.

Missy Poe rides herd on our database and our computer programming generally. She is a valued member of the team, has sound, keen ideas, and is there when you need her.

Suzanne Davila is a utility infielder with her heart in the right place. She is one of the "straws that stir this drink," and we would be sad without her fine spirit.

I thank Eclipse Press, publishers of my first two books, for their gracious willingness to permit certain material from those books to appear in this one.

PHOTO CREDITS

Printed in the United States
79303LV00003B/92